STUDIES ON ETHNIC GROUPS IN CHINA

Stevan Harrell, Editor

HENRY M. JACKSON SCHOOL OF INTERNATIONAL STUDIES

STUDIES ON ETHNIC GROUPS IN CHINA

Cultural Encounters on China's Ethnic Frontiers
Edited by Stevan Harrell

Guest People: Hakka Identity in China and Abroad
Edited by Nicole Constable

Familiar Strangers: A History of Muslims in Northwest China
Jonathan N. Lipman

Lessons in Being Chinese:
Minority Education and Ethnic Identity in Southwest China
Mette Halskov Hansen

Manchus and Han: Ethnic Relations and Political Power
in Late Qing and Early Republican China, 1861–1928
Edward J. M. Rhoads

Ways of Being Ethnic in Southwest China
Stevan Harrell

Governing China's Multiethnic Frontiers
Edited by Morris Rossabi

GOVERNING CHINA'S MULTIETHNIC FRONTIERS

Edited by

MORRIS ROSSABI

University of Washington Press

Seattle and London

In Memory of Michel Oksenberg

University of Washington Press
P.O. Box 50096-5096
Seattle, WA 98145, USA
www.washington.edu/uwpress

Library of Congress Cataloging-in-Publication Data

Governing China's multiethnic frontiers / edited by Morris Rossabi.
      p.   cm. — (Studies on ethnic groups in China)
    Papers presented at conference "China's Management of Its National
Minorities," held in Washington, D.C., Feb. 2001.
    Includes bibliographical references and index.
    ISBN 0-295-98390-6 (alk. paper)
    1. Minorities — Government policy — China — Congresses.   2. China —
Ethnic relations — Political aspects — Congresses.   I. Rossabi, Morris.
II. Series.
JQ1506.M5G68   2004
323.151 — dc22   2003064505

Contents

Preface
vii

Introduction
MORRIS ROSSABI
3

1 / White Hats, Oil Cakes, and Common Blood
The Hui in the Contemporary Chinese State
JONATHAN N. LIPMAN
19

2 / The Challenge of Sipsong Panna in the Southwest
Development, Resources, and Power in a Multiethnic China
METTE HALSKOV HANSEN
53

3/ Inner Mongolia
The Dialectics of Colonization and Ethnicity Building
URADYN E. BULAG
84

4/ Heteronomy and Its Discontents
"Minzu Regional Autonomy" in Xinjiang
GARDNER BOVINGDON
117

5/ Making Xinjiang Safe for the Han?
Contradictions and Ironies of Chinese Governance in China's Northwest
DAVID BACHMAN
155

CONTENTS

6/ Tibet and China in the Twentieth Century

MELVYN C. GOLDSTEIN

186

7/ A Thorn in the Dragon's Side
Tibetan Buddhist Culture in China

MATTHEW T. KAPSTEIN

230

Bibliography
270

Contributors
285

Index
287

Preface

The essays presented in this volume evolved from a conference that was inspired by conversations between Michel Oksenberg of Stanford University and myself in 1999. Professor Oksenberg suggested that I invite leading specialists on the minority *minzu* (ethnic groups) of China to write essays appraising the Chinese government's administration of the minority regions, an important lacuna in studies of modern China. After discussions with colleagues at Stanford and Columbia Universities, I invited the prospective authors to provide overviews of state relations with the minority peoples since the founding of the People's Republic of China in 1949, analyze the present status of these relations, and suggest policy alternatives for the United States if crises should erupt in a minority region. For publication in the Studies on Ethnic Groups in China series, we have eliminated the U.S. policy dimension.

The conference, titled "China's Management of Its National Minorities," convened in Washington, D.C., in February 2001. The authors met for three days to discuss papers that had circulated well in advance of the meetings to suggest revisions. After the conference, I reread the papers and suggested additional revisions to each author. Later, we made further adjustments in response to comments by those who evaluated the manuscript for the University of Washington Press. These published essays are thus the result of several rounds of criticism and refinement.

Professor Oksenberg's interest in the conference persisted until the onset of his final illness. His contributions to this particular project and to so much else in the field of Chinese studies were so manifold that the authors wish to dedicate this work to his memory. He helped conceive the project, and he actively supported efforts to locate funding for the conference. For this assistance, the authors are grateful.

The Smith Richardson Foundation provided a grant for the conference, a subvention that facilitated our work. Dr. Samantha Ravitch, its former program officer for East Asia, assisted enormously in planning the conference. The Asia Society and its vice president for public and corporate programs, Robert Radtke, administered the grant efficiently and supplied much-appreciated logistical support.

The authors benefited from the suggestions of Stephen Kotkin of Princeton University and Pamela Crossley of Dartmouth College, who acted as discussants at the conference. Professor Kotkin, a historian of Russia, offered comparative insights, and Professor Crossley, a specialist on Qing China, provided historical context.

Morris Rossabi
City University of New York
Columbia University
September 2003

GOVERNING CHINA'S
MULTIETHNIC FRONTIERS

Introduction

MORRIS ROSSABI

Since the first identifiable and attested dynasty in the second millennium B.C.E., China has gradually expanded from its original base along the bend of the Yellow River to incorporate additional territory and to rule over other people. Each accession of land has translated into the absorption and gradual assimilation of native peoples, who have themselves contributed cultural or linguistic traits to the dominant group. Even if a foreign kingdom or khanate managed, through superior weapons or tactics, temporarily to occupy parts of China, it needed, according to historians, to adopt and use Chinese institutions in order to rule. On the other hand, when China acquired land at the expense of other groups, *the natives on occasion preserved their unique traditions and institutions,* challenging the Chinese dictum that they would naturally assimilate.

Nonetheless, as the Han (206 B.C.E.–C.E. 220), Tang (618–907), and other great dynasties gained power, the official ideology of a culturally superior China, surrounded by less sophisticated peoples, developed. According to this view, as the non-Chinese (or non-Han, with "Han" coming to signify the dominant, ethnically Chinese population) recognized the glory of Chinese civilization and the brilliance and goodness of the Chinese emperor, they would gravitate toward the Chinese court and seek to integrate into Chinese civilization; in the Chinese formulation, they would "come to be transformed." The wiser and more virtuous the Chinese ruler, the greater the number of foreigners who acquiesced to Chinese governance and adopted Chinese ways. Even the embodiments of steppe nomadic culture such as the Khitans (who established the Chinese-style Liao dynasty, 907–1115) and the Mongols (who founded the Chinese-style Yuan dynasty, 1271–1368) were reputedly entranced by Chinese civilization, and some assimilated with the Han population. Yet the survival of such groups as the Mongols belies the Chinese view that foreigners, many of whom were nomadic pastoral peoples residing north of China, sought integration with China because of its "more advanced" economy and culture. Instead, relations between China and its northern neighbors alternated between trade, disguised as tribute offerings to the Chinese emperor,

3

in the capital and commerce along the frontier. Unlike its policy in the north, China strenuously attempted to incorporate the non-Chinese peoples of the southwest into the Middle Kingdom.

By Ming times (1368–1644), Chinese officials had reached a consensus that China ought not to compel neighboring peoples to the north into political integration. Instead, these northern foreigners ought voluntarily to seek the benefits of Chinese culture. The officials also agreed that China ought not to initiate aggressive forays to expand into territory beyond its cultural boundaries, though military expeditions designed to overwhelm the non-Chinese peoples in the southwest persisted. Such expansion in the north would have been counterproductive because it would have entailed vast expenditures on military forays and occupation forces to rule over restive and often rebellious foreigners. As the first Ming emperor said to his officials,

> The ancients have a saying: "The expansion of territory is not the way to [achieve] enduring peace, and the over-burdening of the people is a cause of unrest." For example, the Sui Emperor Yang sent his forces to invade Liu-ch'iu, killing and injuring the foreign people, setting fire to their palaces and homes, and taking several thousand of their men and women as prisoners. Yet the land which he gained was not enough to furnish him with supplies and the people he enthralled could not be made to serve him. For vain glory he exhausted China.[1]

The first Ming emperor eschewed military means in the north and opted instead for a Song dynasty (960–1279) policy of being a "lesser empire" and remaining within what was perceived to be the traditional territories of China (which, however, included the southwest).[2] His successors pursued this policy throughout the Ming era, the only exceptions coming early in the fifteenth century with adventurist and abortive military expeditions in Mongolia and Vietnam.[3]

QING EXPANSIONISM AND ITS AFTERMATH

The rise of the Manchu Qing dynasty (1644–1911) witnessed the abandonment of these injunctions. Not bound by the dicta enunciated by the Ming rulers, the Qing embarked upon a policy of territorial expansion. In 1634, even before the Manchus had ascended the throne in China, they had crushed Mongol resistance in the lands now known as Inner Mongolia. Whatever ideological views the Qing emperors had of themselves as universal rulers and of the peoples within their growing domain (a subject that has recently attracted the attention of several scholars), the practical ramification of their military successes was a seemingly inexorable drive toward domination of areas populated by non-Han peoples.[4] In 1691, the various khans of the Khalkha, or Eastern Mongols, accepted a status as vassals of the Manchus, and in 1696, a Qing army defeated the rulers of the Zunghar, or Western Mongols, and added their realm to China. A detachment of Zunghar Mongols fled to and gained control over Tibet, until a Manchu army dispossessed them around 1720. The Qing then established suzerainty over Tibet. Additional threats from the Zunghar Mongols led the court to dispatch a force in the 1750s to the region now known as Xinjiang to destroy once and for all the obstreperous "barbarians." By 1757, the Qing had annexed this vast domain, which comprises one-sixth of the total territory of present-day China and is inhabited mostly by Turkic-speaking Muslims.[5]

Like the Ming, the Qing pursued the same hard-line policy in southwest China. The southwestern province of Yunnan had been brought under the control of Beijing relatively late in history. Khubilai Khan's military campaign prompted the Kingdom of Dali, which controlled much of Yunnan, to submit to the Mongols in 1253, but the region, together with Guizhou and Guangxi, two other provinces in the southwest, continued to resist control from Beijing throughout the Ming and early Qing. Rebellions led by a group labeled the Miao in the Chinese sources plagued the court in the 1720s and 1730s.

By 1760, once the Qing had pacified these non-Han territories, it sought to moderate its hard-line policy in order to avert non-Han resistance. It instructed its officials not to discriminate economically against the native non-Han peoples, not to impose restrictions on their religious practices, and not to permit Han entrepreneurs and merchants to take advantage of and exploit them.[6] The Qing court apparently assumed that the native peoples would gradually be absorbed into China—quite simply, they would come to be transformed once they recognized the superiority of the hybrid Chinese-Manchu civilization. However, it failed to consider the difficulty of attracting qualified officials to assume positions in what they perceived to be culturally inferior non-Han regions; some who ventured to these mostly borderland regions were neither the most competent nor the most honest, undermining the court policy of evenhandedness toward the newly subjugated populations.

The Lifanyuan, the agency responsible for administration of the newly incorporated territories in Mongolia, had many reputable bureaucrats in

Beijing and in the provinces, including Mongols and other non-Han groups, but some local-level officials evaded regulations and permitted considerable exploitation of the native peoples.[7] In the northwest, they interfered with the practice of Islam, on occasion banning the construction of mosques. In Mongolia and Tibet, they tended to collaborate with the Buddhist monasteries, offering monks authority and wealth in hopes that the spread of Buddhism would undermine what they believed to be the military ethos of the Mongols. Yet defying court instructions, they allowed Chinese merchants, entrepreneurs, and bankers to travel without restrictions and sometimes to settle in the non-Han lands. Within a short time, the ordinary people and the non-Han elites found themselves in debt to the Han, leading in Mongolia to the gradual impoverishment of the entire territory in the nineteenth century.[8]

The resulting hostility toward China and the Han resulted in tensions and, on occasion, outright conflicts. The Qing goal of assimilation was not fulfilled. Instead, some of the non-Han regions were extraordinarily turbulent. Revolts erupted as early as 1781 in northwest China,[9] and they continued to bedevil the Qing until the major rebellion of 1862–78, which caused considerable destruction and death. Tibet and both Inner Mongolia and Mongolia remained relatively nonviolent; this was partly due to the influence of Buddhism, but animosity toward the Han and Qing rule was never far beneath the surface.[10] In Yunnan, the so-called Panthay rebellion, led by a certain Du Wenxiu and other Muslims and non-Han in the province, raged from 1847 to 1877.[11] The Qing vision of a peaceful and stable multicultural empire under Manchu rule had simply evaporated.

Facing foreign threats and domestic insurgencies, the Qing fell in 1911; this permitted the non-Han peoples living along the frontiers to seek independence or at least greater autonomy in the ensuing chaos. Despite a lack of unity among their leaders and several incursions by Chinese and White Russian forces, the Mongols of present-day Mongolia broke away from China and with assistance from the USSR, formed the second communist state in the world, the Mongolian People's Republic (MPR).[12] Though China continued, until the founding of the People's Republic of China in 1949, to claim jurisdiction over the MPR, or Mongolia, as it renamed itself in the 1990s, the country has remained free of Chinese control. However, the USSR had great influence over the MPR until 1990, when the Soviet bloc collapsed. Inner Mongolia underwent considerable turbulence from 1911 to 1947, as the Chinese Nationalist Party (Guomindang), the Chinese Communists, the Japanese, and the Mongolians competed for power. In 1947, the People's Liberation Army annexed the area and founded the Inner Mongolian Autonomous Region.[13]

From 1911 to 1949, warlords, the Chinese Nationalist Party, and the USSR vied for influence over Xinjiang, and the native peoples sought independence through the establishment of an Eastern Turkistan Republic in the 1940s.[14] The ensuing turbulence permitted the People's Liberation Army to seize the region in 1949–50, and in 1955, the government set up the Xinjiang Uygur Autonomous Region.

Tibet had achieved real autonomy from 1911 to 1950, though no Chinese government abandoned claims to this remote land southwest of China. In 1950, as in Xinjiang, People's Liberation Army forces occupied Tibet and brought it back within China's sphere. The southwest, including Yunnan, generally remained under Chinese domination from 1911 to 1949, though specific warlords sometimes paid lip service to the central government authorities while themselves governing these regions or provinces. In 1949, the Chinese Communists gained control over the provinces of Yunnan, Guizhou, and Guangxi. Though they founded autonomous regions and counties for the Zhuang (the largest minority group in China), the Yi, the Miao, the Yao, and other non-Han peoples, China remained dominant.

COMMUNIST ADMINISTRATION OF THE MINORITY REGIONS

Once the Chinese Communists had restored control over the Qing non-Han domains, they proclaimed that they differed from previous regimes in China in their policies toward the so-called minority peoples. They pledged to assist in preserving the linguistic and cultural heritage of the fifty-five minority peoples identified in a nationwide survey (altogether, the survey identified fifty-six peoples [*minzu*], the fifty-sixth being the majority Han). One of the more curious entities to be labeled a *minzu* was the Hui, a religious group composed of Chinese Muslims who speak Chinese and are ethnically no different from the Han. Such anomalies characterized other elements of the Communist classification of the fifty-five minority peoples, who currently constitute about 8 percent of the population. Despite such unusual identifications, the Chinese government maintained that its objective was to protect the minorities' right to adhere to their unique customs and practices, including their religions, music and dance, and languages and literatures. It founded so-called autonomous regions and counties, a policy that implied that the minorities would have considerable control over their own destinies. In practice, however, the

7

government has imposed sometimes severe and sometimes less severe restrictions on the autonomy of the minorities, challenging the official version about the independence of the autonomous areas.

The Communist leadership asserted that the rights of the ethnic minorities could be safeguarded only under socialism: ethnic divisions and hostilities would wither away as all groups were treated equally. The government would strive to avoid offending the sensitivities and sensibilities of the various ethnic groups. Yet the major Chinese specialists on minorities continued to refer to the autonomous regions as "backward ethnic-minority areas" and to assert that the Han would help them "accelerate development and achieve common prosperity."[15] It seems clear that the Communist leaders implicitly assumed that the minorities would recognize the inherent superiority of socialism (as earlier they had acknowledged the splendor of traditional Chinese civilization and come to be transformed) and eventually integrate into Han culture.

This assumption has proved to be erroneous. As one specialist on China's minorities wrote thirty years ago, "Minority problems in most societies have proven enormously resistant to easy or rapid 'solutions,' irrespective of the broad goals enunciated or the concrete policies applied. It is not yet clear that the People's Republic of China constitutes an exception."[16]

The Chinese government's wavering policies have contributed to its problems with the minority *minzu*. From 1949 until the later 1970s, the government, via the State Nationalities Affairs Commission and other agencies, veered from professed concern for, or at least benign neglect toward, the minorities' unique cultures and beliefs to repression of their religions, languages, cultures, and practices. It also shifted from offering economic opportunities and high offices to the minorities to granting economic benefits and control over minority regions to the Han. Even when it pursued benign programs, the government, as in Qing times, could not ensure that its local officials would implement such benevolent policies and would avoid a hostile minority reaction. This alternation of policies generated animosity from the minorities, which no doubt led to greater government domination.[17]

There was no alternation in the inexorable drive of Han settlement in the minority regions, a migration that the government fostered. Areas with a majority of non-Han populations in 1949 had a sizable influx of Han migrants by the late 1970s. By 2002, the Mongols were a decided minority in the Inner Mongolian Autonomous Region, outnumbered by more than six to one; the Han, who amounted to about 10 percent of the population of Xinjiang in 1949, now constitute approximately 50 percent;

an increasing number of Han have been assigned to work in Tibet, and some have remained even after the end of their assignments; and in the southwest, the Han are a growing presence in the enclaves of heavily minority districts.

To be sure, the minority regions have benefited, to a certain extent, from Communist rule. Despite the convulsions of the radical Great Leap Forward of 1958–62 and the Cultural Revolution of 1966–76, the Communist period in most regions has been more stable than the previous forty years. In addition, the Communist government has invested in education and health in the minority areas, ensuring a higher rate of literacy and a rudimentary medical system. Among some of the more male-dominated minorities, Communist support has translated into somewhat higher status and greater opportunities for women. Many among the minority peoples have cooperated with the Chinese Communists. Not all have been dogmatically opposed to Chinese rule or scornful of the Han. Some were already disenchanted with the oppressiveness of the religious and political elites in their own societies and regarded the Chinese as potential liberators. Yet the Great Leap Forward and the Cultural Revolution witnessed concerted attacks against the minority peoples' languages, heritage, and customs.

The government's investment and economic-development policies after the end of the Cultural Revolution and the opening to the West, starting in the late 1970s, were even more telling about attitudes toward the minority regions. Nearly all of the initial efforts of the government, international aid agencies, and foreign investors were directed at the coastal regions of China. For almost two decades, the minority regions lagged behind. In the mid-1990s, however, the government turned its attention to the interior, or western, parts of the country—the homelands of the more populous minority groups. It promised greater domestic and foreign investment for these economically deprived areas. Though it is too early to assess the success of this policy, preliminary patterns point to favoritism toward the new Han settlers in the minority regions. Many of the economic benefits of the last half decade have accrued, as David Bachman shows in his chapter on Xinjiang, to the Han immigrants. A more equitable distribution will be required if the Chinese government expects to ingratiate itself with the minority peoples.

The shift in government policy in the mid-1990s (toward more investment in the minority areas) resulted, in part, from developments outside of China. The ending of the USSR's domination over Central Asia in the early 1990s and the ensuing establishment of five independent countries, of which four have a predominantly Turkic population and all five are composed principally of Muslims, concerned China because it set a potentially alarming precedent for the largely Muslim and Turkic-speaking minorities in Xinjiang. Would they attempt to pursue the same route toward independence as their Turkic cousins in Central Asia? To deflect such calls for independence or true autonomy, the government has invested in infrastructure in the minority regions, with roads and railroads linking to China, and has, at least on paper, committed itself to an affirmative-action policy that offers special advantages for minority peoples in education and the economy. It has also become a significant trading partner with, and investor in, the Central Asian countries and has spearheaded the creation of mutual-cooperation agreements with its Turkic neighbors in Central Asia and with Russia (still a major force in the region); in this way, it has successfully limited their support for dissident groups in Xinjiang who demand independence. As of this writing, the effect on China of the greater U.S. presence in Afghanistan and Central Asia, which was a result of the attacks by Islamic fundamentalists on New York and Washington, D.C., on 11 September 2001, is difficult to predict.

At the same time, the emergence of a Mongolia that is free of overwhelming Soviet influence could set the stage for a pan-Mongol movement that would challenge Han interests in the Inner Mongolian Autonomous Region. As China's relations with Mongolia have improved, closer contacts between Mongolians on both sides of the border could embolden Mongolian nationalists in the Inner Mongolian Autonomous Region and encourage them to demand greater autonomy. Once again, part of China's strategy has been to become such a dominant trading partner with, and investor in, Mongolia that the Mongolians cannot afford to support such pan-Mongol aspirations.

The international movement for Tibet has also proved nettlesome to China. Tibetan and Western supporters of the Dalai Lama and of greater autonomy for the Tibetans in the Tibetan Autonomous Region and other ethnically Tibetan areas have been a thorn in the side of the Communist leadership. These advocates have been extremely successful in their public relations and have attracted considerable sympathy for the cause of Tibetan independence by depicting the Han and the Communist government as seeking to destroy Tibetan culture. Placed on the defensive, the Chinese leaders have formulated a policy for Tibet that is similar to the ones in Xinjiang and the Inner Mongolian Autonomous Region. Since the 1990s, they have relied on greater investment and greater opportunities for economic development to deflect dissidence in Tibet.

The Chinese authorities may also be concerned about ethnic disruptions in other parts of the world. The conflicts in the former Yugoslavia have presumably made an impression on world leaders, including the Chinese, but nearer at hand, the Azeri-Armenian wars, the continuing hostilities between Muslims and Hindus on the Indian subcontinent, and the antagonism toward overseas Chinese in many areas of Southeast Asia may have shaped the views of Chinese policy makers concerning the resiliency of ethnic problems. These policy makers no doubt recognize that ethnic insurgencies, or at least disruptions (bombings, demonstrations, etc.), cannot be ruled out in the minority regions, particularly Xinjiang and Tibet.

All but one of the chapters in this book focus on the more politically and strategically significant minority regions in China. Inner Mongolia, Xinjiang, and Tibet have witnessed varying degrees of turbulence over the more than five decades of Communist rule. Because the southwest has generally not experienced similar disruptions, nearly all the contributors emphasized other areas. Thus the book is focused mostly on the northern and western frontiers. Yet Mette Hansen's chapter reveals the increasing involvement of some of the southwestern minority peoples with foreign countries in Southeast Asia, a potentially significant development that could serve as the subject for a separate book based on recent anthropological studies.

CHINA AND ITS ETHNIC MINORITIES: THEIR PRESENT STATUS

Each ethnic minority in China represents a different challenge for Chinese policy makers, and each has reacted differently to Chinese policies. Some have differed in customs and practices from the Han but have considered themselves to be part of China; others have perceived that they are distinct from the Han, but the pressure of immigration and a lengthy exposure to Chinese culture have fostered acquiescence to Chinese rule and some assimilation; still others have retained a strong identity, have rejected integration with China, and have sought independence or at least autonomy.

The Hui, as Jonathan Lipman explains, do not seek independence from China. Unlike most of the other minorities, the Hui are scattered in different locations throughout China. Though the government has established a special Ningxia Hui Autonomous Region in northwest China, most Hui coexist in many of the same areas as the Han. Almost all speak Chinese, their customs are similar to those of the Han, and intermarriage has resulted in physical resemblance between themselves and the Han. Though the Hui perceive themselves to be different from the Han, they cannot readily identify these differences. Moreover, Hui living in various regions in China have adapted to the local cultures and thus differ from each other. Nonetheless, the government has classified the Hui as a minority ethnicity and has contributed, through the promotion of special institutions such as the Chinese Islamic Association, to the Chinese Muslims' growing identification as Hui. Though the authorities have been somewhat concerned that a Hui identity might translate into greater authority for Islamic clerics, they have attempted to portray the Muslims as Chinese citizens and to use the Hui residing along the frontiers as intermediaries in dealing with Tibetans and non-Chinese Muslims. This policy has been effective. Despite some local tensions and violence, the Hui have not developed any separatist movements. Though they identify generally with Islam, the Hui do not share the animosity of the Turkic Muslims of Xinjiang toward the government, and unlike the Turkic peoples of Xinjiang, they consider themselves to be Chinese. Such a fragmented minority group, which has not generated any charismatic national leaders, has certainly not challenged the authorities. According to Jonathan Lipman, the Hui's own brand of Chinese nationalism has deflected and will continue to deflect any attempt to break away from China.

Southwest China, home to an astonishing array of minority ethnicities, also has not posed a serious threat to the government. The Communist policies of encouraging Han migration into the region and of acculturating the minorities through changes in education, language, and religion have been effective. The various minority peoples have differed from, and at times been hostile to, each other, but they have all faced the seemingly inexorable influx of Chinese migrants. The government fostered such migrations from the 1950s through the 1970s to impose greater control, to provide Han leadership in this reputedly "backward" region, to promote Chinese language and education, and to offer work to the unemployed Han laborers on the east coast of China. In short, as Hansen writes, the new settlers "were supposed to teach the minorities to become good Communists and Chinese citizens in the new Chinese state."

Since the 1990s, Han migration has continued as an antidote to the growing unemployment in the central regions of China. Opportunities for employment in trade, tourism, and the exploitation of abundant natural resources in the southwest have lured Chinese settlers, and some minority peoples have become convinced that this will pave the way for the eradication of their culture. An educational system that has been ambivalent about, and occasionally disdainful of, minority languages, history, and cultures, as well as the availability of better schools for Han migrants, has contributed to the minority peoples' fears of the subversion of their cultures. The poorer education for minority peoples has also made it difficult for them to compete with the Han for major positions in society and politics. In addition, many minority people resent the tawdry tourist industry, with its encouragement of prostitution and its depiction of natives as "exotics." Even more galling, the Han have dominated the industry and reaped the profits. Finally, minority theme parks and minority singing and dancing concerts (a Han specialist on the minorities told me recently that they "love to sing and dance when they're happy") have contributed to Han stereotypes about these groups.

Yet Hansen unequivocally states that the ethnic minorities in the southwest "are not interested in (or even considering) seeking independence from the Chinese state." Despite recent contacts between the Tai of China and Thailand because of their shared Buddhist beliefs, the ethnic minorities may resent the involvement of foreign governments on their behalf, and indeed, such intrusions may be counterproductive because they could antagonize the Chinese government.

Nonetheless, despite the efforts of outsiders—the world Islamic community (which has donated funds for the repair and construction of mosques and theological colleges) in the case of the Hui or international nongovernmental organizations in the case of the southwestern minorities—these two groups are increasingly assimilating to Chinese culture. Faced with a condescending Han attitude that minority people are somewhat "backward" and need Han and Communist leadership, both have accepted their positions within the Chinese state. Each recognizes that economic, social, and political advancement requires greater integration into Chinese culture. The growing pressure of Han migrants in the southwest offers added incentives to acculturate, for the government would most likely provide even more opportunities for Han if the minorities remained attached to their heritage and avoided making some concessions to the dominant Chinese culture.

The Mongols of the Inner Mongolian Autonomous Region have, according to Uradyn Bulag, faced similar pressures for the past century. Beginning in 1902, the Qing government and the successive Chinese governments until 1947 opened up Inner Mongolia to Chinese colonization, and as early as 1937, the Chinese outnumbered the Mongols by three to one. The establishment of the Inner Mongolian Autonomous Region yielded even greater opportunities for Chinese, and more of them flooded into the area, making the Mongols "a small minority in their own home-land." During the Cultural Revolution, the Mongols were pressured by radicals from 1966 to 1969 to integrate into Han culture; their resistance to such pressure led to the deaths of more than twenty thousand Mongols. The traditional lack of unity among the Mongols has further hobbled efforts to resist the intrusions of Chinese peasants in what traditionally has been pasture land. Conversion of such land to agriculture has resulted in desertification and degradation of the land, threatening the lifestyle of the Mongols and jeopardizing the environment. Even in animal-related enterprises, the Han now dominate. Mongol goat herders provide raw cashmere wool, but the Han control the processing factories, which earn most of the income in the cashmere industry. Finally, the Chinese frown upon affirmation of Mongol identity and suppress any expression of Mongol autonomy.

As a Mongol, Bulag has strong views about Chinese policy toward the Mongols of Inner Mongolia, asserting that "Mongols have suffered enormously." He notes that neither Buddhism nor their heritage, as reflected in their renowned historical leader Chinggis Khan, has unified the Mongols, and their responses to what he perceives as Chinese encroachment have thus been feeble. The regime has provided the Mongols with better health, education, and social welfare and has improved sectors of the economy; however, Bulag believes that the trade-off has been the erosion of Mongol identity and culture.

Unlike the southwest and Inner Mongolia, Xinjiang has proven to be a more serious problem for Chinese policy makers. When the Communists gained power in 1949, Turkic peoples constituted by far the largest group in the region. By 2000, the Han comprised approximately one-half of the population. Up until the 1980s, the new immigrants had often been induced or coerced by the government into settling in Xinjiang. However, like the second wave of Han migrants in the southwest, the Chinese arriving in Xinjiang in the 1990s came voluntarily, lured by the government's policy of economic development of the interior, mostly western, provinces. This influx of migrants, as well as the hostilities among the various Turkic peoples, which the government in part inflamed, fomented disturbances. Because the government appeared to be deliberately diluting the power of the non-Han and particularly the Uygur segments of the population, dissent in the form of bombings and riots occurred. Gardner Bovingdon demonstrates that the Han dominated the most important government positions in the region and that the Uygurs had a disproportionately small number of representatives in influential posts in the local administration. He also shows that many Uygurs are concerned that the Communist Party "will not allow them to speak freely."

Having to contend with the Han migrants, the Turkic inhabitants of Xinjiang have faced considerable pressure and have simultaneously gained some benefits from government policies. Starting much earlier but with increased efforts in the 1990s, the Han authorities have attempted to foster the use of the Chinese language among the Uygurs and to undercut the attraction of Islam. On the other hand, the government's affirmative-action policy has meant that the minority peoples in Xinjiang have lower standards for admission to higher education, and other special provisions have permitted them to evade the one-child-per-family restrictions imposed on ordinary Chinese since 1980. Such concessions to the Uygur and other Turkic minorities in Xinjiang may reflect the government's eagerness to appeal to the world's Islamic community by adopting a tolerant policy toward Muslims within its own borders.

Yet according to Bovingdon, these beneficial policies have not pacified the Uygurs. Advocates of independence, admittedly a tiny minority, have used bombings, assassinations, and demonstrations to manifest their discontent with Han rule, but the large majority of Uygurs also resent the privileged positions of their Chinese governors, not to mention the greater emphasis on the Chinese language. Yet most Uygurs have not demanded independence, and the Chinese accusations of "separatism" do not apply to them. The majority simply desire the autonomy the Chinese pledged in 1955 when they established the Xinjiang Uygur Autonomous Region.

David Bachman points out that the Chinese government has invested too much in Xinjiang to abandon it to its Turkic inhabitants or to brook what it perceives as Western interference. It is true that the investment that was initiated in the 1990s has principally benefited the Han. Nonetheless, some gains have trickled down to the Turkic population. The government has also emphasized economic relations as a means of discouraging potential assistance to Turkic separatists in Xinjiang from the newly established Muslim, mostly Turkic countries in Central Asia. It has invested funds in several Central Asian countries and has outbid U.S. oil companies in obtaining a license to drill in Kazakhstan and to build a pipeline from there to Xinjiang. Its ensuing economic leverage has translated into a lack of Central Asian support for dissidents in Xinjiang.

Meanwhile, economic development in Xinjiang continues to favor the Han. The areas with the greatest concentration of Han have higher incomes, greater investment from the central government, and larger outlays on education and the social sector. The extraction of raw materials has been the primary objective of investment, turning Xinjiang more and more into a colony of the central government. The mostly Han Production and Construction Corps, which currently constitutes about one-eighth of the population of Xinjiang and has tremendous economic power, is, in Bachman's words, "a vanguard of Han penetration into Xinjiang." Like Bovingdon, Bachman does not foresee a successful independence movement, partly because the mostly Turkic population has not galvanized around a particular leader and partly because China will not withdraw from a region in which it has invested so much and which is vital for its security.

The issue of Tibet is the thorniest and most widely publicized of those involving ethnic-minority groups in China. Tibet's present and future status has become embroiled in international politics. As early as the mid-1950s, the U.S. Central Intelligence Agency assisted Tibetan guerrillas in plans to detach Tibet from China. After the failure of the 1959 rebellion, yet another country became involved when the Dalai Lama subsequently fled to India.

Since then, the Tibetan exile community and the Dalai Lama personally have gained influential allies, a few of whom are celebrities, with access to the mass media. These Western supporters have, in turn, capitalized on their connections in the media to direct attention to the plight of Tibet, and the Dalai Lama, a charismatic and attractive figure, has been a valuable asset in this effort. Organizations that support Tibetan independence have sprouted in the Western world and have intensively lobbied their government officials to pressure China on behalf of Tibet. These international organizations have romanticized traditional Tibetan Buddhism and have fervently promoted the cause of independence (not just autonomy), thereby limiting the options for negotiation and engendering a more hostile response from the Chinese authorities.

As Melvyn Goldstein makes clear, at the outset of their rule, the Communist leadership adopted a moderate policy of governance in Tibet. Although they adamantly opposed abandoning Chinese claims to Tibetan territory (because to do so would eliminate the buffer zone around Sichuan Province, a key economic center), in 1951, they pledged to permit political autonomy in Tibet, as long as the Dalai Lama conceded that Tibet was part of China. This arrangement persisted until the failed 1959 rebellion, when the Communists launched a more radical policy that required economic and political integration with China. During the Cultural Revolution, they limited the expression of Tibetan culture and religion and permitted the destruction or damage of many Buddhist sites. The conclusion of the Cultural Revolution and the accession to power of a more moderate Chinese government offered opportunities for a political settlement in the late 1970s and early 1980s. However, the dominant faction among the Tibetan exiles sought political autonomy and the restoration, with real political power, of the Dalai Lama, a policy that the Chinese leadership could not countenance. China's rejection of these proposals solidified the support of Western sympathizers and caused monks and other Tibetans to demonstrate and riot on several occasions between 1987 and 1989 in the streets of the Tibetan capital.

After the Chinese government finally ended the violence in 1989, it initiated the same policies it had in Xinjiang and the southwest to curtail what it termed "splittism," that is, separatism or a movement for independence. First and foremost, it began to invest substantial sums to foster economic development, assuming that a higher standard of living would facilitate its rule and avert Tibetan dissidence. As in Xinjiang, however, the chief beneficiaries appear to have been the Han migrants who were recruited as laborers and experts for these construction and infrastructure projects. The arrival of additional Han settlers has somewhat diluted the Tibetan flavor of Lhasa, the capital city, and other towns and has been accompanied by an influx of Han bureaucrats and officials. Chinese education and greater use of the Chinese language complements this policy, reflects the need for fluency in Chinese for vocational and professional advancement, and is designed to ensure that Tibetan youth identify with China. The Communist leadership counts on a gradual erosion of Tibetan culture and the greater prominence of Han settlers and officials to foster stable conditions. Yet it cannot afford to ignore the extraordinary influence of the Dalai Lama and of Buddhism on the population, as well as the possibility that Tibetans will not gradually lose their identity in the Chinese melting pot. A negotiated settlement is still a possibility, though Goldstein believes that mistrust and the question of real political authority pose obstacles to such a solution.

As Matthew Kapstein observes, Chinese policy toward Tibetan Buddhism and culture continues to waver. After the 1959 revolt and again after the Buddhist-led disturbances of 1987–89, the Chinese authorities clamped down on religious expression within Tibet, even confiscating photographs of the Dalai Lama in residences and in the monasteries. On the other hand, Kapstein finds that the Chinese leaders have provided greater religious latitude to the Tibetan communities outside of the Tibetan Autonomous Region and even to Chinese converts to Tibetan Buddhism. He concludes that individual Tibetan monks and laymen have fewer Chinese-imposed limitations on their spiritual lives. The paradox of having restrictions on official Tibetan Buddhist institutions while simultaneously granting religious freedom to individuals reflects the uncertainties and disagreements within the Chinese leadership about proper policies.

NOTES

1. Lo, "Policy Formulation and Decision-Making," 52.

2. See Wang Gungwu, " Rhetoric of a Lesser Empire."

3. On two such expeditions, see Woodside, "Early Ming Expansionism"; and Goodrich and Fang, *Dictionary of Ming Biography,* 12–15.

4. See Crossley, *Translucent Mirror;* Farquhar, "Emperor as Bodhisattva"; and Rawski, *Last Emperors.*

5. A handy guide to this expansion is Rossabi, *China and Inner Asia,* 139–65.

6. Fletcher, "Ch'ing Inner Asia," 49–52.

7. On the Lifanyuan, see Chia, " Li-fan Yuan."

8. Sanjdorj, *Manchu Chinese,* 37–38; Bawden, *Modern History,* 173–76.

9. Lipman, *Familiar Strangers,* 103–66; Hsu, *Ili Crisis,* 22–29.

10. See Bawden, *Modern History,* for extensive evidence of such disaffection.

11. This rebellion has not been accorded a full-scale study in English. It deserves a monograph.

12. See Ewing, *Between the Hammer.*

13. A recent sympathetic portrait of one of the Inner Mongolian nationalists (who also collaborated with the Japanese) in this struggle is Jagchid, *Last Mongol Prince.*

14. On events in Xinjiang in the 1940s, see Forbes, *Warlords and Muslims,* and Benson, *Ili Rebellion.*

15. Wang Xien, "Globalization," 348.

16. Dreyer, "Traditional Minority Elites," 450.

17. Astonishingly, the official line is that "there have been no major problems in our ethnic relations over many years" (Wang, "Globalization," 347). The government has ensured that critics of the official line have remained relatively mute.

1 / White Hats, Oil Cakes, and Common Blood

The Hui in the Contemporary Chinese State

JONATHAN N. LIPMAN

A STORY OF VIOLENCE, NOVEMBER 1990

In a market town south of Kunming, the capital of Yunnan Province, some Chinese-speaking Muslims (Hui) from the countryside got into a fight with some non-Muslim Chinese—a Muslim child, playing with firecrackers, had damaged the merchandise in a bookseller's stall—and the Muslims beat up a couple of people. The police arrested them, mistreated them severely, and kept them in detention. After two days, their people wondered what had become of them, and two cars full of Muslims, led by a popular local man, came to town to look for them. Rumors quickly spread that these out-of-town Muslims had come to make trouble, and the police armed themselves in their station courtyard.

When the leader of the Muslims opened the station gate and entered the courtyard to inquire about his friends, the police lieutenant, son of a local power holder, shot him at close range. Fatally wounded, the Muslim leader struggled to his feet, and his companions rushed to help him. All the police then opened fire, killing three of the Muslims and wounding ten (my informant, who went to town the following day, himself saw the wounded in hospital, all of them in terrible condition). The local Muslims came to fetch the corpses, and they took the bodies not to their home village but to a Muslim stronghold, the county town of Yuxi. Muslims converged on Yuxi from every direction in trucks and cars, bringing young men in hundreds and plenty of guns (including Uzis and AK-47s). Vehicles filled with explosives, manned by volunteers for martyrdom, were placed in position to blow up the police stations, if it were deemed necessary. An official of the county Minorities Commission and the Yuxi vice-mayor were taken hostage. Clearly, some of the Muslims were ready to confront the immense power of the state and die in the cause of vengeance for their murdered coreligionists.

The Muslims took over a portion of Yuxi City as their headquarters. After several days, their leaders received word from friends in Kunming that the army had mobilized from provincial bases and was heading for Yuxi. An announcement was made over centrally placed loudspeakers, and some of the men wrote Arabic prayers on white cloths, wrapped themselves in these shrouds, seized their weapons, and prepared to die. But after a dramatic wait, the army, restrained by provincial leaders, stopped short of the city, and the Muslims relaxed a bit. Muslim community leaders engaged in negotiations with civilian officials from the provincial capital, including the Minorities Commission, and succeeded in forcing the state to pay compensation to the families of the dead and wounded. Each aggrieved family was to receive ¥8,000 for a man's death, and the wounded had all their hospital expenses paid by the government. The children of the dead were to be supported by the state to age eighteen. In the end, however, my informant claims to have discovered that the government found excuses to imprison the Muslim leaders by accusing them of drug smuggling, a common enough offense in the Yunnan borderlands, while the policemen were never punished. Though there are no visible signs of tension in Yuxi now, thousands of Muslims will remember the excitement, anxiety, and desire for revenge they experienced in those days.

A STORY WITHOUT VIOLENCE, 1990–1997

A Muslim quarter in the city of Zhengzhou, an important railroad junction in northern Henan Province, was terribly dilapidated—its buildings old-fashioned and rickety, its markets and alleys insalubrious (in fact, nauseating), its people poor. Like other Chinese city governments, the reform-minded Zhengzhou administration wanted to undertake sweeping reconstruction in order to sanitize the city, improve its image and public health, and create significantly enhanced housing stock for the rising middle classes (almost all of them non-Muslim). Not coincidentally, many government officials and businessmen, especially contractors, would be able to make a great deal of money from the project. They recommended that the single-story buildings of the Muslim quarter be torn down, except for a few historic mosques, and be replaced by multistory housing that would be too expensive for the majority of Muslims. This would have resulted, naturally, in the scattering of the Muslims to more affordable suburban neighborhoods. This scenario had already played out in a number of other cities, and the Muslims were well aware of the potential consequences of urban renewal.

The complaints from the Muslim quarter were very loud. Muslims, they claimed, must live together near their mosques and their businesses, so relocation would destroy the solidarity of the local Hui. Sensitive to minority concerns (some claim overly sensitive), the city government negotiated with community leaders, who demanded that the government build *xincun* (new urban villages, equivalent to American public-housing projects), in the same location as the old quarter and at prices the Muslims could pay. Ground was broken in the late 1980s, and now the quarter surrounding the Great Mosque, with its nearby women's mosque, is made up almost entirely of government-built apartment houses. The ten-year-old buildings are already shabby, but the new ones were finished only three years ago and remain beautiful, though their grounds have not yet been entirely finished. The residents are almost all Hui, of the lower and middle classes, and their new homes provide much better conditions than before. At no point in the process did anyone threaten violence.

WHO ARE THE HUI?

In a recent book, Masumi Matsumoto argues that two minority *minzu* (ethnic groups) dominated the Chinese Communist Party (CCP) leadership's perceptions of China's "non-Chinese" inhabitants well before 1949: the Mongols (Meng) and the Chinese-speaking Muslims.[1] She claims that because many Mongols and Chinese-speaking Muslims lived in and around the Yan'an (northern Shaanxi) region, which was the CCP's headquarters from 1935 to 1949, those two, among the fifty-five minority *minzu* currently recognized by the People's Republic of China (PRC), occupy unique places in the PRC's "ethnic policies" *(minzu zhengce)* and "ethnic discussions (or theory)" *(minzu lun)*.[2] As the most familiar minorities, the ones most easily available for study and application of experimental policies before 1949, these two certainly had an impact on the CCP that was out of all proportion to their size.

They also presented the CCP with very different problems of definition and governance. The Mongols strongly resembled Stalin's definition of a *narod*. That is, to the CCP's leadership and their representatives, the Mongols appeared to live almost exclusively in their own historic and well-defined territory, to use primarily their own language, to practice nomadic pastoralism in contrast to agriculture, and to possess a relatively homogeneous culture marked by common folkways such as food, music, horsemanship, and wrestling.

The Hui[3] may have looked similarly well defined from the vantage of Yan'an and its rather limited hinterland, but once the CCP took national power, its *minzu* experts discovered that the widely distributed, culturally diverse, Chinese-speaking Muslims resembled the Mongols hardly at all. Indeed, the presence of considerable numbers of Muslims throughout the Chinese cultural area has created difficulties of both perception and policy for every China-based state since the Ming empire.[4] Living in every province and almost every county of the PRC, the Hui have managed simultaneously to acculturate to local society wherever they live and to remain effectively different from their non-Muslim neighbors. Most of them use the local Chinese language exclusively,[5] and they have developed their "customs and habits" in constant interaction with local non-Muslims, whom they usually resemble strongly in their material life.[6] Intermarriage has made them physically similar to their neighbors (with some exceptions in the northwest)[7] but their Islamic practice and/or collective memory of a separate tradition and history allow them to maintain distinct identities. In short, they are both Chinese and Muslim, a problem that must be solved within many local contexts, for there is no single isolated territory occupied primarily by Hui people that could serve as a model for Hui all over China.[8]

From the fifteenth to the twentieth century, Hui (or the earlier Huihui) was simply the Chinese word for "Muslim."[9] The ethnographers of the Qing empire divided its subjects by language, so that male Chinese-speaking Muslims had to wear the queue, the pigtail that signified Chinese submission to the Manchus. The Turkic-speaking peoples of the Tarim Basin, on the other hand, though also Muslims and subjects of the Qing, were exempt from the queue, except for their leaders, who had to travel to Beijing to pay homage to the Manchu emperor. The Qing empire's northwesternmost territory, created in the mid-eighteenth century, was often called Huibu, the territory of the Muslims. Various types of Muslims received descriptive ethnonyms—the *chantou* Hui (Muslims who wrap the head) were the turban-wearing Turkic speakers of the southern Xinjiang oases (today subsumed within the Uygurs), the Sala Hui were the Turkic speakers of northeastern Tibet (today's Salars), and the Chinese-speaking Muslims now included in the Hui were sometimes called the Han Hui, the Chinese Muslims.

There was no name for what is now called the Hui, and there were few institutional connections among the Muslim communities scattered all over the Qing empire, except for trading networks, which allowed Muslim merchants to find a mosque for prayer and ritually pure (Ar. *halāl,* Ch. *qingzhen*) food as they traveled, as well as teacher-disciple networks of religious professionals.[10] The Manchu center had a powerful interest in discouraging widespread, unofficial organizations within its frontiers, and voluntary associations of all kinds had long been suspect within the Chinese cultural nexus. Islam, with its outlandish sacred texts and unconventional mosque-based community structure, appeared heterodox to many Qing officials (whatever their ethnicity) and thus bore careful watching. Many magistrates and provincial-level functionaries wrote memorials warning the throne about the strong resemblance between Islam and the Buddhist and Daoist sects, which so often caused social disorder. This perception grew stronger when Sufi orders began to spread in northwest and southwest China in the late seventeenth century. The Sufi order (Ar. *tariqa*), with its centralized, hierarchical religious authority vested in the sheikh (Ar. *shaykh*, Ch. *shehai* or *laorenjia*), appeared particularly subversive to Qing officials because of the connections between communities through the peripatetic sheikhs themselves or their representatives. In addition, the sheikh appointed imams to each mosque rather than each community selecting its own religious professionals. These were the first formal structures of extralocal power within the world of Islam in China, and the Qing state proscribed and persecuted those that were perceived to be inimical to social order.[11]

The Sufi orders did not, however, constitute "national" organizations to which all Chinese-speaking Muslims, all over the Qing empire, might turn for redress of grievances or influence at court. Quite the contrary, Muslims remained regional, divided, and pitted primarily against each other rather than attempting to establish Islamic unity. The more "national" type of institution and identity had to await the first glimmerings of "modern" China at the end of the nineteenth century. Urban Muslim intellectuals from Beijing, Nanjing, Suzhou, and other eastern cities received that "modern" impulse, like their non-Muslim intellectual colleagues, from Japan and (more distantly) Euro-America. They discovered that a new world awaited them and that a New China had to be created to survive in that world. In northwest China, in contrast, the modernist impulse arrived initially from the Middle East in an Islamic package, emanating from the Ottoman empire, Egypt, and Saudi Arabia. For both groups of Muslim intellectuals, a national Muslim identity could be found only in the context of a newly emerging Chinese identity. Looked at in this way, the Hui, as a Chinese ethnic group (a self-conscious social entity), could only come into existence once a Chinese nation-state had been created to contain it.[12]

During the last years of the Qing and the chaos of the early Republican period, these Muslim intellectuals struggled to form national Hui organizations to overcome what they saw as the ignorance and provincialism of their coreligionists. Like their non-Muslim countrymen, they relied for debate and consensus on numerous periodicals; these included *Xinghuibian* (Awakening the Muslims), one number of which was published in 1908 by a group of Muslim overseas students in Tokyo; *Islam,* which flourished in Henan in the mid-1930s; and the long-lived *Yuehua* (The [crescent] moon and China), founded in Beijing in 1929, which continued to appear until 1948. In the atmosphere of crisis, Social Darwinist thinking, and powerful Japanese intellectual influence, some of them came to see the Hui as a distinct and genetically defined people (a race), while others continued to claim that Islam (usually called Huijiao, the Hui teaching, in Chinese) constituted the essential binding force. Non-Muslim leftist intellectuals such as Fan Changjiang agreed with the former position, some imams took the latter stand, and the great historian Gu Jiegang concluded that all peoples of the former Qing empire, including Han, Muslims, Mongols, Manchus, and Tibetans, constitute a single Chinese people *(Zhonghua minzu),* or Chinese national family. By the 1930s, the CCP, under Stalin's influence and drawing on detailed research done by its own scholars, had begun to refer to the Chinese-speaking Muslims as the Huizu (or Huihui *minzu*).[13]

Muslim intellectuals were not alone in working to create a national identity for the Chinese-speaking Muslims in a new China. Imams influenced by Islamic modernism from the Middle East also founded institutions to create a new consciousness for the Hui. These institutions included Sino-Arabic (Ch. *Zhong-A*) primary, secondary, and normal schools in which education in both religious subjects and the modern secular curriculum (which was called Chinese, after its medium of instruction) was taken to be the responsibility of Muslim communities. Even in parts of the remote northwest, scholars basing themselves in the Islamic-Confucian canon of the Qing period designed schools to teach a mixed Islamic-Chinese curriculum that rapidly came to include foreign languages, mathematics, science, and other "modern" subjects.[14] Obviously, it was crucial that the Chinese-speaking Muslims be defined advantageously within a new China. The impact of powerful government policies might well depend upon whether they came to be considered "insiders" (that is, fully Chinese) or "outsiders" (that is, members of an exotic minority group) in relation to the Chinese national project(s). Muslims never agreed among themselves: more "progressive" groups claimed status as an independent *minzu,* "conservative" imams held that Islam (religion) alone defined their identity, and scholars in the Guomindang (Nationalist Party) camp argued for a single, comprehensive *Zhonghua minzu.*

On the mainland at least, the CCP won, and these tensions informed the definition of the Hui during the "ethnic identification" *(minzu shibie)* project of the 1950s, when the Hui became one of China's oddest minority *minzu*—both Chinese and not Chinese, encompassing people who speak a variety of languages and live all over the country—and a unique object for minority policies at every level of government. Ideologically constrained by its own commitment to Stalin's criteria, the new PRC could not recognize Islam alone as the distinguishing feature of the Hui, but neither could the state ignore the fact that many of the differences between Hui and their neighbors derived from religion.

Pressing political questions emerged for national, provincial, and local leaders and Party structures: What could be done about the legitimate power of the mosque and its religious professionals within Hui communities? How should the state handle the connections between Hui communities, which made them appear conspiratorially linked in ways that non-Muslim Chinese could not be? How could the long-standing local antagonisms between Hui and their non-Muslim neighbors, or between competing groups of Hui (especially Sufi orders and twentieth-century Islamist groups), be tamed or eliminated? How could Hui neighborhoods, often tightly knit enclaves located cheek by jowl with non-Muslim neighbors, be effectively integrated into China's burgeoning urban life? How might Hui villages—autonomous, sometimes exclusive, and (in some places) habitually resistant to state power—be transformed into sites for socialist development? How might the Hui be brought into China's national project(s) as compliant "minority" participants? That is, what types of organization could the state allow (or impose) that would enable effective control over the Hui, who were generally perceived to be antisocial and prone to violence?[15] Few of these questions have been answered finally or consistently in the PRC, and they continue to trouble the state's local authorities throughout China.

Interviewing Hui all over China in the summer of 2000, I asked dozens of people—professors and cabdrivers, farmers and factory workers, businessmen and imams—What do all Hui everywhere in China share in common? Hui working as "ethnic functionaries" *(minzu ganbu)* gave me the conventional answer dictated by the government's definitions, namely, that all Hui share descent from Arab and Persian sojourners and a host of "national characteristics, customs, and habits." Some informants described an emotional attachment to the genetic claim to homogeneous *minzu* status, the notion that "All Hui under Heaven are a single family." After considerable discussion, however, most people answered, "Not much," for they accurately perceived that Hui-ness, or "doing HuiHui" (Ch. *zuo* Huihui), cannot be dissociated from its local context. Even Islam, with its vision of a universal congregation of believers (Ar. *umma*) no longer touches all Hui. Many have become secularists, atheists, members of the Communist Party, and thus have separated themselves to some extent from the religious life of their communities, though by the CCP's own definition, they remain members of the Hui, people we might call ex-Muslims.

A young urban Hui "salary man" in Yunnan went through a whole litany of differences among his fellow Hui—most of them dictated by geography and local culture—before announcing that there are only three things that all Hui share: the white skullcaps that religious Hui men wear either all the time or (at least) in the mosque precinct; *youxiang,* the deep-fried wheels of slightly sweetened dough that are part of every Hui festival, feast, and life-cycle celebration; and consciousness of common Middle Eastern blood.[16] As for the rest, he said, it depends on where you are and whom you ask. So diffuse and elusive an entity presents the PRC with multifaceted, diverse challenges ranging from military control to urban renewal to ideological uniformity. The remainder of this chapter will address the state's actions and some Hui communities' initiatives, resistances, and compliances.

THE PRC AND THE HUI

The pre-1949 relationship between the northwestern Muslims and the CCP followed no single unified path. It included the allegiance of some progressive Muslim intellectuals to the Party and ferocious Muslim military resistance to the Long March, as well as the cooperation of some local Muslim elites with the CCP's anti-Japanese policy after 1935. In Gansu, Qinghai, and Ningxia, most Muslims belonged to communities dominated by families of Muslim warlords (all surnamed Ma) who joined the Guomindang.[17] Some Muslims, however, joined the CCP—out of poverty, sympathy for the Party's anti-Japanese position, or opposition to the Guomindang elites in their communities. Committed to the broadest possible social coalition against Japan and the Guomindang, the CCP did not, at this point, take a strong stand against religion or religious leadership. After the Long March, Edgar Snow talked to northwestern Muslims fighting in the Eighth Route Army, who told him, "The Chinese and the Moslems [*sic*] are brothers; we Moslems also have Chinese blood in us;

we all belong to Ta Chung Kuo [Da Zhongguo, that is, China], and therefore why should we fight each other? Our common enemies are the landlords, the capitalists, the moneylenders, our oppressive rulers, and the Japanese. Our common aim is revolution."[18]

During the anti-Japanese war, the CCP moved away from the Comintern's earlier policy, which allowed self-determination for minority groups as nations, and toward a United Front policy in which all patriotic elements within the great family of the *Zhonghua minzu* should be encouraged to resist Japan together. Mirroring Stalin's reversal of the right of secession for "ethnic minorities," the CCP proclaimed the indivisible unity of China (by which they meant the entire territory of the former Qing empire) and the responsibility of all citizens to love and protect the motherland.[19] The CCP leadership had already decided that China was to be a multiethnic state, for on their Long March they had met not only Muslims and Mongols but also the culturally diverse (and hard to control) non-Chinese peoples of Guizhou, Yunnan, Sichuan, and eastern Tibet. Following the lead of Sun Yat-sen, they declared the Han, a vast mosaic of peoples living from Siberia to the tropics, the overwhelming majority of China's population, to be a single, undifferentiated nationality, the "children of the Yellow Emperor," sharing blood and history.[20] All the rest became "minority peoples," for they belong to China-the-country and should be regarded as younger brothers in the great *minzu* family. According to the CCP analysis, each people will inevitably follow the most advanced—the Han—toward the light of socialism and communism.

This rosy picture, of course, could never be implemented in practice. Even the process of deciding which peoples of China were to be designated as distinct *minzu* engaged the Party and its ethnographers in contentious and highly politicized debates in the mid-1950s. Over four hundred groups "applied"—that is, they were considered sufficiently like *minzu* that scholars were sent to investigate and report on their conformity to the official definition(s) borrowed from the Soviet Union. Party committees at the central and provincial levels made the final decisions. The case of the Hui, among many others, reveals that Stalin's carefully enshrined terminology, still repeated regularly in academic and popular literature on the minorities, was honored as much in the breach as in practice.[21] The members of the Hui, as currently defined in the PRC, have no common language, no common territory, and no common economic life, though they are widely held to be genetically inclined toward skill at doing business in the marketplace. As for common psychological makeup, or culture, Islam itself constitutes their sole common heritage, and their "customs and habits" tend to differ from region to region, except for those that derive from their religion.

Since the "nationality identification" of the 1950s, and especially since 1978, communication and transportation have improved all over China, and the state's designation of the Hui as a coherent social entity now has considerably more validity than it ever did in the past. Because the state has been willing to fund official *minzu* institutions of all kinds, members of the Hui are now aware of their *minzu* identity (which many certainly were not in 1949) and that their *minzu* has, for example, "*minzu* costumes," "*minzu* folksongs," and "*minzu* literature," both ancient and modern. There are Hui research institutes, Hui exhibits at *minzu* theme parks all over China (as well as in Hawaii and Florida), and Hui variety performances on television on New Year's Eve. After years of "*minzu* work" by state functionaries, many Hui are entirely convinced of the common blood they share with all other Hui.

Some Hui take pride in this institutionalized affirmation of their "national" existence, while others find it false, condescending, or downright silly. According to a young Hui worker, "We all loathe those dreadful '*minzu* village' theme parks; they're just places for Han to go and feel superior to the primitive natives." Pointing to his jeans, T-shirt, and baseball hat, he said, "I'm certainly a Hui, but does this look like Hui clothing to you?" After leading me around a typical "*minzu* costume" room in an ethnographic museum—all such rooms contain exactly fifty-six pairs of life-size mannequins, male and female, dressed in the "distinctive" costumes of each *minzu*—a Hui scholar confessed that the Hui exhibit looked like something out of a stylized costume drama and that "no one wears clothes like that, really." At the same time, many Hui earn their living by research, collection, exhibition, and reification of their "national" traditions; scholars in work units all over China are dedicated to the study of the Hui heritage, dating back to the Mongol period or even the Tang, but heavily focused on the present.[22]

There is no question that the thirteen-hundred-year presence of Islam and Muslims in the Chinese cultural area has produced a remarkable synthesis. The seventeenth- to nineteenth-century Confucian-Muslim texts, for example, constitute a rare example of profound Islamic philosophy in a "non-Muslim" language. Sino-Arabic calligraphy is a striking adaptation of a hallowed Middle Eastern art form to the formal aesthetics of Chinese culture. The PRC's definition of the Hui, however, invariably distorts what have been highly localized evolutionary processes. In virtually any realm of life except religion, we may find as much difference among Hui all across China as between Hui and their non-Hui neighbors.

STRUCTURES AND PERSONNEL OF AUTHORITY: THE MOSQUE AND THE *MINZU GANBU*

As a system of religious authority, Islam has been relatively decentralized since the eighth century. Sunni Islam in particular, to which practically all Muslims in China adhere, has never been led by a centralized church or hierarchically organized clergy. Each congregation or mosque (Ar. *jāmia*) can employ religious professionals to lead prayer, preach, teach, and interpret religious law (Ar. *sharī'a*) and the sacred texts. In controversial or recondite cases, these learned leaders (Ar. *'ulamā*) may refer questions or doubts to famous scholars at majors centers of learning, and they, in turn, may reply with an authoritative opinion (Ar. *fatwa*), but these opinions cannot be implemented by any universal system of religious enforcement. As the Islamic community came to include large numbers, and finally a majority, of non-Arabs (and non-speakers of Arabic), this internal flexibility allowed congregations in the southeast Asian archipelago, in the Atlas Mountains, in the Caucasus, and in China (among many other places) to follow the orthodox tenets of their faith without imitating the social or political forms of Islam's Arabian homeland.

In the vast Chinese cultural area, with its diverse ecologies and social landscapes, Muslim communities have thus fit into many different local scenes without following a rigid blueprint. They certainly share many characteristics that distinguish them from their non-Muslim neighbors — the centrality of the mosque and its professionals, for example, and the sacred texts in Arabic, which mark them as outlandish, however thoroughly they have become "local." Since the fourteenth century, however, Muslims in China have come to use local Chinese as their sole vernacular, adding Arabic, Persian, and Turkish words as an internal lexicon of recognition and authenticity. They have placed themselves in economic niches that take advantage of the connections between their communities, and they rely on one another to provide hospitality, *halāl* food, and a place to pray, as well as to act as trustworthy trade partners in the face of non-Muslim competitors. But except for the Sufi orders mentioned above, they have few formal structures of intercommunity authority, so they have generally been able to adapt to local (non-Muslim) contexts without threatening either social order or the state and its local representatives.

In the PRC, the centralized structures of the Hui, in parallel with those of the other "ethnic minorities," have been created as hierarchies by the state. The *minzu ganbu* of the Hui are organized into at least two sets of organizations—one dealing with religion, the other (in theory, resolutely secular and "ethnic") handling *minzu* problems. The China Islamic Association (Ch. Zhongguo Yisilanjiao Xiehui, shortened to Yixie), which includes members of all ten officially defined Muslim *minzu,* takes charge of Islamic religious affairs and mediates all open, "legitimate" contacts with Islamic organizations and Muslims outside the PRC. The central Yixie in Beijing, for example, allocates places in the government-sponsored pilgrimage (Ar. *hajj*) delegations to Mecca, which are highly desirable to Chinese Muslims because the state foots at least part of the rather large bill for transport, lodging, and food during the month-long journey. In addition, there are branches of the Religious Affairs Office (Ch. Zongjiao Shiwu Ju) at the provincial- and local-government levels to deal more directly with local religious issues. The Central Ethnic Affairs Commission (Ch. Zhongyang Minzu Shiwu Weiyuanhui, shortened to Minwei), on the other hand, deals with political and social issues involving all of the minority *minzu.*[23] The Yixie, Minwei, and Religious Affairs Office all have provincial- and county-level structures, sometimes headed by Han but staffed largely by *minzu ganbu,* and members of these organizations can see their functions as quite separate, though they may have overlapping personnel and might often work together.

In theory, at least, these structures allow members of the Hui to take charge of their own communities. Some informants, however, scoffed at the idea that the *minzu ganbu* and their hierarchical *minzu* and religious organizations have any power or influence. As one Muslim shopkeeper in Xi'an told me, "We solve our problems here ourselves, without any interference from them. The *minzu ganbu* are useless." His neighbor, who also had a shop, claimed that no minority person would ever be given a position with influence. A Muslim worker from Kunming agreed with this conclusion and said that the state authorities use the *minzu ganbu* as a front, as window dressing, while giving all the effective jurisdiction to Han functionaries. "They would never trust a Hui with any real power," he said.

A *minzu ganbu* from Ningxia who held joint positions in the provincial Minwei and Religious Affairs Office disagreed with this opinion. He had participated actively in local conflict resolution throughout his career, and he saw his work as a mediator within the Hui community as a serious contribution to social order, one that had prevented the kinds of conflicts that had polarized the northwestern Chinese Muslims from the

1760s to the 1930s and had led to sanguinary violence. But some Ningxia Muslims openly expressed their contempt for such people, who they said join the Han in oppressing Muslims. The *minzu ganbu* of course denied this, claiming that people who hold such opinions are ignorant of the vital contribution made by the religious- and *minzu*-affairs functionaries.

The construction of top-down bureaucracies to handle Hui affairs might seem to homogenize at least the administration of local Hui communities all over China, and this has indeed been one effect of the PRC's consolidation of effective central power in the last half century. But this has not had much leveling effect on the types of conflicts, problems, and distinctions that confront Hui in their local contexts all over China. As the two stories at the beginning of this chapter indicate, some areas are more violent than others, presenting the authorities with intractable problems of rivalry and a collective memory of conflict stretching back into the distant past. In contrast, some Hui communities are engaged with the state (cooperatively or in conflict) in solving what appear to us to be much more modern, "normal" dilemmas.

The persistence of Islamic authority—the *'ulamā* (Ch. *ahong,* from Per. *akhünd,* "teacher"), Sufi sheikhs, and elders of the local mosque—continues to provide an internal alternative to the formal structures of the Yixie and the Minwei, one that sometimes appears subversive to non-Muslim officials. *Ahong* must be very careful not to tread on the toes of state functionaries or to invade their realm of authority. One elderly religious teacher in Xining, a man of eminent descent and great learning in the Muslim tradition, talked to me for over an hour without admitting that anything ever goes wrong in his community or that religious conflict had ever occurred in the large provincial city in which he constitutes the highest Islamic authority. Though evidence to the contrary exists, he felt he had no choice but to describe the state structures, and his own role in mediation, as entirely successful in keeping social order.

THE PRIMACY OF THE LOCAL: HUI AS MIDDLEMEN

Both Chinese and Muslim, the Hui may be seen as occupying the cultural margin of Chinese civilization, part inside and part outside. More literally, many Hui communities are physically located on the edges of the Chinese cultural area, where it abuts Southeast Asia, Tibet, Central Asia, and Mongolia.[24] In these locations, the Hui often serve as middlemen, brokers between Chinese and non-Chinese cultures. They are not alone, for members of other ethnic and cultural groups can also perform these functions, but the Hui have proved themselves uniquely suited to the position. In Lintan Jiucheng, a market town in southern Gansu, one Hui community has more than a century's experience in economic brokerage between China and Tibet. Tibetan is taught beside Chinese and Arabic in the community's schools, and they have designed their economic activities to maximize exchange between the mountain and grassland products of the Tibetans and the lowland artisan and industrial production of cultural China. Knowing that the Tibetans have particular tastes in textile colors and designs, for example, this Muslim group has purchased two silk factories in Hangzhou, far away in eastern China, where they manufacture cloth to suit Tibetan preferences. They transport the goods by rail and road to Lintan Jiucheng, where they are repacked and loaded onto small pickup trucks, which the individual brokers use to reach their tent-dwelling customers in the high country.

Hui communities like Lintan Jiucheng's can be found throughout the great semicircular frontier that buffers the Chinese cultural area on its inland side. The Hui have also placed themselves throughout China proper—in villages, towns, and cities where they are surrounded by a vast majority of non-Muslims, most of whom are Han. In those locations they constitute a kind of internal frontier, where they sometimes continue their middleman function. For example, Hui families all over China have taken up transporting, carving, and selling jade as their specialty. Even in Beijing and Shanghai, some of the most famous and prosperous jade dealers are Hui. They have undertaken this work in part because the most important domestic source for jade within the PRC (and within the Qing empire in centuries past) lies in Xinjiang, China's huge northwesternmost province, whose population was until the mid–twentieth century overwhelmingly Turkic speaking and Muslim.[25]

More commonplace trades have also attracted Hui entrepreneurs. In part because of their religion's dietary prescriptions, many Hui engage in butchering (eschewing pork, of course), in inn keeping, and most obviously in recent decades, in preparing and selling food. The *halāl* restaurant is ubiquitous in China and is assumed to be cleaner than its non-Muslim counterparts; it serves tasty, slightly exotic specialties such as Xinjiang fried noodles, Central Asian bread, and lamb stew. In the past few years, high-end Hui restaurants have appeared in major Chinese cities, serving *halāl* versions of the same dishes as non-Muslim establishments— roast duck, whole fish, crab, and more. The more common Hui food stall is located in a market street, and its customers sit on stools at small, rickety tables to eat *halāl* adaptations of local everyday foods. Like their non-

Muslim neighbors, Muslims in northwest and north China prefer noodles, steamed bread, and other wheat products as their main grain foods
(Ch. *zhushi*), while Yunnanese, Sichuanese, and other southern Muslims
eat their meat and vegetables with rice.

Xi'an

The Muslim quarter of Xi'an is clearly distinguished from nearby non-
Muslim parts of the city not only by its old-style housing (see below),
but also by its dense concentration of Muslim restaurants, bookstores,
mosques, shops, and schools.[26] In the past twenty years, the residents of
the quarter have prospered in business and rebuilt many of their substantial
mosques. The largest and oldest of them, the Great Mosque, dates from
the Ming period and has been designated as a national historic site by the
PRC government. Since the Great Mosque has been included on the flour-
ishing Xi'an tourist circuit, hundreds of thousands of visitors make their
way on foot through the quarter's alleys each year. Responding quickly
to this potential market, the Hui of the quarter have become souvenir
dealers on an enormous scale—one can buy "Muslim" objects, such as
white skullcaps, calligraphic scrolls in Arabic, or porcelain decorated with
Arabic inscriptions, as well as conventional "traditional Chinese" knick-
knacks from the hundreds of stalls that crowd the narrow walkways.

Conspicuous economic success marks the Xi'an Muslim quarter, but
so does Islam. In the early 1990s, religious leaders became increasingly
uncomfortable about the sale of alcoholic beverages by Hui merchants in
the quarter. Most Xi'an Hui follow the Koranic injunction against con-
suming alcohol, but merchants eager for non-Muslim customers found
it necessary to acquiesce to their clientele's demands for alcoholic drinks
with their food. During his Friday sermons, a courageous *ahong* began
to denounce the sale and consumption of alcohol, and a committee was
formed to ban alcohol from the quarter. This organization, which has few
parallels in other parts of China, agitated openly, held rallies, and confronted merchants who refused to cooperate with the ban. After several
years of success, the committee was suddenly declared illegal by the local
authorities, since it had not applied for permission to incorporate as an
organization. Though it received support from all of the Xi'an area's eighteen mosques and even from non-Muslim merchants operating in the vicin-
ity, the committee would only be allowed to operate if it accepted a CCP
member in its ranks and allowed him to report on all its activities.[27]

This particular conflict, which had still not been resolved in 1998, placed the quarter's Muslims in a potential confrontation with the state, as well as with non-Muslim merchants and customers who resented the alcohol ban. Activist Hui had skillfully used the state's own minority policies, which permit socially acceptable "minority customs and habits" to flourish, but they were unwilling to resist the government's label of "illegal organization" (Ch. *feifa zuzhi*) by either direct confrontation or going underground. No national Hui organizations joined the struggle, though provincial Yixie representatives voiced their support for the alcohol ban. Its substance— alcohol avoidance—was universally Islamic, but this was a local battle, fought by local Hui, over a local issue.

Sanpo

East of Xi'an, on the south bank of the Yellow River in Henan Province, lies Sanpo, an entirely Hui community of forty-five hundred people near Zhengzhou. Sanpo differs from nearby Han communities in the centrality of its ten mosques in collective life and in its devotion to the trades of the tanner and furrier, especially those processing sheepskins and wild animal pelts.[28] These occupations, and the ensuing marketing of furs and leather, have proved most profitable, but they have also given the village a powerful and penetrating smell. Some Sanpo villagers have migrated to the hill country of eastern Gansu, where they raise sheep on barren hillsides, then bring the hides to Sanpo for processing. The products are sold to clothiers and to boutiques in the major cities of eastern China, and more recently to Europe, Japan, and the United States as well. As a sideline, some enterprising Sanpo merchants have also invested in the manufacture of woolen rugs for export.

Marked as different from their non-Muslim neighbors by their religion, their trade in sheep, and their village's odor, the Sanpo Hui are also quite distinct within the world of Islam, for their village has five mosques reserved for, and led by, women. Women's mosques (Ch. *nüsi*), as distinguished from curtained-off women's sections in ordinary mosques, may be found in very few parts of the Muslim world. In China, they exist primarily in the north China plain (with outliers in Xi'an and Lanzhou), and in Yunnan, where virtually every significant Muslim community has at least one. Muslims from elsewhere in the world find the women's mosques peculiar at best and unnecessary or even heterodox at worst, but local Muslims in China defend them as perfectly compatible with Islamic orthodoxy. They believe that women can find a more satisfying spiritual and community life within their own institutions, taught by their own female imams (Ch. *nü ahong*).[29]

From these brief vignettes we may move toward the conclusion that relationships between the Hui (as individuals, as communities, and as an "ethnic minority"), their non-Muslim (or non-Hui) neighbors, and local government are determined more by local issues, conditions, and personalities than by any national agenda on either side.

THE HUI VERSUS THE STATE:
NEGOTIATING URBAN RENEWAL

Xi'an

The Muslim quarter of Xi'an, just behind the Bell Tower at the center of the old city, is distinguished not only by its religious institutions and its anti-alcohol committee but also by its antiquated housing. Xi'an has undergone a thorough urban renewal in the past twenty years, and only the Muslim quarter remains as a remnant of the old days; its many low, run-down buildings constitute a blot on the urban landscape, according to city planners, who much prefer modern apartment blocks with flush toilets. Like the Muslim sections of Zhengzhou and many other cities, this Hui quarter (Ch. *Huiminfang*) has been under increasing pressure to submit to government plans for gentrification and resettlement of some of its population in the suburbs. The Muslims, too, would like to have running water, modern apartments, and wider, cleaner streets, but not at the cost of values and social conditions that they perceive to be essential to their community life.

Like the Muslim urbanites of Zhengzhou, the Xi'an Hui have lobbied their local government, but their negotiations have taken place in an entirely local personal and political context, without involvement by the central authorities and without any systematic reference to experience elsewhere, though several informants referred informally to the positive models of Jinan and Shenyang. They have demanded that any urban-renewal plan leave room for them to maintain their solidarity, and some of them have organized to define their community's interests. Though they certainly desire to be seen as progressive, these Hui also have deep anxieties about the survival of their community life, their extended families, their mosques, and their businesses, fears that neither local nor provincial government planners have been able to allay.[30]

Ma Liangxun, the leader of the Xi'an Hui community in relations with city and provincial authorities, holds the official position of vice-chairman of the Religious and Ethnic Affairs Committee of Shaanxi Province. He is also the brother of a leading *ahong* of the quarter, Ma Liangji, who recently retired as the religious leader of the Great Mosque and now devotes himself to Muslim construction and commemoration projects. But Ma Liangxun is not a businessman, so when plans were first made to rebuild the Hui quarter, the city government sought a Hui business leader to direct the contracting and concentration of capital for investment in renewal, but none could be found. A successful Hui entrepreneur managed to achieve a government position from which to play the middleman, but his efforts failed.

Reacting to the potential transformation (or elimination) of the quarter, a group of local men, including small entrepreneurs, academics, schoolteachers, and religious professionals—not the most visible leaders but solid citizens with credible voices—formed the Xi'an Islamic Cultural Study Society (Ch. Xi'an Shi Yisilan Wenhua Yanjiuhui) in 1995. Their work has included holding conferences, publishing edited volumes of essays, welcoming guests, both foreign and domestic, conducting formal and informal relations with Muslim communities in other parts of China, and, most relevant here, doing research on the Hui quarter in order to provide data to residents and to the local and provincial governments. This formal group, permitted by the state under the category of "popular (Ch. *minjian*) organizations," has worked publicly and openly as an advocate for the Hui community. One of its intellectual leaders, Zhu Songli, thought that he could help to ease the tension and conflict over urban renewal in the Muslim quarter by gathering information and listening to the residents. Everything was done through official channels, in no way resembling the violent confrontation in Yunnan described at the beginning of this chapter:

> We worked out an outline for investigation and research, then submitted it to the superior departments responsible for the work and the relevant provincial leadership. In the past half year, we have invited concerned people from every walk of life in the Hui quarter to several discussion meetings to hear their opinions. We have made a number of specific visits [to individuals] and produced and distributed more than a hundred questionnaires. Naturally, our work is still quite superficial, and the materials we have gathered are very limited and scattered. But undertaking this research has nonetheless impelled us to think about many problems, some from the comments of our members and others dis-

cussed in the reactions to the questionnaire, and it has given us considerable inspiration.[31]

The opinions of Xi'an Muslims on urban renewal, reported both by Maris Boyd Gillette and by the Cultural Study Society, differ by the respondent's wealth and education, by religious affiliation and personal piety, by individual goals, and even by family size. Numerous objections have been raised to the government's plans, but no unified counterproposals have come from the Muslims. Rather, they continue to discuss urban-renewal issues with one another and, through official and unofficial representatives, with the state. As of summer 2000, no renewal projects had yet broken ground in the quarter. Only a few old public apartment buildings had been vacated and torn down, but work had not begun on any replacements for them.

Yinchuan

Facing a similar urban problem, a mosque community in Yinchuan, the capital of the Ningxia Hui Autonomous Region, took a very different path. Their nineteenth-century mosque, built in the old Chinese style, had been desecrated during the Cultural Revolution, and they very much desired a new mosque in the heady, vibrant reform economy of the 1980s. On the same site as their old mosque, they constructed an "Arabic-style" complex with a dome and two towers,[32] and they also built half a dozen large apartment buildings surrounding it. The housing, some of it owned and operated by the mosque as an endowed property (Ar. *waqf*), generates income for the religious institution. It also guarantees that this particular Hui community will not be broken up by gentrification or further urban renewal. Though the complex does not contain retail businesses, there are market spaces nearby where the Muslims can shop and operate their own trades. The flexibility of this community is due in part to the relative anonymity of their location in a small provincial city—Yinchuan, unlike Xi'an, does not lie on the major national or international tourist circuits, and this mosque had been located on the outskirts for centuries.[33]

At least one conflict did mar the mosque's happy renewal. Like most modern mosques, this one broadcast the early-morning call to prayer through an amplifier and loudspeakers located in the tall minarets, just before dawn.[34] Pious Muslims, of course, find this call, which begins with a resounding "God is great!" to be a welcome invitation to communal worship and to the satisfying ritual of the new day. However, non-Muslim families who moved into the nearby apartment buildings, unaccustomed to Islamic religious routine, resented being suddenly awakened by their neighbors' amplified and unintelligible noise. Arguments occurred that were unpleasant but not violent, and the mosque's leaders agreed to a meeting. The city Religious Affairs Office played a part in the negotiations, and a compromise was reached by which the first call to prayer of the day would not be amplified, and the remaining four would be announced as usual through the sound system. This was certainly a far cry from the battles and massacres of the region's past. Sufi orders had flourished and fought one another in the area, and a major Muslim rebellion against the Qing established its headquarters across the Yellow River from Yinchuan in the 1860s. Tens of thousands of people died in the empire's campaign of suppression. By the 1990s, the Muslims of this mosque, at least, had established their presence as legitimate, their religious institutions as an ordinary part of the landscape, and their voice as one of moderation and negotiation.

CONFRONTATIONAL HUI: VARIOUS LOCALES, VARIOUS SOLUTIONS

If people in premodern China knew anything at all about the Chinese-speaking Muslims, they "knew" that they were violent people, prone to ganging up on hapless non-Muslims, to protection rackets and extortion, to feuding among themselves, and to violent crime. In the Qing period, law cases and memorials from the northwest, from the southwest, and from the north China plain—all the parts of China proper in which Chinese-speaking Muslims were concentrated—described "those people" as fierce, brutal, and antisocial. As the story that begins this essay demonstrates, that stereotypical image has not faded from memory in some parts of the PRC. The Yunnanese policemen who opened fire on the Muslims in the police-station courtyard thought they had much to fear from a trouble-making gang of Hui. The army has been called out on a number of occasions in the past decade, in a number of provinces, to deal with violence involving Hui. Many non-Muslims, especially those living near dense settlements of Hui, still fear for their lives and deplore the state's "soft" policies on minorities. One non-Muslim scholar in Beijing claimed that the Hui receive myriad special benefits because local government is so afraid of them, so concerned that "Hui violence" not recur.

Be that as it may, a close examination of a number of recent incidents reveals that "Hui violence" is not evenly distributed, is not simple rapacity or collective sociopathology, and is not always directed at non-Hui. Some Hui do behave violently (so do some Han, of course, but their *minzu* identity is not blamed), but most do not. The Muslims of the north China plain (especially Henan), who were once famous for banditry and predation, have since the 1930s become much calmer. The Muslims of southern Shaanxi, feared for their solidarity and bloody-mindedness in the Wei River valley hinterland of Xi'an, were all killed or driven out during the "Muslim rebellions" of the mid–nineteenth century. So the following cases come primarily from Ningxia, Qinghai, Gansu, and Yunnan, frontier zones in which Muslims remain concentrated and their reputation as inherently antisocial people has persisted.

Ningxia

The Ningxia Hui Autonomous Region occupies barren plains and mountains through which runs a ribbon of green, a narrow plain watered by the Yellow River as it meanders between the Ordos Desert and the Liupan Mountains on the east and the Helan Mountains on the west. Long an area of mixed religions and ethnicities, Ningxia currently has a population about 70 percent Han and 30 percent Hui, with a small number of Mongols in the west of the province. The irrigated areas (mostly to the north) have prospered in agriculture, industry (including coal mining), and trade, while the southern sections, mountainous and arid, have been the site of incredible poverty. Though there are Hui all over the province, for the past few decades "Hui violence" has been isolated in the destitute, water-starved south.

In 1992, a conflict erupted within the Banqiao branch of the Jahrïya Sufi order over leadership of the branch. The violence escalated so fast that more than fifty people had been killed before the army arrived. All of the dead were Hui, and none of the participants had made any overt moves against the state. The army separated the two sides without firing a shot, and the work of pacification, judgment, and reconciliation began with the arrival of a provincial work team made up of fifteen hundred officials, the majority of them Muslim *minzu ganbu*.

The job took eighteen months. By the end, one of the contenders for the leadership of the Jahrïya and some of his followers were doing time in a provincial prison, but they were not executed or locked away for life, as has often been the case with Chinese citizens involved in violent incidents. The work-team members were satisfied that they had dealt with the local antisocial elements, but they came away appalled by the poverty and deprivation they had seen. Within two years, plans had been made to alleviate those conditions, and by the year 2000, road-building projects, newly dug wells, and agricultural-extension stations had been located throughout the three counties of southern Ningxia. Central and provincial governments have both contributed funds to the effort; Muslim institutions and private individuals do so as well.

The situation in Yinchuan City, in the northern part of the province, presents a strong contrast. With a large Muslim population and a long history of internecine feuding among Sufi orders, traditionalists, and fundamentalists, the city could be a hotbed of violence. But informants ranging from imams to professors to shopkeepers told me that the problems had been solved (like the early-morning loudspeakers in the western suburb) and that there had been no violence there for a long time. They attributed this rapid improvement to one of two sources: either the *minzu ganbu* (especially those from the Yixie) had done their propaganda work well, mediated among the potentially feuding communities, and fostered an atmosphere of mutual respect; or that same atmosphere had been created by effective cooperation and negotiation among the *ahong* of the various mosques and the leaders of the competing Muslim interests. All informants agreed that the members of one mosque can attend services at the others, that *ahong* routinely give sermons to one another's congregations, regardless of affiliation, and that the members of one congregation are often invited to others for charitable feasts, funerals, and festivals.

Qinghai

As mentioned above, the most eminent *ahong* in Xining, the capital of Qinghai Province—which contains the northeastern corner of the Tibetan cultural region, where it abuts the Chinese, Mongolian, and Turkic cultural regions—spent over an hour telling me that everything there is fine. Tibetans and Muslims never quarrel, Muslim groups all get along, everyone shares mosque space for festivals, Han never insult Islam, and "unity" (Ch. *tuanjie*) characterizes all *minzu* relationships. Understanding his position as a public leader in a delicate and closely watched frontier zone, I did not press him or present evidence to the contrary (which is plentiful) during our conversation.

The previous evening, a young shop clerk sat with me for over an hour and talked about "what happened back in 1993." That year (my informant was a teenager at the time), a newspaper in Sichuan published arti-

cles and advertising deemed insulting to Islam and Muslims, juxtaposing
Islamic material and pictures of pigs.[35] Protests spread all over the country, and Xining Muslims planned a demonstration. The Xining authorities refused permission for a demonstration, but the Muslims marched
anyway. Already defying the local representatives of the state and dissatisfied
with their reaction, the Muslims decided to take their grievances to
Lanzhou, hundreds of kilometers to the east, and then to Beijing, a place
of immense power to which few if any of them had ever been. The army
moved to block the bridges in the narrow mountain passes, so some of
the marchers decided to swim the river instead. Five of them drowned.

Clearly this was not "Muslim violence," though it certainly constituted
disobedience to local authority. It did nourish an already existing sense
among some Xining Muslims that the army (and by extension the state)
does not care about them, that they were willing to watch Muslims drown,
and that they would not allow Muslim voices to be heard. For non-Muslims,
this incident offered further evidence that Muslims will misbehave if given
the chance and confirmed their prejudice that Muslims will sacrifice themselves instantly and thoughtlessly for their religion or their ethnic group.
Though these stereotypes are not limited to Xining—indeed, they are quite
general in China—this particular incident caused only local upset, and it
is known among ordinary Muslims elsewhere in the country only as a
distant report.

Gansu

Dru Gladney has described recent brawls between members of competing Muslim interests in Linxia, a prefectural city in southern Gansu
Province.[36] It is located on the east side of a mountain range: to the west,
the population is largely Tibetan; to the east, beyond the Tao River, lie
predominantly Han counties. In short, Linxia represents the cultural frontier, a riverside market town where Chinese and Tibetans meet, their economic interactions mediated, to some extent, by Chinese-speaking
Muslims. To this potentially volatile mix of ethnic difference and frontier
location, the modern world has, since the late nineteenth century, added
a new ingredient—illicit drugs. Since 1978, the booming commercial markets, lax law enforcement, and ubiquitous government corruption of the
PRC have reintroduced the drug trade to China, including to the Muslims of the northwest. According to a recent news story, many Linxia Muslims are engaged in smuggling opiates, including heroin, from Yunnan,

near the border of the Golden Triangle; their destinations are as far away as Xinjiang, where some dealers also obtain supplies of opiates from Afghanistan via the former Central Asian republics of the Soviet Union.[37]

In either case, already established transportation networks staffed by Muslims are available for moving the drugs from the frontiers toward markets in China proper, which local people call "the interior" (Ch. *neidi*). This repeats a common pattern from earlier in the century, when Muslim farmers grew poppies and Muslim merchants moved raw or processed opium to market. The same article reports an alarming rise in local consumption, with hundreds of young Linxia Muslims already addicted. In Linxia, as elsewhere in the world, the combination of rapidly acquired wealth and drug use has enhanced the frontier's propensity for tension and violence. In 1996, Linxia informants professed themselves afraid, nostalgically recalling the Cultural Revolution and its strict social controls as halcyon days of peace and social stability.

A hundred kilometers southeast of Linxia, across a stretch of grassland above eight thousand feet in altitude, lies Lintan Jiucheng, mentioned above as a center for Muslims engaged in the trade between cultural China and cultural Tibet. The Xidaotang, a Muslim collective with over ten thousand members, has had its headquarters there for almost a century.[38] Valuing commerce, and therefore social order, the leaders of the Xidaotang have taken a conciliatory stand toward government regulation and the ethnocultural values of both their suppliers and their customers, preferring to deal peacefully as the intermediaries between Tibetans and Chinese.

The Xidaotang has also mediated within the world of Islam in China. Its founder, Ma Qixi (1857–1914), studied the Muslim tradition in Central Asia and was thoroughly conversant with the Arabic canon, but he also received a classical Chinese education. Once he became an *ahong,* that combination led him to focus his teaching curriculum on the Islamic texts in Chinese, the Han *kitab,* which had been produced during the Qing period.

Without watering down their Islamic orthodoxy or orthopraxy, the Hui of the Xidaotang have built China-wide production and distribution networks, including numerous retail shops, using their commercial name, Tianxinglong. As mentioned above, they teach Tibetan in their community's schools, and community informants confirm that they take a relatively respectful approach toward their Tibetan clientele, an attitude not shared by most Chinese. In part because of the Xidaotang's powerful local influence in ethnic relations, Lintan Jiucheng has remained relatively calm for the past half century, and there have been few incidents of communal violence. Though drugs may be smuggled there—the town lies on a major trade route between Yunnan and the northwest—none of my informants mentioned addiction as a social problem.

Yunnan

The ethnic and historical complexities of Gansu, Qinghai, and Ningxia are more than matched by those of Yunnan. China's southwesternmost province, bordering not only several Southeast Asian countries but also the Tibetan cultural region, has been the site of sanguinary confrontations, massacres, displacements, forced migrations, and diverse intermingling of peoples and cultures since it was incorporated into a China-based empire by the Mongols over seven hundred years ago. Muslims came to Yunnan in large numbers just at that time—soldiers and officials in an army commanded by Sayyid Ajall Shams ad-Dïn (Ch. Sai Dianchi), one of Khubilai Khan's most successful generals. They stayed and have been an ordinary part of the social landscape ever since. Their relationship with the state reached a low point in the mid–nineteenth century, when Du Wenxiu (1827–1872), a local Muslim, proclaimed Dali (in western Yunnan) the capital of "the state that pacifies the south" (Ch. Pingnan Guo). Du fought off the Qing armies for years, then perished after a lengthy siege. Many of Du's core followers were Muslims, and the Qing armies (one of them led by a Muslim) killed thousands of Muslims while pacifying the rebellion.

Some parts of Yunnan, especially in the west and south, were more engaged in Pingnan Guo than others, despite a provincewide distribution of Muslims. The Muslims of the poverty-stricken northeastern region (Zhaotong) pride themselves more on their lineage genealogies than they do on their adherence to a nineteenth-century Islamic state.[39] Several informants, including university-based scholars, emphasized that the patchwork, somewhat disconnected quality of the Muslim worlds of Yunnan continues to exist today. A linguist told me that there are at least four distinct dialect zones within the Yunnanese form of Chinese, and that Muslims are residents of all four. My own field experience bore out the contention that very few generalizations can accurately describe the Hui in the region, apart from the obvious unities of religion and mosque-based community structure.

Apart from the violent incident described at the beginning of this chapter, one potent moment stands out in recent history, as narrated by local

Muslims. Everyone in Yunnan (and every Muslim in China) knows that toward the end of the Cultural Revolution, the state destroyed the village of Shadian, a sizable south Yunnan Muslim community of several thousand souls.[40] I could not go to Shadian, but several informants in Kunming and Yuxi were willing to tell me what happened, and their various accounts contain the truth that "everyone knows." In the chaotic days of the early 1970s, conformity to Han standards and values constituted the most important tenet of *minzu* policy in China under the direction of the Cultural Revolution Central Committee. Anything perceived as "different" was maligned as counterrevolutionary and squelched. All over China, mosques became sites of bullying, sacrilege, and even murder and suicide as Muslims were forced to raise pigs in the courtyards, and even aged *ahong* were forced to violate their own religious beliefs by eating pork.

Shadian was no exception. The state, through its local officials, imposed a production quota of pork on the village, and few were willing to resist, since the policy was well known and closely linked to patriotism and love of Chairman Mao. In addition, disobedience would have brought severe penalties. But then local Han officials came to the village and began to browbeat the Muslims. Old *ahong* were made to crawl on the ground and make pig sounds, and local policy demanded that Muslims not only produce but also consume pork in order to be "good Chinese revolutionaries."

Local Han cadres, eager to "help" the Muslims become good Chinese by overcoming their hidebound and antisocial resistance to pork, decided to place pig bones in the wells to accustom the Hui to the taste.[41] Discovering the pollution, the Muslims refused to drink the water and determined to resist what they perceived as murderous, sacrilegious behavior from their Han neighbors and government officials. Shadian, like many Yunnanese Muslim communities, had a long tradition of metallurgy, blacksmithing, and weapons manufacture. Over the next two years, as the county mustered an all-Han militia to oversee the "counterrevolutionary" village, the Muslim men made new guns, which included sophisticated automatic weapons, and organized a Muslim paramilitary of their own. Battles between the two armed groups left a number of men dead. The authorities, not understanding the depth of the Muslims' determination, sent ordinary policemen to deal with the problem, and the Muslims killed them.

The People's Liberation Army (PLA), summoned from provincial frontiers and distant bases, then surrounded the entrenched farmers and small entrepreneurs of Shadian, who had only small arms and no artillery. After negotiations failed to persuade the Muslims to allow the PLA into the village, the army opened fire and razed the village entirely. According to Gladney, the army destroyed the village as a warning to others, but after the fall of the Gang of Four in 1976, the state rebuilt Shadian quickly— one informant thought this was done in hopes of eradicating the memory of the army's brutal suppression. The county and provincial governments provided special grants once reconstruction began, so Shadian developed more quickly than most Yunnan villages and today, because of the incident, it prospers in trade and agricultural production.

Closer to Kunming, up in the central Yunnan hill country, the Muslim village of Najiaying also had a tense confrontation with the state, but with a very different denouement. When Shadian "rebelled," the *ahong* of Najiaying organized the men to withstand a siege and prepared the community for armed confrontation. But the village leaders talked the men out of suicidal resistance and when the army arrived in force, surrendered the village without firing a shot. Najiaying currently has seven thousand indigenous residents, and another seven thousand "outside" workers, mostly from elsewhere in Yunnan, serve as the lower-level labor force. The Muslim community is doing exceptionally well in business.

Shandong

The most recent local violence involving Hui occurred not in a remote frontier region but right in the Chinese heartland, in Shandong Province. In December 2000, international news networks reported deadly clashes there between police, allied with armed non-Muslim paramilitary units, and crowds of Muslim protesters. In Yangxin County, no fewer than five Muslims were killed, and Muslims from all over eastern China were said to be in Yangxin to protect their coreligionists and to seek revenge.[42]

The cause of these violent outbreaks lay in long-term misunderstandings between local Muslims and non-Muslims over what constitutes respectful coexistence. In late September, a non-Muslim street vendor, trying to take advantage of the Muslims' reputation for cleanliness and tasty food, had (in his ignorance) put up a sign advertising "Muslim pork." Agence France-Presse reported that Muslim leaders both staged public protests and attempted to petition local government for redress of this insult, and Lateline News claimed that outraged Muslims killed the vendor and another non-Muslim. Rather than negotiating the removal of the sign, county-level officials accused the Muslims of serious violations of the law (because of their protest gatherings) and arrested several leaders.

In a sad replay of Qing- and Republican-period incidents, by November, Muslims and non-Muslims were polarized, and police clashed several times with unarmed Muslim demonstrators, whom they accused of illegal assembly.

Serious violence, however, did not occur until someone hung a pig's head in front of a mosque on 8 or 9 December. Several days later, hundreds (perhaps thousands) of Muslims from Mengcun, a Hui stronghold in nearby Hebei Province, set out on the road to join the protests in Yangxin. Stopped by armed police and militia at a roadblock, they refused to disperse or return home and (according to police) became rowdy. Fighting broke out, joined by unofficial Han bystanders. As frightened by a Hui mob as their colleagues in Yunnan had been in 1990, the police fired into the crowd of protesters, killing five and injuring as many as forty.

By 18 December, a negotiation process had begun, reparations for the dead and wounded had been offered, and as many as two thousand *minzu ganbu* had descended on the region to calm the violence. No national, regional, or even provincial outbreaks occurred—indeed, the 18 December story is the last news I have been able to find about the incident. Inquiring by e-mail of friends all over China in January 2001, I found that Muslims know about the violence, regret it, and even resent it and openly blame the state for it. But none has any intention of going to Shandong, organizing a national protest, or undertaking any public action. Once again, we find local authorities dealing not with national ethnic conflicts but rather with local Hui problems, which they try to resolve without supralocal repercussions.

CONCLUSION

How can we explain the differences between rebellious Shadian and overtly compliant Najiaying? Between Shadian's fate in the 1970s and that of Yuxi two decades later? Why was the Zhengzhou Muslim quarter able to negotiate construction of new urban villages to salvage its neighborhood's location and structure, while the Xi'an Muslim quarter's efforts have thus far produced no results (though their neighborhood has not yet been razed or "renewed")? It seems to me that all of the stories in this chapter can be understood only by recognizing the local nature of Hui communities, which endures despite their common Muslim religion and (state-defined) *minzu* identity. Chinese scholars unify all of these phenomena in a conceptual universe dominated by the notion of *minzu*. Indeed, they posit two simultaneous interlocking processes—ethnicization *(minzuhua)* and localization *(diquhua)*—as responsible for the formation of the Hui within the Chinese cultural matrix.

Without accepting the conventional timing of these two processes (for Chinese scholars place the former in the Ming period rather than the twentieth century), we may understand their importance to the formation and maintenance of Hui identity in contemporary China. Hui intellectuals emphasize the universal quality of Huiness, its minority *minzu* core, while many other Hui stress the local in discussing who they are. Religious leaders and pious individuals, of course, place greatest importance on the Islamic religion as a unifying valence of identity, but they also recognize its limits. Despite the claim that "all Muslims under Heaven are one family," most Hui *ahong* do not connect themselves easily or comfortably with separatist Turkic-speaking Muslims in Xinjiang and their sociopolitical ambitions. After all, the vast majority of Hui, even some of those who have traveled extensively in the Middle East, are clearly Chinese in their language, material culture, and textual lives outside the mosque. However much they might identify with Muslims elsewhere—even going so far as to don Arab clothing and headgear for photo opportunities—the Hui are not members of Malay or Turkish or Persian or Arab or any other "Muslim" culture in which Islam is a "natural" component of identity. On the contrary, they must distinguish themselves constantly from the overwhelming majority of Chinese speakers, who are not Muslims, while still remaining part of the only culture and polity in which their identity makes sense—that of China.

Seen in that light, this study of the Hui suggests some important conclusions regarding *minzu* and *minzu* policy in contemporary China. First, "the Hui" do not exist as a unified, self-conscious, organized entity. Some would argue that no ethnic group conforms to these criteria, but our commonsensical notion of "the Tibetans" or "the Uygurs," discussed in endless newspaper articles and Web postings, indicates that many of us believe that they do (or should). The Hui have national leaders, but they all, to some subjective extent, lack legitimacy because of their empowerment through some intimate association with the state—through the Yixie, the Minwei, the universities, and other government-approved organizations. If the above analysis is correct, then the separatist Eastern Turkestan movement in Xinjiang, the Republic of Mongolia, and the Dalai Lama's leadership of a substantial portion of Tibetans—all headquartered outside of China—set a model for *minzu* identity that the Hui (and, I would suggest, at least some other *minzu*) do not (indeed cannot) follow.

Second, some Hui communities are more difficult, sensitive, volatile, and potentially violent than others. This could be due to a historical memory of confrontation and the desire for revenge, to bellicose or inflexible Muslim leadership, to local geographical or economic conditions that militate against harmony with non-Muslim neighbors and/or the state, or to insensitive or downright discriminatory policies or behavior from functionaries at several levels of government. We have seen negotiation between Muslim leaders and state authorities succeed in Zhengzhou, prevent confrontation in Yinchuan, and allow Hui survival in Najiaying, while Yuxi, Shadian, and southern Ningxia exploded in violence. If communities as similar and geographically proximate as Shadian and Najiaying could have such different histories, how much more disparate must community histories be in Gansu, Henan, Beijing, or elsewhere?

Third, we cannot ignore the power of *minzu* policy and its underlying vision of "the minorities" (including the Hui) as primitive peoples who require the leadership of the advanced Han *minzu* to advance toward the light of modernity. This mixture of condescension and fear toward non-Chinese people has much power in Han society. There can be no question that some Hui resent this attitude and its attendant policies. But others do not, or at least, they mute their enmity by concentrating on Hui achievements and successes, in both the past and the present. Though this persistent ethnocentrism will always produce small-scale confrontation, and even rage and violence, there are no Hui leaders or organizations calling upon all Hui, all over China, to reject the authority of the current system in favor of Hui hegemony or emigration. In this, the Hui of China strongly resemble the Muslims of India, who persist in their homeland despite constant tension and occasional open ruptures with a majority society that to some extent denies the validity of their sense of belonging and brands them as dangerous and foreign. But the Hui have no Pakistan, no Bangladesh to which they can turn as a "more authentic" homeland, and they constitute an incomparably smaller percentage of the general population.

Finally, as far as most Hui are concerned, no separatist movements or Islamic fundamentalism should undermine the unity of China as a nation-state. We may conclude from the above arguments that the Hui can only be Hui in China, however orthodox they may be in their Islamic lives. Even if increasing international communication raises the consciousness of Middle Eastern issues and Islamic identity among the Hui, this will not result in more than superficial Arabization and calls for "authentic" religion. The small communities of Hui living outside of China—in Turkey, for example, or Los Angeles—have not attempted to set up governments in exile but rather *halāl* Chinese restaurants, thus conforming to the pattern of other Chinese emigrants in those parts of the world. Thus, despite the Hui being defined as an "ethnic minority," we must nonetheless regard them as unequivocally Chinese, though sometimes marginal or even despised Chinese. Some among them, especially young and militant *ahong*, might claim that the unity of the Islamic *umma* overrides national (Chinese) identity, but this contention is not shared by most Hui. Like African Americans or French Jews, the majority of Hui participate as patriotic citizens in the political and cultural life of their homeland, even when antagonistic elements in the society or state challenge their authenticity or loyalty.

NOTES

1. Matsumoto, *Chūgoku minzoku*. See esp. chap. 4.2, in which the author focuses on the Shaan-Gan-Ning Border Region government's changing policy toward minority *minzu*.

2. The word *minzu* (Jap. *minzoku,* Kor. *minjok*), usually translated as "ethnicity," "ethnic group," or "nationality" in English, has a long and checkered history since its invention (in Japan) in the 1870s as a translation of the German *das Volk.* In contemporary Chinese, it usually refers to either (a) one of the fifty-six officially recognized and defined ethnic groups in the PRC (fifty-five of which are minorities; the fifty-sixth—the Han—is the majority) or (b) a putatively consanguineous social entity characterized by common language, territory, economic life, and psychological (i.e., cultural) makeup. These criteria, devised by Stalin to define a *narod* (people) in the newly formed Soviet Union, can differ considerably from more anthropological Euro-American definitions of an "ethnic group." Nonetheless, the idea of *minzu* is very powerful in China and is held to define national and individual character in the same way that "race" has done in the United States (especially in the nineteenth century).

3. In this chapter, which focuses on the contemporary, I shall use the commonly accepted term "Hui" because the PRC defined the Chinese-speaking Muslims as a *minzu* and gave them a nationally determined identity in the 1950s.

4. For a general history of the Chinese-speaking Muslims, see Lipman, *Familiar Strangers.*

5. Muslims in China who speak variants of Turkish, Persian, and Mongol have been classified as members of their own distinct Muslim *minzu* (of which there are nine, apart from the Hui); Muslims who use local non-Chinese, non–Central Asian languages—in Yunnan and Guizhou Provinces, for example, where they speak Tibeto-Burmese languages, and on Hainan Island, where they speak Malay—have been included within the Hui. Most Hui cannot actively use or even passively understand Arabic or Persian, though they might know some liturgical Arabic by rote and include many Arabic and Persian words in their local version of Chinese as markers of Hui authenticity.

6. "Customs and habits" *(fengsu xiguan)* is the Chinese term used to describe "folkways" or other markers of ethnic or local difference among China's wildly diverse sociocultural groups. In the case of the Hui, virtually all such markers derive either from their (or their ancestors') adherence to Islam or from their physical location on state or cultural frontiers.

7. Sun, "Qinghai Huizu," 12–21, argues that the Chinese-speaking Muslims of northeastern Tibet (formerly Amdo, in modern Qinghai Province) came directly from Central Asia to the region without a gradual process of intermarriage and acculturation elsewhere in China and therefore appear to be far more foreign— that is, Turkish—than do the Hui of neighboring Gansu or Sichuan Provinces.

8. The Hui do constitute a majority of residents in some locales, though few are larger than a township *(xiang)*. The population of the Ningxia Hui Autonomous Region, home to many Hui institutions because of its supposedly autonomous Hui status, is only about 30 percent Hui, the bulk of its residents being Han. Unlike many *minzu*, the Hui do not have an ancestral homeland to which they can look or return.

9. Scholars now agree that this word derives from the Ming term Huihe, or Huihu, which referred to the modern Uygur people and meant, at that time, people from the frontier regions northwest of the Ming empire (who were not necessarily Muslims, though most were).

10. Ben-Dor, "'Dao of Muhammad.'"

11. Some Sufi orders, to which the pejorative "New Teaching" *(xinjiao)* was usually ascribed, were branded as heterodox and antisocial; others, lumped together as the conservative, responsible "Old Teaching" *(laojiao)*, were permitted to exist as long as they sided with the state against their New Teaching coreligionists. See Lipman, "Sufism," 553–75.

12. Lipman, *Familiar Strangers*, 200–11.

13. The first detailed internal CCP study of an individual minzu, written primarily by Li Weihan, was titled *Huihui minzu wenti* (The problem of the Huihui *minzu*) and was published in 1940.

14. Lipman, *Familiar Strangers*, 186–99. For the Islamic-Confucian synthesis, see Ben-Dor, "'Dao of Muhammad,'" and Jin, *Zhongguo Yisilan*.

15. Lipman, "Ethnic Conflict," 65–86. As early as the mid-eighteenth century, Chen Hongmou, the governor of Shaanxi Province, had seen fit to impose a covenant on Muslim communities under his jurisdiction. By its terms, the Muslim elders of a village or town would be held responsible for the conduct of the young men in their community who engaged in antisocial behavior. Chen himself believed the Muslims to be violent, brutal people by nature. See Chen, "Huahui Huihui tiaoyue" 30:13a–22a.

16. The claim to consanguinity does not depend on DNA analysis or visual recognition but rather on the growth of ethnic consciousness, which has been encouraged by the *minzu* policies of the Chinese state.

17. Lipman, "Ethnicity and Politics," 285–316.

18. Snow, *Red Star*, 321–22. At that early date in the CCP's relationship with what would become the "ethnic minorities," Snow's informants did not mention *minzu* or *minzu* policies in their declarations.

19. Matsumoto, *Chūgoku,* 278–79, calls this a move from a doctrine of (potentially independent) "nations" to one of (Chinese) "nationalism."

20. This definition includes within the Han a variety of very distinct groups for which scholars have invented the term "subethnic"; the Hakka is one such example (see Constable, *Guest People*). James Watson holds that everyone who is Han may be identified by a common culture unified by orthopraxy. See Watson, "Rites or Beliefs?" 100.

21. For another "unconventional" case, see Harrell, "Nationalities Question," 274–96.

22. In 1999–2000, "Hui studies" was being considered as a new field within the Chinese academy, and so conferences were being held and articles were appearing all over the country to define the parameters of this emerging discipline.

23. I was able to interview high-ranking Hui functionaries at both the Yixie and the Minwei. Sophisticated, well-educated ex-academics, these men assured me that the clear lines of responsibility often bend pragmatically to allow effective solutions to problems in which "religious" and "ethnic" issues intermingle. They expressed frustration at the ponderousness of central government bureaucracies, but they did not believe that Han *ganbu* (functionaries) were routinely given more power than *minzu ganbu.* There are no Han *ganbu* at the Yixie, and many of the highest positions at the Minwei are held by *minzu ganbu.* We should not conclude, however, that these "self-government" structures are in any way free from the constraints of the higher-level central organs of the PRC. They are not, and the Central Committee and its powerful executive are staffed almost entirely by Han.

24. These terms do not designate political states but rather cultural zones. Some frontiers between their territories and Chinese culture are well within the national borders of the PRC, in places such as western Ningxia, southern Gansu, western Sichuan, and most of Yunnan. As scholars of southern China have shown in recent work, the PRC south of the Yangzi also contains numerous internal frontiers, pockets of cultural non-China (usually deep in the hills or mountains) surrounded by cultural China.

25. Hui have been going to Xinjiang for centuries in a variety of social and economic roles, from impoverished farmers to wealthy merchants and religious pilgrims. Often bilingual and successful in the marketplace, the Hui in Xinjiang are nonetheless regarded by Turkic-speaking locals with considerable mistrust, despite their Muslim heritage, because they are Chinese Muslims and therefore seen to be complicit with the incorporative projects of the Qing, the Republic, and the PRC. In the eyes of many Turkic speakers, Hui are "them" by culture and language rather than "us" by religion.

26. See Gillette, *Between Mecca and Beijing.*

27. This account is taken entirely from Ibid., chap. 6.

28. Allés, *Musulmans de Chine.* This trade is associated with Hui all over north and northwest China, as is commerce in beef, mutton, and other halāl meat products.

29. See Jaschok and Shui, *History of Women's Mosques,* for a comprehensive view of these mosques in their Chinese context.

30. Gillette, *Between Mecca and Beijing,* chap. 2. Probably a nationwide distrust of the promises of the state and its functionaries plays an important role here.

31. Zhu, "Guanyu Xi'an," 256–57.

32. This "Arabic" style, which has become very popular among Hui communities all over China in the past thirty years, is actually a peculiar hybrid of Anglo-Indian and Middle Eastern Muslim architecture.

33. Wu, *Zhongguo qingzhensi,* 187–88.

34. The only exception to this practice that I have found is in Xinjiang, where local Uygur mosques are not permitted to use loudspeakers, so the muezzin must rely on his own lungs to issue the call to prayer.

35. Incidents such as these have occurred in China since the 1920s, with the rise of modern publications. Newspapers and magazines that have printed insulting articles—repeating, for example, the conventional calumny that Muslims do not eat pork because their ancestors were pigs—have been picketed, attacked in print, or even had their offices physically assaulted by angry Muslims. In the most famous recent incident, an offensive 1989 book was banned and forcibly removed from bookstore shelves (despite its lively, pornographic contents) and its authors and publishers punished by the state after extensive Muslim protests.

36. Gladney, "Salafiyya Movement," 102–49.

37. Associated Press, 2 August 1997.

38. Lipman, *Familiar Strangers,* 186–99. Because of its remarkable economic success and its long-term collective existence, the Xidaotang has become the subject of a large and growing ethnographic and Islamic literature in China, most of it by Hui scholars. The Xidaotang's headquarters and a number of its subunits are often compared to the Israeli kibbutzim.

39. One Zhaotong informant, now living in Kunming, showed me his family's mimeographed genealogy (Ch. jiapu) and claimed that they had not participated in Du's rebellion, on either side. He complained that ethnographers, both Chinese and foreign, have ignored the Muslims of Zhaotong because they never rebelled or did anything else interesting. They just followed the rules and lived in poverty. That this might not be true does not make it less interesting as a self-perception and identification.

40. The most accessible account in English remains Gladney, *Muslim Chinese,* 137–40.

41. One informant claimed that the Han cadres did not intend to "educate" the Muslims by putting pork bones in the well; they did it just because they were Hans. I have no verification of either possible motivation from written sources.

42. The news stories are not entirely consistent, but the general narrative line may be taken as accurate. See Associated Press, "Chinese Police Fire on Muslim Demonstrators"; Agence France-Presse, "Chinese Muslims Bury Five"; Lateline News, 15 December 2000; and Lateline News, 18 December 2000. The last-cited story includes some information on the resolution of the conflict.

2 / The Challenge
of Sipsong Panna in the Southwest

Development, Resources, and Power in a Multiethnic China

METTE HALSKOV HANSEN

The southwestern minority areas, like the rest of China, have undergone tremendous political and social changes in the past twenty years. Economic reforms and the opening of trade have created new opportunities for the many minority *minzu* (ethnic groups) in the region. At the same time, issues such as unequal development, the exploitation of natural resources, mass immigration, and poorly developed education create tensions and constitute new challenges in people's lives and to the local and central political leadership. Compared to the Tibetans, Uygurs, and Mongols, whose relations with the state have been turbulent, the southwestern minorities are less confrontational. Yet by studying them, we notice the continuing problems the PRC faces in dealing with even the less truculent minorities.

In this chapter, I discuss some major consequences of the political and social changes during the last two decades on social developments and ethnic relations in the multiethnic southwest. I argue that political approaches toward China's minorities in the southwest need to take into account the multiethnic character of the area, rather than focus exclusively on a few selected minorities. Many minority intellectuals in the southwest (and elsewhere) are intensely engaged in struggles to rediscover the histories of their own ethnic groups, histories that may contrast with the prevailing image of minorities as "backward" and create for them a place in the national history of China. Rural minority members, on the other hand, often are concerned with more mundane issues, such as production, loss of income as a result of environmental degradation or new policies of environmental protection, or the limitations on upward social mobility for minorities. Based on data collected largely during periods of fieldwork in local areas of the southwest, this chapter mainly deals with Chinese migrations to minority areas since the 1950s, policies of education and language, the management of natural resources, religious practices, and the impact of tourism. These are all issues of intense negotiation between different minority groups—stratified in terms of class, gender, and generation and obviously having different social interests and changing cultural practices—and local mediators of state policies, the Chinese Communist Party (CCP), and the political elite in general.

The southwestern part of China (Yunnan, Guangxi, Guizhou, and southwest Sichuan) is characterized by strong variations in cultural practices and ethnic identities. Most of China's fifty-six officially recognized ethnic groups inhabit this area, which is generally among the poorest in the country. Yunnan Province alone is home to twenty-six officially recognized *minzu,* including the majority Han. Disregarding the official classification of *minzu* and counting instead local (and flexible) concepts of ethnic boundaries, the number of ethnic groups in the southwest would increase by many times. Several ethnic groups often inhabit the same administrative area, which complicates the state's approach to, for instance, minority autonomous rule and minority education. Adding to the historically complex ethnic composition of the southwest, most minority regions have experienced considerable immigration of people belonging to the ethnic majority, the Han, since the founding of the People's Republic in 1949. These Han immigrants and their descendants (who often consider themselves to be "locals" in the minority area)[1] need to be taken into account when analyzing social and political relations and developments in those areas. Just like the ethnic minorities, the immigrant Han are stratified in terms of class, social status, gender, and age. And contrary to common ways of representing Chinese immigrants in minority areas, they do not have uniform political and cultural interests or similar relations with the state and the local minority people they encounter.[2]

Many of the minority peoples living in the southwest are relatively small in number, some with populations of less than one hundred thousand (the Jinuo, Premi, Bulang, and Dulong, for example), but others have populations of more than one or even several million (the Zhuang, Miao, Yi, and Tai, for example). The total number of people belonging to minority ethnic groups in the southwest exceeds 44 million, and in Guangxi, Guizhou and Yunnan Provinces, the minority population constitutes over 30 percent of the total population. Nevertheless, the minorities in the southwest are often disregarded in Western and international debates about minority rights and issues in China because they rarely make strong demands for autonomy or independence and because they lack an influential international lobby such as that of, for instance, the Tibetans in exile. However, locally these groups often struggle to accommodate to new policies and economic changes and raise issues that relate to their own cultural, religious, and economic rights as minorities and citizens. Though they are less visible than minority groups with organized representatives in exile and those that use violent means of expression, the southwestern minorities' various ways of negotiating their own positions and creating room for maneuver within the political system illuminate some important aspects of how China operates as a so-called multiethnic state.

As becomes clear in a comparison of the different minority areas, the minority ethnic groups in China cannot be regarded as a homogenous group of people, but as officially categorized minority *minzu,* many of them are faced with a number of similar cultural and political challenges in their lives. The social and political issues raised in this chapter are all closely related to China's national policies on minorities and to the development of global markets and increasing international contacts. The discussion is mainly based on the situation in the Tai Autonomous Prefecture of Sipsong Panna, in Yunnan Province, and derives from long-term fieldwork carried out mainly among the Tai people[3] and Han immigrants in various minority areas of China. However, the issues raised illustrate current trends that may be observed in many other minority regions in southwest China, which are inhabited by several different ethnic groups.

THE TAI AND OTHER MINORITY GROUPS IN SIPSONG PANNA

People who call themselves Tai in China have gained official recognition as the Dai *minzu,* or Daizu. This *minzu* consists of 1,025,402 people (1990 figure), who traditionally live in Yunnan Province.[4] They belong to a much larger group of Tai-language speakers in China,[5] and they are normally divided into two main groups: the group often called the Tai Na in the Dehong region and the Tai Lüe in Sipsong Panna.[6] Historically, these two groups of Tai lived in different regions, had different rulers, followed different branches of Buddhism, and used the forms "Na" and "Lüe" only on those occasions when it was necessary to distinguish between them. Nevertheless, because of their cultural and linguistic similarities especially, researchers in the 1950s decided that they all ought to be officially classified as one Dai *minzu.*

The region known today as Sipsong Panna (or simply, Panna),[7] on the border with Burma and Laos, was historically ruled by a Tai (Tai Lüe) king. A Chinese administration was established in Sipsong Panna after 1911, but in practice, the Tai king and local princes continued to rule the area in most internal matters. When the CCP started to operate in the mountains of Sipsong Panna in the mid-1940s, during the Civil War, the ruling Tai elite was split over which side to support—the Communists or the Nationalists.

When, in 1950, the CCP gained firm control over the area, it allied itself with parts of the Tai elite and treated the influential Buddhist leadership gently so as to assure the loyalty and cooperation of the Tai people. The CCP promised the ruling elite autonomy in a new prefecture ruled by a local government dominated by members of the Tai ethnic group. In 1953, the Tai Autonomous Prefecture was established with people belonging to the traditional Tai elite occupying the most prominent positions of government. However, the local CCP branch was, and continues to be, headed by a Han. This division of power is common in all minority autonomous areas of China and has profound consequences, partly because the head of the Party is generally acknowledged as having more power in practice than the head of the autonomous government.

The establishment of a Tai Autonomous Prefecture was not uncritically welcomed by all ethnic groups. Though the Tai people's king had historically ruled the region, there were other peoples living in the area who would have liked to gain more representation in a new autonomous government under Communist rule. The Tai in Sipsong Panna inhabit the green and fertile subtropical valleys, but higher up in the mountains live people belonging to other *minzu* such as the Akha, the Blang, the Lahu, and the Jinuo. These people have traditionally been hunters and have practiced slash-and-burn agriculture. They have traded with the Tai, but rarely have they engaged with them socially or intermarried. The Tai have tended to regard them as inferior, and even today, many Tai are firmly against their children marrying members of these groups.

At the time of the establishment of the autonomous government, some Akha people (officially classified in China as Hani) raised the issue of more groups sharing power, but this was rejected. To prevent uprisings against Communist rule, it was first of all necessary for the CCP to gain support from important members of the Tai elite and, through their influence, the majority of Tai commoners. However, by the mid-1950s—even before the disastrous Great Leap Forward of 1958-59—the policy of cooperation with traditional Tai and religious elites was turned into a policy of struggle, in which Tai and other minority peasants were encouraged to fight against their local headmen and traditional authorities. The goal was to obtain a socialist system wherein the CCP had a monopoly on power. Many monks and laymen fled, mainly to Thailand. This trend continued during the Cultural Revolution (1966–1976), a period characterized by the heavy and undisguised repression of all religious activity and expressions of ethnicity. Monasteries were closed down or smashed, monks and novices were forced to return to lay life, and all other so-called remnants of feudal society (including the Tai script) were repressed.

Granting autonomous rule to officially recognized minority ethnic groups in provinces, prefectures, counties, and sometimes even townships has been an important strategy of the Communist government to ensure the cooperation of minorities and gain their support. In the reforms that followed the end of the Cultural Revolution, minority autonomous rule was again emphasized as the legal structure in minority areas. Nowadays, although there are obvious and strong limitations to the actual nature of "autonomy," local elites may sometimes find room within the law to create flexible policies on, for instance, the language of instruction, religious practices, and birth control.

Today, Sipsong Panna functions as an autonomous prefecture whose government is run mainly by Tai representatives. According to official statistics, the population is 820,000. Approximately one third are Tai, one third are Han, and the rest are mainly Akha, Blang, Lahu, and Jinuo. However, the actual number of inhabitants is much larger because of the ongoing unregistered immigration of mainly Han into the area. Religious practices have revived since 1978, especially among the Tai, who (together with the Blang) follow Theravada Buddhism. Many rural Tai parents send one or more sons to be novices in a local monastery for a period of time. The other non-Han groups in the area practice other local forms of religion and have no monastic traditions. Living standards have generally improved in the area since the reforms began, but as in the rest of the southwest, many of the mountain areas especially remain poor, with underdeveloped communications and education. In the mid-1980s, this area (like other border regions in Yunnan) was opened up for cross-border trade, and tourism became an important industry. This resulted also in a considerable immigration of Han people seeking work. The reform policies have led to improved opportunities for Tai and other minorities to reestablish contact with family members—in Thailand especially, where most Tai families have relatives—and to develop international relationships with Buddhist organizations, researchers, NGOs, and development organizations. Trade has increased, and state-owned rubber plantations have developed into large enterprises.

However, the development of different parts of Sipsong Panna has been very unequal, and there is a tendency for Han immigrants, rather than local minorities, to control and profit from the tourist industry and trade. Some serious side effects of development have arisen within the last fifteen years: drug smuggling (from the Golden Triangle into China), drug abuse, and prostitution (with the ensuing problem of the spread of HIV and AIDS). As often noted in Chinese publications, Yunnan was the first province to develop a serious HIV problem, and with the high number of prostitutes (mainly Han immigrant women) and Han male tourists (often participating in conferences or official meetings), Sipsong Panna has its share of the problems that accompany the virus.[8]

RECENT MIGRATIONS TO MINORITY AREAS IN THE SOUTHWEST

The influence of recent large-scale Han migrations to minority areas such as Sipsong Panna on local policy, development, education, the environment, and ethnic relations can hardly be exaggerated. Immigration is a direct (and in some periods, indirect) result of Chinese policies and needs to be considered when analyzing the social situation of China's minority peoples today and their relation to the state and government. Therefore, minority studies in China needs to integrate the study of the Han immigrants to a much larger extent than it has so far.[9]

Migrations from central China to the empire's peripheries have taken place throughout China's history, sometimes as government-organized colonization, sometimes as individually motivated resettlement. Migration was often seen as a means of establishing control over, and curbing unrest in, the outlying areas, as well as easing the population pressure on land in China proper. Individually motivated resettlements took place often, as a result of overpopulation, famine, wars, epidemics, and natural catastrophes.[10] The history of southwest China has to a large extent been formed by ongoing migrations and immigrations of different peoples, and the ethnic pattern of the region today is extremely complex and fluctuating. In the 1950s, the aim of the CCP was to determine, on the basis of what were presumed to be objective criteria, the number and names of all the minority ethnic groups in China. Not least in the multi-ethnic southwest, this turned out to be an insurmountable task, even for researchers who themselves believed that objective criteria could determine people's ethnic affiliation. China's most prominent anthropologist, Fei Xiaotong, acknowledged that the ethnic complexity of the southwest, especially the highland region of Yunnan and Guizhou, constituted a special obstacle to the researchers' aim of identifying distinct ethnic groups. Of the more than 400 groups that publicly asked to be recognized as *minzu* in the 1950s, more than 260 were from Yunnan Province alone.[11] Official recognition of a *minzu* was supposed to be objective—based on historical and linguistic facts; recognition was important because it became the basis for determining which groups would get the right to form local, autonomous governments. Later, one's status as an officially recognized minority person could in some cases also be a factor in allowing easier access to education or special treatment with regard to birth control. Therefore, the children of Han immigrants married to minority women were normally registered as minority *minzu*.

In spite of a long history of Han migration to the southwest, many of the areas today designated as minority autonomous counties and prefectures experienced large-scale Han immigration only after the establishment of the PRC, and especially since the mid-1950s. Immediately after the Communist takeover in 1949, the government started to transfer personnel to the border provinces in order to establish control. Between 1950 and 1958, nearly five hundred thousand people moved or were transferred to Yunnan Province alone—as military personnel, cadres, or workers reclaiming wasteland.[12]

With plenty of natural resources, a sparse population, and not least, a potential for developing rubber production, the border region of Sipsong Panna was of special interest to the new government. In the early 1950s, the Han in Panna made up only a few percent of the population. They had come in the early twentieth century to trade and develop tea plantations, and by the time the Communists arrived in the region, most of them had either left or settled in the mountains among the various hill peoples. Today, the locals of Panna and the Han immigrants who arrived much later (after the 1950s) regard these early Han settlers as a special group. They are known locally as the "mountain Han" *(shantou Hanzu),* and they are generally not seen as having any special connection with the more recent immigrants apart from their common ethnic status.

In the mid-1950s, the Chinese government started to transfer people to Panna on a large scale to set up and run new rubber plantations. Initially, the plantations were organized by the military, and the first groups to arrive were mainly soldiers and military personnel. After a short time, they were reorganized as state farms *(nongchang),* and large numbers of new cadres and workers, mainly Han, were recruited from outside Panna. During the Cultural Revolution, thousands of young intellectuals *(zhishi qingnian)* from Chongqing, Shanghai, Beijing, and Kunming were also sent "up to the mountains and down to the villages" to work in the state farms of Panna. They rarely settled in ordinary Tai or other minority villages, and most of them left again in 1978. The majority of the earlier state-farm settlers, on the other hand, remained in the area with their children, who are now known as "the second generation" *(di er dai)*.[13]

By 1995, people officially registered as Han made up 26 percent of the total population of Panna. In the prefectural capital, Jinghong, they made up as much as 48 percent.[14] However, this figure excludes a large number of unregistered settlers and temporary migrants. Local government cadres interviewed in 1997 estimated that the unregistered population of Jinghong County alone was at least 30,000 to 50,000 people (in addition to the registered population of more than 350,000 people).

From the 1950s to the late 1970s, Han immigrants were almost exclusively government-sponsored workers and cadres with their families. Today, the majority of Han in Panna are still somehow connected to the state farms, which produce mainly rubber and have developed into major enterprises. These state farms function as work units, with their own medical services, their own schools (the best in the region), and their own housing facilities.[15] However, since the early 1980s and especially in the 1990s, the development of tourism and trade has attracted large numbers of individual migrants and workers who either have been actively recruited to work in new private enterprises or have decided on their own initiative to try their luck in one of the developing border regions.

Interestingly, many of them come from the same regions of China as the earlier, government-organized immigrants. Most are from two specific counties in Hunan Province, namely, Liling and Qidong, from which tens of thousands of state-farm workers and cadres migrated in the 1950s and 1960s. Relatives and neighbors of previous migrants from these counties are naturally well informed about the developments in Panna and the growing demand for labor. The current migratory pattern of people individually moving from certain areas of Hunan, for instance, to specific parts of Yunnan is therefore an indirect result of the earlier government-organized large-scale migrations.

In addition to the individual migrants from Hunan, many others have come to Panna from Sichuan, the most populous province of China, where millions of workers have been laid off in the recent reform of state-owned enterprises. Although the government has done nothing to organize or directly support the Han migration to Panna, the trend will continue as long as there are working and trading opportunities for immigrants. But with the immense Han immigration of recent years and the simultaneous decline in Chinese tourism (thanks partly to new opportunities for Chinese to visit even more exotic places, such as Thailand), Han immi-

grants are moving into more remote areas of Panna and many are cross-
ing the border into Burma.

By and large, both the state farms and the Han cadres in the local administration have been supportive of the new immigrants, although some
cadres have also raised concerns about their impact on the environment
and the social atmosphere in the area. The government no longer consciously transfers large numbers of Han to the southwestern minority areas,
but generally, it regards the increase in Han immigration to the western
parts of China as a positive development—in terms of improving the economy of these areas, expanding political control, and easing population
pressure in the eastern provinces, where both rural and urban unemployment is increasing. Some people in the minority areas, as well as some
Chinese researchers, have pointed out that the grand new national plan
to "develop the western regions" *(xibu da kaifa)* will lead to even more
immigration because of the need for trained experts and the plan's limited focus on long-term local education.

In Sipsong Panna, the recent large-scale Han immigration is a direct
result of the opportunities there to develop trade and tourism, as well as
the relaxation of the former restrictions on internal migration. Many of
the recent settlers from China's rural heartland had previously migrated
to the large east-coast cities. Many of them reported in interviews that
they were used to being treated badly in the large cities by both the locals
and the local administration; in the border region, on the other hand, they
found that they were relatively well received. Indeed, many local officials
expressed a generally positive attitude toward the ongoing immigration
of Han peasants. Though they regarded them as poor and uneducated,
they considered the minority areas to be even more backward than the
rural areas in China proper. Therefore, they emphasized the more advanced
methods of trading and doing business these peasant newcomers were
bringing, as well as their more advanced culture (understood mostly, but
not entirely, in terms of their level of Chinese education). According to
many local officials, the peasant migrants' level of "civilization" *(suzhi)* and
education was "higher" than that of the local minorities. In the large coastal
cities, to the contrary, these rural Han migrants had been commonly seen
as poor, dirty, stupid peasants, useful only as long as they were willing to
take on work that no city folks wanted.[16]

In Sipsong Panna, several creative and successful entrepreneurs were
consciously recruiting Han workers from some of the poorest areas of
Yunnan and neighboring provinces rather than attempting to work with
local minority labor. Minority workers were often described by Han entre-

preneurs as being demanding and less willing than the Han to accept poor housing and long working hours. One cadre and entrepreneur, interviewed in 1997, expressed his preference for Han labor in the following way:

> The Tai in the plains have fields and they have money. They are not interested in working for us. They do not want to work for others at all, and many of them rent out their own fields in the dry period, and then just plant rice when there is water enough. Or they let their fields the whole year. Now, the minorities in the mountains—they have fields but no money. They do not mind working for others, but the problem is that when they come here, they cannot stand it, they cannot eat this kind of bitterness [chibuliao zhei yang de ku]. For the town and township enterprises[17] we get most of our workers from poor places outside Panna. Most are from Mojiang or Jingdong, where people are really poor. We deliberately go to poor areas to keep our costs down, and we recruit Han workers. We rarely employ people from poor minority areas such as Lancang or Ximeng because then we encounter the same problems as with workers from Panna. They cannot "eat bitterness," and whenever we tried to hire some, they quickly left. They are not stable, and they are even quite lazy. Mostly we ask poor Han couples to come and work for us because they are more reliable. When they come here, they have absolutely nothing. Just a simple backpack and nothing more. They stay here because they have come together and because they can make more money than they were able to do at home. They endure the hardship in the beginning, and after some time, if they work well, they start to make money. These workers from poor places in Yunnan really have an impact on the economic development here in Panna.[18]

In spite of being regarded as absolutely essential for the economic exploitation of the tourist potential and the development of local markets and enterprises in the minority area, the peasant migrants were not seen by local cadres, administrators, and Party leaders as having any other special mission in the area. In this regard, they differed significantly from the earlier Han migrants who were transferred or recruited by the government to the Panna region and other minority areas in the Mao period. The earlier migrants were not merely expected to bring in a new political system and the means to exploit hitherto unused natural resources but also to promote a common Chinese language, a Chinese education system formed by the Communist Party, and systems to train minority cadres

capable of gradually taking over the administration in ways fully acceptable to the new regime. On a more abstract level, they were supposed
to teach the minorities to become good Communists and Chinese citizens in the new Chinese state. This implied spreading the Chinese language, gradually eradicating religion, establishing celebrations of Chinese
national festivals, promoting symbols of a unified Chinese nation, such
as the flag, the anthem, and national day, and suppressing cultural practices (e.g., those related to marriage and religion) that were incompatible with Communist ideals. The Communists in the early period held high
the ideal that all nationalities should be treated equally under Communist rule and that traditional "Han chauvinism" *(da hanzuzhuyi)* should
be eradicated. But locally, the civilization campaigns were often regarded
more as an attempt by Han people to eradicate minority cultures than as
expressions of Communist Party policy. The vast majority of people sent
to the minority regions in the southwest to direct development, establish
governments, and organize education were Han people, and mostly they
were prepared, through descriptions in the media, in literature, and during meetings, to encounter backwardness, poverty, and ignorance of Chinese culture and civilization in the minority areas they were sent to.

Among Han officials, it is common to encounter strong perceptions of
the minorities as childlike, backward people in need of help from what is
regarded as more advanced ethnic groups. To deepen our understanding
of how ethnic relations are evolving in the southwestern areas, it is necessary to focus on the much more complex aspects of the actual relationships
today between Han immigrants and minorities. In the dominant Western
discourse on Han migrations to minority areas of China, the Han are often
pictured as a homogenous group of colonizers with more or less similar
(racially discriminating) views, goals, and perceptions. However, the Han
immigrants are, just like the minorities themselves, highly stratified in terms
of class, gender, age, and level of education, and they have very different
degrees of access to political and economic power. Therefore they also
engage in different kinds of relationships with the different minority people
they encounter locally. Many of the poorest Han peasants have taken up
jobs in the service sector, which very few Tai people will accept. Many minority people therefore regard these Han peasants as being at the bottom of
the local social hierarchy. Differences in social class and level of access to
power are so profound among different Han immigrants that they cannot
be regarded as a common, unified group of "colonizers." There is no doubt
that the massive immigration of Han to the minority areas of the southwest since the mid-1950s continues to play a very important role in the way

63

that relations are developing today; therefore, the processes of developing local relations between different ethnic and social groups, including the immigrant Han, with various social positions, need to be thoroughly analyzed to better understand the consequences of China's political "management of the minorities."

LOCAL RESPONSES TO POLICIES
OF LANGUAGE AND EDUCATION

The establishment of a standardized education system in all areas inhabited by minority ethnic groups was an important political aim of the CCP when it first gained control in the border areas. Through their participation in a state-controlled education system, minorities were expected gradually to become better integrated into the political system and able to take up various positions within the administration of their local regions—positions that were initially occupied by trained Han. The obligation to participate in state-organized education was seen as a basic means for the minority peoples to achieve equality with the Han and to make them equal citizens in the Communist state. Mass participation in the state education system was regarded as fundamental for promoting the spread of a standard Chinese national language, for developing feelings of national identification among minorities through the teaching of China's history and Communist ideology, and for eventually changing social and cultural practices and habits that were considered unhealthy and undesirable in the "new China."[19] Thus, in regarding its purpose as partly geared toward fostering national feelings, identifications, and loyalties, the CCP's view on minority education did not, in fact, differ significantly from most other modern state-education programs in the world.

Under the Law on Regional National Autonomy, minority autonomous areas in the PRC have the right to organize special training in minority languages based on local needs and demands. During radical leftist periods, this right was often suppressed. In the early 1980s, in the wake of the disastrous Cultural Revolution, which had created strong resentment against the Han among many minority members, it was essential for the government to regain the trust and cooperation of the minorities. Religious practices were again allowed to flourish, and decisions on whether or not to establish special language programs for minorities were to a large extent left to the local autonomous governments. Since 1980, special minority education has been reestablished in a number of regions, although with varying success.[20]

In Sipsong Panna, this created new kinds of largely unexpected tensions. Just as religious practices resumed, the contract land system was introduced, and the result was that people's living standards generally rose. People were eager to rebuild destroyed temples, and most Tai villages collected money to make it possible for Tai boys once again to become novices for some years, as had long been the custom among the Tai Theravada Buddhists. For about twenty years, it had been impossible to train monks in Panna, and therefore knowledgeable monks who were willing to teach in the numerous small temples that emerged were in high demand. Consequently, several villages took the initiative to invite monks from Thailand and Burma to come to Panna to teach, and rural Tai people started again to send their sons to the monasteries at the age of seven or eight or even older. This became a problem for educators and the local Bureau of Education. Within a few years, the number of Tai girls in many village schools south of the Mekong was far larger than the number of boys, who were often spending time in the monasteries rather than in school. Newspaper articles and government reports criticized what was perceived as irrational behavior by the Tai: they were chastised for spending money on temples rather than on developing the market economy and for following old habits by providing boys with Buddhist training rather than sending them to the Chinese state school. Attempts to experiment with special schools for Buddhist novices gained national interest and attracted a number of scholars and bureaucrats who praised local educators' creative efforts to combine state education and religious practice. But the experiments stopped after a few years, and there were no attempts to restart them. Although researchers in China had found the experiments interesting, local educators and monks alike considered them rather fruitless, and they never managed to establish constructive cooperation between the schools and the monasteries. Today, the educational level of the Tai in Panna is relatively low, and even with affirmative-action policies that give them extra points on university entrance examinations, the Tai have not been very successful in this regard.

Language is a core issue in the debate over education for the Tai, as well as for many other minorities in China. In the 1950s, as part of the central government's effort to promote literacy among some of the officially recognized minorities and construct written languages for others, the Tai script was simplified. After that, Tai language classes were carried out in the new simplified script, whereas teaching in the monasteries continued to be in the traditional script in which all the Buddhist texts were written. By the 1980s, the trend was clear: to the degree that Tai children learned any Tai script at all, the boys learned traditional Tai in the monasteries and sim-plified Tai in short-term courses in the schools; the girls, on the other hand, never attended classes at the monasteries and therefore learned Tai script only if they attended a course in simplified Tai at school.[21] Then, in 1986, apparently after pressure primarily from the older generation of Tai men who were related to the previous elite, the local government decided to abandon the teaching of simplified Tai and return entirely to the use of the traditional script. School materials had to be rewritten, and the local newspaper had to start publishing in traditional Tai. Some intellectual Tai were firmly against this because they had learned only simplified Tai, but by the mid-1990s, amid growing contacts with Thai and Tai people from Thailand, Burma and Laos, and with increasing concern for maintaining Tai culture among younger Tai intellectuals, opinions generally seemed to change in favor of the traditional script. It was therefore surprising when the government in 1996 decided to return to the use of the simplified Tai script. Once again, school materials had to be rewritten, and Tai language classes were cancelled for a long time. Although these decisions were taken at the local-government level, the confusion surrounding the teaching of Tai in schools is still partly an expression of the limited willingness of all levels of government and of the Party administration to expend resources on language classes for minorities. Since the 1980s, the number of Tai classes set up by schools in Panna and supported by the local government has generally been very small. They are mostly voluntary, only Tai chil-dren participate, and classes normally amount to only two hours a week. My interviews with teachers and headmasters in Panna in 1994 revealed that several (Han) headmasters were not even aware that the Tai classes in their own schools were taught in traditional, rather than simplified, Tai script.

In addition to short-term classes in the Tai language, at least one vil-lage school in Panna has carried out a comprehensive experiment in which Tai was used as the language of instruction for other subjects, and the Tai script was taught as the first written language for students in the lower primary grades. The Chinese language was then gradually introduced from the first year as the children's second language. The experiment also included a "control" group of students who were instructed in Chinese and who learned the Tai language only in a special class. When I visited the school in 1994, the teachers and the headmaster were enthusiastic about the project and found the results of the experiment very encouraging. Based on the children's examination results and teachers' reports, they were con-vinced that the children in the experimental class developed a stronger knowledge of, and confidence in, not only their own language but also Chinese. Within the local government, however, there was strong resistance to the project, and it was stopped after a few years because of lack of financial (and seemingly political) support. When I revisited the school in 1997, no Tai courses were offered at all, and the school authorities were rather disappointed about the lack of economic and political support for what they regarded as a successful experiment.

But if one focuses entirely on the Tai minority and their opportunities for pursuing education in their own language, one loses sight of a number of other issues related to education in Panna and most other ethnic-minority areas in the southwest. For instance, although the Tai have their own language and script, other minority groups in the area have their own language but no traditional script. They are therefore normally not entitled to receive instruction in their own language and no special classes are available. Some teachers and educators in fact regarded this as an advantage for minorities such as the Jinuo, the Akha, and others. Unlike the Tai, they had no history of being the ruling ethnic group; they had no monastic tradition, no script, and no tradition of teaching in their own language. Therefore they were, in the eyes of many teachers, more willing than the Tai to adapt to the Chinese school system and abandon their own cultural practices. At the same time, many local educators were very concerned that they were not able to provide teachers who were actually able to communicate with the children in their own language, at least during the first year of schooling. One of the biggest obstacles for the local governments has been to recruit qualified teachers for these remote villages, and it has proven difficult to make those who are recruited stay and endure the poor living standards and low wages. Thus, teacher training is one of the priorities of many local governments, but teacher training in itself does not solve the problem of poverty and poor living conditions that makes especially the mountainous areas unattractive for teachers of any nationality. Furthermore, a recent study of education in another rural minority area in the southwest (Yanyuan County, in Sichuan's Liangshan Prefecture) has demonstrated that the language of instruction in schools is not necessarily an important factor in determining the different levels of educational attainment by children belonging to ethnic minorities. As is known from other parts of the world as well, factors such as distance to school, social status, and traditions of formal education as a means of social mobility are often far more important than the language in which classes are taught.

Since the mid-1980s most people in Panna have been aware that the best schools—normally perceived as those that produce students capable of continuing on in the education system—are the schools connected to the state farms. These schools are not administered by the local Bureau of Education and may recruit their own teachers. Being directly connected to the state farms, they have better funding than most ordinary schools in the region, and they are organized specifically for children in the state farms, most of whom are Han. A few minorities are allowed access, but they have to pay tuition. Other good schools are the local so-called key schools *(zhongdian xuexiao)*, where nearly all the teachers and the majority of students are Han or children of minority cadres. The local secondary "minority schools" *(minzu xuexiao)*, on the other hand, are popular not because they are considered to be especially good but because students there receive financial support from the government. The minority schools have their own admission rules and take in a number of students from all the officially recognized *shaoshu minzu*, even when they do not have the examination points normally required. All the schools I've mentioned have no special curriculum or language training for minority students. Educators generally consider this useless because by the time they reach secondary school, the students already have a sufficient knowledge of the Chinese language. This exemplifies how the study of minority languages in Panna and other areas of the southwest is regarded as a mere transitional tool for reaching the higher levels of standard Chinese. Thus, the tendency is to organize courses in minority languages only if they are considered indispensable for improving children's adaptation to Chinese or for preventing indirect local resistance toward a school system that largely ignores local minorities' cultures, languages, and beliefs.

The Law on Regional National Autonomy explicitly states: "Schools where most of the students come from ethnic minority groups should, whenever possible, use textbooks in the students' own languages and use these languages as the medium of instruction."[22] In practice, minorities in the southwest generally have few possibilities of studying their own languages in the context of the standardized school system. Compared to, for instance, many Tibetan areas, they have fewer opportunities to pursue education in their own languages even at the most basic levels. In addition to the problem of resources and some local officials' skepticism toward organizing special programs for minorities, national attitudes and policies concerning the relationship between the national language and minority languages influence to a very great extent the practical possibilities and willingness of schools to experiment with specialized programs. This is not necessarily due to specific orders or regulations from above but is more often a result of limited resources and self-censorship (related to awareness of the need to adapt to new trends at the higher political levels of decision). Furthermore, since the language of educational success and upward social mobility within the administrative system is standard Chinese, many minority people themselves—and especially those with a Chinese education—are first of all interested in assuring their children's proficiency in Chinese. They are not necessarily especially concerned with promoting their own language through the state education system. In this respect, there are profound differences between minority areas, between different minority groups, and even between different people belonging to the same minority group. In the immediate aftermath of the Cultural Revolution, when the government was eager to improve relations with the minorities, a positive attitude toward the development of special minority language courses prevailed, though at the same time, the authorities wished to strengthen the general level of Chinese. In recent years, a number of bureaucrats and educators have taken a somewhat different stand and argue more strongly that the whole debate on bilingual education (*shuangyu jiaoyu*) has failed to focus on the fact that only a high level of proficiency in the Chinese language can help minority areas develop to the same economic and educational levels as most Han regions. In the mid-1990s, most education officials and many teachers in Sipsong Panna were disappointed that the non-Han generally still had a very low level of Chinese. Some of them argued that the purpose of learning minority languages in school was above all to promote the transition to Chinese and that this process was currently going much too slowly. Although several Tai educators were unsurprisingly extremely positive toward the various experiments with teaching Tai as the first language, many Han teachers and officials thought that only a much stronger focus on Chinese at the expense of bilingual or mother-tongue education would speed up the economic and educational development of the minority regions. This view has also found expression in recent debates among some Chinese legislators on how to regulate standard Chinese and make it obligatory for all citizens to use. Several minority people engaged in local education in the southwest have pointed out that research material on bilingual education has decreased considerably in the last two years. Financial support for developing teaching and other materials in minority languages is also limited. Most publishing houses now need to earn money, and it is sometimes difficult to get material in minority languages published because it is rarely sold in large quantities and used mostly in relatively poor areas anyway. Furthermore, many local officials now shy away from bilingual education, fearing that it goes against the political tide, which stresses the need to strengthen the national language and build national unity, rather than engage in costly projects to promote what are often regarded as insignificant languages that lack a modern vocabulary.

THE MANAGEMENT OF NATURAL RESOURCES

In the whole of southwest China, the management of natural resources is vital for the Chinese government, which needs timber, minerals, rubber, and the like to promote and maintain the industrial development of the PRC. At the time of the Communist takeover, many important natural resources were still largely unexploited in areas traditionally inhabited by ethnic minorities. As a result, numerous conflicts arose over the right to exploit them. Today, with new environmental concern on the part of the government and with legislation to provide new environmental safeguards, disputes related to the control and use of resources are on the increase in many minority areas in the southwest.

As in other regions of China, large tracts of forest have been cut down in the southwestern minority areas since the 1950s, and deforestation has been blamed for the disastrous floods of recent years. People in the rural southwest are increasingly complaining that the climate has changed, that floods and drought are ruining their economy, and that the government has not taken full responsibility for the effects of its own policies. The main periods of decline in forest quantity and quality (according to Chinese scientists, whose findings are supported by peasant accounts) were during the Great Leap Forward, when everybody had to produce steel and needed wood for charcoal; in the late 1960s and early 1970s, when government policies on grain production forced peasants to open up forested areas for agricultural production; and in the early 1980s, when land had been contracted but many forested areas were not managed very well and private individuals were able to log them with impunity. After 1984, new laws ensured that the logging of forested areas in the southwest (and in other parts of China) was more efficiently controlled by the government, but by that time, many areas had already seen a considerable decrease in the number of trees. The Law on Regional National Autonomy states that the organs of self-government in minority autonomous areas "shall protect and develop grasslands and forests and organize and encourage the planting of trees and grass." At the same time, it instructs them to "place the interests of the state as a whole above anything else and make positive efforts to fulfill the tasks assigned by state organs at higher levels."[23]

Thus, local control of natural resources in minority areas has generally been subordinated to broader national interests and central policies. In Sipsong Panna, the state's control of large forested areas through the state farms was firmly established in the mid-1950s.

In the late 1990s, as part of the central government's attempts to prevent future disasters, projects have been initiated to replant trees, and a total ban on logging in many of the most deforested areas has been enforced since 1998. People in many districts in the southwest now have to return the land that was opened up on hill slopes, and sometimes on grasslands, to the government, as part of its reforestation programs. In private conversations, peasants as well as township administrators today often express concern that the compensation for land returned to the government is insufficient to provide the peasants with a reliable income. Often, compensation is paid out as financial support over a fixed number of years; for many peasants, this is a short-term solution that compares unfavorably to the long-term consequences of their loss of land. Although from an environmental standpoint, the government's efforts to reforest the southwest are essential, they create at the same time new social problems, not least in poor, remote minority areas. The ban on logging was introduced suddenly and with no prior investigation of the social impact on those border regions that depend on timber production for income. When efficiently enforced, the ban causes many areas to lose their main source of income, and local unemployment rates rise significantly. This has already happened in several of the poorest minority areas in the southwest in Yunnan and Sichuan.

In state-owned plantations, which traditionally handled the majority of state logging operations, tens of thousands of mainly Han employees have been retrained to plant and maintain forests. However, many plantations also used to employ local minority peasants, on a contract basis, to assist in the most physically demanding labor of felling trees. With the sudden ban on logging, these peasants lost their jobs—in areas where there is often no other industry or alternative way of sustaining a family. The logging industry also indirectly supported minority people: some had invested in trucks to transport the timber, and others had started restaurants and small hotels for the truck drivers along the transportation routes. Taxes from the timber industry used to provide many counties in the southwest with an important part of their revenue, and some counties (for instance, Meigu and Muli Counties, in Liangshan Prefecture, in Sichuan) lost up to 85 percent of their revenue from the sudden ban on logging. Even with state compensation, this has had serious consequences for those areas with no alternative industries and underdeveloped means of communication and transport. Although the state's interest in timber ensured a certain degree of government investment in building and maintaining roads and electricity in these remote areas, this is no longer economically viable, and the economic responsibility is now, to a large extent, left to the prefectures and counties, which have few resources. Thus, local governments and leaders in a number of minority areas have turned their interests to the development of tourism, which some regard as one of the most realistic ways (and sometimes the only way) of generating alternative revenue.

Subtropical Sipsong Panna is one of the few regions in China where it is possible to produce rubber. Since the mid-1950s, national policies have been aimed at achieving self-sufficiency in strategic materials such as rubber; beginning in 1956, the government organized migrants (from Hunan Province especially) to settle in Panna and develop new rubber plantations in formerly forested areas. The local Tai were allowed to maintain their fields in the plains, but conflicts arose over sacred forest areas in the mountains, and people who depended on swidden agriculture and hunting for their livelihood clashed with state-farm employees whose primary task was to provide the country with rubber. As one early Han settler said, "The biggest problem was to explain to the minorities that all land and all forest in fact did not belong to them, but to the country." There have been several serious clashes between the mountain people and the new state-farm settlers, but these have been rarely reported. The media always stress the idea of mutual understanding between the state farms and the locals and the need for unity and sacrifice to develop the motherland. Economic reforms after 1978 have made it possible for local state farms to develop quickly into large enterprises that produce not only rubber but various consumer goods. Recognizing that the state farms have been successful, more Tai people have also become interested in rubber production, and some have now contracted forested areas from the state farms to engage in private production.

TOURISM, RELIGION, AND INTERNATIONAL CONTACTS

After 1980, in the new economic climate of reform, many minority areas—not least in the southwest—proved to have a potential for tourism. Although most Chinese tourists in the early 1980s were either male cadres attending conferences and meetings or honeymooning couples, huge numbers of urban Chinese now have the means and are anxious to see their country. They are supported in this desire by the government, which has encouraged the building of tourist facilities all over the country. Having visited China's most famous historical and cultural sites, including Beijing, Xi'an, Hangzhou, and Suzhou, an increasing number of tourists has begun to look farther afield, toward areas that are considered exotic and culturally distant from their daily lives. Remote border regions have long been featured in the media, which represent their minority inhabitants as colorful, cheerful, and exotic. Sipsong Panna was well known before the 1980s as a place of beauty, hospitality, and even danger (from wild animals or malaria). Many Han settlers who moved there in the 1960s and 70s recalled having read a popular novel, *Song of Dawn at the Borders*,[24] which describes the heroic and zealous young people who volunteered to go to this inaccessible area and develop it. When the area was opened up to foreign visitors and border restrictions were eased, investments in new hotels, dance bars, shops, and other businesses related to tourism quickly grew. The sleepy capital of Jinghong became a construction site for four-star hotels, minority theme parks, monuments, and new streets. Today nearly 1.5 million tourists a year—the vast majority of them Chinese—visit this area, which has approximately 800,000 inhabitants. Businessmen from the rich southeastern cities of China have invested in the tourist industry, and the state farms have their own hotels and activities related to tourism. Conferences and meetings of various levels of government officials from all over China are organized in the pleasant surroundings, and visitors have access to more small private restaurants and shops than ever before. In fact, tourism has developed so fast in Sipsong Panna that some visitors have started to complain— as do many Western visitors in heavily developed tourist areas—that tourism has ruined the original atmosphere of the place. Whereas earlier, in the mid-1980s, tourists were excited to visit Tai and Akha villages and see the jungle, visitors in the late 1990s often expressed deep disappointment over the lack of hospitality and the absence of beautiful women bathing freely in the floods, as they had seen so often featured in TV programs. The much publicized Water Splashing Festival also tended to pale when tourists realized that it was celebrated (for their sake) nearly daily in various leisure parks and resorts. By the late 1990s, the number of tourists going to Sipsong Panna was slowly decreasing, partly because of the renewed possibilities for Chinese tourists to buy affordable trips abroad to countries in Southeast Asia—trips that most tourists I interviewed found potentially much more exciting than a visit to Sipsong Panna.

Still, Sipsong Panna remains one of the most popular tourist destinations in southwest China, and other minority areas in the southwest have started to follow similar paths of development. In areas where government and Party cadres find that there is a potential for attracting Chinese and foreign visitors, and where other resources are scarce, tourism is often seen as the only realistic way out of poverty. As shown in Tim Oakes's comprehensive study of tourism in Guizhou, many local village leaders also share that belief.[25] To this end, they are willing to commodify and market their culture.[26] At the same time, the experiences of those minority areas that already have a developed tourist industry suggest that local minorities are not necessarily the ones who profit most from this industry. Even in an area such as Sipsong Panna, with a developed tourist industry, only a few towns and villages near the most popular tourist destinations directly benefit from tourism, and there have been many instances where the interests of local peasants have been sacrificed for the sake of promoting an industry that benefits other sectors of society. Disputes over land and land use are common in many of the areas that have focused their development on the tourist sector. Locals have raised concerns about mass tourism's impact on the environment, about the large-scale immigration of Han Chinese, and about the frequent conflicts of interest between peasants and local traders on the one hand and well-connected entrepreneurs and government officials on the other. Local reactions against mass tourism in Panna have mainly taken the form of scattered and quiet criticism of developments that many people feel they have had no control over. Nobody, including the local government, has been in control of how the tourism industry has evolved, but quite a few people outside the political elite in Panna have, in different and often indirect ways, expressed their dissatisfaction with the government's handling of specific issues connected to the development of tourism. Admittedly, tourism brought an airport to Panna, but those who lost their land because of the new airport were far from satisfied with the meager compensation they were offered. The nightlife in Panna is famous, but many locals were more than disturbed by the daily sight of state employees eating and partying at the country's expense in the many bars and restaurants. Prostitution has become a major business in Jinghong, and many locals despise the women sex workers, who are mainly Han from Sichuan and other provinces. Most new shops and restaurants in Jinghong are run by immigrant or second-generation Han who know better than most locals how to cater to the needs and wishes of Chinese tourists, and competition is very tough.

On 4 December 1997, I carried out a street survey in Jinghong to find out who ran the various shops in one of the major shopping streets at the

TABLE 2.1
Privately Owned Businesses*
on a Selected Jinghong Shopping Street:
Owner's Ethnicity

	Number	Percent
Han	84	91.3
Tai	4	4.3
Hani	3	3.3
Yi	1	1.1
Total	92	100

Source: Author-conducted survey, 4 December 1997.
*This includes the small private stalls that were run simply by a person sitting on the pavement. It does not include three state-owned enterprises.

time, where they came from, and which ethnic group they belonged to. I chose that particular street because it had a whole range of different kinds of shops, and it was not, as were some other streets, lined with mainly one type of enterprise.[27] Here, people from different parts of China were running different kinds of shops, and in addition, there were many small-scale traders with stalls or simply selling or repairing goods from a seat on the pavement. In each shop or stall along the street, at least one person was asked to participate in the survey, which inquired only about the shop or stall owner's place of origin, gender, age, and ethnic affiliation. In cases where people had time and interest in talking further, they were asked about the history of their migration to Panna and their reasons for starting a business there. As can be seen from tables 2.1 and 2.2, there were altogether ninety-two privately owned or privately contracted (*chengbao*) shops and small stalls along the street. Two (maybe three) were brothels disguised as beauty parlors; the others were restaurants, food stalls, repair shops, pharmacies, jewelry stores, shops with electronic articles, clothes shops, and so forth. Of the ninety-two privately run shops, eighty-four were run by Han (of whom thirty-five were from Panna, which meant that they belonged to "the second generation"). Three shops were run by members of the Hani *minzu* (two Akha and one who called himself a Biyao), four by Tai (one of whom was not from Panna), and one by a Yi. The survey found that many shops changed ownership relatively frequently within a short period of time, something that was explained as mostly a result of rather fierce competition. Many interviewees explained that it was becoming increasingly difficult to do business in Jinghong, and

TABLE 2.2

Privately Owned Businesses on a Selected Jinhong Shopping Street: Owner's Place of Origin

	Number	Percent
Sipsong Panna	42	45.7
Yunnan (outside Sipsong Panna)	11	12
Sichuan	24	26.1
Guangdong	5	5.4
Hunan	4	4.3
Zhejiang	2	2.2
Shanghai	1	1.1
Burma	1	1.1
Guizhou	1	1.1
Fujian	1	1.1
Total	92	100.1

Source: Author-conducted survey, 4 December 1997.

many were considering moving to the Panna county towns of Mengla and Menghai or to smaller towns in these counties. In the other shopping streets of Jinghong, shops and restaurants run by Tai or other local minorities constituted a small minority, though there was still a considerable number of Tai and other minorities selling vegetables and food products (rather than clothes) in the market. According to the government office responsible for the administration of private enterprise, an estimated 80 percent of people selling goods (including clothes and vegetables) at this market were people from outside Panna who mainly bought goods through contacts in larger cities and brought them to Panna to sell.

The reason so few shops were run by members of local minority groups, according to most shop owners, was that local minorities were neither interested in nor capable of running businesses. Many local minority people I interviewed partly agreed with this view, but they explained that first of all, minorities were unable to compete with the more experienced Han businesspeople. They did not have the economic backing and contacts in the larger cities needed to set up modern shops or restaurants. Many thought the Han immigrants had benefited more from the boom in tourism because minority people did not know how to exploit the economic opportunities that presented themselves and were not willing to take up unattractive jobs in the service sector. Moreover, many of them had land and therefore found it unnecessary to engage in business.

Because of the lack of a forum for public expression of dissatisfaction, the only ways people were able to voice or display their opinions about development were through occasional contacts with cadres higher up in the administrative system, through their local village leaders, or through informal talks with neighbors, friends, or relatives about the behavior of the elite. Dissatisfaction was mainly directed against specific, concrete aspects of development and never manifested itself in the form of spectacular outward collective expressions.

In the southwest and other minority areas of China today, the development of tourism is often connected to government policies on religion. Any attempt to understand how local governments and Party organizations approach religion must take into account the fact that many minorities' religious practices constitute a resource for developing tourism. Although the central government's religious policies (including its support for the rebuilding of temples destroyed during the Cultural Revolution) are not primarily geared toward developing tourism in minority areas, local governments' policies in areas such as Sipsong Panna are often geared to do just that. The Buddhist Tai, especially in rural areas south of the Mekong River, in Panna, have transmitted their religion through generations, while constantly reworking it to accord with changing political and economic circumstances. Since the 1980s, when people's incomes were raised, they have rebuilt a lot of old temples and monasteries, and they have invested in a number of new buildings and monuments related to their Buddhist practices. As in many other minority areas, the government supported the rebuilding of destroyed temples both in recognition of the disastrous effects of the Cultural Revolution and as a means to heal some of the wounds it inflicted on relations between the minorities and the Han. For the local people who have revived and renewed their religious practices and other activities (such as education) connected to the monasteries, the rebuilding of temples since the 1980s has obviously had nothing to do with a need or wish to develop tourism. But for local governments in areas with a clear potential to develop large-scale tourism, governments facing decentralization and decreased economic support from the state, beautiful temples were clearly something to offer urban Chinese visitors. For the average outside visitors to Panna, the religious practices of the Tai constitute a strong visual encounter with a culture and people different from their own. Tourists going to Panna expect to find—and do find—young boys wearing yellow robes, beautiful temples, and Buddhist celebrations where colorful monks perform exciting rituals. Now that more and more Tai are building their traditional Tai houses in new, modernized versions—

against the will of the government, which sees this as a threat to local culture—and now that much of the jungle has been cut down, the visual images generated by religious practices remain an important asset for an area whose 1.5 million tourists annually may not be content to visit an organized "minority village" or be entertained in one of the many "traditional" restaurants run by Han immigrants.

The more relaxed political climate since the early 1980s has also paved the way for religious contacts across borders, and every year, monks from Panna travel to receive training and expand their contacts in monasteries in Thailand. This trend has been prompted partly by the development of tourism, which has allowed a large number of people from Thailand, especially, to visit Panna and support the local monasteries. Today, financial support from organizations in Thailand for the reestablishment of monasteries and construction of Buddhist statues plays a very important role in the religious revival in Panna. The study of standard Thai has become popular among young Tai, not only because of religion but also because of the development of trade with Thailand and the new international contacts with investors, businesspeople, and Thai tourists.[28] Some monasteries have started to teach standard Thai, as well as other modern subjects such as mathematics and Chinese language. The government tries, through the local Bureau of Religion, to keep track of the number of novices and monks, and monks have to apply for permission to go to Thailand to study in other monasteries. The government also tries to regulate the content of the curriculum at the largest monasteries, which it insists should include the Chinese language. At some points during the 1980s and 90s, it tried to prevent foreign monks from staying and teaching in Panna. At the same time, the government accepts that the monasteries receive donations from Thai and other Buddhist organizations, and since the Tai have not politicized their religious practices, they are generally not perceived as a threat to the government's demand for unity.

However, the renewed practice of sending boys to monasteries at a young age in Panna poses new problems for the government. It directly contravenes both the government's policies on education and the Law of Regional Autonomy, which states: "The state shall protect normal religious activities. No one may make use of religion to engage in activities that disrupt public order, impair the health of citizens, or *interfere with the educational system of the state*."[29] The practice of sending boys to monasteries does interfere with the educational system of the state, mainly because the monasteries and the school authorities have never found a way to reconcile religious tradition with the modern demand for attending a state-controlled school. The schools now allow religious novices to attend them, even while connected to the monasteries, but few novices actually do. Most monks do not encourage novices to attend the state school. At the same time, the reform era has brought with it demands that parents pay for schoolbooks, as well as various other expenses (including, sometimes, tuition), and this has increased the popularity of a monastery education for some people. Parents pay monasteries too, but they would do this anyway, since it is regarded as a normal way of supporting the monastery and performing good deeds as Buddhists. In practice, there is currently no connection between the state educational system and the Buddhist monasteries. To a certain extent, they compete for pupils. Those educated in the Chinese system are at least to some extent equipped to obtain social mobility in China. Those trained in the Buddhist monastic system receive support for their cultural and linguistic traditions from Thailand and from other Tai peoples, as well as from Buddhists and Buddhist organizations in and outside of China. The fact that the best Chinese schools are attended mainly by Han children and the children of minority cadres, while the less prestigious ordinary schools are attended mainly by minority children, together with the fact that it is practically impossible for most minority children to receive any training whatsoever in their own language or to learn about their own culture and history, means that minority children grow up less able to voice their demands or influence political and economic decisions locally.

CHINA'S POLICIES TOWARD MANAGEMENT
OF MINORITIES IN THE SOUTHWEST

Many of China's southwestern minority areas are characterized by the peaceful coexistence of numerous minority ethnic groups, although a range of issues—large-scale immigration, environmental degradation, and unequal access to power and resources, to name a few—may eventually divide them. Some of these minority peoples are relatively unknown in the West. However, an increasing number of NGOs—both Chinese and foreign—have established bases in Yunnan Province especially and are dealing mainly with environmental and poverty issues. The educational level of minority peoples in the southwest is often low compared to the Chinese average; this is partly because minorities are usually not very successful in voicing their demands or advancing local causes before Chinese state organizations. The vast majority of minority people in the southwest are not interested in (or even considering) seeking independence from the Chinese state. Perhaps partly for this reason, they are hardly visible in the dominant Western-media images of China's minority ethnic groups. In the multiethnic southwest, groups with different histories, religions, languages, and relations to the Chinese state live together and interact socially. Many are struggling to improve their lives through creative local initiatives in trade, religion, education, and production, and by establishing contacts with various organizations and institutions nationally and abroad. Support for these local initiatives may increase the visibility of these groups and strengthen their attempts to ensure their own cultural, political, and economic interests and rights.

The Chinese government's campaign to develop the western regions means that considerable state resources will be redirected toward that part of China (which comprises more than 60 percent of the nation's territory). The western regions contain China's poorest areas; they are inhabited mainly by ethnic minorities and are sites of potential social and ethnic conflict. The government is trying to attract more foreign investment to these areas, and large, prestigious workshops and conferences are being held to promote the campaign. The government's emphasis is on infrastructure, industry, and urban development. Within the western regions, the campaign is being actively promoted in the press and through meetings of cadres at different levels. Local people are discussing the project and joking about it: "Will it simply bring a mobile telephone to everyone?" they ask. Criticism has already been directed against what is seen as the campaign's first and foremost interest: building up the infrastructure to move natural resources out of the west and into the central and eastern parts of China. Insufficient attention has been paid to building a better educational system so as to achieve economic development, the critics argue, and they worry that the campaign may result in new immigration of skilled labor from eastern China.

Government plans aside, the campaign has provided a political framework for some minority cadres, teachers, and administrators to initiate projects they think will promote local development, such as the translation of an English encyclopedia for children. Foreign NGOs and aid organizations have been permitted to support these local initiatives, which has led to greater cooperation and mutual understanding in places where these kinds of contacts are often weak but strongly desired. Examples of such local initiatives, many still in their preliminary stages, may be found all over the southwest.

Environmental concerns—specifically, the loss of forested areas—have led the state to establish more and more nature reserves in the southwest.

However, the lack of a public forum for debate makes it difficult to ensure that local people's interests are being heard and considered. A similar problem exists in regard to industrial development and the government's attempts to attract foreign investment. It is common to hear businessmen complain about the lack of skilled labor when companies are set up in areas other than the larger cities or east-coast areas of China. In the west, and not least in the southwest, this is a problem that is largely connected to the low levels of education in many of the towns and villages. Villagers often live in remote areas, and it is not uncommon for rural children to attend primary school for only the first three years or to not go to school at all. Since 1949, the Chinese government has achieved remarkable results in the field of education, but today, a number of regions are still lagging far behind the national average, and many minority people in the southwest are complaining about the dwindling resources spent on minority education. It is becoming increasingly difficult to publish material in minority languages because publishers now have to make money, and books in minority languages rarely become best-sellers. Furthermore, most teaching material in minority languages has tended to focus on issues of local culture, stories, heroes, and specific customs. Some minority intellectuals have started to argue that although this kind of material is badly needed, there is an equally urgent need to develop a modern vocabulary in minority languages to ensure that minority children are able to learn about the modern world in their own language as well as in Chinese. Another major concern is the lack of qualified teachers. In a number of minority areas, educators and education bureaus have tried to improve teacher training, including training in minority languages, but scarce resources make this very difficult. Generally, minority ethnic groups in the southwest see education as a way to preserve and develop their own languages, promote knowledge of their histories, improve their means of expression, improve their opportunities for finding jobs, and lay the basis for further economic development that they themselves direct.

In other words, most minorities in the southwest are not concerned with political independence but rather with how to advance their own interests, which include raising their communities' living standards and increasing control over their own lands, cultures, and customs. I am convinced that in addition to the already existing and expanding contacts between foreign entities and government organizations and educational institutions at the central and provincial levels, there is a need in these areas for more support for local initiatives, as well as more contacts with local elites, policy makers, teachers, and researchers.

NOTES

I am grateful for the suggestions for improving this chapter made by Matthew Kapstein, Morris Rossabi, Koen Wellens, and the outside reviewers for the University of Washington Press.

1. Some of them call themselves "local people" *(bendi minzu)*.

2. See also Hansen, "Call of Mao or Money," and *Majorities as Minorities*.

3. The Tai of Sipsong Panna speak a Thai language, and according to common transcriptions of Thai, they should be called "Thai." This is pronounced like the Chinese phoneme transcribed in pinyin as *dai*.

4. Economy Department of National Minority Commission et al., *Zhongguo minzu tongji*, 53.

5. Of which, the Dai, Zhuang, and Buyi languages are closely related to the standard Thai language of Thailand and the standard Lao of Laos.

6. Transcribed according to the common practice of transcribing the Thai language.

7. Xishuangbanna in Chinese.

8. On prostitution and the marketing of Panna as a "sexy tourist destination," see Hyde, "Sex Tourism Practices."

9. Fieldwork-based studies of China's southwestern ethnic minorities include Harrell, *Cultural Encounters* (several articles); Brown, *Negotiating Ethnicities;* Cai, *Une société;* Litzinger, *Other Chinas;* Schein, *Minority Rules;* Wellens, "What's in a Name?"; and Hansen, *Lessons in Being Chinese.*

10. See, for instance, Lee, "Migration and Expansion."

11. Fei, *Fei Xiaotong xuanji*, 285.

12. See, for instance, Li, Shi, and Gao, *Jindai Zhongguo yimin shiyao*, 364.

13. This is a common way of referring to the offspring of those Han (and to a limited extent, those Hui, and other minorities) who after 1949 were sent to minority areas to help establish control of the vast borderlands. These early immigrants are often presented as pioneers who contributed even their children and grandchildren to the cause. See, for instance, Li, *Neidi ren zai Xizang.*

14. According to a local, unpublished report from the statistical bureau.

15. Increasing competition from Southeast Asia is expected to result in serious economic strains for the rubber-producing state farms, with their many employee benefits. Although the schools are still generally regarded as the best in the region, the average age of state-farm employees is high, and providing for the large number of retirees presents a formidable challenge.

16. For an elaborate and interesting study of rural migrants in large cities, see especially Solinger, *Contesting Citizenship*. See also Davis, "Never Say 'Dai.'"

17. Mainly hotels, the sugar factory, tourist enterprises, and contracted rubber plantations.

18. This man was born in 1962 on a state farm. He had participated in a short-term course to become a cadre in a minority area, which secured him an influential administrative post, as well as opportunities to engage in private enterprise.

19. I have previously described and discussed Chinese minority education in the southwest in much more detail in Hansen, *Lessons in Being Chinese*. See Postiglione, *China's National Minority,* for a number of recent articles concerning minority edu-

cation in China, especially Harrell and Ma, "Folk Theories of Success," for a study of education among rural minorities and Han in the southwest.

20. After the Cultural Revolution, the Law on Regional National Autonomy was revised, and the revisions were made effective in 1984.

21. See Hansen, "Ethnic Minority Girls," for a discussion of the relation between gender and language training among the Tai.

22. *Zhonghua Renmin Gongheguo Minzu Quyu Zizhifa,* article 37.

23. Ibid., articles 28 and 7.

24. Huang, *Bianjiang.*

25. Oakes, *Tourism and Modernity.*

26. See also Schein, *Minority Rules,* on ethnic tourism in Guizhou.

27. In the restaurant district, small-scale restaurants were very obviously run mainly by Sichuanese, while Shanghainese ran the larger restaurants, hotels, and bars. Shops in the garment district were run mainly by entrepreneurs from Zhejiang. The market area had many people from Hunan selling vegetables, meat, and fish.

28. Sara Davis even suggests that a pan-Tai ethnicity might be growing, especially among Tai monks and musicians who have traveled to Thailand and Burma. See Davis, "Never Say 'Dai.'"

29. National People's Congress, *Law of the People's Republic,* article 11 (emphasis added).

3 / Inner Mongolia

The Dialectics of Colonization and Ethnicity Building

URADYN E. BULAG

Chinese minority policies emphasized assimilation during the 1960s and 1970s, but it is often debated whether China still openly practices such a policy today. Has the Chinese regime given up its ambition to assimilate its minorities and moved toward more tolerance and democracy in governing them, or has it simply adjusted its strategy to ensure its own survival? The question of whether China is a *minzu* (ethnic group) builder or a *minzu* destroyer is an important one because it has implications for assessing China's human-rights record. Because some minority ethnic groups in China, such as the Hui, the Zhuang, and others, were creations of the Chinese state, one is reluctant to consider any nationalist resurgence among them as a human-rights issue.[1] Indeed, this is the case with the Western attitude toward ethnic issues in the former Soviet Union and Yugoslavia.

Inner Mongolia presents a paradox for understanding contemporary ethnic politics in China. Unlike the Tibetans and the Uygurs, whose ethnic nationalist movements have attracted great attention and invited speculation about an ethnic challenge to the Communist regime, thus anticipating a Soviet-style scenario of national disintegration, the Mongols apparently exhibit no such independent spirit. There is a great disjuncture between the historical image of the Mongols as some of the most ferocious conquerors the world has ever seen and their current "peacefulness" or "sheepishness." Despite its link with the Republic of Mongolia, Inner Mongolia seems to be a quiet backwater. The following passage is typical of many Western reports on Inner Mongolia. It expresses disappointment and perhaps still more, a search for hopeful signs of Mongol resistance to Chinese rule:

> Inner Mongolia, a large Chinese region southeast of Mongolia, has only a minority population of ethnic Mongolians. A small number have expressed ambitions to reunite the Chinese-controlled territory with Mongolia, which shed Communist rule and became

a democracy in 1990. But there has been little sign of anti-Chinese unrest since the early years after the 1949 Communist takeover and the 1966–76 Cultural Revolution when dissent was crushed. Inner Mongolia has been less restive than Tibet and Xinjiang, western regions with strong movements seeking independence from Chinese rule. However, in late 1995, authorities in Inner Mongolia arrested 12 people who had demanded more democracy and greater autonomy. In December 1996, China jailed two Mongolians for up to 15 years on charges of separatism and espionage.[2]

The purpose of this chapter is not to portray Inner Mongolia as either pro-China or pro-Mongolia but rather to point out that the Chinese regime, which has granted unified autonomy to the Mongols, has also instituted various mechanisms to undermine the Mongols as a viable community. The Mongol ethnicity generated by these mechanisms is so perplexing that the Mongols aspire not only to maintain an ethnic political entity but also to live as normal citizens of the Chinese state. Furthermore, they simultaneously emphasize group cohesion and individualism. Contrary to the current dominant view that the Chinese regime is a builder of *minzu,* in fact, it builds in order to destroy.

MAPPING A MONGOLIAN AUTONOMY?

One looks in vain for Inner Mongolia on the map of the Republic of China in Taiwan. There, Inner Mongolia does not exist at all; rather, Outer Mongolia substitutes for Mongolia as a whole, and Inner Mongolia, along with Tibet, constitutes a special administrative zone under the Mongolian-Tibetan Affairs Commission.[3] The map demonstrates the raison d'être for the beginning of Inner Mongolian nationalism in the early years of the twentieth century. Maps are emblematic of nationalism, for ultimately, the existence of a nation must be certified by occupying a space on the Earth, marked with a logo. The appearance of a regional-cum-ethnic entity named the Inner Mongolian Autonomous Region on the map of the People's Republic of China has led to both an arduous struggle against colonial erasure and a continuing battle for the maintenance of Mongolian identity. However, the logocentric aspect of the map may be seriously at odds with what is hidden from its artistic surface; behind the Mongol place-names on the map are different realities.

The Qing conquest and division of Mongolia into Outer and Inner Mongolia is a familiar story. The disappearance of Inner Mongolia from the Chinese map was indicative of a long process of interaction rather than a sudden takeover. In fact, so-called Inner Mongolia was never a "unified" administrative unit, even in the Qing, as was Outer Mongolia. By contrast, Outer Mongolia gradually began to attain a unified identity thanks not only to its having a more homogeneous population based on the Halh and a unified Buddhist church (since the seventeenth century) under the various reincarnations of Jetsundamba Hutagt but more importantly to the objectifying effect of the Qing administration.[4] On the other hand, Inner Mongolia was fragmented into various mutually exclusive leagues and banners directly controlled by the Qing court. Instead of allowing a native unified church that would serve as the focal point for all the Mongols in Inner Mongolia, the Qing court controlled the Buddhist churches directly by placing them under the Jangjiya Hutagt, the imperial teacher. After two and a half centuries of stringent divide-and-rule policies that not only imbued each Mongol banner with a territorial location in which Mongols exercised a high degree of autonomy but also made Mongols pledge fealty to the Qing,[5] various Inner Mongolian banners began to bear the brunt of unrestrained Chinese migration as the Manchus identified more closely with Chinese interests. A new style of colonization was initiated in 1902 to officially reclaim Inner Mongolian pastures for agricultural development in order to raise funds that the Qing could use to pay for the Boxer Indemnity. This pitted the Mongols against both the Qing and the Chinese, as Mongols could no longer control the land, nor could they tax the incoming Chinese settlers. The wave of Chinese migration provoked a host of Mongolian rebellions, some led by banner princes, culminating in the massive but unsuccessful attempt of the Inner Mongolian princes to join the independence movement initiated by Outer Mongolia in 1911.[6] However, this did not prevent some Mongol aristocrats from selling land to Chinese. Their loss of salary following the demise of the Qing, together with their need to pay for the modern amenities they enjoyed in Beijing and other cities, required their finding a source of extra income. As a result, popular Mongol nationalism targeted two enemies: externally, land-grabbing Chinese, and internally, land-selling Mongol aristocrats.

One of the first signs of Inner Mongolia's incorporation into Republican China was the setting up of Chinese administrations on Mongol territories. As early as 1914, the three Chinese "special administrative zones" of Suiyuan, Chahar, and Rehe were created in the central part of Inner Mongolia, areas with high concentrations of Chinese settlers. By 1928, after Chiang Kai-shek "unified" China, the three special administrative zones were dissolved, their western parts apportioned to Gansu and Ningxia and their eastern parts to Fengtian, Jilin, and Heilongjiang Provinces, thus completing the Chinese administrative colonization of Inner Mongolia and erasing Inner Mongolia completely from the map of the Republic of China. The precise number of Chinese in Inner Mongolia in the early nineteenth century is difficult to gauge but may have been approximately 1,000,000. In 1912, it exceeded 1,500,000, and in 1937, there were over 3,000,000 Chinese in the former Inner Mongolia. In comparison, there were more than 1,000,000 Mongols in Inner Mongolia at the beginning of the nineteenth century, but by 1912, their number had declined to 877,946. By 1937, they had further dwindled to 864,429 because of wars and venereal diseases.[7]

The Chinese colonization of Inner Mongolia had many of the characteristics of the American opening up of the native Indian frontiers, though it less frequently involved either ethnic cleansing or genocide. The reclaimed "wasteland" (pasture) was settled by Chinese farmers, who were administered by specially established county governments. The counties soon expanded, separating banners and leagues from each other. For instance, Linxi, Lindong, and Jingpeng Counties effectively divided Inner Mongolia down the middle, into western and eastern parts. Kailu and Lubei Counties were wedged between Jirim and Jo'uda Leagues, Wuchuan County separated Tumed Banner from Da Muminggan and Durben Huhed Banners, and the Houtao region (north of the Yellow River) formed a buffer between Yekeju and Ulaanchab Leagues.[8] Moreover, many historic monastic centers were inundated with Chinese settlers, and they became "towns" or "cities," thus rapidly transforming the political, economic, and cultural landscape of Inner Mongolia. This reflected increasing demographic disparity. Thus, by 1947, the Chinese had become the overwhelming majority, constituting over 85 percent of the total population of 5,617,000 people. Mongols numbered only 832,000.[9]

The establishment of the provincial administration and the abolition of the banner and league systems were predicated on the principle that the Mongol system was anachronistic and feudal and hence should be eliminated. In destroying Mongolian "feudalism," Chinese republican revolutionaries may have thought they were doing the Mongols a service, but it provoked violent resistance, not only from Mongol aristocrats but also from Mongol intellectuals, who vowed to defend Mongolian "autonomy" or achieve "independence," redefining Manchu-imposed institutions as "Mongol." This was ironic, for Mongol nationalism was also "democratic" and "progressive" in character and aimed to modernize the "feudal" characteristics of Mongol life. The Chinese assault on the Mongols put on hold the internal reform by Mongol nationalists; the priority of the nationalist imperative demanded abolition of the Chinese provincial establishment, defining it as colonialism. What can therefore be said is that Inner Mongolia, which was the creation of a Manchu colonial administration that separated it from Outer Mongolia and colonized it and which was targeted for destruction by Mongol nationalists seeking reunification with Outer Mongolia, took on a life of its own precisely because of the Chinese colonial onslaught. Inner Mongolian nationalism was thus energized, and its ultimate objective was "restoration" of lost Mongol territory.

Mongol nationalist movements can be divided into three periods: 1911–1913, 1925–1929, and 1931–1947. Briefly, 1911–1913 saw a pan-Mongolian movement, led by Mongol nobles, to reunite Inner Mongolia with Outer Mongolia. The increasingly sedentary habits of the population facilitated the growth of this movement, as nationalist leaders capitalized on the fixed presence of larger numbers of people. In 1925, an Inner Mongolian People's Revolutionary Party demanding independence for Inner Mongolia was launched under the influence of the third Communist International (Comintern). Though based, unwittingly, on the Manchu and, later, Chinese colonization efforts, this was the first "Inner Mongolian" institution, but it proved to be short lived.[10] The Japanese occupation of Manchuria and eastern Inner Mongolia turned out to be more significant for Inner Mongolian nationalism. For some Mongols, desperate to escape Chinese colonization, Japan was a necessary evil. Conversely, the Japanese cultivated the Mongols' anti-Chinese nationalism but fell short of supporting them wholeheartedly.

This third period requires more elaboration to illustrate Inner Mongolian territorial nationalism. Three nationalist groups were active during this period; differences notwithstanding, they were unified in their common goal of removing Inner Mongolia from Chinese provincial administration. The most important group was led by Prince Demchugdongrob,[11] who initiated an autonomous movement as early as 1931 in the Silingol region, in response to the establishment of the provincial administrations. Demchugdongrob was increasingly drawn to the Japanese, whom he hoped to use to curb Chinese colonization. However, the Japanese defeat in 1945 deprived him of his political legitimacy.

The Mongols in Manchukuo did not have a leader like Demchugdongrob, but they proved to be politically savvier after the war. One can say that Manchukuo played an important role in creating an "eastern Mongolian" identity, thanks to the Mongols' common experience of colonization and unified administration. Moreover, the military organization of the Mongolian Hingan Army in Manchukuo provided the Mongols with an organizational structure. After a failed attempt at unification with the newly independent Mongolian People's Republic (MPR) in late 1945, the eastern Mongols organized an Eastern Mongolian Autonomous Government in early 1946, a force that had to be reckoned with by the Chinese Communist Party (CCP) and the Chinese Nationalist Party (Guomindang, or KMT).

There was also an active resistance force consisting mostly of Communist Tumed Mongols led by Ulanhu. The Tumed, a numerically insignificant Mongol group that had played a prominent role in supporting the Dalai Lama in Tibet, had once occupied the most fertile ground in Inner Mongolia. However, by the early twentieth century, the Tumed were largely Chinese speakers because of massive Chinese migration into their region starting as early as the late eighteenth century. Nonetheless, many became staunch Communists, fighting not only the Chinese Nationalists, but also the Japanese.

When the CCP and its Red Army moved to northern Shaanxi, which borders on the Ordos region of Inner Mongolia, in late 1935, the Mongols became strategically important to the very survival of the Chinese Communists. Desperate to win over the Mongols, Mao made a historic declaration in December 1935 in which he promised to return Inner Mongolia to the Mongols and called upon them to join in the common struggle against both the Japanese and the Chinese Nationalists.[12] It was this statement that persuaded Ulanhu and his Tumed cohorts to move to the Communist base in Yan'an in 1941; by 1945, Ulanhu would emerge as an alternate member of the CCP Central Committee, the highest rank achieved by any minority in the Communist movement.

The establishment of the pro-independence Eastern Mongolian Autonomous Government and the KMT's occupation of Manchuria after the Anti-Japanese War were important considerations in the CCP's ultimate decision to support Inner Mongolian autonomy. An autonomous Inner Mongolia, it was reasoned, would fight to defend itself from KMT penetration. Though motivated by strategy rather than by unconditional support for Mongolian autonomy, the CCP sent Ulanhu and Mongol Party members to eastern Mongolia, where they successfully founded an Inner Mongolian Autonomous Government in May 1947. Based on the territorial jurisdiction of the Eastern Mongolian Autonomous Government, its capital was Wangiin Sume, now called Ulaanhot.

The CCP support for Mongolian autonomy was attractive to the Mongols, especially when the eastern Mongolian quest for unification with the MPR was rejected and when the Eastern Mongolian Autonomous Government was threatened by the Chinese Nationalists. It was attractive also because the CCP supported Inner Mongolian autonomy, which, though short of complete independence or unification with Mongolia, was predicated on the future unification of fragmented Inner Mongolia. Surely the Mongols were intoxicated by the prospect of eastern and western Mongolian unification, but few predicted what kind of autonomy it would be under the Chinese Communist leadership.

The Inner Mongolian Autonomous Region was a product of the Chinese Communist need for Mongol support in the Civil War rather than simply an example of Chinese Communist support for Mongol "nationalism"; the Chinese Communists did not promote or create Mongolian nationalism.

REMAPPING INNER MONGOLIAN AUTONOMY

Did the Inner Mongolian Autonomous Region encourage a sense of separate nationhood for Mongols or did it in fact contribute to the integration of Mongols into the Chinese state? This question echoes recent debates among Sovietologists regarding the effect of the Soviet nationality policy in destroying the Soviet Union. Yuri Slezkine, for instance, blamed Soviet policy and what he calls "compensatory 'nation-building'" for fostering the localism and nationalism that eventually brought down the Soviet Union.[13] Francine Hirsch, on the other hand, argues that for Soviet policymakers, colonization and "making nations" went hand in hand, through a process of what she calls "double assimilation"—the assimilation of diverse peoples into official nationality categories and the assimilation of nationally categorized groups into a unified political, economic, and ideological whole. This is a participatory process: "As new dominant nationalities and national minorities used a common vocabulary and standardized administrative procedures to fight for resources and assert their rights, they also become increasingly anchored in the Soviet state and society."[14]

The territorial-administrative demarcation of the Inner Mongolian Autonomous Region resulted in the Mongols becoming increasingly integrated into the Chinese state. Ironically, it was their ambition to "recover" Inner Mongolian territory that resulted in closer integration. The Mongols have not been able to solve the demographic imbalance within Inner Mongolia. From the outset, when the Inner Mongolian Autonomous Government was founded with the support of the CCP, Mongol nationalism was curtailed by the class-nation concept, in which the Chinese peasants were rendered class victims of the KMT and thus could not be treated as colonialists. Therefore, the Mongol efforts to recover lost territory and dismantle the Chinese provincial administration did not result in a Mongol majority within the autonomous territory, nor did it result in the expulsion of the Chinese migrants, who by 1949 numbered more than 4,000,000. On the contrary, the more territory the Mongols recovered, the more Chinese were incorporated into Inner Mongolia.[15]

The Inner Mongolian Autonomous Government began its westward expansion from eastern Mongolia as soon as the People's Republic of China was proclaimed. In 1949, Jirim League of Liaobei Province and Jo'uda League of Rehe Province were incorporated into Inner Mongolia, and the Inner Mongolian government moved from Ulaanhot to Zhangjiakou, the capital of Chahar Province. In 1952, three ethnically mixed counties were incorporated into the autonomous region when Chahar was dissolved. However, it proved difficult to move further west into Suiyuan Province. Suiyuan, an overwhelmingly Chinese province, had two prefectural-level autonomous Mongol regions, Yekeju and Ulaanchab. Since the Chinese leaders of Suiyuan were mostly locals, who had strong ethnic prejudices, conceding to Mongolian power was an affront to them. For Ulanhu, this constituted at best a partial success; his homeland Tumed region, located in the center of Suiyuan, was precisely the area that had been most colonized by Chinese. Determined to reclaim his homeland for the Inner Mongolian Autonomous Region, he moved the Inner Mongolian government seat to Guisui (renamed Hohhot in 1954) in 1952. Only through a protracted negotiation and because he feared Mongol discontent during the Korean War did Mao personally intervene on behalf of Ulanhu. However, the so-called autonomy of Inner Mongolia was compromised by mutual concessions — in a schema called the "two doors" by Mao, Suiyuan was persuaded to open its door to the Mongols, and the Mongols agreed to allow the Chinese to stay in an enlarged Inner Mongolia. In 1956, the two westernmost Mongolian banners in Gansu Province were also incorporated into the Inner Mongolian Autonomous Region. In the same year, six banners and counties, including Chifeng, which was previously part of Rehe Province, were taken over by Inner Mongolia. At long last, an Inner Mongolian Autonomous Region took the shape that we know today; however, some large chunks of Mongol land were lost to neighboring provinces, though in some cases, they were organized as Mongolian autonomous counties.[16]

This territorial expansion increased the existing demographic disparity between Mongols and Chinese, causing further unforeseen problems
for the Mongols in terms of their cultural survival. Particularly problematic for many was the choice of Hohhot as the capital of the Inner Mongolian Autonomous Region. Hohhot, once a monastic center, became a
Chinese trading town at the beginning of the nineteenth century. With
few Mongol residents in and around the city, and with no Mongolian
ethnic "enclave," the Mongol administrators who were newly arrived from
eastern Mongolia and who had been recruited from pastoral areas were
dispersed in various residential units throughout the city, together with
members of their work units; there, they comprised a minority. Within
a few years, the children of Mongol cadres lost their Mongolian language,
and thus began a voluntary assimilation process.[17] The same thing happened in lower-level league and banner centers.

The territorial expansion of the Inner Mongolian Autonomous Region
was soon accompanied by a severe reduction in autonomous rights as the
Party's program of land reform, agricultural collectivization, and nation-
alization of industry proceeded throughout China. A massive influx of
Chinese migrants arrived in Inner Mongolia; they came as a result of land
reform and collectivization, as well as the transfer to Inner Mongolia of
large- and medium-size factories from coastal and inland China. Inner
Mongolia was a favored spot for Soviet aid, especially in the building of
heavy-industrial plants, and the new plants were mainly staffed by an influx
of workers from north and northeast China. The implications were profound for the creation of a Mongolian working class, so much desired by
Mongols as a sign of socialist modernity. Between 1950 and 1957, 1,536,100
Chinese migrated into Inner Mongolia. An additional 1,926,600 Chinese
moved in between 1958 and 1960 as a result of famine.[18] More pastures
were reclaimed for agriculture during this period than at any other previous time.

Faced with the loss of a wide range of autonomous rights so recently
won or promised, Mongol cadres and intellectuals began to call for implementation of autonomous rights, the right of equality, and so on. But
these demands were rebuffed by the Party in 1957–58 in the Antirightist
movement that followed the Hundred Flowers campaign, in which many
Mongol intellectuals were labeled "ethnic rightists" *(minzu youpai)*. The
increasing demand for autonomy coincided with the escalating tension
between China and the Soviet Union in the late 1950s and early 1960s.
Soon, Inner Mongolia was at the forefront of border clashes between China
and the Soviet Union (and its ally, the MPR). The historical association

between Inner Mongolian Communists and the Soviet Union and Mongolia, hitherto the Mongolians' strategic credential in obtaining autonomous rights, now became a liability. Mongols were forced to choose either to unequivocally support Chinese national unity, a route that would require the drastic reduction of Mongol autonomous rights, or to insist on ethnic difference to resist Chinese state penetration, thereby risking Chinese repression. Ulanhu and his Mongol supporters chose the latter and were thus accused of siding with the Soviet Union and the Mongolian People's Republic in their confrontation with China. Their demand for autonomy was then attacked as treasonous to China and as undermining Chinese national unity. Chinese officials accused Mongols, especially Mongol Communist officials, of conspiring to create a pan-Mongolian state. More than twenty thousand Mongols were killed and more than three hundred thousand injured during the turmoil in Inner Mongolia from 1967 to 1969. This is by far the highest number of officially acknowledged casualties among any single ethnic group during the Cultural Revolution.[19]

In 1969, as Sino-Soviet tension escalated, the territory of the Inner Mongolian Autonomous Region was drastically reduced, and several leagues were turned over for administrative purposes to Heilongjiang, Jilin, Liaoning, and Gansu Provinces and Ningxia Hui Autonomous Region. It was only in 1979 that these territories were returned to Inner Mongolia. But this territorial adjustment never resolved the demographic disparity. It remains an insoluble problem for the Mongols, who are today a small minority in their own homeland.

WHOSE AUTONOMY IN INNER MONGOLIA?

The post–Cultural Revolution era has seen Mongols playing a minor role in Inner Mongolian "autonomy." The irrelevance of the Mongols in the political domain may be observed in the changing ethnic composition of members of the Political Consultative Congress (PCC). The PCC is part of the state's United Front apparatus, which encompasses non-Party elites, such as nobles and senior monks, as well as intellectuals. In recent years, however, it has become what one Mongol figuratively calls a "concentration camp" of discredited Mongol Communist officials. For instance, the chairman of the PCC is Qian Fengyun, a prominent Mongol who wielded considerable power in Inner Mongolia in the early 1980s before falling afoul of Zhou Hui, the Party secretary of Inner Mongolia, in 1981–82, when he refused to obey Zhou's order to punish Mongol student-protest leaders. His deputy is another prominent Mongol leader whose opposition to attempts to divide the historic Ordos tribe and relocate its western banners to Wuhai, a coal-mining city, led to his "promotion" in the mid-1990s. In other words, if in the past, the Party treated the non-Party elites as United Front allies, today, they have placed their own Mongol Communist officials in such roles. As "traditional" Mongol elites decline in number, two groups staff the PCC: discredited Mongol officials and Chinese economic elites, who increasingly pursue political power to protect and promote their interests.[20]

The most serious challenge to Mongol autonomy lies in the People's Congress of the autonomous region, the highest organ of self-government. While the Law on Regional National Autonomy stipulates that the chairman of the regional government must be a member of the titular nationality, Article 16 is ambiguous as to the ethnic identity of the chairman of the People's Congress: "Among the chairman and vice chairmen of the standing committee of the People's Congress of a national autonomous area shall be one or more citizens of the nationality exercising regional autonomy in the area." Given the fact that the People's Congress is the highest political organ exercising autonomous rights, the ambiguity opens the door for Chinese, as members of a nontitular nationality, to become chair of the People's Congress of the autonomous region. After two Mongols served as chairmen from 1982 to 1992, Wang Qun, a Chinese and the former Party secretary of Inner Mongolia, assumed the chairmanship. It has apparently become a rule for the Party secretary to be concurrently chair of the People's Congress. The incumbent Party secretary, Chu Bo, a Chinese from Anhui, succeeded Liu Mingzu, another Chinese, in December 2001 as Party secretary and in January 2003 as chairman of the People's Congress of Inner Mongolia.

Mongols do not even constitute the majority of the deputies of the People's Congress. According to a senior Mongol leader working in the People's Congress of Inner Mongolia, when Ting Mao, a Mongol, was the leader of the People's Congress (1982–1984), only 40 percent of the seats were held by Mongols, the highest number to date. Because Chinese form the majority in the People's Congress, it is not surprising that it has not drafted "regulations on the exercise of autonomy and separate regulations in light of the political, economic, and cultural characteristics of the nationality or nationalities in the areas concerned," as required by the Law on Regional National Autonomy. There have been no legally binding regulations defining the exercise of autonomy in Inner Mongolia, despite the efforts of two Mongol chairmen, Ting Mao and

Batubagan (1984–1992) , who were known for their strong pro-Mongol sentiments.

We now see an interesting development in Inner Mongolia: the Mongols seek the rule of law while the Chinese emphasize majoritarian "democracy." As more Chinese are represented in the Party Committee, the government, the People's Congress, and the PCC, the Inner Mongolian Autonomous Region becomes increasingly a misnomer. The autonomous region now emphasizes "region" as opposed to "ethnicity." In a recent major policy-oriented publication, Beijing-based sociologist Ma Rong and anthropologist Zhou Xin redefined the relationship between autonomous regions and the state this way:

> The great majority of the "minority group regions" or "ethnic regions" are in actual fact multiethnic regions par excellence; ethnic regional autonomy is not an ethnic autonomy separate from the designated territory, rather it is an ethnic regional autonomy that takes account of the interests of both the self-governing ethnicity within the autonomous region and all other non-self-governing ethnicities within the autonomous region. Those ideas that aim to establish independent ethnic "economic" or "political" systems not only misunderstand ethnic regional autonomy but are also ignorant of the basic condition of China. The unhealthy trend that exists today, that is, understanding ethnic autonomy to mean, or mainly to mean, the ratio of cadre allocation or positions, is good neither for the healthy growth of minority cadres nor for the unity between self-governing ethnicities and non-self-governing ethnicities in an ethnic autonomous area.[21]

MANAGING MONGOLIAN OFFICIALS

In June 2000, learning that Deng Nan, the daughter of the late Deng Xiaoping, would arrive in Silingol League with funds to invest to "cure" the desert that had been caused by overgrazing, Yun Bulong, the chairman of the Inner Mongolian Autonomous Region, drove to meet her. But on the way, a local train rammed into his car, and he was killed. This immediately posed a problem for the political succession in Inner Mongolia. Seeking to balance Chinese and Mongol interests, the central government took more than two months to appoint an acting chairman.

The first reaction to Yun's death was disbelief. Various political jokes and stories circulated.[22] His death seemed to have surprised even central leaders such as Premier Zhu Rongji. Zhu was known to have angrily remarked that this was unprecedented in Chinese history *(kuanggu qiwen)*. People interpreted this as Zhu merely expressing his alarm at the poor security protection of even a provincial-level leader. But his concern went further: Yun's untimely death had caught the central government unprepared. Since he was halfway through his five-year tenure, the central government had not yet thought out his replacement. According to the Law on Regional National Autonomy, the successor had to be a Mongol. The real issue was that the central government had to determine from which Mongol tribal group the chairman should be picked.

Yun Bulong was a "western" Mongol, and his predecessor was an "eastern" Mongol, so the politics of tribal balance appeared to determine that his successor should be an "eastern" Mongol. However, since Yun had not completed his term, the possibility remained that a western Mongol could be appointed interim chairman until the formal reappointment of a chairman two years later. Various names were circulated. Some speculated that Baatar would be a strong candidate. The son of Jargal, a prominent eastern Mongolian leader, Baatar was a former chairman of the Inner Mongolian Youth League. Others insisted that Bayanchuluu, an Ordos Mongol, had a better chance. He was the first deputy chairman of the All China Youth League in Beijing. Talented and seen as having powerful connections with the central leadership, he seemed to have a strong chance. His only disadvantage was that he lacked leadership experience at the local level; but others insisted that experience is secondary and a political network is primary. Three more names were circulated. Bayin, an eastern Mongol who followed closely the Party line, was not known to be sympathetic to the Mongols. Wang Fengqi, another eastern Mongol, was the favorite choice for legalists because he was the Mongol vice-chairman next in rank to Yun Bulong; he was known to be intelligent and articulate. The third was Oyunchimeg, a woman and eastern Mongol, who was also a vice-chairman and was famous for propaganda work. No names of "western" Mongols were circulated.

The political division of "eastern" and "western" Mongols is a relatively recent configuration. The so-called western Mongols consist almost entirely of the Tumed Mongol Communists who came to political prominence in Yan'an during the Anti-Japanese War. The eastern Mongol leaders are Nationalists and Communists who were once colonial subjects under the Japanese in Manchukuo. These two Mongol political groups, together with the Chinese, constitute the three political factions in the Inner Mongolian Autonomous Region; they are united in some respects but also divided along ethnic and tribal lines. Mongols from other leagues and banners have been marginalized because of their lack of Communist credentials. After the Cultural Revolution, the Ordos Mongols formed a third Mongol faction, though they have often been considered allies of the Tumed Mongols because of their geographical proximity.

This tribal and ethnic configuration could clearly be seen in the structure of the Inner Mongolian CCP Working Committee formed in May 1947. Ulanhu, the secretary and a Tumed Mongol, had a Chinese deputy, Liu Chun; in addition, the members of the Party Standing Committee were one eastern Mongol, one western (Tumed) Mongol, and two Chinese.[23] The tribal and ethnic balance was even clearer in the structure of the Inner Mongolian Autonomous Region People's Government formed in December 1949, a government not elected by people's deputies but appointed by the central government. The chairman of the government was Ulanhu, and the deputies were Hafenga, an eastern Mongol, and Yang Zhilin, a Chinese. This pattern continued to the eve of the Cultural Revolution.

For the first fifteen years of the autonomous region, the leadership position of the Party and the government were dominated by Communist veterans, appointed by the central government and reflecting their regional and ethnic origins. The small number of senior Tumed Mongols such as Ulanhu, Kuibi, and Biligbaatar were undisputed leaders because of their Communist credentials; so were Hafenga and other senior eastern Mongols such as Tomorbagan and Jargal, who played prominent roles in unifying eastern and western Inner Mongolia. Yang Zhilin and Su Qianyi, two senior Chinese Communists, were leaders of Suiyuan Province. This triangular balance began to crumble in the early 1960s. As a result of the Socialist Education campaign, class factors assumed increasing importance in one's political career. Up to 1964–65, Ulanhu, in his effort to maintain Mongol supremacy in Inner Mongolia, had relied on many young eastern Mongol Communists, who were far better educated under Japanese rule than the majority of the Tumed Mongols, many of whom, except for some senior leaders, such as Ulanhu, Kuibi, and Biligbaatar, had been trained in Yan'an. Moreover, the eastern Mongols, who spoke both Mongolian and Chinese fluently—some even spoke Japanese—were a formidable force; many were intellectually superior to their Chinese counterparts. The new class emphasis suddenly undermined their political credentials, however; their experience of having served in the Japanese-controlled Hingan Mongolian Army became a liability. Because of this, the junior Tumed Mongols, trained in Yan'an and, up to the early sixties, holding middle-ranking positions in the Party and government, began to be promoted. As a result of Ulanhu's new maneuver to strengthen his own power base by building up trusted Tumed officials, many senior Chinese leaders, such as Su Qianyi and Yang Zhilin, were also removed from Inner Mongolia although they were given higher positions elsewhere.

In February 1966, in an administrative reshuffle to abolish various departments, Ulanhu formed five encompassing commissions, all headed by Tumed Mongols. A thirteen-member acting standing committee of the Inner Mongolia Communist Party formed in January 1966 (to strengthen Ulanhu's control of the increasingly volatile situation in Inner Mongolia) had seven Tumed Mongols, three eastern Mongols, and three Chinese. This effectively destroyed the ethnic and tribal balance among Communist leaders in Inner Mongolia. Ulanhu's installation of his Tumed Mongols in the face of increasing Chinese political penetration, together with the worsening international relations between China and the Soviet Union and its ally, the MPR, was resented by both eastern Mongols and Chinese and was considered a political coup d'état. The Cultural Revolution initially targeted the Tumed Mongols for their "tribalism" and "nationalism" and resulted in the permanent removal of Ulanhu from Inner Mongolia, but it soon turned toward uprooting an alleged Mongol conspiracy against China.

The legacy of the Cultural Revolution has been both negative and positive. Some of the *minzu* practices have been institutionalized. For one thing, the CCP has become a Chinese "colonial" institution, represented by a "Chinese" Party secretary appointed by the central government. Moreover, the position of the Organizational Department (Zuzhibu) of the Party Committee has been in the hands of Chinese since the Cultural Revolution. The sinicization of the Party institutionalized the subordination of and distrust toward ethnic minorities.

On a more positive side, Ulanhu, who was removed as Inner Mongolia's preeminent leader in 1966 and subsequently sent to Beijing, in the early 1980s, in his capacity as a vice-chairman of the National People's Congress, led a team to draft the Law on Regional National Autonomy. This was an effort toward constitutionalizing autonomy for minority ethnic groups. As far as Inner Mongolia was concerned, the law initiated sharp struggles over the nature of national autonomy.

According to the Law on Regional National Autonomy, the people's congresses and people's governments are "organs of self-government." Chapter 2, Article 17 stipulates that "the chairman of an autonomous region, the prefect of an autonomous prefecture, or the head of an autonomous county shall be a citizen of the nationality exercising regional autonomy in the area concerned." One would have expected that, in the aftermath of the Cultural Revolution, Mongols would be more united than previously because of their common experience of persecution. They did attain a degree of internal unity, but only briefly. Rehabilitated Mongol leaders, with Ulanhu's support from Beijing, managed to reclaim the lost territories in 1979. But with the appointment of the chairman subject to manipulation by the central government, the historic eastern and western divide between the Mongols quickly deepened, with a devastating effect on Mongol unity. Buhe, the eldest son of Ulanhu, served as chairman from 1982 to 1992; he was succeeded by Ulji, an eastern Mongolian, who was followed by Yun Bulong. In August 2000, Yun was succeeded by Oyunchimeg.

What are the criteria used to select a specific candidate? None of the above-mentioned leaders was known to have been effective or decisive in leadership style. All were known for their obedience to the central government, if not for their lack of ability. The central government's repeated appointment of leaders who are popularly deemed weak reinforces the impression that Mongol leaders are genuinely of low quality because of their cultural upbringing, if not their genetic makeup. And since Mongols are perceived to be incapable of governing their autonomous region effectively, they deserve only to serve as symbols of autonomy, for which the quality of obedience is an asset. As a corollary, since the post-Mao priority in Inner Mongolia is economic development, "smarter" Chinese leaders have to be promoted. As a result, in the past decade, the vice-chairman who runs the day-to-day affairs of Inner Mongolia has been a Chinese; so has the vice-chairman in charge of finance and planning.

The Mongol officials' incapacity can be seen more clearly in contrast to Tibet. Tibetan officials have consolidated their power vis-à-vis the Chinese central government through upholding China's Law on Regional National Autonomy and manipulating China's morbid opposition to the Dalai Lama. They have successfully presented themselves as the only alternative to the Dalai Lama, a role that cannot be hijacked by Chinese cadres. This unique position enables them not only to protect some of the rights accorded to minority ethnic groups under China's laws but also to bargain for economic benefits from the central government.[24]

Inner Mongolian officials had earlier played a similar role because of the geopolitical position of Inner Mongolia between China, the MPR, and the Soviet Union. Ulanhu's and other senior Mongols' special credentials as revolutionary veterans were important factors in their success in securing relative "autonomy" for the Mongols. However, this was a dangerous position, requiring careful management. Indeed, the Sino-Soviet rift ultimately deprived the Mongols of their political capital. As the Soviet Union and the MPR emerged as powerful enemies of China, the links between the Soviets and Inner Mongolian officials became a liability for the latter; they were perceived as a threat to the Chinese government. Since the Cultural Revolution, and with Ulanhu gone, the second generation of Mongol officials has not been able to influence the Soviet Union (or its successor, the Russian Republic) or the MPR (or its successor, the Republic of Mongolia). Moreover, the Mongolian "people," in general, have not been able to form any autonomous constituency outside of the state power and are in no position to put any pressure on Mongol officials.

The Chinese government employs Mongol officials whose main function is not to govern Inner Mongolia but to secure Mongol loyalty to the Chinese government and oppose any Mongol dissidence. Many Mongols, then, do not respect them. Because they do not command a constituency, Mongol officials face obstacles in bargaining with the Chinese state.

HOW SHOULD INNER MONGOLIA BE DEVELOPED?

The history of the Inner Mongolian Autonomous Region has been punctuated by a struggle on the part of the Mongols and their leaders against both agricultural expansion and the concurrent Chinese immigration. The emotion that pastoralism conjures up for Mongols derives from its importance as the quintessential historical cultural marker of Mongol-ness (as opposed to Chinese-ness, which is associated with agriculture). As one of the most important criteria in defining Mongolian ethnicity, pastoralism informs a Mongol sense of morality in resisting further attempts to introduce agriculture, despite or because of the fact that the majority of the Mongols in Inner Mongolia are already farmers.[25]

The initial concession to the Mongol resistance to agriculture that resulted in the Inner Mongolian Autonomous Region was soon rescinded. Land reclamation in Inner Mongolia began in earnest in 1957 to produce grain for northern China. In 1958, without the approval of the Inner Mongolian Autonomous Region, the Ministry of Land Reclamation pushed into Hulunbuir. By 1960, one million *mu*[26] of pasture had been reclaimed for agriculture; this was followed by massive Chinese immigration. Criticism of land reclamation became politically risky as Chinese took charge of frontier defense, which was aimed at the Soviet Union. In 1958, Mongols who opposed land reclamation were denounced as "ethnic rightists." By 1962, however, the escalation of border tension between Mongolia and

China led some Mongol herders who lacked pasture lands to flee to the Mongolian People's Republic; the Inner Mongolian Autonomous Region then closed some of the newly opened fields and restored them to pasture. This Mongol resistance was suppressed, however, during the Cultural Revolution, when land reclamation resumed in earnest.

Chinese land reclamation was justified because the pastoral economy was considered to be of less significance than agriculture. Grassland, upon which Mongol herders made their living, was considered wasteland, subject to "development." The advancement of the Mongol ethnic group was deemed possible only by their adopting Chinese agriculture. In this pursuit for "modernization," the Chinese state not only legally and openly reclaimed pastureland but sent in millions of Chinese immigrants.

In the face of this new socialist drive, Mongol officials developed new strategies for defending their land and their ever-shrinking pastoral economy. First, they argued that pastoralism and agriculture were not two stages of social evolution; rather, they were complementary sectors of a national economy. Moreover, the kind of agriculture practiced by Chinese in Inner Mongolia was denounced as *younong,* or nomadic agriculture, a kind of slash-and-burn agriculture that moves to a new location whenever a field becomes infertile. *Younong* was considered an anomaly, in violation of the basic characteristic of agriculture, which, in the Mongol view, must be sedentary and intensive. Mongol officials did not support pastoralism for the Mongols alone; rather, they promoted it as a contribution to the Chinese national economy. They argued in environmental terms, attributing the worsening desertification in Inner Mongolia to agriculture. Most of the soil of Inner Mongolia is known to be unsuitable for agriculture; the thin topsoil, when exposed to wind, quickly turns to desert. The promotion of ecologically unsustainable agriculture at the cost of environmentally appropriate pastoralism was thus denounced as destructive of the Chinese national economy rather than the Mongol economy.

Second, a number of cultural initiatives were launched to improve the image of pastoralism in the early 1960s. Ushenju, a pastoral area of Ordos facing desertification, became the center of a model effort, led by a Mongol woman, Boroldoi, to grow shrubs to control the desert. Ushenju thus became the pastoral counterpart to the agricultural model Dazhai. In addition, two little sisters were crowned with heroic titles for saving the commune's flock of sheep by braving a blizzard.[27] A mobile cultural troupe was developed in the same period to propagate the socialist spirit, not only among dispersed herders but also in other parts of China. Pastoralism began to attain a new life as the ultimate cultural marker of Mongol identity and a barometer to measure the degree of autonomy Mongols could exercise in their autonomous region.

During the 1950s and early 1960s, two Mongolian epic poems extolling the Mongol struggle against Chinese land grabbing in the 1920s and 1930s became popular. The historical events depicted in these poems—Sine Lama's Duguilong movement and Gada Meiren's anti–land grabbing struggle—must be appreciated not so much for themselves but for their ideological significance in presenting Mongol identity in class and ethnic terms. The story of Gada Meiren is particularly emblematic; a song about his struggle titled "Gada Meiren" has become the unofficial anthem of the Inner Mongolians. For a long time, the epics and the song were promoted to remind people not only of the "revolutionary" genesis of the Mongolian Communist struggle but also of the CCP's role in helping the Mongols to regain their land.

Because of this campaign, the pastoral areas of Inner Mongolia bore the brunt of the Cultural Revolution. Denounced as a Mongolian cultural stronghold, the pastoral areas became the sustained target for land reclamation and immigration. According to an official description, initially young male peasants from inland China pioneered in migrating to Inner Mongolia:

> Some of them moved in in teams, concentrating in one place or dispersing in several. Sometimes, a production team, a brigade, or even an entire commune moved in. They chose lush grassland as their destination; there, they reclaimed wasteland and grew crops, built roads and houses, and built a village. Then, they sent all their household records to the local government for registration in order to obtain the status of legal residents.[28]

Many of these migrants participated in attacks against Mongol herders accused of plotting independence. They formed the "poor- and middle-peasant propaganda teams" to struggle against alleged Mongol class enemies. These immigrants were not limited to those coming from the rural areas of inland China. Large numbers of demobilized soldiers and urban sent-down youth were also dispatched to rural Inner Mongolia to establish military farms.

There was no Mongol "backlash" against the Chinese immigrants until after the Cultural Revolution, when Mongols attempted to repatriate them. The Chinese central government abruptly halted this effort and denounced the Mongols for having waged a movement to "fan Han pai wai" [oppose the Chinese and reject outsiders]. In the 1980s, in an attempt to protect the remaining Mongol pastureland and preserve the Mongol cultural heartland, Mongol leaders adopted the Chinese agricultural reform method, namely, allocating pastureland to individual households. The official rhetoric was similar to Chinese developmental rhetoric, that is, it provided an incentive to individuals, who, as property-holders, would be more interested not only in raising productivity but in protecting the pastureland from degradation. Naturally, the settlement of Mongols onto permanent pastureland and the division of the pastures among households would prevent Chinese from entering the pastureland. Granting clear, individualized entitlement to pastureland, the Mongols thought, would reduce the likelihood of the arbitrary administrative reallocation of pasture to outsiders, who were mostly Chinese immigrants.

The proponents of land division inadvertently violated one important principle of pastoral production: that ecologically balanced pastures are achieved only through nomadic culture, which requires larger grasslands. The household system, combined with the market-economy principle of exploitation for maximum profit, quickly degraded pastureland. It placed Mongol households in a constant battle between a market logic driven by profitability and the limit set by ecological constraints. This, to no small degree, contributed to the accelerated desertification of the pastureland, thus sabotaging the earlier Mongol ecological argument. In other words, static market-economy pastoralism, unlike nomadic pastoralism, worked to produce environmental degradation.[29]

Simultaneously, this household pastoralism became a venue to reintroduce agriculture through the back door by creating new demands for fodder. Fodder was necessary to make up for the lack of grass within the restricted pasture allocated to each household. Since Mongols were not used to agriculture, many pastoral households invited migrant Chinese farmers to become resident laborers. Increasing numbers of Mongol households also leased their pastures to Chinese peasants indefinitely for quick cash, and some lost their land as a result. Thus fodder production reintroduced not only agriculture but also migrant Chinese peasants from neighboring provinces. In recent years, while the Inner Mongolian grassland has been swamped with Chinese settlers, many Mongols, in turn, have become "nomads." The modern-day Mongol nomads do not herd animals, though; nor do they ride horses. Rather, they roam the cities in pursuit of glamour and pleasure, which is often missing in the dismal countryside. A new kind of Mongol migrant class is quickly forming. Many Mongols are low-wage workers in Chinese factories, and many young women work as singers or waitresses in restaurants or as prostitutes. Many middle-aged parents or grandparents move to the banner centers with their children or grandchildren to avoid sending them to boarding schools; they hope that one day, the children will be able to escape the grassland. Some of these middle-aged Mongols also hope to find jobs in the banner centers. Thus, the market mechanism has induced some Mongols voluntarily to sell their land. Admittedly, the transition is not so smooth; historical memories and cultural values continue to inform the Mongol sensibility toward land and pastoralism.

Let me use the municipality of Ordos (formerly known as Yekeju League) to illustrate this. In recent years, Ordos has moved from being one of the most economically "backward" areas of Inner Mongolia to being its most developed region; this is partly due to its abundant natural resources. Since the early 1980s, the league has developed three major industries: cashmere, coal mining, and chemical products. By the late 1990s, all three were represented in the Shanghai and Shenzhen stock markets, thereby signaling the economic success of the region. To the west of Ordos is the coal-mining city of Wuhai; to the east, the steel-producing city of Baotou. The municipality of Ordos boasts the largest open-pit coal mines in the world. They are a major source of conflict between Inner Mongolia and the Chinese central government. The mines are directly controlled by the Ministry of Coal in Beijing, which recently built a large coal-mining town with workers coming mostly from outside of Inner Mongolia. Local Mongols and Chinese not only lost their land, they were not even compensated with jobs in the mine.

With the clarion call to "develop the western regions" [xibu da kaifa] in early 2000, major tensions began to develop. In the spring, some developers in Ejen Horoo Banner, close to the Chinggis Khan Mausoleum, bulldozed a large stretch of fertile grassland for cultivation. It turned out that the land is a Mongol cemetery, thus causing organized protest from Mongol herders. To placate the herders, the banner administration paid ¥1 million to a Mongol lama from Kumbum Monastery to build a stupa in the middle of the cemetery. Meanwhile, the banner administration plans to lease the land surrounding the mausoleum to some Chinese tourist agencies to build an international airport and theme park. Mongols fear that they will be evicted from their historic homeland.[30]

The grasslands, over which the Mongols have struggled for much of the twentieth century, have now begun to be opened up for further "development" according to market conditions. In 1997, Otog Front Banner leased several hundred thousand *mu* of grassland to a Shenzhen developer for agricultural development, without even compensating the evicted residents. In the first half of 1998 alone, Dalad Banner leased 320,000 *mu* to people outside Inner Mongolia, attracting ¥125 million ($25 million).[31] Other banners designated various "development zones" or "experiment zones," many of which are of dubious value. Lured by short-term benefits, officials at various levels have been more eager to sell or lease anything valuable. In this process, the Mongol administrative units of banner and league have been considered a hindrance. In summer 2000, people in Yekeju League were enthusiastic about the prospect that soon it would be renamed Ordos Municipality.[32] As municipalities, the local officials could bypass any reference to Mongol minorities. Since then, Jirim League and Jo'uda League have changed their names to Chifeng and Tongliao Municipalities, thinking that Chinese rather than Mongol names, and "municipality" rather than "league," would provide more of an "advanced" flavor of development.

This current desire to erase the Mongolian characteristics of the banner and league system stands in sharp contrast to the strenuous fight to preserve them in the first half of the twentieth century. Even as late as the early 1990s, when the former premier Li Peng recommended splitting up Yekeju League and giving the western two Otog banners to the newly built coal-mining city of Wuhai, a predominantly Chinese municipality in Inner Mongolia, the governor of Yekeju League opposed the decision, insisting that the historical integrity of the league must not be undermined. He was subsequently removed from his position and, as Party secretary of Wuhai Municipality, assigned to carry out the division. But he refused. So he was again removed.

Given these dramatic changes, it is not surprising that the two epic poems and the song mentioned above have attained new lives and meanings. In 1993, during my visit to Inner Mongolia, many Mongols confided to me that it was no longer politically correct to sing "Gada Meiren" when Chinese were present. In summer 2000, I had hoped to collect some local Ordos revolutionary histories, particularly regarding Sine Lama and his Duguilong campaign, but such materials were then considered "top national secrets." Not only were books I mailed through the post office intercepted by state security personnel, but when I protested that such materials were Party history, I was reprimanded and told that studying the history of the Duguilong was intended to incite Mongols to rebel against China. Clearly, the two epics have acquired new significance in legitimating potential resistance. In summer 2000 two volumes of the selected works of Ulanhu were published. Instead of imbibing the intended propaganda message that Ulanhu helped Inner Mongolia become part of China, some Mongols read between the lines and told me that Ulanhu had protected Mongolian interests against encroachment. Indeed, Ulanhu now enjoys a reputation among Mongols as the only Communist Mongol to champion pastoral economic development in the face of the Chinese onslaught. His 1950s slogan "Developing pastoralism is the number one priority of Inner Mongolia" has become a mantra for those who defend the pastoral economy and way of life.

Ethnic conflicts have not been limited to those between Mongols and Chinese. Every autumn, beginning in the 1990s, the Inner Mongolian grassland has been subjected to attacks by gangs of poor Muslims from the neighboring Ningxia Hui Autonomous Region and Chinese peasants from surrounding provinces. They are attempting to dig moss or *facai,* a vegetable whose homonym means "to get rich," that is in great demand in Singapore, Malaysia, Hong Kong, and development-crazy Guangdong Province in south China. Often the gangs consist of hundreds or thousands of people. Since they use rakes for efficiency, they pull out the roots not only of *facai* but of all the vegetation. Since Mongols live dispersed throughout the grasslands, and each plot of land is now separated by wires fencing off pastures, they can protect neither the grasslands nor themselves from such invasions. According to a recent American Embassy report, most of the grassland areas that have been raided have become desert.[33] There have even been "turf wars" between Mongols and Hui, with both sides using whatever weapons available, including guns. The hardest hit areas have been the Ordos, Ulaanchab, and Silingol regions.

However, the development of the pastoral industry in recent years in Inner Mongolia has not benefited the Mongol herders. The industry has been divided into two sectors according to ethnicity: Mongols are the providers of the raw materials, such as cashmere and wool, and Chinese control the industrial plants that process the materials. Ordos boasts the world's largest cashmere processing plant, producing more than one million cashmere sweaters a year. However, the plant does nothing to help pastoral Mongols protect their pasture. The demand for cashmere has encouraged Mongols to breed more goats, but that in turn has resulted in severe grassland degradation, as well as disputes between neighbors. Goats have been banned by local governments in most of the Ordos region so that the pastures can recover. But instead of focusing on how to improve the pastures and ensure a sustainable local source of supply, the Ordos cashmere plant has abandoned Ordos herders and turned to the Republic of Mongolia for raw cashmere. The Republic's cashmere plants cannot compete with the Ordos group and have lost their raw cashmere to the latter. Thus, Chinese industrialists have managed to destroy not only cashmere production in the Ordos region but also the Republic of Mongolia's budding cashmere industry, thereby causing international conflict.

The events of spring 2000 dramatized the consequences of grassland degradation in ways that could no longer be ignored by the central government. About a dozen sandstorms swept across Inner Mongolia, striking nearby Beijing, Japan, and even the United States.[34] Ignoring the fact that the roots of the problem were in the land-distribution program, Chinese officials were quick to heap the blame on Mongol herders and to impose measures that had devastating effects on their livelihood. In Ordos, for instance, government directives were issued to close off the fenced pastures to animals, and animals were allowed only in walled pens. In Bayanbuur, mountain goats in the Daqing Mountains were driven out of the mountains, ostensibly to protect the mountains. If this bizarre measure remains in force, we may reasonably predict that more Mongols will either be forced to turn to agriculture or to give up their grassland and move into cities.

UNIMAGINING INNER MONGOLIA;
OR, CAN MONGOLS BECOME JEWS?

For the Mongols, the socialist revolution promised territorial autonomy, which was supposed to bring about the regeneration of the Mongol people, but over the past fifty years, this high hope has been compromised by the ethnic, territorial, political, and administrative considerations. Instead of forming a strong *minzu,* Mongols have become further fragmented internally and integrated into Chinese society in all aspects. This has been brought about both by the growing demographic disparity between Mongols and Chinese and more importantly, by the intolerance of the Chinese regime to any sign of Mongol dissent. The Inner Mongolian Autonomous Region has become in fact a region of Han autonomy, although the Mongol veneer will continue to serve a useful political function for some time to come.

For a few years, from 1978 to 1981, former Mongol officials who had survived being purged during the Cultural Revolution returned to power and controlled some of the key areas, such as the finance, planning, and education departments, of the Party and the government. Today, Mongol officials look back with nostalgia to those few years; one told me that he felt for the first time he could make decisions without having to defer to the Chinese. There is also nostalgia for the period from 1947 to 1966, when Inner Mongolia enjoyed some form of autonomy despite many problems. However, the good times did not last long. In 1981, Inner Mongolia was rocked by a month-long strike by regional-college and middle-school faculty and students opposing Document 28, a central-government directive increasing the number of Chinese immigrants to the area. The strike revealed the basic cause of tension in Inner Mongolia, that is, ethnicity. It was suppressed with severe repercussions for the Mongols. Not only were the student leaders punished, more than two hundred high-ranking Mongol officials were sacked or demoted for being sympathetic to the student demands. They were replaced by either more "obedient" Mongols or Chinese.

The 1981 crackdown has had two far-reaching consequences: First, Mongol officials were further convinced that Mongolian autonomy could not be guaranteed by Marxist principles. Autonomy, many came to believe, could only be guaranteed by law. The sacking of Mongol officials in 1981, according to some accounts, incensed Ulanhu and other high-ranking Mongol cadres in Beijing, prompting them to draft the Law on Regional National Autonomy to legally protect minority rights. Second, the crackdown alienated many Mongol students and intellectuals, who no longer placed their hopes on Mongol officials to protect their rights. In recent years, some Mongols have repeatedly criticized Mongol officials for placing their own interests above Mongol interests, and in some cases, they have even been denounced for betrayal of the Mongols. However, demands for autonomy from outside the Party have not been tolerated by the Chinese regime. In 1991, two cultural organizations in Ordos were criminalized and their leaders imprisoned for several years. In 1996, a Mongol democratic organization was crushed, and two of its leaders were sentenced to fifteen and eleven years' imprisonment respectively on charges of secessionism.

Sustained Chinese colonization through agricultural expansion, the drastic reduction in the right of autonomy, the difficulty of Mongol cultural production, given the demographic disparity between Mongols and Chinese, and the eagerness of the Chinese state to criminalize the assertion of ethnic identity have all given rise in the last decade to two Mongol sentiments. The first is the feeling of living in a diaspora in their own homeland. Inner Mongolia, as it stands, can no longer be thought of as "Mongolian." The independent Republic of Mongolia offers some Mongols a beacon of hope as a nation where Mongols can live and reproduce as "pure" Mongols in a "pure" Mongolian cultural milieu. The normalization of relations between the Republic and China in 1989 unleashed an unprecedented desire on the part of Inner Mongolians to go and visit Mongolia. But this enthusiasm was soon dashed. Though Mongols from China flock to Mongolia in search of a glimpse of pure Mongol-ness, instead of being greeted as brothers and sisters, they have been seen as a source of cultural pollution and a threat to the sovereignty of Mongolia.[35] A frosty relationship between the two Mongol groups has ensued, each accusing the other of being non-Mongol in behavior and ethics. This has led to the immigration of many disillusioned young Mongols to Western Europe and the United States and to the growth of a nationalism that agitates for farther-reaching objectives, including full nationhood for the entire Mongol region.

The second sentiment is the call to establish Mongolian "reservations" (baoliudi) similar to those of the native Americans in North America. This is, of course, a very much romanticized notion, out of context with history. And it is ironic because the fate of the American Indians used to figure prominently in the Mongol imagination as a worst-case scenario. Refusing to be confined to their banner enclaves within the Chinese provinces, Mongol nationalists and Communists dismantled the provinces and reclaimed Mongol sovereignty over certain counties that had formerly been banners. In recent years, however, problems of cultural survival have pushed many Mongols to question the very structure of Inner Mongolian autonomy.

The idea of "reservations" came not from Mongol cadres but rather from the ranks of Mongol dissidents. In 1995, the mood I sensed from my fieldwork in Inner Mongolia was that the basic problems confronting the Mongols derived principally from the fact that they had been dispersed widely and there was no viable community in which they constituted a majority. Some Mongols suggested that given the severe environmental degradation in western Inner Mongolia and the small number of Mongols there, the Mongol population should be relocated to the better pastureland of Silingol[36] and Hulunbuir Leagues. Moreover, some argued that the eastern Mongols, who have long been disparaged for their adoption of agriculture, which is regarded as proof of their sinicization, might actually prove to be the bulwark of resistance to assimilation, thanks to their compact communities of Mongol villages. It is not agriculture but communal village life, which is lacking both in pastoral areas and cities, that is seen as offering a glimpse of hope for long-term Mongol cultural survival. Not surprisingly, this small-and-compact-is-beautiful sentiment is accompanied by strong criticism of Ulanhu. Ulanhu, it is argued, did more harm than good to the Mongols by moving the capital of Inner Mongolia from Ulaan-hot to Hohhot, thus further dispersing the Mongols in that vast expanse of land, with no consideration for the logistics of such an enterprise.

So whither the Mongols in Inner Mongolia? In the face of such over-whelming assaults on their ethnic rights, what have been the new Mongol strategies, if any? As stated in the beginning of this chapter, Inner Mongolia has not seen large-scale ethnic violence in recent years, although the Chinese state has not ceased being paranoid of potential Mongol nationalist movements. Nor have Mongols become sullen pacifists, try-ing to hide and nurse their wounds in monasteries; indeed, they have no such retreats. Buddhism, unlike in Tibet or the Republic of Mongolia, has not become a rallying point for an Inner Mongolian identity. Indeed, Inner Mongolian nationalism has been antithetical to Buddhism, which has long been defined as alien and held responsible for reducing Mon-golian prowess. There has been no single Buddhist church or leader identified with Inner Mongolian interests; rather, Buddhist leaders have historically served Manchu or Chinese interests, helping the latter to pacify and control Mongols.

Nor has Chinggis Khan become a banner Mongols can carry to rally for their interests. Ironically, the Chinese have co-opted Chinggis Khan as a pan-Chinese hero and ancestor whose military feats purportedly brought glory to the Chinese nation. Numerous novels about Chinggis Khan have been published in recent years, often portraying him as the only Chinese to defeat the Europeans. In 1999, a movie titled *Chinggis Khan* was shown in New York to celebrate the fiftieth anniversary of the founding of the People's Republic of China. In 2000, Chinese archeolo-gists announced that they had found the tomb of Chinggis Khan in Xin-jiang, thus sabotaging Mongolian efforts to find his tomb in Mongol territory.[37] In this competition, Mongols in China are in a dilemma. As a minority, they are happy to see their ancestral hero hailed, even wor-shiped, by the Chinese, but they are also unhappy because their cultural heritage is being appropriated by the Chinese state, which leaves them unable to claim exclusive rights to their national hero. By supporting Mon-gol claims, they risk accusations of treason from the Chinese state; by sup-porting Chinese claims, they betray their ancestral roots.

If neither Buddha nor Chinggis Khan is their role model or savior, who is? The buzzword today is *jinghua* (cream, or elite). Who are the elites of the Mongols? Who is to shoulder responsibility for the Mongols in the new millennium? The devaluation of Mongol officialdom comes not only from ordinary Mongols but from Mongol officials themselves. Many high-ranking officials have devoted themselves after retirement to promoting education and scholarship among the Mongols. Batubagan, the former chairman of the Inner Mongolia People's Congress, now the most widely respected Mongol official, has become the patron of two monumental publishing projects: a series of Mongolian literary classics and an encyclopedia of the Mongols. Other former officials admonish young people to devote their energy to academic study and to take pride in achieving excellence outside of Inner Mongolia or better yet, outside of China. Politics is seen as a dangerous zone.

In the classificatory scheme of a former official, there are now three kinds of *rencai* (talented individuals), who together constitute 30 percent of the Mongol population: 10 percent are high-ranking officials, 10 percent are scientists and scholars, and the remaining 10 percent are ordinary cadres. The official singles out scientists and scholars as *minzu jinghua* (ethnic elites), whereas the others are just *rencai*. The difference, he explains, lies in the different contributions *rencai* make for the Mongol *minzu*. Whereas officials have to be "in agreement with" the central government, helping China rule the Mongols, and working little on behalf of the Mongols per se, scholars and scientists can act as "individuals" and win "glory" for the Mongols.

Mongol scholars and scientists are urged to demonstrate to the Chinese that the Mongols have intellectuals and some of them are world class. Mongol intellectuals are also supposed to serve as an inspiration to the many Mongol youth who have developed inferiority complexes and see no hope for the future, either for themselves or for the Mongol people. Not only can they be successful in Inner Mongolia, they can also achieve prominence abroad. Some prominent internationally known Mongol scientists are the ultimate role models. They are used to illustrate what Mongol scholars can do; not only do they make Mongols shine *(loulian)* in the eyes of the Chinese, they also, through their intellectual networks, achieve more for the Mongols than the officials have ever dreamed of in the way of improving educational possibilities for Mongols. More importantly, as prominent scientists, they cannot be denounced as "ethnic splitists" *(minzu fenliezhuyi fenzi)* because of their activities. Thus, their scholarly careers are considered politically safe. This is the politics of "knowledge is power" par excellence. Being a scientist not only leads to individual achievement but contributes to the *minzu*'s fund of knowledge, and only knowledge can transform the Mongols from being powerless today to becoming a major force in the future.

The inspiration for such a new individualism derives from the Jewish diaspora. Many Mongols marvel at the Jews' putative ability to influence American political and economic policies, including securing powerful support for Israel. Jews represent an enigma for the Mongols, especially given their geographical dispersal, which is deemed analogous to the Mongol situation in the world. Some Mongols explained to me that without having to worry about maintaining territorial boundaries, a native language, or a separate economy, the Jews thrived in interaction with other peoples. They marveled that after a dispersal of over one thousand years, the Jews, partly through their religious faith, were able to come back to their homeland and build a nation-state on Jewish cultural foundations and with Hebrew as the national language.

In this new drive to salvage the Mongol people through individual intellectual effort, the "traditional culture" is deemed an obstacle. What is needed is no more than a consciousness of being a Mongol. Whether a successful and cosmopolitan "Mongol" with little or no cultural grounding would still fight for Mongol rights is a moot question for the new apostles of "knowledge is power." What is certain is that there has been a general relaxation of efforts to retain Mongol-language educational programs. This attitude accelerates the loss of Mongol culture. Convinced that a Mongol education would devalue its recipients or make them unemployable in the modern (Chinese) market economy, the overwhelming majority of urban Mongols, and even many rural Mongols, send their children to Chinese schools.

There is a naive romanticism in this new endeavor, and one cannot help but ask whether every Mongol will be able to compete on unequal terms with the Chinese. What is clear is that the Mongols are pursuing a passion for "the Jewish path" as a means to gain power in modern times. A question that remains is whether they can be "superior" within a Chinese cultural framework without destroying their own cultural identity.

CONCLUSION

In this chapter, I have discussed the processes of Mongol assimilation into the Chinese state and society despite or because of the kind of autonomy they have been allowed to exercise. Mongols have suffered enormously. Ironically, socialism, once the Mongols' best hope for survival, has led to greater pressure for them to assimilate. And yet, the socialist principle of equality still remains an ultimate ideal. At the core of the problem is the fact that China is a nationalizing state in which minorities such as the Mongols have been torn between two mutually conflicting needs: the need to be recognized as citizens and the need to maintain their *minzu* identity.

The fact that the Mongols insist on the Chinese honoring their promise to uphold minority autonomy even as the Chinese attempt to undermine Mongolian autonomy defies any simple dichotomous understanding of China as either a *minzu* destroyer or a *minzu* builder. Nor can ethnic violence be addressed as simply a human-rights violation. The attitude of the Mongols in China cannot easily be pigeonholed into any preconceived analytical category as either pro-China or anti-China.

Whatever hopes Tibet or Xinjiang may have for achieving independence from the People's Republic of China, it is difficult to imagine any similar success for the Mongols. To cling to such hopes would only mean further frustration and danger for the Mongols. Nevertheless, despite the increasing despair Mongols feel as to whether they can maintain a viable community, there is no reason to accept this gloomy scenario at face value and come to the conclusion that the Mongols are indeed doomed.

We ought not to treat China's ethnic minorities, including the Mongols, as "problems" for the state. As a result of the misdiagnosis of the ethnic dimension of the Soviet collapse, minorities everywhere are seen as a potential source of trouble or a threat to regional stability or national sovereignty. Many Westerners, influenced by the Soviet experience, have credited China for preserving a multinational state and have criticized it merely for violating "human rights."

In light of the Soviet collapse, the Chinese state has adopted a new way of managing its multinational empire. Despite its multicultural guise, China is actively reviving the notion of a single Chinese people *(Zhonghua minzu)*, which the Chinese Communists earlier condemned as Han chauvinism. In this scheme, ethnic minorities would be depoliticized and their cultures appropriated as part of "Chinese" culture. It is not surprising therefore that a systematic effort has been made to strip the minorities of many of the rights guaranteed by the Law on Regional National Autonomy.[38] In recent years, Chinese scholars, including anthropologists, have sounded alarmist warnings against an affirmative-action policy, insisting that a poor country like China cannot possibly mete out favorable treatment to one hundred million minority people. Moreover, efforts have been made to reduce ethnic consciousness *(ruohua minzu yishi)* and increase the minority peoples' self-identification as citizens of the Chinese state.[39] The diminution of minority rights in China does not come from a regime that wishes to emphasize a civic political culture; rather, minorities are to be assimilated and brought under the rubric of a new Chinese nation that, like Japan in World War II, defines itself racially as opposing so-called imperialists.

NOTES

I thank Morris Rossabi, Melvyn Goldstein, and other conference participants for their comments. My gratitude also goes to Mark Selden, Pan Jiao, and Wurlig Bao for commenting on an early version of this chapter. The mistakes are mine alone.

1. See Gladney, *Muslim Chinese,* and Kaup, *Creating the Zhuang.*
2. Reuters, "Hijack Foiled."
3. Although a legitimate question can be raised with regard to the status of independent Mongolia and the Inner Mongolian Autonomous Region in the event of unification of Taiwan and mainland China, I leave it to the constitutional experts to answer that question.
4. See Bawden, *Modern History,* for additional details.
5. See Atwood, "'Worshiping Grace.'"
6. See Onon and Pritchatt, *Asia's First Modern Revolution.*
7. Song, *Zhongguo renkou,* 50–54.
8. Chindamani, "Shi lun Menggu minzu," 31.
9. Hao, *Nei Menggu Menggu minzu,* 55–56.
10. See Atwood, "Revolutionary Nationalist Mobilization."
11. See Jagchid, *Last Mongol Prince.*
12. See Schram, *Mao's Road to Power,* for more detail.
13. Slezkine, "USSR as a Communal Apartment."
14. Hirsch, "Toward an Empire," 225.
15. What was curious about this expansionist autonomy was that it dismantled the local autonomy enjoyed by the Mongol banners. Eager to overturn what was called the *yi di er zhu* (one land with two masters) system, the Mongols fought to restore "sovereignty." They were convinced that under a generic Mongolian autonomy, local autonomy was no longer necessary.
16. Whether or not this territorial expansion of Inner Mongolia was a success depends on the criteria by which we judge it. Compared to the Tibet Autonomous Region, it may be considered a success. The Dalai Lama's map still includes areas that are now parts of Gansu, Qinghai, Sichuan and Yunnan Provinces. For the Dalai Lama, including Qinghai (historically, Amdo) is emotionally important because both he and the late Panchen Lama were born there.
17. See Bao, "When Is a Mongol?"
18. Song, *Zhongguo renkou,* 66–67.
19. Asia Watch, *Crackdown.* See also Tumen and Zhu, *Kang Sheng.*
20. For an incisive analysis of the new social structure in China, see He, "China's Listing Social Structure."

21. Ma and Zhou, *Zhonghua minzu,* 458.

22. According to one story, Yun Bulong, as chairman of the autonomous region, should not have driven to meet Deng Nan, who had a lower official position; he should have sent a deputy instead. By making this gesture, it was argued that Inner Mongolia had devalued itself politically. The investment to control the desert was the duty of the Chinese government; it should not have been treated as a bestowal of favor on the poverty-stricken people of Inner Mongolia.

A second story claimed that it must have been an alien invader with a laserlike weapon who killed the chairman. How could the grassland train, which runs only three times a day across Shuluun Höh (Zenglan) Banner kill a heavily protected chairman driving in a motor cavalcade? The fault must have lain with the chairman's driver, who was renowned for ignoring all traffic controls in Hohhot. He may have assumed that the train would stop to make way for his car.

Another story had it that as the chairman's motorcade passed by Shuluun Höh Banner, local Mongols lined the road, holding ritual scarves and wine cups to bless him. However, he responded, "E mo sijian" ["I don't have time"], and rushed off. Mongols were angry, for the banner is the site of Khubilai Khan's summer capital, Shangdu. How dare he refuse to accept blessings from the Mongols who safeguard the old capital? Had he stopped for only a minute, he would have missed the deadly collision.

23. *Zhongguo Gongchandang Nei Menggu,* 81.

24. See Wang, *Tianzang.*

25. See Khan, "Who Are the Mongols?"

26. 1 *mu* is equal to 0.165 acres.

27. See Bulag, "Municipalization and Ethnopolitics."

28. Song, *Zhongguo renkou,* 177.

29. Cf. Humphrey and Sneath, *End of Nomadism?* For a critical analysis of the contribution of fencing to desertification in Inner Mongolia, see Williams, "Barbed Walls."

30. Already, some Darhad Mongols, the priestly people who officiate in the rituals dedicated to Chinggis Khan at the mausoleum, have been dismissed and replaced by outsiders in order to better control the content of Chinggis Khan worship. Recently, the Xinhua News Agency reported that Inner Mongolia plans to invest ¥200 million to build the area of Chinggis Khan's Mausoleum into "a world-class tourist destination." The project will take two years to complete and cover eighty square kilometers. See Xinhua News Agency, "Genghis Khan's Tomb."

31. Chen and Wang, *Zhongxibu,* 89.

32. Yekeju League changed its name to Ordos Municipality on 28 September 2001.

33. U.S. Embassy, Beijing, "PRC Desertification."

34. Sandstorms originating in China and reaching the United States were documented even before spring 2000. According to research conducted by California-based meteorologists in 1998, "Huge volumes of dust from the Gobi Desert in Mongolia and other Asian deserts . . . traveled in a cloud across the Pacific, reaching as far east as Texas" (Verrengia, "No Real Public Health Threat"). As environmental destruction and predatory "development" intensify in Inner Mongolia,

there may be major regional or ethnic conflict or even famine lying ahead (see Brown, "Dust Bowl").

35. Bulag, *Nationalism and Hybridity*.

36. Much of the best pasture in Silingol League has been turned into desert in recent years. Many settled Mongol herders, long touted as a poster child for China's modernization of the Mongols, began wandering again in 2001 in pursuit of pasture for as many as one million head of livestock.

37. See "Chinese Tomb."

38. The Law on Regional National Autonomy was amended on 28 February 2001 to provide a legal framework for resource extraction and major infrastructure construction, which are now the main priorities for minority areas.

39. See Ma and Zhou, *Zhonghua minzu*.

4 / Heteronomy and Its Discontents

"Minzu Regional Autonomy" in Xinjiang

GARDNER BOVINGDON

By 1950, the Chinese Communist Party (CCP) ruled in Xinjiang, the vast region in the northwest corner of the People's Republic of China (PRC). The Uygurs, Turkic-speaking Muslims who today number roughly eight million, claim Xinjiang as their historical homeland; Chinese officials have long considered it part of China. In the 1940s, CCP theorists proposed a system of regional autonomy to give Uygurs (and other non-Han peoples) control over their own affairs, while not compromising China's sovereignty. Though the Party claimed that the establishment of Xinjiang as a "Uygur Autonomous Region" gave Uygurs unprecedented political sway in the territory they had historically occupied, in fact it minimized their political influence in a number of ways. The chapter documents both the initial structure and the historical development of the system of regional autonomy in Xinjiang and shows how it has diminished, rather than augmented, the Uygurs' say over their individual and collective lives.

In particular, the chapter demonstrates the success of one of the more obscure intentions of this policy of regional autonomy. To counter Uygur claims that Xinjiang belonged to them, Chinese officials in the Republican period (1911–1949) announced that thirteen different groups, including the Han, had long occupied the territory. After the Communist victory over the Nationalists in 1949, CCP administrators adopted this stance instrumentally. In assigning to each of the originally recognized thirteen groups representation in the government and control over some part of the territory, the Party intended to create divisions among the peoples of Xinjiang, thereby setting them up for co-optation by the Chinese state. In this aim it succeeded. There are now substantial antipathies within and among the various non-Han groups, so that the government need not fear a concerted effort by all groups to fight for independence. Yet the tactic also isolated and alienated the Uygurs, still the largest group. In the last two decades, Uygurs have waged numerous protests, peaceful and violent, against the system of autonomy and its attendant ills. The Chinese government has proclaimed Xinjiang peaceful and its inhabitants happy; it has vaunted Xinjiang and the system by which it is governed as a model for the world. Yet episodes of popular protest and violence over the last two decades call this depiction into question. I argue that the system of administration itself, rather than placating popular dissatisfaction with CCP rule, has instead exacerbated it.

HETERONOMY

The Xinjiang Uygur Autonomous Region (XUAR) was established with great fanfare in October 1955. While, in principle, the Uygurs thereby received title to the entire territory, in reality, they were confronted with a condominium of nested autonomies. The Uygurs occupied a patchwork of lands in the east and south, and they were divided and surrounded by lands assigned to the Mongols, Kazakhs, Hui, Kirghiz, and others. This division of the territory had taken place in a series of steps begun in 1953, and it presented the Uygurs with a fait accompli at the time of the XUAR's establishment.

The division of Xinjiang into a number of smaller autonomies was a stroke of administrative genius. In parceling out various "subautonomies," the CCP simultaneously satisfied two goals: to reinforce the idea that Xinjiang belonged to thirteen different *minzu*[1] and to counterbalance the overwhelming political and demographic weight of the Uygurs.[2] The political and material interests of each of the other recognized groups were therefore, to a certain extent, aligned with the central government and against the Uygurs. By the end of 1954, more than 50 percent of the area of the (then) province[3] had been allotted to autonomous townships, districts, counties, and prefectures. In fifteen out of the twenty-seven units established, the titular *minzu* constituted less than 50 percent of the population; in Tacheng and Emin County Autonomous Districts, the titular *minzu* (Daghuor and Mongol) made up, respectively, less than 17 percent and 12 percent of the population. Bayinguoleng, which comprises nearly one third of Xinjiang's area, was designated a Mongol autonomous prefecture, though Mongols constituted only 35 percent of the prefecture's population.[4] In a recent officially sponsored study of *minzu* relations in Xinjiang, analysts Mao Yongfu and Li Ling noted that

> Kirghiz, Tajik, and other *minzu*, despite the small size of their populations, nevertheless have their own autonomous prefectures and counties; in those areas, they belong to the self-governing *minzu*.

Map 4.1 Autonomous Prefectures in Xinjiang

> By contrast, in [those places] the Uygurs have once again become
> non-self-governing *minzu*. . . . This is something we must look
> into diligently.[5]

The authors' apparent surprise at this situation is disingenuous in the
extreme; the order of establishment of the autonomies demonstrates that
this had been precisely the intention forty years before. But the passage
begs the question, in what sense are the various *minzu* "self-governing"?

One cannot read three sentences into any official text on *minzu* regional
autonomy *(minzu quyu zizhi)* without encountering the boilerplate
expression "dang jia zuo zhu" (masters of their own house), which is what
the system of autonomy advocated by theorists and enacted by the CCP
since 1949 supposedly makes the non-Han peoples.[6] In Xinjiang, the purpose of this system has not been to make the non-Han masters of their

own house but rather to keep them in the house. The granting of Uygur influence over affairs in the Xinjiang Uygur Autonomous Region has taken a back seat to the consolidation of CCP control, as well as to the crushing of any movements advocating independence or even the more modest goal of "real autonomy."

A Taiwanese analyst, critical of particular policies but still favoring the retention of Xinjiang in China, evaluates the system succinctly:

> The leaders of the autonomous regions are essentially all deputed or appointed by the CCP authorities and have a firm grip on power. The system is called "self -government" [*zizhi*], but in reality it is "we are in charge" [yi wo wei zhu]. At this point, to force separation would not be easy.[7]

This is not an idle potshot from across the Straits. In a document for internal circulation promulgated in the mid-1990s, CCP strategists used the same phrase in advocating changes in Xinjiang policies: "We must firmly adhere to the principle that we are in charge [and we allow only what is] advantageous to us."[8]

The expression "dang jia zuo zhu" supposedly captures the world-historical privileges *minzu* enjoy under the PRC's current system. Though advertised as providing autonomy—that is, self-government—to the Uygurs and others in Xinjiang, the system in fact enacts heteronomy, or rule by others.[9] Maintaining publicly that power stems from the people, the CCP leadership has always taken pains to extend authority from the top down and has therefore given no quarter to power organized locally. Officials have regarded the Uygurs, as a group, to be politically untrustworthy and have therefore allotted very little power to them.[10] The Party leadership has selected and promoted Uygurs to exercise power only in a fashion consonant with CCP goals, and it has reserved the decisive authority at virtually all levels for trusted Han, who have been imported from posts in China proper. In administrative terms, this is a frankly colonial apparatus.

This system of rule has failed to serve the Uygurs in a variety of ways. If Uygurs truly did rule themselves with minimal interference from the central government, local dissatisfaction and anti-Party agitation would be hard to understand and merit little sympathy. Given that the Uygurs are ruled by Han on instructions from the center, that same unrest is quite comprehensible.

Yet political disenfranchisement and economic exploitation are only two of the causes of popular unrest. Cultural pressures, status hierarchies, and ingrained prejudice have proven just as powerful as more obvious forms of oppression in motivating activism. Nor is exploitation or inequality the sole criterion for understanding discontent. Beyond the tangible and measurable goods of daily economic life, intangibles, such as self-respect and a sense of belonging, which cannot (or cannot easily) be measured, nevertheless figure powerfully in popular evaluations of governance.

For the remainder of this chapter, I first discuss Communist Party rule over Xinjiang and the Uygurs since 1949, then analyze Uygur responses to that rule. I attempt to illuminate Chinese *minzu* policies *(minzu zhengce)* through a careful reading of the policy texts themselves in order to shed light on what problems Chinese officials believe they confront and what they hope to accomplish. At different times over the last five decades specialists on *"minzu* problems" have officially pinned their hopes on cultural tolerance, pressure to assimilate, or indoctrination in socialist internationalism to draw Uygurs more firmly into the Chinese fold. For most of that period, the same officials have privately relied upon military force and Han immigration to suppress and then submerge Uygur resentment.

MINZU POLICIES: CHRONOLOGY, 1949–2000

Limited space prevents the recounting of political events in Xinjiang prior to 1949. Two features of the social climate of the Republican period must be noted, however, as they figured prominently in Communist Party leaders' calculations of strategy. Anti-Han sentiment was deep and widespread among Uygurs, partly as a consequence of decades of harsh, exploitative rule by Han warlords and local officials. At the same time, collective anti-Han sentiment that might have drawn Uygurs and other Turkic peoples (principally Kazakh, Kirghiz, and Tajik) together was counterbalanced by religious, political, and cultural differences of long duration. Turkic peoples had cooperated several times in the twentieth century to establish independent governments—for example, in the Turkish Islamic Republic of Eastern Turkistan (TIRET) of 1933–34, which controlled the southern third of the region from Kashgar, and in the Eastern Turkistan Republic (ETR) of 1944–49, which governed the northwest from Gulja. Yet those governments covered only part of the vast territory of what is today Xinjiang, and they fell apart as much from internal disagreements as from external attacks.[11] Anti-Han sentiment posed a challenge to CCP strategists, but antagonisms within the Turkic population provided an opportunity to pit groups against one another and thus to manage that challenge.

Following the "peaceful liberation" of Xinjiang in 1949, the Party demobilized thousands of Nationalist (Guomindang) and People's Liberation Army (PLA) soldiers and redeployed them on paramilitary farms (later called the Production and Construction Corps, or PCC)[12] throughout the province. Having installed a tractable leadership headed by the Tatar Burhan Shāhidi and the Uygur Sāypidin (Saifudin) Āzizi, the Party set about establishing policies for managing non-Han groups.

A generation ago, Donald McMillen captured the central dilemma confronting Xinjiang's rulers. On the one hand, out of security considerations, the Party had to develop policies that respected the Uygurs' (and others') cultural and religious differences—though not, McMillen adds parenthetically, "their right of self-determination"—to avoid provoking popular antagonism. On the other hand, nation-building concerns led to policies such as forced Han immigration and language reforms "designed to undercut gradually the very ethnic and cultural uniqueness which the Party outwardly promised to safeguard. . . ." The ultimate aim was assimilation. According to McMillen, the path chosen by Wang Enmao, who by 1965 was both military commander and first party secretary of Xinjiang, was "to maintain actively the facade of regional autonomy for [the various *minzu*] . . . while at the same time adopting measures that would gradually [make] them, and the territory they inhabited, unquestionably Chinese."[13]

In the early 1950s, these policies were relatively tolerant. The CCP strategy of the "united front" *(tongyi zhanxian)* counseled the establishment of links with "progressive members" of social and religious elites, which in turn required minimal interference with business, religious practice, or social norms. The Party did, however, gradually take control of religious institutions through the China Islamic Association, as well as through the confiscation of mosque lands and the forcible replacement of religious courts with "People's Courts."[14]

In the same period, the Party dealt uncompromisingly with separatists and those who tried to use religion to stir resistance to Communist authority.[15] CCP leaders also inveighed against the evil of "Han chauvinism": "Han cadres were told to respect the customs and habits of the minorities . . . and to listen to the opinions of their non-Han counterparts."[16] That there would still be official criticisms of (to say nothing of Uygur complaints about) Han chauvinism three and four decades later indicates the message had little effect. There was an obvious tension between placing Han in charge and then telling them not to be arrogant.

By the mid-1950s, as Mao pressed regional leaders to make more sweeping economic changes throughout the country in the so-called socialist tide, the Xinjiang leadership faced resistance to such initiatives. Collectivization required antagonizing the "progressive elites" with which the Party had previously cooperated, and, as would happen many more times, the attempt to mobilize the exploited classes (mostly peasants, in this overwhelmingly agrarian region) against the elites instead drove many Uygurs and others together against the Party. In China proper, Mao invited criticism of CCP policies from the masses in the 1956 Hundred Flowers campaign; the vehemence and volume of the resulting protest shocked the leadership, which then unleashed the Antirightist movement in 1957 to silence the opposition. In Xinjiang, the Antirightist movement quickly turned into an "anti–local nationalist" movement targeting those who allegedly sought to "rule Xinjiang as an independent country" or resist CCP rule. Particularly irksome to Party officials were voices condemning PCC soldier-farmers as "Han colonialists." Faced with such challenges, the Party reinforced its efforts to mobilize class against *minzu* interest.[17]

Mao's radical Great Leap Forward, begun in 1958, led in Xinjiang to calls for rapid cultural homogenization to accompany and facilitate the Leap. This naturally meant much reduced tolerance for difference. Ethnicity itself became an "obstacle to progress." The Party stepped up attacks on Islam and other "backward customs."[18]

As is widely known, the policies of the Great Leap Forward, in combination with bad weather and the central government's ill-chosen decision to export grain to meet its debts to the Soviet Union, brought on a terrible famine. Party leaders temporarily prevailed on Mao to restore a more moderate economic course, producing a Thermidor in the early 1960s. The government's cultural policies in Xinjiang relaxed during this period, as calls for tolerance replaced the earlier emphasis on speedy assimilation.

There were, however, complicating factors. In addition to the Party-mandated population flows, vast numbers of people fleeing famine in the interior of China proper ended up in Xinjiang, driving Han immigration to over eight hundred thousand per annum, its highest level ever, in both 1959 and 1960.[19] Many of the refugees were welcomed on PCC farms, provoking increased resentment by Uygurs and others. In 1962, over sixty thousand Uygurs and Kazakhs fled across the border into the Soviet Union, prodded by exasperation with CCP policies and pulled by ceaseless radio propaganda advertising the far superior living conditions on the Soviet side of the border. The central government was already grappling with the Sino-Soviet split. Soviet consular officials had apparently connived in this mass exodus by passing out travel papers that had already been prepared. The flight of so many posed for Xinjiang and central-government officials the frightening prospect of hostile former citizens receiving military training, then assisting in the cause of "Soviet social imperialism" by helping to take Xinjiang by force. In response, the government sealed the border and forcibly relocated thousands of families away from the border zone.[20]

Minzu policies changed course again in the mid-1960s, with the advent of the Socialist Education campaign and then the Cultural Revolution. Officials appointed to the Cultural Revolutionary Small Group (which replaced the XUAR Party Committee for several years), as well as the initially mostly Han Red Guards, harbored extreme intolerance of cultural difference. In the interior, Red Guards answered their leaders' exhortation to "destroy the four olds" by burning books and paintings, smashing temples, and the like. In Xinjiang (as in Tibet and other non-Han regions), they targeted non-Han culture; difference was once again seen as backwardness. They destroyed mosques, forced many religious leaders and ordinary Muslims to raise pigs, and frightened the various Turkic peoples into shedding their habitual clothes, adornments, scarves, and hats and donning Mao suits.[21]

The punishments Cultural Revolutionaries visited on intellectuals betrayed particular truculence toward Uygur culture: the famous linguist Ibrahim Mutte'i was tortured by having the huge volumes of a multilingual dictionary he had helped edit (with full CCP support at the time) dropped on his head.[22] Ordinary citizens were not exempt. My informants[23] described witnessing men being shaved in the streets, for even beards were interpreted as signs of defiance. A Kazakh woman raising a towheaded Uygur boy dyed his hair black and shaved his eyebrows to avoid persecution. Uygurs meeting each other in the street learned to initiate every greeting with "Long live Chairman Mao" (in Chinese).[24]

Hard-line policies reached their extreme in the Cultural Revolution. After Mao's death and the arrest of the "Gang of Four," Party leaders faced a crisis. The Cultural Revolution had alienated a large segment of the population in China proper and in Xinjiang as well. Resentment was particularly grave among Uygurs and other non-Han people, for whom it had been not merely a political and social assault but a cultural one. To continue the hard-line policies seemed destined to provoke increasing discontent and thus instability. But more tolerant policies, by allowing cultural exploration, freer religious practice, and so forth, might similarly provide opportunities for individuals and autonomous organizations to exploit. Consequently, policies have charted a zigzagging but narrow course between openness and control since then.

In 1980 one of the younger leaders in the Party Central Committee pressed vigorously for openness. Hu Yaobang, soon to be promoted to the post of secretary general, traveled to Tibet to investigate local conditions. He reportedly came back horrified at the poverty of the region. To remedy Tibet's situation he advocated "genuine autonomy, economic policies suited to local needs . . . the revival of cultural, educational and scientific projects and the phased transfer to the interior of Han officials." He made similar proposals for Xinjiang in July 1980. At the time, Hu thought Xinjiang presented less of a separatist threat (and was thus perhaps of slightly lesser concern) than Tibet because it lacked exiled religious or political leaders like the Dalai Lama and had no "overseas support" for independence.[25]

Held responsible for the increasing student and popular demonstrations of 1986, Hu Yaobang was purged in 1987. Former Xinjiang military commander Wang Zhen, who had fought openly with Hu over his proposed changes, now scrapped the more accommodating policies promulgated under Hu's influence. A Han official siding with Wang is reported to have said, "You give them autonomy and they will only turn around and create an East Turkistan." The official was disgusted with a proposal to send Han back to China proper and insisted that only "hard-liners like Wang Zhen" could keep Xinjiang stable.[26]

The conservative leadership of Xinjiang initially sought to block the implementation of Deng Xiaoping's economic reforms there, fearing that they would destabilize the region. To many, the pace of the reforms that did come was frustratingly slow. People would still joke wryly in the mid-1990s that although the interior had wholeheartedly embraced capitalism, socialism was still being pursued, if not realized, in Xinjiang. Nevertheless, by 1992 the XUAR leadership had come to an agreement that reform was inevitable. In that year, the popular Uygur official Isma'il Āhmād announced that, responding to the call for reform and openness, the central government would cede more autonomy to Xinjiang. This would include "power [to approve] projects of foreign trade, border control and administrative management." The reporter covering the story interpreted this also as an attempt to counter the appeal of separatists, particularly in the face of the Soviet Union's collapse and a March 1992 bus bombing in Urumqi attributed to Uygur secessionists.[27]

But the Party complemented the loosening of economic policy with political tightening, something that has remained true through 2000. Two central components of that tightening have been the yearly "strike hard" *(yan da)* campaigns and the periodic attempts to shore up central-government control in each locality under the rubric of "comprehensive management" *(zonghe zhili)*.[28] A number of my informants received orders from their work units to take part in comprehensive-management activities in 1997, as the Party fretted about the return of Hong Kong to mainland control. One ardently anticommunist man told me he was simply informed a week in advance that he would be traveling to southern Xinjiang to spend two months singing the praises of the CCP. He was to go from house to house within "suspect" villages, chaperoned by two Han to make sure he passed the right message, patiently correcting people's misconceptions and erroneous political views. It was, he said to me, like being forced to eat a steaming plateful of pork. Another informant told of being sent more regularly on short trips to areas around Urumqi, again without any choice in the matter. Interviews with a third informant revealed that the strategy did not involve surveillance and propaganda alone. A doctor, she was dispatched for several months (with little warning and no choice) to several poor rural areas to treat patients and pass on the Party line while doing so.[29]

Not content to limit its efforts at control to domestic policies, the Party has also gone on an international offensive since soon after the Soviet breakup. It has pressured the other members of the "Shanghai Five" (Kazakhstan, Kirghizstan, Russia, and Tajikistan), as well as Turkey, to crack down on Uygur separatists who are active within their own territories, even demanding (often successfully) the extradition to China of suspected separatists.[30]

POPULATION

One of the Party's most effective tactics for "managing" the Uygurs has been, in effect, to pass the responsibility on to another group. Government-sponsored immigration of Han into the region has been a central component of CCP policy in Xinjiang. Between 1950 and 1978, the Party cajoled, induced, or ordered several million Han to move to Xinjiang, many to the PCC farms.[31] This increased the Han proportion of the population from roughly 5 percent in 1950 to over 40 percent in 1978. But while moving Han into Xinjiang was relatively easy in the pre-1978 period, making them stay after that time became increasingly difficult.

One of the first major disturbances in Xinjiang in the period after the Cultural Revolution involved Han agitating to return to China proper. During the Cultural Revolution, many Han youths had been "rusticated," or "sent down" *(xiafang),* from Shanghai and other major urban centers. Some had already returned home clandestinely, discovering to their dismay that the local authorities were unprepared to find them jobs or housing; their residence permits had been permanently transferred to Xinjiang. In February 1979, Han youths unwilling to return to Xinjiang and other "remote" areas rioted in Shanghai. In late 1980, thousands of resettled Shanghai youths in the town of Aqsu demonstrated to protest both local conditions and the government's refusal to allow them to return home. The Party responded by dispatching former regional military leader Wang Zhen to stifle the disturbance; Wang "requested" that local units improve conditions for young Han settlers, and he increased propaganda stressing how important the youths were to countering Soviet designs on the region. Nevertheless, emigration topped immigration for the first time the following year.[32]

The 1990s saw a new wave of immigrants pour into Xinjiang on their own initiative. This was the result of a combination of market forces, state policies that modestly favored the western half of China, and the declining significance of the *hukou,* or household registration. Deng Xiaoping's economic reforms had enabled farmers to lease land, individuals to strike out in private businesses, and underemployed rural and urban workers to seek jobs in new enterprises. Though both geography and central policies initially encouraged migration to the coastal regions, by the early 1990s, the government had announced favorable land-lease rates and tax abatements in the interior—the so-called west-leaning policies—and labor and capital were being lured to the west. Finally, the burgeoning markets in food, land, and labor had greatly diminished the power of the household-registration system, which tended to fix people in one place. The combined effects were plain to see in the thousands of simply dressed, heavily burdened people pouring out of the Urumqi train station each day, drawn by rumors of land and jobs in the "great northwest."

The Party's newest concern is the scarcity of the most desirable kinds of immigrants: educated youths, technical workers, and committed, politically reliable cadres. It has tried a variety of stratagems to remedy those deficiencies, including subsidies to college graduates willing to immigrate and temporary "swaps" of cadres from the Chinese heartland with cadres in Xinjiang. Perhaps most strikingly, the Party announced quietly in April 2000 that it was reassigning one hundred demobilized army officers from China proper to head local CCP branches responsible for "political, legal, military, and recruitment affairs."[33] There is no doubt that the Party also pins high hopes on its 2000 "Go West" initiative *(xibu da kaifa)*, which will pump billions of yuan into infrastructural improvements and business ventures in Xinjiang and neighboring regions, to attract Han immigrants of all types in large numbers.

THE PRODUCTION AND CONSTRUCTION CORPS

The redeployment of demobilized Guomindang and Red Army soldiers in the PCC produced a subtler compartmentalization of sovereignty than that effected by the division of Xinjiang into a number of subregional autonomies. PCC units that were set up along the margins of "troubled" regions, along key road and rail lines, and around transportation hubs enabled the government to control traffic and isolate regions with very modest manpower. Heavy concentrations of PCC farms in Kashgar, Aqsu, and Kumul districts further diluted or counterbalanced the overwhelmingly Uygur population in those regions. Though the PCC was billed as a force to protect Chinese sovereignty in sensitive border regions, the pattern of deployment of PCC units makes plain that defense against foreign invasions was never the principal concern of planners. The concern of first importance was and would continue to be to counteract Uygur agitation for an independent Xinjiang.

The ethnic complexion of the PCC underscores this point. Official historical accounts of the dynastic era refer repeatedly to the "concerted actions of the various *minzu* to repel imperialist incursions," implying always that the Uygurs and others felt loyalty to "China." Though the Party retrospectively trusts the historical loyalty of the non-Han peoples, since 1949 it has left nothing to chance. The efficacy of the PCC is not predicated on further cooperation among *minzu* groups. It has been overwhelmingly Han since its establishment and even today has roughly 90 percent Han membership. We should note that the PCC was not only completely insulated from local control, it was not even subordinated to the national farming or military bureaucracies; rather, it had its own ministry in Beijing.

Population figures may give an idea of the weight of the organization in Xinjiang. In 1974, the PCC membership reached 2.26 million, or one-fifth of the total population of Xinjiang; this was two-fifths of the Han population in Xinjiang. By 1994, the organization had apparently shrunk somewhat: in that year, the PCC claimed 2.22 million members, of whom 1.96 million, or 88.3 percent, were Han. Han members of the PCC thus constituted 35 percent of the total Han population in 1994.[34]

The compartmentalization of sovereignty in Xinjiang has given the non-Uygur populations a stake in the status quo. Leaving aside all logistical and military issues, which decisively favor the PLA, were the Uygurs to join together to demand independence tomorrow, they would be opposed not only by the nearly 7 million Han but also by the other Turkic, Xibo, and Mongol groups.

The Party has further co-opted the nondominant groups into the current system through a targeted recruitment that mirrors and reinforces the effects of the territorial compartmentalization. By insisting on a sort of Noah's ark principle, in which each political organ must include members of all or most of the thirteen "indigenous" *minzu*, the system dilutes the already meager influence of the Uygurs and gives other groups disproportionate authority in the system.

In these and other ways, the CCP has pursued an effective balancing strategy that pits the Uygurs against other groups. On several occasions, I saw Kazakh policemen exploiting the modest amount of power they enjoyed to make trouble for Uygurs. The Uygurs in those encounters complained that such treatment was typical. Many Uygurs pointed out that Kazakhs have since 1991 taunted them by saying, "We have our own country and you don't." I witnessed several brawls between Kazakhs and Uygurs in the college dormitory where I lived. One brawl pitted several dozen Uygurs with chains, metal bars, and stones against a roomful of Kazakhs; it ended only when police intervened.

CADRE RECRUITMENT

Without doubt, the Communist Party has successfully co-opted many Uygurs, as it has members of the smaller groups. Through careful selection, training, and promotion of loyal Uygur cadres, the CCP has added substantial numbers of Uygurs to the government without compromising its policy-making autonomy. Uygurs in regional and local government are frequently called upon to announce the Party's unpopular policies, thereby blunting the criticism that Han alone rule the region. The recruitment has followed a familiar pattern.

By mid-1961, more than 85 percent of county magistrates and deputy magistrates were non-Han; more than half of the commissioners and deputies at district, prefectural, and regional levels were non-Han. Yet according to McMillen, "The key departments and organs of Xinjiang administration . . . largely remained in the hands of Han CCP members. . . ." Moreover, every government organ and enterprise from the regional level down had a Party official, "normally a Han," who exercised real control. In October 1965, non-Han comprised 106,000 of 190,000 cadres, or 55.8 percent of the total. However, a closer look at these figures reveals a decided imbalance in distribution: fewer than 10 percent of non-Han cadres were leaders at the county level or above.[35]

Those numbers would drop dramatically during the Cultural Revolution. A 1985 text presenting the "overall situation" in Xinjiang informs us that over 99,000 of the 106,000 non-Han cadres received damning political "labels" and were dismissed from their positions between 1966 and 1976. By the end of 1983, nearly 100,000 non-Han cadres, now considered to have been "wrongly labeled," had been reinstated. Their return to official positions and the quickened selection and training of minority candidates for office brought the number of minority cadres up to 181,860, a substantial increase. On the other hand, the text does not cite the percentage figure for 1985 and neglects to inform the reader that despite this vast increase in raw numbers, the percentage of non-Han cadres actually had fallen over ten points, to 43.1 percent. Instead, the text ends on a positive note: after the latest elections, the heads of five autonomous prefectures and the capital, Urumqi, as well as the standing committee of the Xinjiang People's Congress, were all members of minority ethnicities.[36]

Even in the era of reforms that began with the downfall of the Gang of Four in 1976, the pattern of non-Han recruitment has been as important as the quantity. One source observes that while there are substantial numbers of Uygurs in both low-level and high-level offices, they are very seriously underrepresented at the middle levels.[37] One can draw two inferences from this. First, if the premise of proportional representation is that people belonging to a particular group will be particularly attuned to the needs and aspirations of that group and can therefore work to represent those interests, the configuration in Xinjiang structurally attenuates any representation of Uygur interests at the middle level, making it harder for messages to reach the top level. Second, if we assume (probably not entirely correctly) a model in which officials at each level are recruited from the pool of leaders at the lower level, then the talent pool of mid-level leaders is far too small to enable selection of especially talented leaders for the top level; we can infer that the top leaders are not promoted through the system on the basis of talent but take accelerated trips to the top because of their tractability. In one of the few studies of elite recruitment in Xinjiang, Stanley Toops has attributed the speedy ascents of key Uygur leaders to their contacts: Tömür Dawamät rose as a protégé of Wang Enmao, and Isma'il Āhmād with the support of his patron Sāypidin.[38] We do well to remember that Sāypidin had attained top positions because of his support for and identification with the "Han-dominated Party (and its policies)."[39]

While trotting out a long series of figures on non-Han officials at various levels of government, books that vaunt the system of self-government delicately sidestep the core figure: non-Han Party committee heads are still exceedingly scarce after two decades of reform. Indeed, the percentage of non-Han Party *members* remains far below the non-Han proportion of the population. In 1987, only 38.4 percent of Party members in Xinjiang were non-Han, though non-Han comprised over 60 percent of the population. And far from increasing, these numbers have only fallen since then. In 1994, the percentage of non-Han Party members had decreased to 36.7 percent.[40] To be sure, there are at least two plausible explanations for the low proportions. One is that Han leaders systematically exclude non-Han from the Party. The other is that many non-Han view the Party with antipathy and therefore choose not to join even if invited. Both explanations are consistent with the premise of a Party that is at best indifferent, and at worst hostile, to non-Han interests. My interviews support both conclusions, though the former more strongly than the latter: Uygurs widely believe that as a group, they face discrimination by the Party, and some Uygurs told me privately they had no wish to associate with it.

Uygurs are well aware of recruitment policies. Every year, the class of several dozen Han students learning Uygur at university (among the lowest scorers on college-entrance exams, most are reluctant Uygur-language majors) travel to a Uygur area in the countryside for their practicum, in which they build language skills and learn about living conditions at first hand. Musing on this phenomenon, one rural cadre said ironically that "in the future, these people will be leaders and Party secretaries" [bular kālgūsidā bashliq, shujiy], so that local governments must always take pains with the practicum arrangements.[41]

Recruitment policies have in a sense dovetailed neatly with the policy on immigration. The Party has clearly hoped that the more Han there are in the province, the less difficult it will be to justify Han predominance in government. Han I interviewed universally approved of recruitment patterns. All Uygurs willing to discuss the matter strongly objected, arguing that the system of recruitment specifically and intentionally deprives Uygurs of the power to exercise any conceivable autonomy.

CULTURE, LITERATURE, HISTORY

On consolidating his authority in 1978, Deng Xiaoping announced a new era by calling for new openness to cultural exploration. In the interior this elicited a wide variety of cultural products, from "scar literature" *(shanghen wenxue),* to cinema, to Democracy Wall musings. In Xinjiang, Uygur authors began to write novels, essays, and poetry. Themes that had previously been forbidden and perspectives that would have been harshly punished only a few years before cautiously appeared in print. Works exploring the past and conjuring a politicized collective identity—which Justin Rudelson, following Richard Fox, called "nationalist ideology"[42]— poured forth in the several oases. Over the decade of the 1980s, for example, the poet Turghun Almas wrote a number of historical articles and books claiming (often rather creatively) that the Uygurs had a long history as a "nation" and had established many independent states. Officials initially tolerated these heterodox writings, either from inattention or out of confidence in Deng's wisdom.

As with so many other facets of *minzu* policies, this changed after the Baren incident of April 1990, in which several dozen armed Uygurs laid siege to a police station and demanded the end of CCP rule in Xinjiang. A huge rally in Urumqi in 1991 criticized Almas and unnamed others for fanning the flames of Uygur separatism and promulgated a message of renewed control. The leadership of several presses was shuffled, as in the case of the Kashgar Youth Press, or replaced wholesale, as was the editorial board of the journal *Kashgar Literature.* Since that time, censors have read submissions to journals with close scrutiny; a code indicating the subeditor responsible for each article is affixed to the bottom of the article for quick reference. Novel manuscripts face strict barriers to publication. Even works already published in Chinese, such as the novels of Zhang Xianliang, have been turned down for translation out of fear, in one would-be translator's words, of the "social effects."[43] Some Uygur intellectuals complain that nothing of quality gets through and that what is published is virtually worthless. The reform-era novels of Abdurehim Ötkür are rare exceptions in receiving great popular acclaim.

Other forms of popular culture also face censorship. Films confront even more stringent limits than texts. Uygur actors must perform in Mandarin, the films are vetted by Han censors, and only then can they be redubbed in Uygur for popular consumption. Audio tapes, whether of poetry or music, meet similar obstacles. It has often happened that allegorical works with hidden or ambiguous messages, and perhaps even works to which listeners attribute meanings not originally intended by their authors, have passed the censors, circulated widely, and then been banned for having "unhealthy social effects." This was true, for instance, of a two-volume collection of Ötkür's poems that had previously been published legally but was released as dramatic recordings after his death in 1995; of an anthology of poems (discussed below) with potentially subversive meanings distributed in 1993; and of a long poem titled *Dehqan bolmaq täs* (It's hard to be a peasant). A number of famous Uygur musicians have produced tapes with songs they were later forbidden to perform in public.

In sum, the limits placed on Uygur cultural production have convinced Uygurs from various walks of life that the Party will not allow them to speak freely or speak the truth. These people therefore conclude that the Party has much to hide. Once again, the atmosphere of suspicious rancor adds depth to every metaphor, so that readers and listeners attribute extra weight to the subtlest signs of dissent. Where criticism is forbidden, every heretical remark is a triumph.

LANGUAGE

If officials worried from the first about what Uygurs might write or say in popular media, they initially promised broad tolerance toward the language itself. Here, I first consider language planning and script reform and then turn to language use policies. The Party made language planning one of the centerpieces of its *minzu* policies. Officially, each *minzu* had the right to develop or reform its own language; at the same time, the Party announced right away its intention to propagate Chinese as the national language. In the early 1950s, Han anthropologists and linguists traveled to non–Chinese speaking regions to document languages and to develop scripts for those peoples that lacked them in order to pave the way for socialist modernization.[44] Uygur and the other Turkic languages in Central Asia claimed sophisticated literatures, which had for centuries been written with a modified Arabic script. From an official perspective, the Turkic languages presented two problems: First, Turkic speakers in no way regarded their languages as inferior to Chinese and thus could not be persuaded that attaining modernity entailed shedding their own languages in favor of the latter. Second, as the script of the Koran, Arabic was invested with a religious significance that posed an obstacle to the antireligious aims of the Party. A third problem emerged as the growing rift with the Soviet Union dashed hopes of socialist internationalism and the Chinese government pursued more strongly nationalist policies: the Turkic languages had no regard for political boundaries and thus linked peoples the CCP wanted to separate.

In the mid-1950s, with Soviet guidance, regional leaders mandated a change from Arabic to Cyrillic script for all the Turkic languages, apparently aiming thereby both to enable Turkic peoples to "learn modern science" and to diminish the influence of Islam by making old religious texts illegible to new generations of students.[45]

Some ambitious planners looked beyond script reform to the wholesale scrapping of the Turkic languages. One of the key elements of the Great Leap Forward in Xinjiang was a call to abandon non-Chinese languages as obstacles to modernization. It soon became clear to provincial leaders, however, that wholesale linguistic conversion would require much more time than expected. Makers of language policy began a program to eliminate foreign (i.e., Russian) loan words in the Turkic languages and to replace them with Chinese terms. The push for all non-Han people to learn Chinese was dropped by the midpoint of the Leap in favor of a new slogan: "Mutual study."[46] Though it would be raised repeatedly in ensuing decades, the slogan never had much effect. For one thing, after the initial fervor of the first Han "volunteers" died down, and as successive waves of far less willing immigrants entered the region, most Han had no interest in learning "local" languages.

Between 1960 and 1962, in direct response to the Sino-Soviet split, language policy again took an abrupt turn. Officials now implemented a change in the script from Cyrillic to Roman, once again with a double goal, though this time to sever textual links to the Central Asian peoples and as part of a longer-term plan to initiate fusion with (romanized) Chinese.[47]

It was during the early Cultural Revolution that Uygurs and Kazakhs replaced the standard greeting "Salam aläykum," now regarded as tainted with religious flavor, with the plainer "Yaxshimusiz" or "Jaqsimusiz" [How are you], translated directly from the Chinese salutation "Ni hao." Language planners pressed for more: one of the oddest products of the Cultural Revolution was a new "hybrid language" consisting of Chinese lexical items—principally slogans and political terms—with Uygur grammatical endings. Though at the time, it flourished in newspapers, at rallies, and in the language of activists, this hybrid ultimately proved infertile and died out by the late 1970s.[48] Soon enough, the script reforms were abandoned as well. Though the Party had proclaimed the conversion to Roman script as permanent, it reinstated the Arabic script in 1980 as part of its bid to regain the loyalties of those alienated by the Cultural Revolution.[49]

Policies on language use would seem, in principle, to provide more latitude for compromise than those on economics, governance, and even culture. The Party initially fulfilled its promise of broad linguistic tolerance. Since the establishment of the Uygur Autonomous Region in 1955, Xinjiang has had two official languages — Uygur and Chinese. In the first decade, Uygur could be heard in government bodies, all documents were translated, and (many) Han officials endeavored to learn some Uygur. Han college students studied Uygur as a required course. But the campaigns of the Great Leap Forward and the Cultural Revolution banished the previous linguistic tolerance. The great mass of Han immigrants, too, altered the language map of the region. By the mid-1970s, the Han population had nearly reached parity with that of the Uygurs. New immigrants had little inclination to learn Uygur, nor did the government press them to do so. In the early 1990s, there was for a time a Uygur-language program called *A Sentence a Week,* pitched to offer ordinary Han minimal familiarity with daily Uygur speech. Though well received at the time, it has since been dropped.

Previous minicampaigns to bring about mutual language study had come to virtually nothing. In 1986, an article in the *Xinjiang Daily* discussed mutual language study in a manner that made the objective clear. While the title suggested that "all *minzu* should study each others' language," the intent was unmistakably to emphasize the Uygurs' learning Chinese. Former Uygur Autonomous Region chairman Wang Enmao, then-chairman Song Hanliang, the Kazakh leader Janabil, and several others visited a hospital and an elementary school in Zepu County—both were chosen as "*minzu*-unity model work units"—to inspect the state of "*minzu* unity" there. After interviewing a number of bilingual workers, Wang announced happily: "Han study Uygur, Uygurs study Han. Excellent! I will learn from you!"[50] Without announcing it directly, the article conveyed the message that some languages are more equal than others. The Han doctors speaking Uygur were given five lines, while the non-Han doctors speaking Chinese received sixteen lines. Wang's ceremonial comment suggested the emptiness of the encounter.[51]

A Chinese report analyzing data collected from a cooperative Chinese-Canadian study of language use offers the following national statistics:

in the early 1990s, there were slightly more than one million bilingual Han and roughly twenty-seven thousand bilingual Uygurs. This gave Han and Uygurs among the lowest incidence of bilingualism of any *minzu* in the country, 0.11 percent and 0.45 percent respectively. Unfortunately, this document does not offer regional breakdowns of these figures, so while the figure for Uygurs is certain to include almost exclusively residents of Xinjiang, the Han figure must cover every region of China. We could speculate that at a maximum, one-third of all bilingual Han in the country live in Xinjiang. Even this improbably high proportion would indicate a rate of Han bilingualism in Xinjiang of less than 6 percent.[52] It goes without saying that the data collected in this case can be accorded only impressionistic significance, particularly given the well-known imprecision built into surveys of language use.

By 1995, the government was deeply dissatisfied with the state of Chinese instruction in primarily Uygur areas. The mid-1990s saw renewed emphasis on a long-brewing initiative, the plan to induce all Uygurs to learn Chinese. At a major conference, Uygur Autonomous Region leaders complained of the deplorable level of Chinese competence among Uygurs and demanded urgent measures to rectify it.[53] Though the official slogan "Equal competence in Chinese and minority languages" [*Min Han jiantong*][54] suggested that both Han and non-Han would be held to the same standards, it did not work out that way. A new campaign to train cadres in all work units to be bilingual was announced with much fanfare in early 1997. Although two volumes of a Chinese-language textbook for non-Han were published immediately, months later, only one of the projected two volumes of a Uygur-language textbook for Han had been published.[55]

Even more telling, in a recent volume of essays titled *Language Contact and Influence*,[56] eleven of the twelve chapters address Chinese-language use among non-Han people (all but one of those chapters relating to the Uygurs). The twelfth, titled "An Investigation of Attitudes toward the Bilingual System in the XUAR," seems at first to promise a balanced perspective. The author begins by noting that given a Uygur population of 7.1 million and a Han population of 5.6 million, "Uygur and Chinese have both become commonly used languages of social intercourse." Yet we learn a page later that the population interviewed consisted of 136 Uygurs, 32 Kazakhs, and 2 Kirghiz. The author offers, among the rationales for selecting this "target population," the principle that "compared with Han, minority peoples are more sensitive to the bilingualism question." A likelier reason is that Han are not pressed to become bilingual in school. As he acknowledges, "Because of the single-minded pursuit of grade advancement and for many other kinds of reasons, the minority-language classes that were once established in Chinese-language schools have all been eliminated." And despite a series of tendentious questions that telegraphed the officials' intention to push Chinese-language study on non-Han (but not minority-language study on Han), 45.9 percent of those polled managed to get across that "Han comrades do not learn Uygur well."[57]

Purely from a state-building perspective, in the interest of bureaucratic, educational, and social efficiency, forcing Uygurs to learn Chinese makes good sense. It is, indeed, the national language of China. Yet if we recall once again that the agreement governing the incorporation of the XUAR specifically stipulated language equality and remind ourselves that Xinjiang is not simply "another province in China" but an autonomous region, we must acknowledge that the current one-sided campaign contravenes the spirit of the XUAR charter.

A report on conditions in southern Xinjiang declares that minority cadres and ordinary minority people are "basically satisfied"—which could be read as not completely content[58]—with the linguistic environment in the XUAR's Party Committee, People's Congress, and government. However, the report goes on to say that in some offices at XUAR department *(ting)* and bureau *(ju)* levels, as well as in some district *(diqu)* offices, "it is impossible to maintain written communications in both Mandarin and minority languages, and they do not provide translators for meetings. . . . This prevents minority cadres from putting their capabilities to good use."[59] This passage directly conveys the relative importance of the two languages: it is the non-Han cadres, not their Han counterparts, who are discommoded by the lack of translators.

RELIGION

In the journal of the Xinjiang Academy of Social Sciences, which is widely read by policy makers, a recent article warning of the dangers of illegal religious belief succinctly expressed the challenge officials believe they face: for *minzu* for whom religious belief is essentially coextensive with group identity, "the believing masses consider attitudes toward their religion to be attitudes toward themselves."[60]

While government control of religion has noticeably relaxed in many areas of the PRC (on the Dai in Yunnan, on the Hui in the north and southwest,[61] and to some extent, on the Tibetans in Tibet as well), Xinjiang is not one of them. To be sure, the Party did loosen control of religion in

Xinjiang in the early 1980s as part of its overture to the Uygurs and others after the antireligious excesses of the Cultural Revolution. A great number of mosques were rebuilt and new ones constructed as well. Many villages had increased resources as a consequence of the agricultural reforms of the early Deng era, and many of those communities decided to build mosques with the new wealth.

But after the 1990 Baren incident, and in response to the shocking collapse of the Soviet Union (which brought about the independence of the Central Asian states), the government reversed its previous policy of tolerance. Officials prosecuted "illegal religious activities," defrocking suspect clerics, breaking up unauthorized scripture schools *(mädräsa)*, and halting the construction of mosques. In 1991, 10 percent of roughly twenty-five thousand clerics examined by officials were stripped of their positions.[62] After a decade of turning a blind eye to mosque building, officials felt that construction had exceeded acceptable limits. In Akto County (where Baren is located), in 1990, officials closed fifty mosques judged to be "superfluous" and cancelled the construction of one hundred more, out of fear that religion was getting out of control.[63]

A 1995 propaganda text from Kashgar complained of "indiscriminate construction of mosques": in 1995 Kashgar District had some ninety-six hundred, "already enough to satisfy the needs of normal religious practice by the believing masses." Certain religious personnel, the text warned, engaged in wanton building with the excuse that the number of religious sites was inadequate. Even worse, "some religious personnel, without seeking approval, have set up their own Koran study schools and study classes, or have taken on *talip* [religious pupils]." According to the text, there were more than four thousand *talip* in the district.[64] The source of the writers' alarm was clearly the role such groups were playing in the politics of neighboring Central Asian states.

The constitution maintains, and textbooks on religious policy repeat, that every citizen has two freedoms with respect to religious belief: the freedom to believe or not to believe. Yet the Party has for years been sensitive to the threat of religion to Party authority and even more grave, the role of religion in dividing populations, even providing a breeding ground for ideas of Uygur independence. Its chosen strategy has been to protect the freedom of people not to believe and "dilute religious consciousness" in the population.[65] The principal aim of official policy in securing both freedoms, as every textbook explains, is to make religion a "personal matter" *(sishi);* but this is, of course, a recipe for eliminating the avenues by which religion is transmitted throughout society and across generations. The "privatization" of Islam, in turn, serves the larger project of reducing the distinct (and oppositional) identities of Uygurs and other Turkic Muslims.

To that end, the Party has placed special emphasis on eliminating the pull of religion on two groups: Party members and students. Resurgent religiosity among cadres and pupils has been a matter of growing concern. Since 1978, large numbers of Uygur and other Muslim Party officials have become religiously observant. Though the constitution guarantees the two freedoms described above, Party cadres and students are now openly denied the right to believe. The following passage provides a classic example of power overwhelming principle:

> Ordinary citizens are permitted two freedoms. Though Party members are also citizens, they are first of all members of the party of the proletariat and therefore *enjoy only one freedom* — the freedom not to believe — and absolutely do not enjoy the freedom to believe. They cannot have feet in two boats.[66]

The presentation of the requirement to be atheist as a single, compulsory "freedom" gives some flavor of the normative regime citizens in Xinjiang still face.

While in theory, students are also citizens, they are now also limited to the single freedom. Official explanations stress both the crucial importance of education to the prosperity of the nation and the importance of allowing youths to make a free, "scientific" choice to believe or not to believe, once old enough to choose. For example,

> youths and children are in the growing-up stage; their worldviews have not yet formed. They lack scientific knowledge and life experience. They cannot yet make responsible and *scientific* choices appropriate to their goals. To irrigate the minds of immature youths with religious thought is to allow someone to impose belief in a particular religion on them.[67]

The author fails to point out that to prevent youths from practicing religion and others from teaching them about it is to allow another agent to impose unbelief. But intervention has by no means stopped there. Post-Baren policies that prosecuted religious activity and expressly forbade the teaching of religion on school campuses were judged insufficient. Party strategists decided to go one step further and make classes in atheism mandatory.

An Amnesty International report on Xinjiang claims that the CCP began the "Education in Atheism" campaign in 1997.[68] A textbook I purchased in Kashgar demonstrates that it began much earlier. The text of the book makes clear that students no longer enjoy "freedom of religious belief." The fifth lesson is devoted entirely to the bald assertion that "teenagers must become atheists."[69] When I bought the text, a Uygur man who was delighted to see that a foreigner could read the language opened the book to identify it. As soon as he saw its contents, he raised his eyes to mine and moaned, "No!" Even antireligious intellectuals, who are critical of the conservatizing influence of Islam on Uygurs, criticize the Party even more stridently for persecuting the religious.

Students at Xinjiang University were fully aware of the increasing stringency of official policy. They told me privately that many classmates continue to perform five prayers *(namaz)* a day and participate secretly in study groups. But the costs of doing so were readily apparent. In spring of 1997, at the entrance to the campus computer building, a series of posters with gaudy vermilion stamps indicated that six students from Hotan had been arrested for attending religious study groups and that they had received substantial prison sentences.

Because the Party has worked so hard to reduce the believing proportion of the population or, at minimum, to keep it constant, officials have shown considerable concern in the 1990s about the spread of Wahhabism in southern Xinjiang.[70] This strict and politically charged form of Islam is popular among those who were previously alienated by the conservative, traditionalist Islam the Party supported. Thus, Wahhabism threatens to reverse the trend of a shrinking and, more important, increasingly politically irrelevant religious population. Investigations by the United Front Department in Hotan District determined that of 81 Wahhabist imams, 61 had "good attitudes" *(biaoxian hao)*, 11 were neutral, and 9 had bad attitudes; of those 9, 3 had committed "errors of political stance." An investigation of 319 Wahhabist *talip* determined that 249 had good attitudes and 70 had bad attitudes. In addition to fearing doctrinal disputes (historically, Wahhabists have held the view that those who practice Islam improperly are not true Muslims and may be killed), Party officials worry about proselytizing. Some suggest that the Third Plenum of the Eleventh Party Congress, widely hailed as the meeting at which Deng Xiaoping initiated economic reforms, opened the way for problems by underscoring the freedom to join different religious sects. They argue that it "provided Wahhabism with policies favorable to its propagation." Those same persons warn of the specific concern that Wahhabists seek to wrest control of mosques from "patriotic clerics with traditional [religious] views."[71]

Barry Sautman has argued that the so-called preferential policies (youhui zhengce) governing family planning, education, job hiring, and cadre recruitment leave Uygurs better off than they would otherwise have been.[72] Viewed from the perspective of China as a whole, this argument is uncontroversial: Uygurs can have more children, enter college with lower examination scores, find jobs in state-owned enterprises with fewer qualifications, and join some government bodies more easily than their Han counterparts in Xinjiang. But Xinjiang is not simply another province of China, and the fate of Uygurs there should not be judged according to national standards.

Indeed, as Sautman often acknowledges, the preferential policies fail to address the real inequalities between Han and Uygurs. Though the autonomous regions were "ostensibly established to create a sense of territorial proprietorship for their autochthonous peoples,"[73] in Xinjiang, Uygurs are less likely to go to high school and college, are less urban, are poorer, and have fewer job prospects than Han. The disparities are particularly acute in the oil industry and in private enterprises, where official quotas have no sway. This means that Uygurs are all but excluded from the most dynamic and profitable sectors, and thus the gap will widen with economic growth.

Nor should we assume that having political representation is the same as having political influence. Sautman suggests that preferential recruitment into officialdom has given some Uygurs political power, but he also says that Uygur officials "may increasingly abandon their quiescence and seek additional preferential policies" and that "it would not be surprising . . . if they were to become more vocal over economic and social issues."[74] Minor officials I interviewed suggested that these possibilities are still remote. They still fear punishment for speaking out. And ordinary Uygurs complained that there is precious little evidence of Uygur officials advancing Uygur causes with any success.

The case of Isma'il Āhmād is instructive. Made a Party secretary in 1973, political commissar of the Xinjiang Military Region in 1975, and chairman of the Uygur Autonomous Region in 1979, he was dismissed from office in December 1985, ostensibly as part of a drive to reduce the average age of the leadership corps, and replaced by Tömür Dawamät. The dismissal provoked a demonstration by Uygur students at Xinjiang University, who boycotted classes in protest; some five thousand marched on the government offices in Urumqi demanding (among other things) that Isma'il be restored to his position. Perhaps because of the protest, Isma'il was appointed head of the national *Minzu* Affairs Commission.[75] In 1996, several Uygur informants, still angry about these events a decade later, shared with me the widespread view that he had been "kicked upstairs" to a relatively powerless post in Beijing after pressing too vociferously for policy changes in Xinjiang.

Finally, specialists on *minzu* problems appear to argue that it has not been possible to transfer the powers of self-government and decision making to the minority peoples themselves, as called for under the policy of regional autonomy. While cadre recruitment since 1980 has brought about a quantitative change in *minzu* representation, it has not effected a qualitative change. Despite nearly fifty years of special treatment and twenty years of reform, Uygurs and other non-Han in Xinjiang experience heteronomy, not autonomy.

RELATIONS BETWEEN THE UYGURS AND THE GOVERNMENT

In the modern era, southern Xinjiang has been a troubled [*duoshi*] region. The reasons are admittedly complex, and the most evident tendency has been *minzu* separatism. *Minzu* separatists use religion to stir up trouble in *minzu* relations and harm *minzu* unity; drawing lines according to *minzu* and religion, they openly clamor for the expulsion of "infidels." The local masses [*minzu* unspecified] feel that in the fifties and sixties, and even until the end of the seventies, *minzu* relations were good. After 1979, a new atmosphere prevailed: *Minzu* relations became tense, and Han commonly experienced a "feeling of being unsafe." The minority peoples also felt "unsettled"; they felt they were frequently "being labeled" or were "not being trusted"; they felt that Han had all the power, while they served as gofers and flunkeys. The Han lived in the city, their lives a class above those of the minorities. Feelings were brittle on both sides, making cooperation very difficult.[76]

Since 1979, then, relations between the Uygurs and the Han have worsened, according to this analysis, and accounts of violent conflicts in both the foreign and domestic media would seem to support this conclusion. The report goes on to express the view (common among Han) that reform-era policies are to blame.

However, a closer look suggests that there are at least three alternative explanations: First, the deterioration of relations might be only apparent—a consequence of changes in reporting. Friction and conflict seldom appeared in newspaper and radio reports before 1979 because of official policy, but the openness ushered in by Deng's reforms extended to the media, as well as to other cultural realms. If this is the case, Uygur-Han relations need not have changed because they were already hostile long before Deng gained power. Nor need the level of violence have risen, only the level of reporting such incidents. Second, there were resentments long before 1979, but political and military repression kept them in check. The looser political controls unleashed pent-up frustrations. If this is the case, there *was* increased conflict, but it was the result not of worsening relations but of other factors. Third, some combination of immigration, discrimination, widening inequalities, and other factors aggravated relations that were already made fragile by the excesses of the Cultural Revolution. Only in this case does the record of much more frequent conflicts after 1979 accurately reflect increasingly antagonistic relations between the Uygurs and the Han.

My interviews with Uygurs suggest that the true situation was a combination of the second and third scenarios. Though not conclusive (because they rely on fallible memory and may be colored by present concerns), the testimonials of Uygurs indicate a growing resentment of the government beginning in the 1960s, which was due to both Han immigration and the Cultural Revolution. There was widespread agreement among my informants, however, that the economic reforms did further harm to the relationship. Many informants also cited the ferocity with which the government has greeted Uygur proposals of any sort, be they bold calls for independence or modest requests for employment and the distribution of oil profits.

Today, relations between the government and the Uygurs are poor. We might divide the evidence of this into three categories: planned acts of violence, riots and demonstrations, and ordinary resentment. The implications of each are different.

Bombings, assassinations, and other planned acts of violence are one indication of dissatisfaction, but they are by nature the work of small, marginal groups. This is true both in the simplistic sense that small groups commit them and in the more complex sense that because the government so energetically seeks out and destroys such groups, the numbers of those that engage in such behavior are limited: many have been jailed and some executed. The frequent prosecution of such groups and the individuals that belong to them has undoubtedly deterred others from following their example. Bombings and assassinations have occurred in 1990, 1992, and 1997.

Demonstrations and riots indicate broader-based discontent. Large student demonstrations in Urumqi in 1986 and 1989 in many ways resembled those in the Chinese heartland, though many of the issues they raised bore more directly on regional issues: immigration, atomic-bomb testing, unemployment, the suppression of religion, and the lack of substantive autonomy. In 1989, there was a mass demonstration against the publication of *Sexual customs (Xing fengsu)*, a mass-market book that likened Muslim minarets and burial mounds to genitalia and insinuated that the pilgrimage to Mecca resembled an orgy.[77] The protest against this book posed a greater threat because Uygurs, Kazakhs, Hui, and other Muslims participated jointly. The Baren incident of 1990, the Hotan riot of 1995, and the Gulja incident of 1997 demonstrate a depth of animosity toward the government sufficient to mobilize large numbers. These episodes are more profound indicators of popular sentiments because of the greater numbers of participants and because spontaneous outbursts indicate long-brewing and widespread tensions.

The third category of evidence for the poor relations between the government and the Uygurs is the grumbling and myriad acts of "everyday resistance" committed by ordinary Uygurs. Many individuals who would not dare to commit violence or join in overt collective action nevertheless express dissatisfaction and defy the ruling regime in small ways. I have written extensively about such quiet defiance elsewhere, suggesting that the majority of the Uygur population engages in one form or other of everyday resistance.[78] The volume and the content of this kind of resistance by ordinary Uygurs indicate great dissatisfaction with the government. Here, I include a single example of literary dissent that reached a wide and appreciative Uygur audience.

A poem from a recent audiotaped anthology, *Pighan,* contains language and imagery that is at once carefully abstract and unmistakably critical of the Han regime. The text on the tape jacket notes carefully that "the bulk of these works were written during the periods when the reactionary KMT [Guomindang] government and the Gang of Four were committing acts of oppression." The purpose of preparing the tape, it continues, is "to help us not forget our people and the past [*ötmüsh*] and to sing the praises of the contemporary period after the Third Plenum."[79] Such placatory language initially enabled the tape to pass the censors.

For many years, a statue of a PLA soldier stood in a park near Beimen in Urumqi. It commemorated the army's "peaceful liberation of Xinjiang." The poem below responds to that statue. Originally published in the Uygur-language edition of the *Ürümchi kechlik gäziti* (Urumqi evening news), it was banned after censors learned of the poem's target.[80]

Häykäl

Bir häykäl turuptu baghda tik tänha,
üstidä yepincha, qolida yaraq.
män uni tonattim; tonumidi u,
chünki u egizdä, män pästä biraq.
ikkimiz uchrashqan pada baqqanda.
däl mushu mäydanda kerip käng quchaq.
bügün u ötüptu, törgä bir özi
män pästä qaptimän chaqqanda yangaq.
"Ayrilmas qoshmaq biz"—digining qäni?
äjäba untughaq bop qalding qandaq.
ming äpsus ichidä turimän baghda
közümdin ot yänip—bilipla biraq.

Statue

A statue stands in the park, tall and alone,
a cloak on his shoulders, in his hand a weapon.
I recognize him, but he doesn't know me
because he is up high, while I'm down low.
The two of us met when there was work to be done;
on this very field we embraced each other with open arms.
Today, he alone takes the seat of honor and enjoys all the fruits,
while I'm left standing empty-handed at the base.
Where, now, are your fine words: "We're inseparable twins"?
Could it be that you have become forgetful?
I stand in the park, immured in a thousand regrets,
my eyes on fire—if only I'd known.

The poem employs the solitary statue and its position relative to the narrator as a metaphor for Han-Uygur relations. It crystallizes the popular Uygur perception of a social reality in which Han are elevated and celebrated, while Uygurs are left below and behind. Originally, when there was work to be done—the liberation of the region from the KMT and the economic development of the region—the two cooperated. Since then, only the Han have enjoyed the benefits. The phrase "inseparable twins" alludes to one of a panoply of rhetorical flourishes conceived by propagandists to express a familial relationship between the two groups. It mocks the slogan "the two inseparables" *(liang ge libukai)* promoted by the government in the 1980s.[81] The soldier does not recognize or refuses to acknowledge the narrator because the latter is below him. Claiming the seat of honor for himself and savoring the fruits (walnuts, actually)[82] that are symbolic of the rich resources of Xinjiang, the soldier thus simultaneously betrays Uygur hospitality and the CCP's claim that it has made everyone better off. The scornful reference to forgetfulness substitutes for a more direct accusation of hypocrisy. What the narrator regrets in the final lines is clearly the Uygurs' cooperation with PLA soldiers. He unmistakably implies another choice was possible at the time. Nowhere is the soldier directly described as PLA, nor is the statue identified. Although the censors initially missed the reference, Uygurs did not, and after the government discovered this, the tape was suppressed and the statue quietly removed.

Uygurs deeply resent the presence of Han in Xinjiang, as well as the government they regard as the proxy of those Han. One can find a litany of Uygur complaints by visiting Internet sites maintained by dissidents in Europe and the United States. But privileged dissidents and intellectuals living beyond the reach of the Chinese state are not the only ones to complain. It is possible to hear similar complaints from people living in Xinjiang right now, the fear of speaking out notwithstanding.

Doctors are angry at what they consider extraordinarily high rates of cancer, not only in towns surrounding the Lop Nor nuclear test site but also in areas affected by pesticides and other chemical pollutants; two different doctors told me that statistics on morbidity are either not collected or kept secret. I interviewed lawyers who are angry that the national "law on autonomy" has not been answered by the passage of statutes in the autonomous regions. Many professors and other teachers are furious that history must be cut to fit a Chinese nationalist mold, that literature must be published and interpreted according to Chinese nationalist principles, and that at the college level, "modern subjects," such as math and science, must be taught in Chinese (even by Uygur teachers), while classes in Uygur cover only language and literature. Businessmen complain about the favoritism shown PCC enterprises and Han corporations from the interior. Officials complain bitterly at being passed over for promotion because of suspicions that they are politically unreliable or lack skills. Students bemoan discrimination in job recruitment.

But dissatisfaction reaches far beyond the educated and professional classes. Shop workers, restaurant staff, farmers, and factory workers speak of a similar range of issues: oil and mineral extraction without adequate compensation (there is a widespread, though farfetched, belief that the revenue from taxes on oil production alone would make every Uygur rich for years to come), family-planning policies, and past and continued Han immigration. Farmers complain that PCC farms and urbanization have drained the water table, making farming increasingly costly and difficult. Nearly all my informants complained about the suppression of religious activities they consider integral to Uygur social and cultural life. Even those Uygurs who distanced themselves from radicalism fumed quietly about the network of spies and traitors *(xayin)* who not only betray separatist plots but inform on those who express reasonable gripes. There is a widely held view among Uygurs that the government systematically lies about every issue that matters. It is this climate of deep and pervasive suspicion that gives wing to every rumor and lends credence to even farfetched complaints.

Only a few of my informants openly voiced a wish for independence.[83] The desire for "real autonomy," or even a system of autonomy that lives up to the original promises of the Party, is near universal. Without conducting an opinion survey or popular plebiscite, it is very hard to say whether a majority of Uygurs support independence, and such measures are obviously impossible at present.

CONCLUSION

The CCP has not only claimed domestically that its policies for managing the minority peoples have proven successful. It now vaunts them as a model for other countries to follow, boasting that it has solved the "*minzu* question." Yet the study of *minzu* relations in Xinjiang quoted several times above clearly articulates the mixture of confidence and apprehension with which Party analysts view developments in Xinjiang. The key passage is worth quoting at length:

> What people with relatively strong *minzu* consciousness really care about is not "separatism," but the vigorous development of Xinjiang and the carrying on and promotion of *minzu* culture. It is precisely on this score that our past work efforts were insufficient.
>
> All we need to do is serve the various *minzu* in Xinjiang heart

and soul, take economic development as the crux, lift up the economy, lift up education, and do a good job with United Front work and *minzu* religion work. In that case, no matter how *minzu* separatism roils the place, no matter how much enemy forces exert themselves, they will not be able to create a real threat for us. Time and opportunity favor us. Only the development and progress of Xinjiang and the collective prosperity of all the *minzu* can truly *weaken* minzu *consciousness,* help strengthen the cohesiveness of China's *minzu,* and aid the unification of the motherland.[84]

I have emphasized the key phrase "weaken *minzu* consciousness" to underscore a constant theme in Chinese writing on Xinjiang, one familiar to scholars of ethnic separatist movements around the world. The state hopes to weaken not *minzu* consciousness in general but one particular kind: the group consciousness of Uygurs. It hopes simultaneously to strengthen the *minzu* consciousness of Uygurs as "Chinese," which would enhance the cohesiveness of the imagined "Chinese nation."

Neither the original system of *minzu* regional autonomy nor its subsequent modifications have enabled the Party to achieve this aim in Xinjiang. The system has not made Uygurs "masters of their own house." It has kept them in the house, but it has not made them any happier to be there.

I argued at the beginning of this chapter that Party officials intended the policy of *minzu* regional autonomy to satisfy two goals. One was to preserve the territorial integrity of the Chinese state. The other was to reverse a legacy of oppression by giving non-Han control over their own affairs—as long as that control did not conflict with the broader policy aims of the Party-state. In other words, the system was intended to defuse the non-Han peoples' potential dissatisfaction with being ruled by a Han state. The chapter has chronicled the military and demographic steps officials took to counter the threat of Xinjiang's separation. The presence of a vast, well-armed military and an enormous and growing Han immigrant population essentially neutralize that threat.

The remainder of the chapter illustrates that having satisfied the first goal, Party officials have shown less and less enthusiasm for, and at times decisively repudiated, the second. The system of cadre and Party recruitment has not ensured the dominance of Uygurs and others over affairs in Xinjiang, nor has it even given them representation proportional to their populations. By installing Han first party secretaries at all levels, and by promoting tractable Uygur officials, the Party leadership has ensured that the concerns of Beijing hold sway in political deliberations. And generous early promises about cultural latitude have given way to the tight restriction of publications, performances, and religious observations. Officials today have little patience with the most obvious and basic expression of Uygur autonomy, language use.

Thus, the dominant sense among even those Uygurs who were once sympathetic to the CCP project is that of betrayal. The land has been firmly occupied by the military and the PCC; the region has been flooded with Han, who have enjoyed disproportionate benefits from economic development to date and will almost certainly continue to do so in the future; and most fear that the Uygur culture that was once guaranteed protection is destined to disappear. Instead of inducing Uygurs to shed their collective identity in favor of a broader identification with the Chinese people, the CCP's policies have alienated them and strengthened their separate identity.

NOTES

1. I join with a number of scholars in preferring to leave the Chinese word *minzu* untranslated. Dictionaries offer, variously, "ethnic group," "nationality," and "nation" as translations. Because these English terms carry such different political connotations, and because in Chinese the term is functionally ambiguous, I intentionally leave the term unresolved.

2. In 1955, the 3.2 million Uygurs comprised roughly 73 percent of the total population (5.11 million) of Xinjiang, according to official statistics.

3. Xinjiang was made a province in 1884 and would remain one until 1955, when the XUAR was established.

4. To be sure, the Mongols had faced similarly flagrant gerrymandering in their own "home districts" long before 1949, and they would see the shape of their "autonomous region" manipulated several times in the post-1949 period. When the Inner Mongolian Autonomous Region was founded in 1947, the Han were already the majority population.

5. Mao and Li, "Nanjiang san dizhou," 173.

6. One dictionary of Chinese idioms explains that it means the subject "has a leadership position in politics or has the power to make decisions." The illustrative example shows that working people, particularly proletarians, have attained this position in New China. That this idiom is allotted to the "state politics" section of the dictionary demonstrates, as does the example, that it has been completely claimed by the state for rhetorical purposes. In a response to an earlier talk from which this chapter has grown, James Seymour objected with justification that "jia" denotes family, rather than physical abode. Since my concern is with connotations and implications, I stand by my usage.

7. Long, "Cong Yining shijian," 24. Throughout this chapter, I use the terms "self-government" and "autonomy" interchangeably to translate *zizhi*. I do this both from stylistic concerns and to underscore the etymological origins of the term. As I point out below, the term "autonomy" is glossed in English dictionaries as "self-government."

8. Zhang, "Xinjiang jiefang yilai," 362.

9. All discussions of ethnically segmented rule introduce the thorny issue of identity. In the service of parsimony, this chapter will sidestep the important relationship between identity formation and politics. Important recent work has illuminated the role of the state in constituting ethnic and other identities (for examples, see the works of Dru Gladney and Justin Jon Rudelson on the Uygurs; Jonathan N. Lipman and Gladney on the Hui; Pamela Crossley on the Manchus; and Mark Beissinger, Rogers Brubaker, Ronald Suny, and Yuri Slezkine on groups in the Soviet Union). In contrast to the work on the Soviet Union, that on China has not explored the political implications so fully. That is, it has not specifically analyzed the political consequences of the state's substantial role in constituting *minzu* as such. See Bovingdon, "Strangers."

10. Though there are substantial populations of Kazakhs, Hui, and other non-Han peoples in Xinjiang, this chapter focuses primarily on the Uygurs. The principal justifications for this narrow focus are (1) that having been identified (or invented) as a group by a Soviet ethnology conference in the 1920s (see Gladney, "Ethnogenesis of the Uighur," and Rudelson, *Oasis Identities,* 149), the Uygurs constituted nearly three-quarters of the population when the CCP won control of the province in 1949, and (2) that my research concentrated on the Uygur population. It is reasonable to fear that on the basis of conditions in post-Soviet Central Asia, should the Uygurs ever establish their own state, non-Uygurs within their borders would not be much better off than they are now (and might be a good deal worse off).

11. See Benson, *Ili Rebellion,* and Forbes, *Warlords and Muslims.*

12. PCC units were also established in Mongolia and the other "border" regions; all but those in Xinjiang were subsequently disbanded. See Dreyer, "PLA and Regionalism"; Esposito, "China's West"; McMillen, *Communist Power,* "Xinjiang and the Production and Construction Corps," and "Xinjiang and Wang Enmao"; and Seymour, "Xinjiang's Production and Construction Corps."

13. McMillen, *Communist Power,* 128–29.

14. Ibid., 113–14.

15. Ibid.; Dreyer, *China's Forty Millions,* 94.

16. McMillen, *Communist Power,* 115.

17. Ibid., 116, 117; Dreyer, *China's Forty Millions,* 150–57.

18. Dreyer, *China's Forty Millions,* 157–63; McMillen, *Communist Power,* 118.

19. See Hannum and Yu, "Ethnic Stratification," 324.

20. Dreyer, *China's Forty Millions,* 169–70; McMillen, *Communist Power,* 120–23.

21. Author interview, Urumqi, 23 October 1996.

22. William C. Clark, "Ibrahim's Story," 17.

23. Over the course of twenty-two months of field research in Xinjiang between 1994 and 1997 I conducted unstructured interviews with more than 160 individ-

uals, among them 95 Uygurs, 50 Han, and a small number of Xibo, Hui, Uzbeks, Mongols, and Kazakhs. I interviewed Uygurs and Uzbeks in Uygur, the others in Mandarin. My informants included clerks, service workers, students, teachers, professors, lawyers, businesspeople, office workers, police, bureaucrats, editors, reporters, writers, and farmers. The group was weighted heavily toward educated urbanites aged nineteen to fifty. As a young male, I had easier access to men than to women, and men therefore constitute roughly two-thirds of my interview sample. Groups underrepresented among my informants include farmers and very religious people.

24. Author interviews, Urumqi, 10 October 1996, 1 April 1997.

25. Dillon, "Xinjiang," 4.

26. This passage quotes from and paraphrases ibid.

27. Cheong, "'More Autonomy.'"

28. The first "strike hard" campaign took place in 1983. Each campaign is a national endeavor in which the police make an all-out effort to round up thousands of suspected criminals within a few months. The suspects face accelerated trials, and for those convicted, summary executions at the end. While strike hard campaigns have generally aimed at capturing "conventional" criminals, in Xinjiang and Tibet they have also targeted so-called splittists.

In its narrow sense, according to a dictionary of new Chinese terms, "comprehensive management" refers to "comprehensive administrative measures taken to resolve problems of social order. Comprehensive management takes place under the unified leadership of the various levels of the Party and government and relies on society's strength, fully using political, economic, ideological, educational, cultural, administrative, legal, and other measures to attack evil trends, crimes, illegality, and breaches of discipline; it [involves] propagandizing socialist spiritual civilization and provides a stable and harmonious social environment for reform and socialist modernization" (Wen, Wang, and Li, *Dangdai xin ciyu*, 676).

29. Antiseparatist propaganda activities have continued. See "China Reports Popular Support" and Hewitt, "China Clampdown."

30. See Human Rights Watch, "China: Human Rights Concerns."

31. Exact figures are hard to come by, and statistics are notoriously unreliable. Using statistical yearbooks and census data, Emily Hannum and Yu Xie have compiled a chart of Xinjiang's immigration and emigration between 1954 and 1985. It shows that at the same time as hundreds of thousands of migrants flowed in— 502,000 in 1954, over 800,000 in both 1959 and 1960, and never fewer than 250,000 in any year—similar but smaller numbers flowed out. Only between 1981 and 1985 (where the data stop) did the numbers of emigrants exceed immigrants. See Hannum and Yu, "Ethnic Stratification," 324. For reasons that would take too long to explain here, it is understood that virtually none of the migrants were Uygurs or other Turkic peoples.

32. McMillen, "Xinjiang and Wang Enmao," 574–76.

33. Agence France-Presse, "China to Deploy Demobilized Officers."

34. It is highly likely that a substantial proportion of the remaining 11.7 percent were not native to Xinjiang. The CCP typically conflates all 55 ethnic-minority groups in China into one large non-Han group for the purpose of statistical analysis. This blurs the distinctions between groups and serves to inflate the figures to prove a

high degree of indigenous control. Thus, a fully assimilated Bai or Manchu serving in Urumqi or Gulja counts as a *minzu* cadre. This is one of many subtler practices reviled by Uygur intellectuals.

35. McMillen, *Communist Power,* 48.

36. XUAR Gaikuang Bianxiezu, ed. *Xinjiang Weiwuer Zizhiqu gaikuang.*

37. The figures indicated "a definite Han predominance on the upper and mid-
dle-level Party committees in the region" (McMillen, *Communist Power,* 75–6).
Guo Zhengli concurs: The real situation of non-Han cadre recruitment is "quite
uneven; its principal manifestation is the scarcity of non-Han core cadres (*gugan
ganbu*) at the county level and above" (Guo, *Zhongguo tese,* 89).

38. Toops, "Recent Uygur Leaders," 95. Toops analyses the career trajectories
of a number of high-level Uygur officials.

39. McMillen, *Communist Power,* 80. I am grateful to Jay Dautcher for a particularly fruitful discussion of this matter.

40. XUAR Difangzhi Bianzuan Weiyuanhui, *Xinjiang nianjian, 1988,* 72, and
XUAR Difangzhi Bianzuan Weiyuanhui, *Xinjiang nianjian, 1995,* 66.

41. Author interview, village outside Kumul, 7 May 1997.

42. See Rudelson, *Oasis Identities.*

43. Author interview, December 1966. Zhang Xianliang is a highly successful
experimental writer whose novel *Half of Man Is Woman* received popular and critical acclaim. Much of Zhang's work has been published since the end of the Cultural Revolution, and it insinuates that chaotic Party politics ruined the lives of
countless Chinese. The point, my informant told me contemptuously, was that
themes considered safe for Han audiences were still thought too dangerous for
Uygurs to encounter.

44. Underlying these ostensibly altruistic gestures was a grand long-term plan
to fuse all the languages together into a single socialist tongue via the pinyin roman-
ization scheme developed for Chinese. See Seybolt and Chiang, *Language Reform.*

45. These paragraphs draw on Wei Cuiyi's thorough analysis of the politics of
script changes in Xinjiang. See Wei, "Historical Survey."

46. Dreyer, *China's Forty Millions,* 178–79.

47. McMillen, *Communist Power,* 119–20; Dreyer, *China's Forty Millions,* 180–82.
See also Ma, " Relationship."

48. Author interview, Urumqi, 21 June 1996.

49. McMillen, "Xinjiang and Wang," 574–77.

50. The expression "I will learn from you" [*Xiang ni xuexi*] has become purely
phatic from ritualized use. But the idea of "mutual study," here already highlighted
in 1986, prefigures the later formulation "the two inseparables" (*liangge libukai*).

51. "Wang Enmao."

52. See Guo, *Zhongguo shuangyu renkou goucheng.* I arrived at the 6 percent figure
by dividing 330,000 (roughly one-third of the million or so bilingual Han nationwide) into 5.5 million (the Han population of Xinjiang). This is, of course, a purely
speculative figure. On the other hand, the number of bilingual Uygurs seems incon-
ceivably low and casts further doubt on the reliability of the statistics. The problem may lie with an overly restrictive definition of "bilingual." The title of the
original Chinese-Canadian study, back-translated into English, is *The World's
Literary Languages: An Outline of Degree and Manner of Use,* vol. 4, *China.* The

author's surname is McConnell (?) (Maikekangnaier), and it was published in 1955.

53. Author interview with a conference participant, Urumqi, 30 April 1997.

54. Wurlig Borchigud notes that a similar slogan, "Meng Han jiantong," was deployed in Inner Mongolia from 1958. See Borchigud, "Impact of Urban Ethnic Education," 289. My guess is that the slogan was originally promulgated much earlier in Xinjiang but not initially pushed so hard; the drastically different population ratios in the two regions may explain the gap in timing.

55. The two textbooks were *Hanyu duben* (A Chinese reader), vols. 1 and 2, and *Weiyu duben* (A Uygur reader), vol. 1, both published by Xinjiang Qingshaonian Chubanshe in March 1997. Volume 2 of *Weiyu duben* had not come out by July 1997, when I left Xinjiang; subsequent inquiries revealed it still had not appeared a year later. This, despite the fact that two much shorter textbooks were made available in February 1997, when the XUAR *Minzu* Language and Script Work Committee (Yuweihui) published *Uygurchä sözliridin jümlü* (Five hundred sentences of daily conversation in Uygur) and *Hanyu richang huihua 500 ju* (Five hundred sentences of daily conversation in Chinese).

56. Xu, *Yuyan de jiechu.*

57. Liao, "Dui Xinjiang Weiwu'er Zizhiqu," 407, 408, 411. One finds, for example, questions beginning "Since Chinese is the national language . . ." and "Since Chinese is one of the languages used in the UN. . . ."

58. Indeed, a former official in the Urumqi city government, for instance, reported widespread anger that all business was expected to be conducted in Chinese.

59. Yin and Mao, *Xinjiang minzu,* 157.

60. Liu, "Feifa zongjiao huodong," 67.

61. On the southwest, see Hansen, *Lessons in Being Chinese;* information on the Islamic communities comes from a personal communication with Jacqueline Armijo-Hussein.

62. Harris, "Xinjiang," 120–21.

63. Dillon, "Xinjiang," 29.

64. Kashi Xiwei Xuanchuan Bu, *Fandui minzu fenlie,* 37.

65. Yin and Mao, *Xinjiang minzu,* 233.

66. XUAR Party Committee Propaganda Bureau Report, 52; emphasis added.

67. Luo, *Zongjiao,* 171; emphasis added.

68. Amnesty International. "People's Republic of China," n. 52.

69. The book (Ma, Li, Li, and Zhang, *Ate'izm*) had a print run of at least seventy-nine thousand volumes. The introduction indicates that it was originally written in Chinese in 1991 in response to calls from the Fifteenth Plenum of the Third XUAR Party Congress to deal with the threat of *minzu* "splittism" and was translated into Uygur within six months. It was prepared for use in political-study classes at the high-school level.

70. Wahhabism originated in Saudi Arabia and is the officially sponsored form of Islam there; it has spread widely in Central Asia in recent years. For a discussion of Saudi-funded *mädräsäs* in Pakistan, Xinjiang's neighbor to the southwest and one likely source of Wahhabist influence, see Nasr, "Rise of Sunni Militancy," 139–80.

71. Yin and Mao, *Xinjiang minzu,* 160–61, 163; the term *biaoxian,* familiar to

students of Chinese politics, is difficult to render into English. Technically, it refers not to attitude but to "expression" of attitude. Those with good *biaoxian* are regarded as more reliable by Party functionaries, and individuals with particularly good *biaoxian* are rewarded with promotions and other perks. See Walder, *Communist Neo-Traditionalism*.

72. Sautman, "Preferential Policies."

73. Ibid., 101.

74. Ibid., 99.

75. Toops, "Recent Uygur," 85–86.

76. Yin and Mao, *Xinjiang minzu*, 173–74.

77. See Gladney, *Muslim Chinese*, 2–3; and Xu, "Pingxi '5–19.'"

78. Bovingdon, "Strangers."

79. *Pighan: Tallanghan she'irlar* (Wail: Selected poems). N.p.: Shinjang Ünsin Näshriyati, n.d. Although the tape jacket offers no copyright date, the ISRC number indicates it was released in 1993.

80. Cristina Cesaro, personal communication. I am most grateful for the information.

81. Short for "the Han are inseparable from the minority peoples, and the minority peoples are inseparable from the Han." The expression was first raised in the CCP Central Committee in July 1981; it "quickly received the support and welcome of the broad ranks of cadres and masses of every *minzu* throughout the country, and in short order was accepted by everyone," according to a primer on *minzu* theory and practice (XUAR Minzu Shiwu Weiyuanhui and XUAR Laodong Ting, *Minzu lilun*, 61). One might just as well translate *libukai* as "cannot leave." In an exoteric rendering of the slogan, "do without" better conveys the meaning, but the phrase also implies that the minority peoples—for instance, the Uygurs—cannot leave the Han in the sense that they cannot establish an independent country.

82. The passage has an embedded set phrase: "Pada baqqanda dost iduq/ yangaq chaqqanda ayrilduq" [literally, We were friends when pasturing the animals, but when the walnuts were cracked, we separated; figuratively, You were happy to have me help with the work, but when it came time to enjoy the spoils, you wanted nothing to do with me]. The first and second parts of the phrase are separated by two lines in the poem.

83. I hasten to add once again that given the sanctions against voicing such sentiments even in private, the fact that only a few people expressed them is hardly diagnostic.

84. Yin and Mao, *Xinjiang minzu*, 254; emphasis added.

5 / Making Xinjiang Safe for the Han?

Contradictions and Ironies
of Chinese Governance in China's Northwest

DAVID BACHMAN

In 1949, when the troops of the People's Liberation Army (PLA) entered Xinjiang, less than 10 percent of the population was Han. Historically, Chinese control over Xinjiang was sporadic, and more or less continuous control came only during the Qing dynasty (1644–1911). Xinjiang did not obtain provincial-level status until 1884 (not coincidentally, the same year Taiwan did). This occurred after Zuo Zongtang led a military expedition to Xinjiang to put down the Yakub Beg–led rebellion and reassert limited central control. In the Republican period (1911–1949), Han nominally continued to lead the province, but the central government's reach was limited, and Xinjiang was arguably the least-integrated province in China under the weak Republican regime. Soviet "diplomats" provided support to rebel movements and various local potentates. So when the People's Republic of China (PRC) was established in 1949, the connections between the Chinese heartland and Xinjiang were extremely weak.

Josef Stalin did not let Mao Zedong forget how weak those ties were. In a secret protocol to the Valentine's Day (1950) Treaty of Friendship, Alliance, and Mutual Assistance between the PRC and the Soviet Union, both countries pledged that "citizens of third countries [would not be allowed] to settle or to carry out any industrial, financial, trade, or other related activities in Manchuria and Xinjiang." Similar restrictions were to apply in the Soviet Far East and Central Asia.[1] Soviet-Chinese joint stock companies were soon set up to explore for uranium and other rare-earth metals useful to the Soviet nuclear-development program, as the Soviet leadership thought that it lacked abundant uranium resources.[2] The agreement struck the Chinese leadership as yet another unequal treaty, imposed on China this time by an ostensible ally. In addition to giving the Soviet Union special economic privileges in China, the treaty allowed the Soviet Union to maintain a number of consulates in Xinjiang; these consulates had ties with the non-Han population.[3]

The realization that integrating Xinjiang more fully into China proper was crucial to national security was reinforced by several circumstances and events: the 1962 migration of more than sixty-two thousand minority people into the Soviet Union in response to discrimination against minorities and Islam in the period from 1958 to 1962, the existence of road access to Tibet via Xinjiang, the Sino-Soviet battles of 1969, and the scattered military confrontations of the 1970s. The migration, or flight, of the sixty-two thousand minority people across the border, which came, according to the Chinese version, at the instigation of Soviet diplomatic personnel, reinforced traditional Chinese concerns regarding the linkage between external threats and internal disorder.

For much of its history, the PRC regime has been highly concerned with integrating Xinjiang economically, militarily, and politically into a modernizing Chinese state. Xinjiang has been the site of extensive investment by the center. But the economic activities of the Chinese state and its representatives in Xinjiang have not been ethnically neutral. Rather, they have overwhelmingly benefited the Han in Xinjiang, and many seem deliberately designed to encourage Han immigration. Today, the military presence in Xinjiang is extensive, and the overwhelmingly Han-dominated Production and Construction Corps (PCC) is an empire almost to itself, exercising production, military, paramilitary, and "judicial" functions. This unusual organization, which was composed initially of the Communist troops who occupied Xinjiang in 1950, has the equivalent of provincial status in Chinese economic planning and is not under the control of the Xinjiang Uygur Autonomous Region (XUAR) authorities. Chinese agricultural policies in Xinjiang appear to be creating an environmental disaster as the short-term need to encourage migration comes at the expense of sustainable development (if such a thing is possible in a region where no urban area receives more than ten inches of rain a year). It should come as no surprise to anyone that policies designed to increase the Han population of Xinjiang—policies that include offering Han economic incentives and reserving well-paying jobs for them—have solidified minority ethnic identities and increased anti-Han feelings (especially in the reform period from about 1978). Such feelings, which arose periodically even before Xinjiang was incorporated into China, have stimulated oppositional activities and led to a classic action-reaction pattern of violence.

This chapter focuses on a number of the economic aspects of what can only be seen as Han economic imperialism in Xinjiang. In comparison to other parts of northwest China and other nominally autonomous provincial-level units, Xinjiang has done quite well economically. The Han, however, have been the major beneficiaries of this process, and the trend appears if anything to be growing stronger. But economic colonialism (or internal colonialism) in Xinjiang can be understood only as a response to Han–perceived security threats, both internal and external to Xinjiang. This chapter also examines the role of the PCC in exerting control over and developing Xinjiang. The PRC has invested so much in, and so much depends on, Xinjiang that the regime will do what it must to retain undisputed control over this vast region.

FOREIGN POLICY AND XINJIANG SECURITY POLICY

Comprising a sixth of all Chinese territory and bordering on eight foreign countries (five, prior to the collapse of the Soviet Union), and with a longer border with foreign countries than any other provincial-level unit in China, Xinjiang poses security issues that have always been a major concern of the central government in China. The Xinjiang Production and Construction Corps was established in the early 1950s to help open up land and provide paramilitary and/or reserve-military support for regular military units in Xinjiang. At least in its early days, the PCC was composed overwhelmingly of demobilized soldiers, both from the PLA and from Guomingdang units that had surrendered in Xinjiang. It appears that Xinjiang was relatively pacific through mid-1957, though campaigns against counterrevolutionaries and other "bad elements" took place.[+] With the Antirightist Campaign of 1957, policies of accommodation toward national minorities began to give way to campaigns that attacked local nationalism. Although these attacks would ebb and flow with general policies toward class struggle in the Chinese heartland, for the next twenty years there were regular attacks, and sometimes extended campaigns, against the leadership and culture of the non-Han peoples of Xinjiang.

The deterioration of Sino-Soviet relations, coupled with the flight of 62,000 people from northern Xinjiang in 1962, led increasingly to the militarization of Xinjiang's extensive borders with the Soviet Union and Mongolia. Wang Enmao, then the leader of Xinjiang, desired moderate policies that would prevent ethnic conflicts from emerging and make managing Xinjiang's increasingly serious external-security concerns easier. Despite Wang's efforts to limit the effects of the Cultural Revolution, widespread violence and near chaos were at times common in Xinjiang. Indeed, though it is hard to say where the Cultural Revolution was the most violent or the most disruptive, it appears that in many, if not all, of the PRC's "autonomous regions," policies aimed against minority individuals and minority members of the Chinese Communist Party (CCP) were severe.[5] As a result of the central government's Third Front policies, Xinjiang militarized, and nine ordinance factories were built in the region, including a major one in Urumqi, north of the Tianshan mountain range, and another major one in Korla, south of the mountains.[6] The ordinance industries of more populous border provinces such as Guangxi, Yunnan, and Inner Mongolia do not appear to have undergone such extensive development.[7] By comparison, the ordinance enterprises in Xinjiang may have made up 10 percent of all the medium- and large-scale enterprises in Xinjiang in 1985.

Xinjiang was slow to recover from the Cultural Revolution, and there were reports of widespread conflict in the early post-Mao period. Ethnic conflict was reported in Aqsu, a border clash with the Soviets occurred in Tacheng, and agitation among youth sent down to the countryside who were anxious to return to their native places was widespread.[8] This slow recovery also seems to have characterized the situation in many of the PRC's autonomous regions. With the reform period after 1978 (perhaps best symbolized by Hu Yaobang's visit to Tibet in 1980), the central government appears to have presented a "new deal" to the autonomous regions: it authorized some accommodations to minority culture, central subsidies to all autonomous regions appear to have increased, and as with the rest of the country, economic development became the priority task. It helped Xinjiang that beginning in 1982, China and the Soviet Union gradually began to improve their relations. The external-security threat diminished, and Han leaders tried to improve the internal-security environment.

During the 1980s, extensive efforts were made in Xinjiang to compensate for prior failings. From 1982 through 1996, non-Han students constituted a majority in Xinjiang colleges (though their percentage never matched their numbers in the general population). Central-government subsidies constituted one-half to three-quarters of all spending in Xinjiang. Greater efforts were made to create a better balance between light and heavy industry. Between 1979 and 1991, the ratio of heavy industry to light industry fell from 59–41 to 50–50, implying a greater concern for producing consumer goods and raising popular living standards. From 1980 to 1993, the overall membership of the PCC remained constant, while its Han membership declined marginally from 90 percent of the total to 88 percent.[9] Reports of unrest in Xinjiang declined, and little information is available about social disorder until 1990 or so. Thus, the combination of improving relations with the Soviet Union and the granting of greater scope for minority people's religious and cultural beliefs and practices appears to have improved the security situation in and around the region.

But this improvement in the security situation was gradually undermined by a variety of factors, many of which were extrinsic to Xinjiang. First, China's demand for petroleum began to exceed its internal supply around the mid-1980s. China's established fields in the east were not increasing production, there were few on-shore untapped reserves or promising geological structures in eastern China, and hopes for off-shore development were not matched by actual, exploitable finds. Xinjiang became the major locus of assumed on-shore potential. As a result, resources began to flow into Xinjiang in significant quantities in the mid- to late 1980s. Not only were prospecting and exploration carried out, but the heavy equipment needed for oil development called for enhancement of the infrastructure. On-shore oil development was at that time under the Ministry of Petroleum (now the China National Oil Corporation), a central-government organization that was dominated by Han. The new exploration teams in Xinjiang increased the Han population, and their wages were relatively high. Xinjiang's potential oil thus became China's last hope for petroleum self-reliance and an essential component of national economic security. But though there has been substantial expansion of Xinjiang's production, huge new finds have not occurred.[10]

Second, the reemergence of Tibetan opposition to Chinese rule, which culminated in the protests of late 1987 and early 1989, prompted conservatives in the central leadership to question whether allowing somewhat greater latitude for differing cultural practices and identities was good policy, not just in Tibet, but elsewhere. Militant Islam, especially as seen in Afghanistan after the Soviet withdrawal, was also viewed as threatening. The 4 June 1989 crackdown on student protesters in Tiananmen Square dealt a crippling blow to all approaches for dealing with social and political issues in China that were not hard-line.

Finally, the collapse of the Soviet Union and communism in Europe further heightened the fear of Chinese political elites for future developments. Was communism doomed to failure? What had led the Soviet Union to collapse? Was a similar collapse in China inevitable? Was the fact that the Soviet Union was widely perceived as an empire, with a rapidly growing population of non-Russians, a major cause of its collapse? These questions reverberated throughout the leadership from mid-1989 until mid-1992.

Although the Soviet Union had been poised between 1969 and the early to mid-1980s to invade Xinjiang (in a way that would have been almost impossible to stop until the Soviet Army reached Gansu—if then!), the very existence of the Soviet Union (and Sino-Soviet tensions) kept the borders more or less closed and prevented strong cross-border links from developing between the Turkic peoples of Xinjiang and those of Soviet Central Asia. The Chinese leadership was unsure whether the Soviet Union's successor states would abet "local nationalisms" within Xinjiang and whether the independence of Central Asia would echo among those believing in an independent Xinjiang or East Turkistan (or any other name).

China's energy needs, the reemergence (from the center's point of view) of restive minorities, and the collapse of the Soviet Union raised new security concerns in Beijing. The central government responded to these concerns in ways that were both innovative (in its external diplomacy and international economic relations) and reactionary (in its handling of internal security concerns within Xinjiang). It also adopted new economic policies in Xinjiang that greatly increased Xinjiang's integration into Han China.

China moved quickly to recognize the new states of Central Asia and to initiate economic and other relations with them. In short, China attempted to co-opt them into contributing to China's economic growth and political stability. Within three years, China, Russia, Kazakhstan, Tajikistan, and Kirghizstan had initiated a process of annual consultation, border delimitation, and mutual cooperation. The acceptance of and support for this "G-5" process was an unprecedented development in Chinese foreign policy. This cooperation has led to significant gains for Chinese security: the PRC has extradition treaties with the states of Central Asia, which have returned independent activists to China (where they were probably executed); it has obtained the agreement of these states not to support independence movements in Xinjiang; and it may have secured the right to engage in "hot pursuit" across international borders to destroy guerrillas who are working for independence or true autonomy for Xinjiang. The Chinese leadership can and should be well pleased with how its diplomacy has limited transnational political linkages between the Turkic peoples in Xinjiang and those across the border. This has given the agents of coercion in Xinjiang a generally free hand to employ extreme measures to try to suppress separatist trends; they have had mixed success.

The independence of Central Asia provided China with another opportunity to deal with its energy problems. The China National Oil Corporation successfully bid on the opportunity to develop a major oil field in western Kazakhstan and to build a thousand-mile pipeline to bring the oil from Kazakhstan to Xinjiang, where it would link up with an expanding pipeline network feeding into the rest of the country. Given the cost of the project (about $10 billion), one can assume that the central government stood firmly behind this deal. Actual progress on the oil field and pipeline has been slow, though Kazakh-produced petroleum is entering China by rail and truck. Provided the project actually gets built, access to the output of the large reserves in western Kazakhstan will have a major positive effect on China's petroleum supply. But it may also increase China's security fears. Pipelines are highly vulnerable, and they obviously have fixed paths and locations. A thousand-mile pipeline across Central Asia makes a good target for oppositional violence to Chinese rule in Xinjiang (whether the violence takes place there or in Kazakhstan). Bombing the pipeline might not kill anyone, but it could create an environmental disaster. Given the often barren, mountainous, and remote nature of the territory that the pipeline will traverse, it will be next to impossible to patrol it all constantly. In effect, though helping to fulfill China's demand for petroleum, investment in Kazakhstan increases Chinese security concerns. A disruption of supply and shipments would obviously have very serious consequences for the Chinese economy; this, in turn, could seriously affect the regime's legitimacy. The central government will have to ensure the security of the pipeline through all of Xinjiang and be deeply concerned about its security in Kazakhstan. The logical consequence of increased dependence on oil originating in Kazakhstan is tightened security in Xinjiang, as well as the perception that China's security interests extend well beyond the Chinese border into Kazakhstan. This, in turn, may encourage a buildup of PLA forces in Xinjiang, especially along the border, in areas with large ethnic-minority populations.

Security concerns set a general context for PRC policy in Xinjiang. Both for its own petroleum (and other raw materials) and its links to external sources that will be increasingly vital for the Chinese economy, Xinjiang looms increasingly large in China's geo-economic and geo-strategic thinking. This will require greater investment in and development of the infrastructure in Xinjiang and greater integration of Xinjiang into the Chinese heartland. Although Xinjiang is likely to be an economic beneficiary of Chinese energy policies, it will be more firmly supervised and controlled by the center, which will focus its concerns on the suppression of opposition and protest in the XUAR.

ECONOMIC DEVELOPMENT IN XINJIANG

As stated above, Xinjiang has done relatively well economically since 1949, and it is becoming increasingly essential in the eyes of the central elite to keep Xinjiang part of the PRC. Although energy plays a particularly important role in this today, the desire to integrate Xinjiang into the national economy and national transportation and communications networks stretches back to the early years of the PRC, as is suggested by comparative statistics.

Table 5.1 shows the national rankings for per capita capital construction (investment) and per capita income for the provincial-level units of the Northwest and for China's provincial-level autonomous regions (Ningxia and Xinjiang fall into both categories). The data suggests that except for in the period 1971–1975 (the Fourth Five-Year Plan), Xinjiang has ranked among the top ten provincial-level units in the country in terms of per capita investment. Qinghai has done even better, and Ningxia also has done well. Guangxi, the most populous autonomous region, has fared poorly, even in the reform period after 1978, despite its nominal "coastal status."[11] Shaanxi, Gansu, and Inner Mongolia were major recipients of investment during the Mao period, in part because they were important centers of defense industrialization. Little can be said about the data on Tibet, except that much of it is missing.

In terms of per capita income, the data are less enviable. Xinjiang ranks in the top half of all provincial-level units. However, in recent years, the rankings for per capita income of the northwestern provinces and all autonomous regions have declined, compared to other provincial-level units, though perhaps some limited Open Door effects are seen in Guangxi's recent relative improvement.

Other things being equal, per capita investment should, perhaps with a lag effect, generate roughly comparable per capita income, as investment is a major determinant of income. Here, the differentials between investment and income rankings suggest a number of possibilities: first, investments were used very inefficiently; second, significant amounts of investment may have been devoted to improving the basic infrastructure and not to directly productive activities; and/or third, given the lower levels of economic development in the provincial-level units of the Northwest and in China's provincial-level autonomous regions, the same amount of capital generates a lower rate of return than in the more developed regions. It is likely that all three hypotheses are true to some extent, but there is no obvious reason why Xinjiang seems to outperform Qinghai, to say nothing of the other provincial-level units considered here. Is there any reason to believe that more investment went to directly productive activities in Xinjiang than in the other provincial-level units? Or that Xinjiang can use investment more efficiently than other autonomous regions or units in the Northwest? Or that Xinjiang invests less in

TABLE 5.1
Average National Rank: Capital Construction per Capita and GNP per Capita

Average National Rank: Capital Construction per Capita

	1953–57	1958–62	1963–65	1966–70	1971–75	1976–80	1981–85	1986–90	1991–95	1996–98
Xinjiang	5.8	3.2	4	9.4	11.8	6.6	5.8	6.2	3.2	5
Shaanxi	10.6	15	18	11.6	6.8	13.2	13	15.2	19.2	23.3
Gansu	7.6	8.2	5.3	5.4	7.6	11.6	15.6	13.6	19.2	23
Qinghai	2.8	2.4	1.3	1.2	2.6	3.4	4.4	2.6	6.2	7.7
Ningxia	20	6.8	11	2	4.8	6	9.6	6.4	13	12.7
Tibet	n.a.	n.a.	n.a.	n.a.	n.a.	6.75*	6	19.2	12	7.7
Inner Mongolia	9.8	8.4	8	15.4	17	15.2	11.2	13.2	9	17.7
Guangxi	26.4	27	22	22.2	24.8	24.2	28.8	29.6	27	26.3

Average National Rank: GNP per Capita

	1953–57	1958–62	1963–65	1966–70	1971–75	1976–80	1981–85	1986–90	1991–95	1996–98
Xinjiang	6.6	5.8	6	9.4	16.8	15.4	13.4	11	11.2	12.7
Shaanxi	16.3	16.6	19.7	20.6	18	20.2	23	21.6	23.4	27.7
Gansu	11.2	21.2	17.7	19.4	13	13.6	21.2	25.4	28.8	29.3
Qinghai	12	8.2	8.3	6.8	6.4	7.1	13.6	14	16.2	23.3
Ningxia	15.8	11.8	12.7	12.4	7.6	10.2	16.8	18.6	19.8	25.7
Tibet	n.a	n.a.	n.a	n.a	n.a	n.a	n.a	19.4	25.6	29
Inner Mongolia	6.4	7.6	7	8.6	12	16.2	15.6	14.2	16.2	16.7
Guangxi	27	26.8	26.3	27.4	24.6	25.2	27.8	29	21.8	22.7

Sources: *Quanguo ge sheng, zizhiqu, zhixiashi lishi tongji ziliao; Zhongguo guonei shengchan zongzhi hesuan lishi ziliao; Zhongguo guding zichan touzi tongji ziliao, 1950–1985; Zhongguo guding zichan touzi tongji nianjian, 1995; Zhongguo tongji nianjian* (1996, 1997, 1998, 1999).

Note: This table uses rank orderings because I have not been able to locate a consistent series of data for investment and gross domestic product using the same prices.

*=77–80

infrastructure? The answer to all these questions is probably no. However, though Xinjiang's superior performance vis-à-vis other northwestern provincial-level units (and other autonomous regions) cannot be fully explained, its poorer performance in terms of the effect of investment on income compared to "core" Chinese provinces can be explained by the higher levels of preexisting infrastructure in those provinces, their smaller geographical size, their more plentiful rainfall and therefore more productive agriculture, and probably their more highly educated populations.

It might be objected that per capita rankings skew the results because, with the exception of Guangxi, the provincial-level units under consideration are among the least populous in the PRC. Even Guangxi is not among the ten most populous provincial-level units. There is some validity to this point, but aggregate investment levels or rankings based on all provinces as equal units would be more distorted. Is it reasonable to compare the fewer than 5 million people in Ningxia with the 90 million or so in Henan (which would be one consequence of comparing aggregate provincial investment or incomes)? Tibet, Ningxia, and Qinghai, the three least-populous provincial-level units, are highly unlikely to have aggregate investment or income rankings above the lowest three. Per capita figures are more illuminating regarding investment priorities and income results because if aggregate figures were used, the gross disparity between large and small provinces would obscure shifting emphases in the allocation of capital and in provincial incomes.

Assuming that these figures are valid, we are left with the question of why Xinjiang has done better in terms of investment and per capita income than the other autonomous regions or provinces in the Northwest. As the rankings indicate, this pattern of results is not simply the product of the reform program (though market allocation processes may explain why other provinces have clearly seen their rankings drop off).

Unfortunately, no good answer suggests itself, and Xinjiang's superior rankings are not easily explained. We might speculate that the independence of Soviet Central Asia has convinced Beijing of the need to build up Xinjiang, or there might be something unusual about the nature of economic development in Xinjiang, such as the important role of the PCC. These ad hoc hypotheses remain problematic. There really isn't much difference between the investment rankings for Xinjiang during and after the Mao period. At the same time, there is nothing obvious in the nature of the PCC that makes it a more efficient user of investment and generator of revenue than other enterprises or organizations in China.

We are left with the fact that Xinjiang, in terms of the national rank-

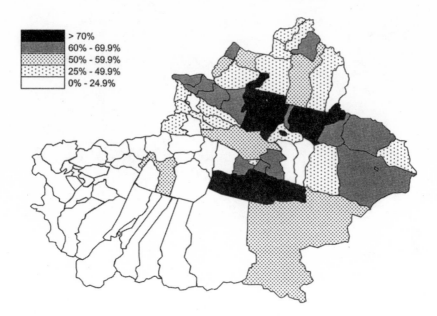

■	> 70%
▨	60% - 69.9%
▦	50% - 59.9%
░	25% - 49.9%
□	0% - 24.9%

Map 5.1. Percentage of Xinjiang Population Classified as Han by County, 1998

ings for per capita investment and per capita income for the entire period from 1953 to 1998, had the best results among the northwestern provinces and autonomous regions. There is no explanation for this. Although the overall pattern of results lends some credence to the view that the coastal provinces are getting rich at the expense of the interior provinces, at least in terms of investment, the evidence is not conclusive.

But though Xinjiang's performance is satisfactory, provincial-level rankings hide huge disparities in the distribution of gross domestic product at the county and city level in Xinjiang. Map 5.1 shows the distribution by county-level unit of Han in Xinjiang in 1998. The areas where Han are in the majority are in the north and east (or generally north and east of the Tianshan mountain range). In other northern areas where Han are not the majority, such as in the Ili district, they are nevertheless a substantial minority. The only area where Han are the majority south of the Tianshan mountain range is in Aqsu municipality. In many counties in the south and west, especially in the Kashgar and Hotan districts, Han make up less than 10 percent of the population.[12] Map 5.2 shows the distribution of the Uygur population in Xinjiang; clearly Uygurs overwhelmingly predominate in the south and west.

There has been a general stability in the composition of county popu-

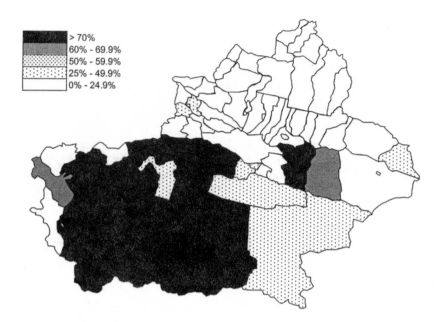

Map 5.2. Percentage of Xinjiang Population Classified as Uygur by County, 1998

lations, at least according to the population data in the Xinjiang Statistical Yearbook. Comparing the population data for 1988 and 1998 reveals that only one area switched from a bare Uygur minority to a place where no ethnic group was in the majority. However, that was Yining, an area of great unrest. The number of Uygurs as a percentage of the overall population in Xinjiang declined slightly, while the percentage of Han increased minimally. There was a minor increase in the percentage of Han in the Uygur heartland, in southwest Xinjiang, particularly in the Kashgar district. Nonetheless, in most cases, Han remained less than 20 percent of the population. Such figures, however, do not include migrants whose housing registration *(hukou)* was not transferred with them.[13]

Map 5.3 shows that the areas where per capita annual income is below ¥4,000, or less than two-thirds of the regional average, are concentrated in the southwest. In three regions (prefectures) — Kizilsu (Kezilesu), Kashgar, and Hotan — there are no Han-majority counties or cities and no areas with per capita income above ¥4,000. This area comprises twenty-four cities and counties, or more than a quarter of the eighty-seven cities and counties of Xinjiang. In 1998, forty-five of the eighty-seven major subregion jurisdictions had per capita incomes below ¥4,000. Han were the

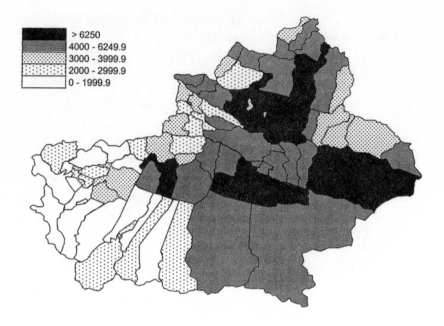

■	> 6250
▨	4000 - 6249.9
▦	3000 - 3999.9
⠿	2000 - 2999.9
□	0 - 1999.9

Map 5.3. Xinjiang Per Capita GDP by County, 1998

majority in only four of these areas, meaning that forty-one of these areas were ones where ethnic-minority peoples constituted the majority of the population. In the entire region, thirty-two counties and cities were Han majority. As noted, only four of those units had per capita incomes below ¥4,000. Forty-one of fifty-five counties and cities where ethnic-minority people were the majority of the population (or almost 75 percent of such areas) had per capita incomes below ¥4,000. In only two counties where ethnic-minority peoples were the majority of the local population was the county per capita income above the regional average. Those two were Urumqi County, which surrounds the regional capital (45 percent Han), and Shanshan County, the location of a major coal mine and an oil field (31 percent Han). Fourteen of the Han-majority counties and cities had per capita incomes above the regional average of ¥6,229. Thus, there is a very strong correlation between areas of Han majority and high per capita income (and conversely, areas with a large percentage of non-Han and low per capita income). Moreover, it is likely that this is not just a correlative relationship but a causal one.

Han economic dominance was manifest in other areas as well. In the 1995 PRC industrial census, 191 large- and medium-sized enterprises in Xinjiang were identified (some key enterprises related to national security may not have been reported). Of those 191, 180 were state-owned industrial enterprises. In none of the large enterprises (40 in number) were their managers unambiguously members of ethnic minorities (one was surnamed Ma, which is often a Hui surname but not always). Of the 151 medium-sized enterprises, the managers of 2 were unambiguously minority, 3 were surnamed Ma, and 1 was unclear (someone named Xuanyuan Guoxin). The rest were almost certainly Han.[14] Only 6 of the 40 large enterprises were in ethnic minority–dominant areas (all in and around Yining). Two were PCC enterprises, and all 6 were apparently managed by Han. With the exception of one enterprise in Korla and another in Ruoqiang County (also a PCC enterprise) no large enterprises were located south of the Tianshan mountain range. Eighteen of the 40 were in and around Urumqi, and no other place had more than 3 large enterprises. Medium-sized enterprises were somewhat more broadly distributed, but they remained concentrated in the north as well. Fifteen of the 151 medium-sized enterprises were located in ethnic minority–dominant units. Only 6 were south of the Tianshan mountain range: 3 in the Korla district, 1 in Kashgar, and 2 in Hotan. Four enterprises were in Han-dominant Aqsu (2 of them were PCC enterprises). Fifty-nine of the 151 medium-sized enterprises were located in Urumqi. Overall, large- and medium-sized enterprises accounted for almost three-fifths of industrial output in Xinjiang in 1998 (a year of major decline in Xinjiang industry. In 1997, large- and medium-sized enterprises accounted for two-thirds of industrial output).[15]

Since the overwhelming majority of large- and medium-sized enterprises in Xinjiang are state owned, their location, in part, reflects conscious state choice. In addition, as state-owned enterprises, managers are appointed from the appropriate *nomenklatura* lists. The lists for centrally "owned" enterprises are unlikely to contain the names of many ethnic-minority members. Those for PCC enterprises, of which there are 49, are also unlikely to contain many names that are not Han, given that the membership of the PCC is about 90 percent Han. Thus, it is not surprising that for the most part, non-Han are not factory managers. Indeed, the distribution of large- and medium-sized enterprises in Xinjiang and the selection of managers who are overwhelmingly Han reflect deliberate state choices. For whatever reasons, the state has not invested heavily in western and southern Xinjiang, and these areas remain predominantly agricultural, poor, and non-Han. Consequently, the privileged position of Han in Xinjiang's political economy is strongly reinforced by decisions concerning allocation.

Although China has been engaged in economic reform since the late 1970s, Xinjiang looks more and more like a centrally planned region with a "traditional" colonial economy. In 1997, almost 68 percent of all industrial output came from large- and medium-sized enterprises.[16] Also in 1997, 1,288 of 7,634 industrial enterprises in Xinjiang were controlled by the center. At a time when central control over industrial enterprises has dropped dramatically, such a large number of centrally controlled enterprises is extraordinary.[17] Whereas nationally, in 1997, the state sector produced about a third of all industrial output in the country, in Xinjiang, it produced more than half of the state's industrial output. Overall, the state sector accounted for three-quarters of all industry in Xinjiang.

Except in 1959, 1975, and 1976, heavy industry never constituted more than 55 percent of the total output of light and heavy industry combined during the Maoist period. Only in 1959 did heavy-industrial output exceed 60 percent of total industrial output. However, in 1995, heavy-industrial output was 64 percent of total industrial output; in 1996, it was 67 percent; in 1997, it was almost 69 percent; and in 1998, it exceeded 69 percent.[18] In short, in recent years, Xinjiang's industry has been oriented more toward heavy industry than ever in its past; in other words, it has become more economically imbalanced. Such a concentration on heavy industry is usually equated with a planned economy, but for China as a whole, even in the heyday of state planning, heavy-industrial output did not consistently rise above 60 percent of the total output of light and heavy industry combined.

The reason for this increasing concentration on heavy industry is that natural-resource development, especially petroleum products, has been the core element of central-government plans for Xinjiang for some time, and for statistical purposes, natural-resource development is by definition a branch of heavy industry. Heavy industry is more capital intensive than light industry, is often less labor intensive, and has higher embodied technology, which means that it requires a more educated workforce. In most cases, natural-resource development, especially on a large scale, is a task for the central government or a central corporation, as opposed to being a task for a regional or provincial government or below. This is particularly true of petroleum. In statistical terms, extractive and raw-materials industries accounted for almost 60 percent of industrial output in Xinjiang in 1997.[19]

However, with the independence of Soviet Central Asia, there was some hope that Xinjiang might profit from the Open Door Policy in the way that coastal provinces had. (The coastal provinces had switched to labor-intensive light-industrial production and encouraged extensive exports, often by foreign-funded enterprises.) Foreign trade has grown substantially throughout the entire 1978–97 period in Xinjiang, at a rate of about 25 percent per year, which exceeds the growth of GDP (about 11 percent) by a significant margin. However, it appears that in the 1990s, the rate of growth of total foreign trade has slowed, and that imports have been growing substantially faster than exports. As table 5.2 shows, total foreign-trade growth has slowed substantially, especially since 1995, and the growth of exports has been slower than the growth of regional GDP.[20] Imports have grown dramatically, especially in the early and mid-1990s. In 1996 and 1997, Xinjiang had a negative trade balance. In the five years (1994–98) for which statistical information is available, the border trade has been in deficit as well. Although a number of the border traders doing import business may be PRC citizens, it appears that trade and export promotion have not played a major role in Xinjiang's economic development. Moreover, almost 75 percent of all of Xinjiang's foreign trade came from Urumqi and the PCC.[21] It would be hard to argue that foreign trade will be a major stimulus to economic growth in Xinjiang, especially in the poorer areas where ethnic-minority populations predominate.

In recent years, the key agricultural priority in Xinjiang has been to promote the cultivation of cotton, and Xinjiang is the country's leading cotton producer.[22] Cotton is one of the few agricultural crops in which China's price structures approximate international market conditions. If international prices are set equal to 100, for China as a whole, prices for rice average 101, and cotton, 107. For most other crops, China's prices are considerably higher. With WTO accession, much of Chinese agriculture faces severe competition.[23] China has vast amounts of cotton in warehouses, and supply grossly outstrips demand. Farmers in Xinjiang are not making a profit on cotton.

Of equal importance to the economic difficulty of raising cotton in Xinjiang are the potential long-term ecological effects. A direct parallel can be drawn between efforts to promote cotton production in Xinjiang and the "virgin lands" program promoted by Nikita Khrushchev in the 1950s and 1960s. The program pushed for extensive land reclamation in Soviet Central Asia, with the new fields to be used primarily to grow cotton. Water from the Aral Sea was to be the source of irrigation. The topographical and hydrological conditions were roughly similar to those in Xinjiang, though the Soviets may have had more available water than the PRC has in Xinjiang. However, the result in the former Soviet Union has been a massive environmental disaster. The Aral Sea is disappearing at an alarm-

TABLE 5.2
Xinjiang Foreign Trade (in US$1,000,000)

	Total Foreign Trade	Exports Total	Ordinary Exports	Border Trade Exports	Imports Total	Ordinary Imports	Border Trade Imports	Balance
1990	410	335			75			260
1991	459	363			96			267
1992	750	454			296			157
1993	922	495			427			68
1994	1,040	576	291	239	464	160	273	112
1995	1,423	769	445	276	659	176	419	110
1996	1,404	550	303	186	854	260	545	-304
1997	1,497	665	361	230	781	241	520	-116
1998	1,532	808	323	376	724	210	493	84
% increase, 1990–98	30.38	15.66			96.26			-7.54
% increase 1994–98	9.45	8.05	2.17	11.42	11.19	6.16	16.11	-5.03

Note: For reasons not explained in the statistical yearbook, ordinary trade and border trade do not equal total trade or total imports or total exports.

Source: 1999 Xinjiang Statistical Yearbook (figures round up to the nearest million).

ing rate. What was once the world's fourth largest freshwater lake has lost between 50 and 60 percent of its volume; its salinity has increased from 1 percent to 11 percent.[24] Since we lack precise hydrological information on aquifers in Xinjiang, we cannot make a definitive assessment on whether the water resources there are being used in a less exploitative fashion than was the case in Soviet Central Asia. It would be surprising, however, if long-term cotton production did not lead to similar kinds of environmental problems in Xinjiang.

The major parts of Xinjiang where cotton is planted in large areas are in non-Han regions, especially the Aqsu and Kashgar districts. (Aqsu municipality has a Han-majority population, but the counties in the district do not. Since PCC farmers are 32.6 percent of the population in Aqsu municipality, without them, even Aqsu municipality would not have a Han majority.) Combining local *(difang)* production with PCC subregional production reaffirms this: together, Aqsu and Kashgar districts account for more than half of all the cotton acreage in Xinjiang. Although the locations of PCC subunit headquarters are known, it is unclear whether PCC subunit boundaries follow those of the political administrative divisions of the XUAR. It is therefore impossible to apportion precisely to the districts of the XUAR the acreage sown in cotton in PCC subunits.[25]

Thus, cotton is planted predominantly in areas inhabited by ethnic-minority peoples. It appears to be unprofitable and potentially environmentally unsustainable. It also appears to be promoted by the PCC in both northern and southern Xinjiang, and the amount of cotton acreage seems to be growing in tandem with the increasing Han population in northern Xinjiang.

Another indicator of ethnic inequality and the predominance of central-government authority in Xinjiang is in the budget. In the 1980s and 1990s, Xinjiang was a major recipient of central-government budget subsidies, with Beijing providing the equivalent of approximately 50 percent of expenditure in the region. The statistical materials do not explicitly demarcate the central government's subsidies for earlier years, but 1966 was the last year that local revenues exceeded expenditures in Xinjiang. In theory, local governments are not supposed to run budget deficits, so the difference between local revenues and local expenditures (when there is a deficit) is a de facto form of central-government subsidy to the locality. Between 1973 and 1986, expenditures were at least 3 times local revenues in Xinjiang; from 1987 to 1997, they were closer to about 2.5 times local revenues. Expenditures in Xinjiang were thus highly subsidized, but since 1987, the rate of subsidization has been declining. Either the center has grown weary of providing such extensive subsidies, or the expenditures in Xinjiang are beginning to pay off with higher rates of revenue generation.[26]

It is also possible to look at where revenue was generated and where it was spent within the XUAR in 1997. In per capita terms, ¥323 of revenue was obtained through taxation and fees, and ¥528 was spent. (It should be noted that almost ¥4.5 billion of overall expenditure is unaccounted for, whereas only ¥200 million of overall revenue is not. Perhaps the PCC is not included in expenditures, but PCC budget figures are lacking.) In places where national minority peoples constitute a majority of the population, especially Ili, Aqsu, Kashgar, and Hotan, per capita expenditures were below ¥400, or about three-quarters of the provincial average. There were some Han areas with low per capita expenditures, for example, Shihezi and Kuytun, but both have high per capita GDPs. One area with a high percentage of minorities had a higher than average rate of per capita expenditure: Kizilsu, the least populated prefectural-level unit in Xinjiang. Han areas generally had higher per capita spending than the provincial average. It should be noted that in all minority areas, income was less than expenditure, indicating a certain degree of subsidy. Urumqi, Karamay, and Kuytun were the only places in the XUAR where income exceeded expenditures.[27]

The consequences of this pattern of expenditure are easily understood. Expenditures are used for many purposes, which include schools, public health, and economic development. If per capita expenditures in Ili, Aqsu, Kashgar, and Hotan were at best three-quarters of the regional average, it follows that in the most profound sense, life chances in those areas were substantially poorer than elsewhere in Xinjiang. The educational and economic disparities between Han and non-Han were made clear in a comparative analysis of the findings of the 1982 and 1990 censuses in China.[28] There is no reason to assume that the situation has improved, and it may even have deteriorated further.

The meaning of these economic factors in Xinjiang's developmental history and current status should be obvious. The central and regional governments appear to be pursuing a classic policy of economic imperialism, or internal colonialism, in the XUAR. The region is deeply dependent on the center for capital. This capital is used primarily to invest in the excavation and exploitation of raw materials. The center's role in industrial ownership is also extensive. Investment is concentrated in heavy-industrial, raw-material sectors. Economic opportunities seem overwhelmingly to benefit Han, and there is a high correlation between above-average regional income and Han-majority populations in counties or cities. In general, there are higher rates of spending in Han-majority areas. The Han population tends to be urban; the ethnic-minority populations, rural. The government has apparently forced many farmers, a majority of whom are from national minorities, to pursue a cash crop, cotton, rather than grain or other forms of agriculture that may be better suited to local conditions.

Many characteristics of the reform period in the coastal areas are not present in Xinjiang. Despite the independence of the Central Asian states, Xinjiang has not seen a rapid growth of regional exports in recent years. It does not have a large private or collective sector. It does not have a balanced pattern between light and heavy industry. It is not basically reliant on itself for its investment and expenditures.

This is not to say that other forms of colonialism are not present in Xinjiang as well.[29] However, economic colonialism may be as important as they are, and it may serve as the basis upon which other forms are based. Economic colonialism may also have consequences for political control and political action.

In a recent essay, Barry Sautman challenged the view that Xinjiang should be seen as an internal colony.[30] Sautman's argument is too complex to be addressed fully here; however, to an important degree, it hinges on intention—the intention of the colonizers to exploit the colonized. He argues that many outcomes in Xinjiang can and should be explained by general Communist Party policies toward the countryside, by geography and climate, and by "the politics of anti-separatism," which keeps the Han in charge. But this last point undermines his argument. He notes that all the minority areas of China are part of China because they were conquered by the Han core. But in my opinion, it is the Han presence alone that keeps Xinjiang, Tibet, and other regions in the PRC, and PRC leaders have pursued policies designed to tie border and minority regions to the Chinese heartland. These policies have sometimes been relatively benign. In aggregate economic terms, Xinjiang has done reasonably well. It does not appear, however, that the central government has gone out of its way to support minority areas in Xinjiang, and both deliberately and unconsciously, its policies have reinforced a pattern of dominance by which the Han disproportionately benefit. To my mind, such a pattern of rule is characteristic of imperialism and internal colonialism.

The Han project to turn Xinjiang into an internal colony has been at least partially successful. Over the last twenty years or so, northern Xinjiang (Dzungaria) has been largely integrated into the PRC. Much of northern Xinjiang is composed of Han-majority administrative divisions. There has been substantial economic development in this area. But though the

Han presence has undoubtedly been greatly magnified in northern Xinjiang since 1949, it is far from clear that the national minority groups are reconciled with political and economic integration. As it was throughout much of the 1900s, the Ili region appears to be less than happy at the prospect of deepening integration into China. The Han are not a majority in the Ili district, but they are present in substantial numbers, and one should not doubt the extensive presence of the People's Liberation Army and the People's Armed Police in Ili. Nonetheless, Ili has remained a center of protest and violence throughout much of the history of the PRC (and of prior Chinese regimes as well), and it has been perhaps at the core of what the central and regional authorities call "splittist activities" in the 1990s. Economic imperialism and internal colonialism may have achieved the center's aims in Xinjiang, but they have not reconciled relations between Han and non-Han. Quite the contrary, they may have solidified ethnic identifications that resist either economic or political accommodations and perpetuate cycles of protest, violence, and repression.

THE XINJIANG PRODUCTION
AND CONSTRUCTION CORPS AND MIGRATION

The Xinjiang Production and Construction Corps is a state within the state in Xinjiang. It is widely seen as comparable to Tang and Qing dynasty institutions that created farms in border areas manned by soldiers. These encampments would increase the Han presence in these regions, provide manpower with some military training to defend these sensitive areas, and above all, extend China's imperial domain to areas that were strategically significant but sparsely populated, thus providing a buffer between the nomadic tribes of Central and Inner Asia and the Chinese heartland. When PLA troops entered Xinjiang in 1949, their commander was Wang Zhen. During the Yan'an period, Wang commanded the 359th Brigade in Nanniwan, south of Yan'an. Mao had extolled the unit for its combination of military skill and political consciousness and for its willingness to engage in extensive agricultural land reclamation.[31] Inspired by a similar strategic logic imbued with socialist consciousness (as well as by more immediate concerns, such as the difficulty of returning PLA and surrendered KMT troops to the Chinese heartland, and perhaps also by Wang Zhen's careerist interests), the PCC was informally created in 1952 and formally established in 1954.[32] It was and is an overwhelmingly Han organization.

During the 1990s, the PCC constituted more than an eighth of the entire population of Xinjiang, and its membership (about 2.4 million) was about 90 percent Han. Since 1990, it has had the equivalent of provincial status in terms of planning *(jihua danlie)*. It controls a very large proportion of the productive assets of Xinjiang, including about 20 percent of arable land devoted to grain production and more than a third of land under cotton. In 1995, at the time of the Third National Industrial Census, the PCC had 2,859 industrial enterprises and production units. This constituted an increase of 639 units since the industrial census of 1985. The output of these enterprises was more than 22 percent of the total industrial output of Xinjiang in 1995.[33] The PCC produced more than a third of all the sugar, cloth, canned goods, and machine-made paper in Xinjiang. In 1985, the ratio of heavy industry to light industry was about 7 to 3. In 1995, it was 82.5 to 17.5. In 1995, the PCC controlled 48 of Xinjiang's 195 large- and medium-sized enterprises. This 25 percent figure was a significant decrease from the 1985 census, when 32 of the region's 89 large- and medium-sized enterprises were controlled by the PCC.[34]

The PCC's economic centrality in Xinjiang has been obscured in recent years by attacks on its "labor education" and "reform through labor" camps. Although the number of these penal institutions is not known, the PCC has an unusual range of power over judicial issues, which demonstrates that though it is an economic, military, and administrative institution, it has attributes of territorial administration that are unlike those of any other institution in China.[35]

The PCC serves as a vanguard of Han penetration into Xinjiang. As the figures in table 5.3 suggest, the PCC constitutes a significant proportion of the Han population in southern and western Xinjiang. It is recruiting new members, and it has been encouraging poor Han from interior provinces to migrate to Xinjiang to work the cotton fields. It has military functions and serves as a backstop to PLA and armed police forces in the region.

Although the PCC has been encouraging migration into Xinjiang, it is also true that the economic opportunities for migrants in Xinjiang have themselves stimulated migration. Certainly it appears that the Xinjiang authorities have done little or nothing to discourage Han from migrating into the region. If migratory flows are ranked in four tiers (from most to least in terms of the number of immigrants) Xinjiang ranked in the second tier (with only the coastal provinces in the first tier).[36] Legal *(hukou-transfer)* migrations averaged between 75,000 and 100,000 per year in the 1990s.[37] Figures for floating-population (illegal) migration are at best estimates and are highly inexact. Several sources suggest figures for total

TABLE 5.3
Xinjiang Administrative Subdivisions: Population, GDP, and Ethnic

City/County	Population	GDP (¥1,000,000)	GDP per Capita (¥)	Percent Han	Percent FPCC* in Area	Percent Uygur
XUAR total	17,473,500	11,166,700	6,229	38.58	10.3	46.58
Urumqi City	1,391,896	23,177	13,475	75.89	3.25	13.35
Urumqi County	156,883	1,620	9,404	44.58	3.5	6.64
Karamay	263,069	9,066	35,098	76.63	6.34	14.79
Shihezi	581,952	2,025	7,745	95.02	9.59	1.12
TURPAN DISTRICT	542,960	5,109	9,365	23.47	0.95	69.7
Turpan (Tulufan)	242,501	1,177	4,807	21.01	2.13	70.86
Shanshan County	198,223	3,302	16,528	30.59	0	64.49
Toksum County (Tuokexun)	102,236	461	4,506	15.51	0	77.03
HAMI DISTRICT	471,791	2,848	6,073	67.19	13.16	19.34
Hami	352,929	2,467	7,050	68.81	13.92	23.37
Barkol (Kazakh) County (Bailikun)	100,355	347	3,460	68.06	11.3	0.21
Yiwu County	18,507	79	4,130	31.73	8.72	46.24
CHANGJI AUTON- OMOUS ZHOU	1,456,477	10,703	6,939	74.88	23.45	4.03
Changji	338,739	2,493	7,465	77.09	15.41	2.89
Miquan	167,869	1,231	7,329	62.45	10.79	2.88
Hutubi County	196,794	1,394	7,121	77.77	36.22	2.58
Manas County (Manasi)	159,366	2,429	9,600	82.31	79.13	2.89
Qitai County	227,981	861	3,787	77.47	15.23	6.78
Fukang	147,776	1,390	9,480	73.74	14.99	5.7
Jimsar County (Jimusa'er)	129,717	599	4,584	72.45	13.02	4.8
Mori (Kazakh) County (Mulei)	87,379	291	3,334	69.71	0	4.84
ILI AUTONOMOUS ZHOU	3,819,989	17,330	4,350	44.71	16.82	16.05
Kuytun (Kuitun)	263,942	981	9,203	95.02	5.57	0.35
Ili District	2,067,372	6,532	3,167	32.79	8.96	27.1
Yining	332,022	1,462	4,452	36.04	0	48.37
Yining County	375,486	1,134	3,040	19.57	3.03	49.01
Qagpal (Xibe) County (Chabucha'er)	157,025	411	2,509	34.35	14.62	26.49

continued on next page

TABLE 5.3 *(continued)*

City/County	Population	GDP (¥1,000,000)	GDP per Capita (¥)	Percent Han	Percent FPCC* in Area	Percent Uygur
Korgas County (Huocheng)	334,192	1,037	2,509	45.37	24.29	20.65
Gongliu County	149,146	380	2,562	31.05	4.97	22.86
Xinyuan County	277,386	1,131	4,082	40.69	9.02	9.18
Zhaosu County	147,736	469	3,198	28.36	17.62	9.76
Tekes County (Tekesi)	148,415	352	2,368	24.61	3.75	9.91
Nilka County (Nileke)	145,964	303	2,130	28.41	3.88	11.17
Tacheng District	905,428	7,110	5,698	58.03	43.21	4.64
Tacheng	147,546	912	6,182	63.23	9.93	3.41
Emin County	182,510	1,096	6,006	55	17.92	4.07
Usu County (Wusu)	200,019	2,078	6,725	62.68	72.67	9.5
Shawan County	193,767	2,455	5,852	70.02	96.6	4.23
Tuoli County	82,658	231	2,852	26.58	2.64	1.29
Yumin County	51,008	203	3,984	59.69	10.34	0.4
Hoboksar County (Hebukesai'er)	49,920	222	3,876	36.66	7.79	2.17
Altay District	583,247	2,707	4,788	43.54	8.21	1.72
Altay	210,302	940	5,153	61.71	6.38	2.31
Burqin County (Buerjin)	67,089	276	4147	32.81	0	1.57
Fuyun County	81,571	452	5,539	25.71	0	2.72
Fuhai County	62,396	429	5222	56.17	43.13	0.96
Habahe County	73,407	224	3,028	31.32	5.7	0.47
Qinghe County	53,199	201	3,805	19.57	1.53	1.09
Jeminay County (Jimunai)	35,283	163	4,535	36.04	7.31	1.06
BORTALA ZHOU	394,375	2,115	5,370	66.26	21.47	12.95
Bole	204,704	1,248	6,098	66.13	25.54	16.37
Jinghe County	118,033	624	5,318	69.62	18.87	12.41
Wenquan County	71,638	275	4,131	61.11	14.1	4.09
BAYAN GOL	993,146	10,615	10,605	55.31	14.96	34.24
Korla (Kuerle)	331,976	7,187	21,978	66.52	10.32	29.44
Luntai County	85,435	360	4,242	11.63	0	87.73
Yuli (Lopnur) County	94,698	607	6,410	70.54	42.94	28.68
Ruoqiang County	28,652	174	6,076	58.72	24.72	38.2
Qiemo County	51,701	243	4,692	22.31	0	77.5
Yanqi (Huizu) County	115,823	621	5,408	44.89	7.64	28.85

continued on next page

TABLE 5.3 *(continued)*

City/County	Population	GDP (¥1,000,000)	GDP per Capita (¥)	Percent Han	Percent FPCC* in Area	Percent Uygur
Hejing County	167,410	771	4,572	55.22	23.51	22.87
Hoxud County (Heshuo)	62,240	335	4,769	68.43	19.98	13.86
Bohu County	55,211	269	4,882	65.81	10.68	16.05
AQSU DISTRICT	1,977,086	9,041	4,556	23.74	10.94	74.99
Aqsu (Akesu)	498,937	3,550	7,116	57.89	33.01	40.75
Wensu County	202,838	809	4,025	21.43	13.98	76.17
Kuqa County (Kuche)	368,440	1,625	4,272	9.49	0	89.93
Xayar County (Shaya)	183,042	821	4,519	14.6	0	84.05
Xinhe County	132,299	505	3,842	4.81	0	95.01
Baicheng County	190,248	388	2,042	12.08	0	87.03
Wushi County	173,789	406	2,340	6.73	4.6	90.01
Awat County (Awaiti)	187,505	874	4,664	17.74	8.1	81.59
Kalpin County (Keping)	39,988	62	1,574	2.54	0	97.31
KIZILSU DISTRICT	425,993	654	1,547	5.37	0.96	63.73
Artux (Atushi)	188,224	295	1,577	7.21	1.71	79.68
Akto County (Aketao)	160,621	198	1,245	2.15	0	69.74
Akqi County (Akqi)	34,253	66	1,924	6.8	0	4.59
Wuqia County	42,895	90	2,100	8.24	2.07	18.43
KASHGAR DISTRICT	3,279,450	7,315	2,230	9.1	4.54	89.37
Kashgar (Kashi)	311,141	994	3,197	17.87	0	81.24
Shufu County	348,564	598	1,709	5.02	0	94.69
Shule County	270,663	635	2,363	6.7	2.16	93
Yengisar County (Yingjisha)	211,688	357	1,696	1.79	0.66	97.82
Zepu County	164,898	450	2842	20.76	0	75.29
Shache County	601,815	942	1,565	3.47	0.15	95.71
Yecheng County	373,625	594	1,615	8.18	0.38	90.78
Markit County (Magaiti)	193,672	737	3,807	21.43	12.33	78.36
Yopurga County (Yuepuhu)	127,795	270	2,141	5.28	3.29	94.68
Jiashi County	294,021	623	2,157	3.52	3.33	96.46
Bachu County	351,050	1,131	3,223	16.41	28.87	83.12
Taxkorgan County (Tashiku'ergan)	30,518	43	1,401	5.08	0	6.28

continued on next page

TABLE 5.3 *(continued)*

City/County	Population	GDP (¥1,000,000)	GDP per Capita (¥)	Percent Han	Percent FPCC* in Area	Percent Uygur
HOTAN DISTRICT	1,580,898	30,006	1,920	3.08	1.41	96.91
Hotan (Hetian)	154,352	433	2,922	16.57	0	83.01
Hotan County (Hetian)	245,846	497	2,089	0.46	0	99.41
Moyu County	383,922	598	1,557	1.44	1.02	98.53
Pishan County	208,980	316	1,520	1.32	7.7	97.85
Lop County (Luopu)	220,917	411	1,879	1.36	0	98.6
Qira County (Cele)	130,445	265	2,036	1.51	1.73	98.45
Yutian County	203,869	401	1,965	1.37	0	98.56
Minfeng County	32,567	80	2,482	8.91	0	90.94

*FPCC is the agricultural population of Production and Construction Corps units in the area. Agricultural members of the PCC constituted about 75 percent of the PCC's total membership.

Source: 1999 Xinjiang Statistical Yearbook

in-bound migration in the range of 250,000 to 300,000 per year. All are assumed to be Han migrants.[38]

In official statistics, Han make up a little less than 40 percent of the population in the region. But this probably significantly understates the number of Han in Xinjiang. It probably excludes PLA and armed police-force members who are not originally from Xinjiang. There are no readily available figures on PLA and armed police deployments in Xinjiang, but given Xinjiang's size, sensitivity and importance, and security problems, these forces are likely to be in the 250,000 to 500,000 range, again with the vast majority being Han. In addition, if the flow of migrants is in the order of several hundred thousand per year, and has been for several years, it is not unreasonable to believe that Han may constitute a majority of the population living in Xinjiang at any particular moment.

CONCLUSION: POLITICAL EFFECTS AND THE LEGACY OF HAN COLONIALISM

One of the most often remarked features in theories of international imperialism is the link between local colonial elites and elites in the metropolitan power. For a variety of reasons that do not need to be explored here, nontrivial numbers of ethnic minorities have been co-opted to serve the PRC administration of Xinjiang. For Han leaders and Han elites, they are, in many if not all cases, token examples of what the Hans would like to project as the positive state of ethnic relations in China. For minorities who want little or nothing to do with China, ethnic elites in the military, the government, and the CCP apparatus are traitors.

These local ethnic leaders must conform to the vision of official nationality relations, and they dutifully repeat the official line to outsiders. Thus, in a meeting with foreign reporters, the regional governor (a Uygur) was quoted as saying, "It is good for Nanjiang [southern Xinjiang] for Han to be sent there. They meet the needs of development."[39] The mayors of Yining and Urumqi (both Uygurs) relayed similar views to foreign reporters on a number of occasions. (That foreign reporters were allowed an extensive visit to Xinjiang in the early fall of 2000 suggests the leadership felt the security situation was well under control. Nonetheless, stories filed by these reporters make clear that Uygur antipathy toward Han efforts is not hard to find, despite the often quite controlled nature of these press visits.) The official line implicitly accepts the view that the Uygurs in particular are too poor and ignorant to carry out economic development themselves. Only with an influx of Han migrants (or implicitly, total acceptance of Han/PRC ways by the national minorities) can Xinjiang rise. The fact that the center is investing heavily in Xinjiang is proof of Han/PRC good intentions and impartiality. The remedy for splittism is explicitly stated to be economic development. But this goes hand in glove with extensive suppression of the national minorities, the closing of mosques and Islamic schools, and other actions that make it harder for Uygurs and others to organize for collective action, even if such actions reinforce non-Chinese identities.

Probing the true thinking of minority elites in Xinjiang is impossible. Nonetheless, they are likely to play a key intermediary role between the central-government elites and local Han leaders. Behind closed doors, they may be able to adjust policy marginally and make Han more conscious of the consequences of their policies. Incremental changes of this nature are surely not likely to win support from those who are unreconciled to Han/PRC control. To exercise such possible influence, minority elites must echo the official view in public. They may be perceived as loyal tools of Han imperialism. Yet they may doing what they can to make that imperialism more tolerable, perhaps because they recognize that Han control is not going to go away.

The size of this stratum of minority officials in Xinjiang is hard to determine. Their presence, as long as they remain players in the colonial game, provides evidence for the myth of the "Chinese civilizing project." Ultimately, their example may be powerful enough to attract more minorities into accepting Han/PRC rule.

What can be said about the prospects for independence, or "splittism," in Xinjiang? There is no unified opposition and no widely agreed upon leader who is seen internationally (and even in China) as speaking for Uygurs or Xinjiang in the way that the Dalai Lama speaks for Tibet. Moreover, it is not clear that other minority peoples in Xinjiang would welcome a Uygur-based state. The proponents of independence have been willing to use violence to pursue their ends in ways that have greatly raised the costs of Chinese rule, and they have been met in return with fierce repression.[40] The disorienting effects of economic growth are undermining the "traditional" ways in much of Xinjiang, and divisions among and within minority groups are growing. As one traveler recounted,

> Young Uygurs, educated in Chinese institutions, were following the Han in accepting Western pop culture and mores. Islam forms the basis of Uygur identity, to be sure, but modernizing, secular layers are gradually accruing. Xinjiang's Uygurs may well come to feel as torn between East and West as many Turks are today. Rent by contradictions between Islamic traditions and acquired Western mores, and split along educational and generational lines, they will be more easily controllable by Beijing.[41]

Others appear to dispute this view. But what cannot be disputed is that Xinjiang (along with Tibet) is a core component of China in Han eyes. Increasingly, it is seen as vital for the economic future of China. The Chinese government has invested much more in Xinjiang than it has in Tibet, both in per capita terms and in the aggregate (as table 5.1 shows), and the per capita income in Xinjiang ranks considerably higher. Thus, the PRC will not allow an independent Turkistan to become an option. This is likely to harden non-Han opposition and make Han rule in the short to medium term more difficult and costly, in terms of human rights as well as finances. But over time, the influx of Han, the co-optation of local people, and rising incomes will limit the effectiveness of any calls for independence. For the most part, Uygurs and others will not be assimilated, but increasingly, Han China is giving them a choice: participate in the process of Chinese rule and do better economically or resist and be suppressed (and be economically ignored). This is not an attractive choice. It is hard to think of a time when other options were available to either Han or non-Han in

Xinjiang. But short of a political collapse in the Chinese heartland causing the Han hold on Xinjiang to slip, China has demonstrated the will
and the power (and the diplomatic skill) to impose its control over Xinjiang. It will not be easily displaced.

POST–SEPTEMBER 11 DEVELOPMENTS

The Government of the PRC quickly signified its support for the U.S.
War on Terrorism in the aftermath of the terrorist attacks in the United
States on September 11, 2001. This cooperative approach was linked with
efforts by the Chinese government to brand Uygur organizations in general as terrorist and to associate them with the Taliban and Osama bin
Laden in particular. At the rhetorical level, in mid-January 2002, the State
Council Information Office issued a lengthy document laying out a
litany of alleged terrorist activities undertaken by Uygur independence
organizations. Although many specific acts of violence were detailed, no
supporting evidence was provided. "Incomplete statistics" cited in the
report reveal that 162 people were killed in Xinjiang between 1990 and 2001,
and more than 440 were injured. Interestingly, Uygurs and other non-
Han who worked at low levels in the state administration seem to have
been a special target for attack and assassination, with more than a dozen
examples provided (or close to 10 percent of the incomplete statistics.)[42]
Yet no attacks occurring after September 11 were reported in the document, and despite the purported ties of separatist forces to the Taliban and
other external sources, knives and explosives, rather than guns and other
weapons, seem to have been used most often in "terrorist" activities.

Publication of the State Council document had consequences: Muslim clerics were required to demonstrate their allegiance *(biaotai)* to the
Chinese state, and religious activity was strictly controlled and monitored
by the ever-present police and military forces. China continued its efforts
to extradite Xinjiang opposition figures from the Central Asian states (the
State Council document reported that a dozen or so had already been
returned to China); Beijing received a promise from Afghan interim leader
Hamid Karzai that Afghanistan would return any Muslim separatist with
Chinese citizenship as part of China's $150 million aid package to post-
Taliban Afghanistan.[43] All the while, repression, extensive well before Sep-
tember 11, continued unabated.

These actions serve to illustrate the Chinese view that Xinjiang is an
inalienable part of China and that the state and its agents will do whatever it takes to incorporate Xinjiang into China more fully. Opportunist

actions, such as linking the Uygur opposition with September 11, serve to contain U.S. and human-rights organizations' criticisms of China's ongoing suppression of minority groups. At the same time, its efforts to expand economic development in Xinjiang continue, with Han in the vanguard. Chinese aid to Afghanistan comes with significant strings attached. Every possible means is used to further China's control over its largest "autonomous" region.

NOTES

I owe a special debt to Neil R. Taylor for making the maps. I gratefully acknowledge the assistance of Morris Rossabi and the other conference participants.

1. Goncharov, Lewis, and Xue, *Uncertain Partners,* 121.

2. Holloway, *Stalin,* 177; Li et al., *Dangdai Zhongguo de he gongye,* 19–20; Fu, *Dangdai Zhongguo de Xinjiang,* 393–94, 451.

3. MacMillen, *Communist Power,* 23–24, 122, notes the presence of Soviet consulates in Urumqi and the Ili district.

4. See Fu, *Dangdai Zhongguo de Xinjiang,* and *Zhongguo Gongchandang Xinjiang Weiwuer Zizhiqu* for general background.

5. The case of Tibet is very well known. On Inner Mongolia, see Woody, *Cultural Revolution in Inner Mongolia.* Guangxi's experience during the Cultural Revolution is also known to have been very violent, including reported cases of cannibalism.

6. *Zhongguo binggong nianjian,* 594–98. Information on the location of these enterprises comes from the 1995 Industrial Census. The Third Front was a Maoist policy of military industrialization that began in 1964. Its goal was to build weapons plants in the Chinese interior so that when one or both superpowers invaded and occupied the industrialized heartland, the Chinese people could continue to resist by fighting a "people's war." For details, see Naughton, "Third Front."

7. For more detail on Guangxi, see *Guangxi guofang gongye.*

8. McMillen, "Xinjiang and Wang Enmao," esp. 574–81.

9. For PCC membership figures, see *Xinjiang shengchan Jianshe Bingtuan 1998 tongji nianjian,* 39. Data on heavy and light industry and central subsidies comes from *Quanguo ge sheng, zizhiqu, zhixiashi lishi tongji ziliao* and various Xinjiang statistical yearbooks.

10. On petroleum development in Xinjiang and some of its implications for internal and external security, see Christoffersen, "China's Intentions," and Krekel, "Cross Border Trade."

11. Despite its having a coast, most discussions of coastal provinces exclude Guangxi, and Guangxi has been less centrally involved with (and received fewer benefits from) the Open Door Policy, a policy that signaled China's renewed political and commercial relations with the rest of the world after 1998.

12. My spelling of subregional political units in Xinjiang generally follows the rendering found in *Zhongguo diminglu.* Where these are not obvious, I also translit-

erate the Chinese characters in pinyin. The exceptions are Uygur (Uighur), Kashgar (Kaxgar), Aqsu (Aksu), and Hoten (Hotan).

13. *Xinjiang tongji nianjian* (1989), 60–65; *Xinjiang tongji nianjian* (1999), 60–65.

14. *Zhongguo Disanci Gongye Pucha ziliao guangpan.*

15. *Xinjiang tongji nianjian* (1998), 347; *Xinjiang tongji nianjian* (1999), 347, 480.

16. *Xinjiang tongji nianjian* (1998), 347, 468.

17. Ibid., 347.

18. *Quanguo ge sheng, zizhiqu, zhixiashi lishi tongji ziliao,* 923.

19. *Xinjiang tongji nianjian* (1998), 347.

20. *Xinjiang tongji nianjian* (1999), 347, 480.

21. *Xinjiang tongji nianjian* (1998), 571, table.

22. See Becquelin, "Xinjiang in the Nineties."

23. Yang, "'Ru shi' hou."

24. See Stone, "Coming to Grips"; Micklin, "Desiccation of the Aral Sea"; and Abdiiaev, "Disaster Zone."

25. See *Xinjiang Shengchan Jianshe Bingtuan 1997 nianjian,* inside cover.

26. *Quanguo ge sheng, zizhiqu, zhixiashi lishi tongji ziliao,* 944.

27. *Xinjiang tongji nianjian* (1998), 189–91.

28. Hannum and Xie, "Ethnic Stratification."

29. See, for example, Gladney, "Representing the Nationality"; Dikotter, *Discourse of Race;* and Harrell, "Introduction."

30. Sautman, "Is Xinjiang an Internal Colony?"

31. Selden, *The Yenan Way,* 251–54.

32. For background on the PCC, see McMillen, "Xinjiang and the Production," 65–96.

33. *Xinjiang Shengchan Jianshe Bingtuan 1997 nianjian,* 5–8 and *Zhonghua Renmin Gongheguo 1995 nian,* 1.

34. *Zhonghua Renmin Gongheguo 1985 nian Disanci Quanguo Gongye Pucha ziliao huibian,* 572.

35. See Seymour and Anderson, *New Ghosts, Old Ghosts,* 44–71, and *Xinjiang Shengchan Jianshe Bingtuan 1997 nianjian,* 112–31.

36. Gu Chaolin, oral presentation at the China Colloquium, University of Washington China Studies Program, Seattle, Wash., October 2000.

37. Based on figures from *Xinjiang tongji nianjian* (1990–1999).

38. Tayler, "Foreign Affairs," 4; Pomfret, "In China's Wild West"; and "China: Xinjiang Receives Rising Numbers of Migrant Farmers."

39. Kwang, "Outpost Set to Rise," 4

40. Amnesty International, "Gross Violations of Human Rights."

41. Taylor, "Foreign Affairs," 3.

42. Information Office of the State Council, "'East Turkistan's Terrorist Forces."

43. See Zhongguo Xinwenshe, "Xinjiang Mobilizes"; Xinhua News Agency, "Chinese News Agency Says"; Agence France-Presse, "Muslims Placed under Tight Control"; and Agence France-Presse, "Karzai Agrees to Repatriate."

6 / Tibet and China in the Twentieth Century

MELVYN C. GOLDSTEIN

Chinese policies toward Tibetans and their language, culture, and religion are no longer the esoteric domain of area specialists. They have become a part of American domestic politics and Sino-American relations.

No issue is more difficult or important for the foreign policy and strategic interests of the United States and the stability of Asia than America's relationship with the People's Republic of China (PRC), and Tibet is a part of that. Crafting (recrafting) a coherent and effective China policy in the coming decade(s) is clearly a priority. Accomplishing this will entail reexamining a number of volatile problem areas, such as Taiwan, nuclear proliferation, trade imbalances, and human rights. It will also require addressing Tibet[1] and the Tibet question (the question of what should be the status of Tibet vis-à-vis China).

The Tibet question has attained enormous international visibility and is today a contentious component of American domestic politics. America's long-cherished Wilsonian ideals and the increasing support for integrating universal human rights in international affairs has facilitated moving the Dalai Lama and the Tibet question from the dark recesses of the State Department to the spotlight of domestic politics. Over the past fifteen years, Congress has become the major force pushing Tibet into Sino-American relations and policy. Congressional interest, moreover, is unusual in that it cuts across normal party lines and ideological persuasions (Tom Lantos and Jessie Helms, for example, both support a pro-Tibetan policy for the United States). Congressional activism on the Tibet issue has taken a number of directions, including funding Tibetan-language broadcasts by the Voice of America (VOA) and Radio Free Asia and passing a number of (nonbinding) resolutions that characterize Tibet as a "captive nation."

But Tibet's visibility goes well beyond Congress. In the broader global arena, the Dalai Lama is widely known and respected, draws huge audiences wherever he lectures, and receives favorable coverage in the world's media and editorial pages. In addition, there has been a proliferation of private Tibet "support" groups, such as the International Campaign for

Tibet, Students for a Free Tibet, the Tibet Information Network, and the International Committee of Lawyers for Tibet. These groups have frequent input into the public and political arenas and have lobbied hard and effectively in Washington. Human-rights groups such as Asia Watch and Amnesty International have also repeatedly criticized China's treatment of Tibetans, again raising the visibility of the Tibet question in the United States and in the international community.

Tibet, therefore, is today an integral part of Sino-American relations, and it is an area whose volatility may increase in the future. The Dalai Lama and his government in exile deplore current Chinese policies in Tibet and argue that they threaten the future viability of Tibetan religion and culture. Some Tibetans, therefore, talk of the need for more militancy if progress toward resolution is not forthcoming. Widespread condemnation of the terrorist attacks on the United States on 11 September 2001 has made a turn to violence by radical Tibetan nationalists very unlikely but does not preclude a shift to more militant forms of "civil disobedience," such as hunger strikes. As the United States struggles to craft a stable policy for U.S.-China relations, it will be hard pressed to ignore the situation of Tibetans in the PRC. In 1999, for example, Sino-American relations were shaken when a seemingly innocuous World Bank poverty-alleviation project in China's remote Qinghai Province became a major political controversy because the project would have altered the demographic composition of a Mongolian-Tibetan minority prefecture. The project generated widespread (and organized) criticism from Tibet support groups, members of Congress, academics, and human-rights groups, and this outcry pressured the Clinton administration to vote against funding the measure, despite the fact that this would infuriate Beijing. It also persuaded the World Bank to empower an independent inspection panel to reexamine the proposed intervention, which ultimately led to its demise as a World Bank project.[2]

Reassessing America's China policy in the new Bush administration, therefore, will require addressing the Tibet conflict and developing policy options for it within the context of Sino-American relations. In turn, that will require understanding objectively what has happened in Tibet since it became part of the PRC in 1951, what is occurring there now, and what concatenation of forces has interacted to produce these results. It will also require understanding the strategic options available to the parties in the conflict and the constraints they face in choosing among them.

The Tibet issue today differs from the other core problem areas in Sino-

American relations because not only has there has been relatively little first-hand scientific research in the Tibetan areas in China but there has also been a tidal wave of misleading and often dissembling partisan writing and rhetoric generated by the combatants and their supporters. Both sides have expended an enormous amount of time and effort to spread their representations of past history and contemporary politics, the result being diametrically opposed constructions of reality that make it difficult for any but specialists to assess.

At the core of the conflict is the historical dispute over the status of Tibet. The Chinese vociferously argue that Tibet has been part of China for hundreds of years and therefore properly is a part of China now. Tibetans equally adamantly contend that Tibet was not a part of China until its conquest by the PRC in 1951 and is today a captive nation with the right to independence. While no short essay can adequately explicate the complex history of Sino-Tibetan relations, this chapter will address some of the core issues in this bitter conflict and present a balanced account of how the conflict has evolved during the past century and where it stands now.

HISTORICAL OVERVIEW

All sides agree that Tibet was independent of China until the Mongols arose on the Asian scene in the thirteenth century. Chinese claims over Tibet begin with the creation of the Yuan (Mongol) dynasty in China (1271–1368), when Tibet, already subordinate to the Mongols, became part of that empire. Tibetans, however, do not see this as evidence that Tibet is a part of China because they contend that they were not part of China but rather of a Mongol empire that had also conquered China. Moreover, they argue that the relationship between the Mongol emperors of China and Tibet's lama rulers was that of "priest and patron," the Mongol rulers serving as patrons of Tibet in return for the spiritual guidance of Tibet's great lamas.

The period after the fall of the Mongol dynasty in 1368 is also contested. China claims that the ethnically Chinese Ming dynasty (1368–1644) ruled Tibet, but Tibetans contend that although contacts between Tibetan lamas and the new Ming emperors continued, China exerted no authority over Tibet during this period.

The conquest of China in 1644 by a non-Chinese confederation, the Manchu, soon led to Tibet's subordination to the new Qing dynasty (1644–1911). It sent armies to Tibet four times in the eighteenth century and, in the process, established a loose protectorate over Tibet, which, however, did not become an integral part of China because it was not ruled by Chinese laws, language, and institutions. The Qing dynasty's Tibet policy was aimed at controlling the religious and lay leaders of Tibet and did not seek to incorporate Tibet or to assimilate and sinicize Tibet's culture, institutions, and bureaucracy. Tibet, therefore, continued to be ruled by Tibetans, using their own language and customs.

From the apex of its power in Tibet at the end of the eighteenth century, the Manchu dynasty's hegemony gradually declined. In the nineteenth century, the Qing dynasty was weakened by internal disorder and external attacks by Western imperialists. Tibet became a backwater of little strategic interest, receiving little attention in Beijing. The Qing dynasty continued to post imperial commissioners *(amban)* to, and station a garrison in, Tibet, but by the last quarter of the nineteenth century, Tibet paid only lip service to China. The arrival of the British in the Himalayas changed the situation, threatening China's hegemony and stimulating a renewed Chinese interest in solidifying its position in Tibet.

During the nineteenth century, the British colonial government in India expanded its political influence from the Indian subcontinent to Nepal, Sikkim, and Bhutan in the Himalayas. Through a series of agreements with these kingdoms, it enlarged the territory of colonial India. Darjeeling, for example, was ceded by Sikkim to the British in 1835.[3] However, as British India sought to develop relations and trade with Tibet, it ran into a stone wall. The Tibetan government refused to meet and discuss this with British officials, and when Britain sought to open relations with Tibet through its nominal overlord, China, Tibet still refused.

In 1903, after years of frustration and failure, the British invaded Tibet with the aim of forcing the thirteenth Dalai Lama to negotiate. The Dalai Lama again disregarded Chinese urgings to talk with the British and in 1904, fled to Outer Mongolia as the British Expeditionary Force was about to enter Lhasa. The British troops compelled the Tibetans to sign an agreement granting the invaders a number of important concessions, such as the establishment of trade marts in Tibet and the payment of a large indemnity.[4] Known as the Anglo-Tibetan Convention of 1904, this agreement between Great Britain and Tibet would have excluded Chinese authority in Tibet and made Tibet a virtual British dependency if it had been implemented as originally written.

However, London felt that the head of its expeditionary force had exceeded his mandate and decided to water down the terms of the Anglo-Tibetan Convention. Although it agreed that some concessions secured from Tibet were useful, it did not want to create an international issue by making Tibet its dependency. So when China stepped in and offered to pay the indemnity levied against Tibet, Britain agreed and began negotiating with Beijing to secure China's agreement to the concessions. In 1906, Britain and China signed an Anglo-Chinese convention that confirmed the concessions and reaffirmed the legitimate authority of China over Tibet. Tibet was not consulted about this. This Anglo-Chinese convention was itself "affirmed" in 1907 via an Anglo-Russian agreement on Tibet.[5]

The British invasion of Tibet and the diplomatic aftermath was a defining event in Sino-Tibetan relations. Though the British knew that Tibetans were running their own government and that China had no real authority there, Britain decided to lend diplomatic validation to Beijing's contention that Tibet was subordinate to China.

At the same time, the invasion refocused Chinese attention on Tibet. From Beijing's vantage point, Tibet had almost been lost because the thirteenth Dalai Lama and his government had been ignoring Chinese instructions with impunity. Consequently, although the Manchu dynasty was on its last legs, it responded forcefully, taking steps to increase its direct control over Tibet. A new imperial commissioner was appointed who pursued a more hard-line policy that sought greater control over the government in Tibet. The new Chinese commissioner began to make plans to train a modern army and secularize the Tibetan government by creating lay governmental boards. Discussions were also held to build roads and telegraph lines and to make use of Tibet's natural resources. Similarly, a new Chinese school was opened in Lhasa in 1907 and a military college in 1908; new Tibetan stamps with Chinese script were issued, and more officials were sent to Tibet. At the same time, China (under General Zhao Erfeng) had taken direct administrative control over most of the ethnic Tibetan areas east of the Yangzi River in today's Sichuan Province. In 1909–10, Zhao sent an army to Lhasa, this action precipitating the flight of the thirteenth Dalai Lama to exile in India and his deposition by the Manchu emperor. Had this new integrationist policy continued for long, Tibet would likely have been converted into a directly administered part of China.

Tibet, however, escaped this fate when the Qing dynasty was overthrown by Chinese nationalists in 1911–12. By 1913, the thirteenth Dalai Lama had expelled all Chinese troops and officials and declared complete self-rule. For the next thirty-seven years (1913–1951), Tibet functioned as an independent nation, conducting all governmental functions without interference from China or any other country. However, Tibet's status was far from settled, since the new Chinese Republican government continued to claim Tibet as a part of China. Tibet, therefore, was going to have to negotiate a new status with China or be prepared to defend its de facto independence.

Tibet quickly sought to reach an agreement with China's new rulers and received assistance in this from British India. The government of British India had found China a bad neighbor during the 1905–11 period of direct Chinese power in Tibet and wanted to prevent any recurrence of such direct control. It pressured the new Chinese government to participate in a conference with itself and Tibet in Simla, India, in 1913.

The Tibetans initially asserted their independence from China at this conference, but the final draft of the Simla Convention was a compromise. While declaring that Tibet would be completely *autonomous* from China, it acknowledged Chinese *suzerainty* over Tibet. Tibetans would administrate Tibet with their own officials in accordance with their own customs and laws, and China would not be permitted to station large numbers of troops or officials in Tibet. However, China could maintain an imperial commissioner and an escort of three hundred men there. This compromise was not the independence Tibet wanted, but nonetheless, it was acceptable to the Tibetan elite because it met their nationalistic sensibilities by guaranteeing that they would retain complete control over Tibet's affairs, including the army, currency, and so forth. It would also legitimize a mutually agreed upon identity for Tibet vis-à-vis China. Both sides agreed to this political compromise. What proved impossible to reconcile was the delineation of the border.

Britain proposed a number of compromise solutions regarding the frontier, but in the end, the Chinese government repudiated these and refused to ratify the Simla Convention. Britain and Tibet signed a bilateral note that bound each other to the terms of the unsigned Simla Convention, but since China did not agree to Simla, Tibet's status was not settled. China continued to vociferously claim that Tibet was part of China although it was unable to transform its verbal claims over Tibet into on-the-ground reality because of the Japanese invasion and World War II. But China was enormously successful on the publicity and diplomatic fronts, and Tibet's de facto status as an independent polity was not accepted internationally. The relevant Western countries, such as Britain, Russia (the U.S.S.R.), and later, the United States, refused to alienate China over Tibet. Consequently, as the Chinese Communists came to power in 1949, Tibet was operating as a fully de facto independent polity but was not recognized as independent by the international community, including newly independent India. All, in one form or another, accepted Tibet as a part of China, albeit an autonomous part.

TIBET AND THE PEOPLE'S REPUBLIC OF CHINA

The founding of the PRC on 1 October 1949 began a new chapter in Chinese history and in Sino-Tibetan relations. Tibet's inability to reach a satisfactory settlement of its status with the precommunist governments of China meant it now had to deal with a very much stronger Chinese communist government. The PRC, like previous Chinese regimes, considered that Tibet had been and should again be a part of China and was committed to reuniting it. Its reasons were both nationalistic and strategic. Redressing the humiliations China suffered at the hands of the imperialists was a goal of all nationalistic Chinese, and reunifying the disparate parts of China under a strong central government was seen as a means to that end. One of the stars on the PRC's flag represents Tibet; the idea of allowing such a huge area to go its own way was unpalatable, particularly since not reintegrating Tibet presented serious national-security dangers. The United States' anticommunist crusade and the anti-Chinese bent of Tibet's leaders made it likely that an independent Tibet would be pulled into the American anti–Communist China orbit. If this occurred, China's potential enemies would be sitting right at the edge of Sichuan, China's largest province. The new communist government, therefore, from the beginning, unconditionally asserted its sovereignty over Tibet. And with an army of several million battle-hardened troops, there was little doubt it could impose its views on Tibet.

The question for the new rulers of China was not whether to incorporate Tibet but how best to do so. The early nationality policy of the Chinese Communist Party (CCP) was modeled after the U.S.S.R.'s nationality system, wherein major nationality areas were given the status of republics, with considerable autonomy (on paper) and *theoretically* even the right to secede from the Soviet Union. By the 1940s, however, the CCP had shifted its policy on ethnic minorities to favor what it called "autonomous regions" for minority peoples. Conceptually, these autonomous regions were less "autonomous" than the U.S.S.R.'s republics and did not, for example, have the right to secede. Nevertheless, China's political system gave minority groups living in compact communities the right to exercise authority over an autonomous region where their language could be used and their customs and culture preserved. How much cultural, religious, and political autonomy was allowed, however, differed in each region.

In the case of Tibet, Mao Zedong was willing to militarily "liberate" Tibet if necessary, but he decided from the start that this was to be done only as a last resort. Mao understood that Tibet was very different from other minority areas because it had been operating independently for four decades and because there were no Chinese living there. Mao decided, therefore, that China should make a major effort to "liberate" Tibet peacefully, that is, with the agreement of the Dalai Lama and the government of Tibet. If China could accomplish this, the risk of Tibet's status becoming internationalized as part of the Cold War would be avoided and Tibetans themselves would come to accept the legitimacy of Tibet's being a part of China.

To facilitate this goal, Mao formulated a special policy of moderation and gradualism for Tibet, in which socialist reforms would not be emphasized immediately and the government of the Dalai Lama would be allowed to continue to function internally. Mao's policy focused on first winning over Tibet's religious and aristocratic elites, especially the Dalai Lama, to being part of China and to the value of socialist reforms and modernization. Since Tibet's elites did not consider themselves part of China and were strongly committed to religion, Mao conceded that it would take time to persuade them to change their views.

China tried hard to persuade the Dalai Lama to send officials to negotiate Tibet's reunification with China, offering relatively liberal terms. Tibet, however, was not interested. It was adamantly opposed to giving up its de facto independence and becoming part of an atheist, communist China. Negotiations with Beijing, therefore, never got off the ground, and in October 1950, Mao ordered the People's Liberation Army (PLA) to invade Tibet's eastern province. The aim of this attack was not so much to conquer Tibet as to force the Tibetan government to negotiate "peaceful" liberation. Thus, after quickly vanquishing the Tibetan opposing forces in the east, the PLA stopped, and China again asked Lhasa to negotiate an agreement. Militarily disorganized and bereft of outside help, the fourteenth Dalai Lama sent a negotiating team to Beijing. It reluctantly signed the Seventeen-Point Agreement for the Peaceful Liberation of Tibet in May 1951. This agreement formally recognized Chinese sovereignty over Tibet for the first time. It also allowed units of the PLA to move into Tibet, to defend the borders, to establish a Tibet Military Area Headquarters to gradually absorb the local Tibetan army, and to create a Military Administration Bureau in Tibet to oversee the administration of the agreement. Tibet was now an integral part of China, but it also had a unique status in the PRC, since China agreed not to unilaterally alter the existing political system in Tibet or the established status, functions, and powers of the Dalai Lama. Tibet, it said, had the right to exercise regional autonomy under leadership of the central PRC government. This meant that the CCP allowed the feudal system, with its serflike peasantry, to persist, and it allowed the Dalai Lama's government to continue to rule Tibet internally in accordance with its own language and traditional laws. All issues such as taxes, land tenure, crime, disputes between Tibetans, and appointments were handled by the Dalai Lama's government without consultation with the Chinese generals in Tibet or Chinese law.

However, the Seventeen-Point Agreement also indicated that reforms would come at some time in the future:

> In matters related to various reforms in Tibet, there will be no compulsion on the part of the central authorities. The local government of Tibet should carry out reforms of its own accord, and when the people raise demands for reform, they shall be settled by means of consultation with the leading personnel of Tibet.[6]

But there was no timetable for reforms, and the traditional Tibetan government headed by the Dalai Lama actually continued to rule Tibet internally until the Dalai Lama's flight to exile in 1959.

While these events were unfolding, the United States tried hard in 1951 to convince the Dalai Lama to denounce the Seventeen-Point Agreement and flee into exile. Washington even offered to permit him to move to the United States with a few hundred of his leading officials.[7] The American initiative, however, failed, as the Dalai Lama believed the U.S. offer of support was inadequate. It did not contain a clear commitment to support Tibet as an independent country and also failed to pledge substantial military aid to defeat China. The Dalai Lama, therefore, decided to try to live under the new agreement with China. But the role of the United States as a hostile force trying to drive a wedge between Tibetans and Beijing had begun. Some in China see today's U.S. Tibet policy as a new version of that position.

In the fall of 1951, Chinese troops and officials peacefully entered Tibet, and a sensitive interregnum began, in which both sides coexisted under the terms of the Seventeen-Point Agreement. The Chinese officials concentrated on setting up garrisons, offices, and roads, that is, on stabilizing their position in Tibet. They presented themselves to Tibetans as "new Chinese," who were there not to exploit and abuse the Tibetan people, as had Chinese in the past, but rather to help develop Tibet. The Chinese military administrators in Tibet showed respect for Tibetan culture and religion, giving alms, for example, to all twenty thousand of the monks in the Lhasa area. No attempts were made to incite the poor serfs to challenge the Dalai Lama's government. This gave Tibet a unique status in the PRC.

However, from the beginning, some within the Chinese military in Tibet proposed a different, "hard-line" strategy regarding how China should handle Tibet. General Fan Ming advocated moving quickly to implement political and socioeconomic reforms in Tibet. His faction felt that the CCP should show preference to Tibet's second highest lama, the Panchen Lama, since that lama and his top officials were, in Chinese communist parlance, "progressives." In particular, Fan argued that a separate autonomous region should be set up in the Panchen's area. There, the Panchen Lama on his own would be able to initiate the process of land reform, knowledge of which would spread to the Dalai Lama's region; this would raise the consciousness of the serfs there, who also would quickly demand land reform, thus forcing the Dalai Lama's government to yield.

Mao, however, disagreed. He reasoned that the Tibetan peasantry was too backward and too enthralled with religion for this hard-line approach to achieve China's long-term goal, so he consistently rejected it and in the early 1950s, blocked all attempts at prematurely forcing reforms or favoring the Panchen Lama over the Dalai Lama.

For Tibetans, the Seventeen-Point Agreement and the arrival of a large contingent of Chinese troops and officials created an enormous crisis. Though they knew that they had been independent since 1913 and abhorred the atheism of communism, they had lost the war in their eastern province and, unlike South Korea, had been unsuccessful in securing effective Western support. To prevent a total invasion and the inevitable destruction and bloodshed it would create, they had accepted the Seventeen-Point Agreement and now had to decide how to deal with their new rulers.

The Tibetan government initially had no clear strategy and no unified policy: Should the government now move quickly to modernize and reform Tibet's exploitative traditional system (in the hope that it could devise methods to accomplish this without destroying key religious and cultural institutions, as well as its political autonomy)? Or should it hamper and obstruct the Chinese so that they would find Tibet too troublesome to rule directly and allow it to operate as a protectorate-like entity (as it had under the Manchus)? Issues such as these were not formally decided. The Tibetan government outwardly tried to maintain polite relations with the Chinese, but from the beginning, key Tibetan officials went out of their way to insult the Chinese generals and make life difficult for the Chinese forces. For example, the Tibetan government refused to replace the flag the Tibetan army carried on parade with the Chinese national flag, citing the somewhat disingenuous reason that this was not a Tibetan national flag but only the flag of the Tibetan army. At the same time, a Tibetan People's Party was organized with the covert backing of key Tibetan officials to protest the Chinese presence in Tibet. In 1952, violence between the Chinese army and the People's Party was only narrowly averted. This threat was diffused after the Dalai Lama dismissed the two main anti-Chinese prime ministers in 1952, but anti-Chinese hostility and anger continued among a large portion of the Tibetan elite who considered Tibet's theocratic system exemplary. These anti-Chinese sentiments and activities were encouraged by a small group of former Tibetan officials (including one of the Dalai Lama's elder brothers, Gyalo Thondup) who had gone into exile in India rather than live in Tibet under the Seventeen-Point Agreement. They urged their fellow countrymen not to acquiesce to the Chinese political and military presence in Tibet, dangling the possibility of active U.S. support for Tibet before their eyes.[8]

There was, therefore, no Tibetan consensus among the religious and secular elite as to how to deal with the agreement and the Chinese so as to preserve Tibetan autonomy and institutions. Nevertheless, the Dalai Lama personally favored reforms. In later years, he stated:

> In 1954, when I was in China, I really developed a feeling that Tibet could be transformed into a modern society through socialism, with the help of the Communist Party. Many Tibetan communists felt the same way and very strongly. They made [a] commitment to achieve this. On several occasions, I discussed my impression . . . with Chairman Mao. . . . I personally felt [at] that time that there were very positive signs, hopeful signs.[9]

These progressive views were welcomed in Beijing and Mao believed that the Dalai Lama would be the vehicle through which his "gradualist" plan for winning over the feudal and religious elites (and then the masses) would come to fruition. However, after the Dalai Lama returned to Tibet in 1955, he did not seek to persuade his people to support reforms and a modern Tibet under China. In fact, the situation deteriorated quickly.

China's decision to implement socialist land reform in the ethnic Tibetan areas east of Tibet proper in 1955–56 (in the Kham and Amdo regions of Sichuan and Qinghai Provinces) precipitated a bloody rebellion in these areas. Although these regions were not included in the Seventeen-Point Agreement because they had not been part of Tibet in 1950–51, events there generated enormous sympathy and anger in Lhasa, and when large numbers of defeated rebels and refugees began to pour into Lhasa in 1957, a new, more serious wave of anti-Chinese activity began in Tibet proper. The rebellion in Sichuan also brought the United States directly into the picture, and by 1957, the Central Intelligence Agency (CIA) was training and arming Tibetan guerrillas.

Mao made a last attempt to salvage his gradualist policy in 1957, when he reduced the number of Han cadre and troops in Tibet and cancelled proposed trial reforms there. He also promised the Dalai Lama in writing that China would not implement socialist land reforms in Tibet proper for the next six years, adding that if conditions were not ripe at the end of this period, he would postpone the reforms even further. But the Dalai Lama could or would not quell the unrest within Tibet. In March 1959, despite the fact that the old society continued in Tibet, with monasteries and aristocratic lords still in control of their estates and serfs, and with the Dalai Lama's government still ruling internally, an uprising broke out in Lhasa that ended with the Dalai Lama's flight into exile in India. The Dalai Lama then renounced the Seventeen-Point Agreement and sought support for Tibet's independence and self-determination. The Tibet question reemerged as an international and Cold War issue. Mao's gradualist policy had failed.

At the same time, the Tibetan rebellion also failed dismally. The CIA's support for the guerrillas was ineffective, and the Tibetan guerrilla forces were unable to hold on to any territory within Tibet as a "Free Tibet" base of operations. The CIA subsequently assisted the guerrillas in establishing a safe-haven base of operations in northern Nepal,[10] but this had no impact on the political situation in Tibet.

After the uprising, the Chinese government also renounced the Seventeen-Point Agreement and adopted a diametrically different policy for how it would treat Tibetans and their culture. The central authorities terminated the traditional Tibetan government, confiscated monastic and aristocratic estates, and closed down virtually all of Tibet's several thousand monasteries. The old society was over and a new, hard-line cultural policy installed. The gradualist policy, with its moderation and sensitivity to the continuance of Tibetan culture and values, was supplanted with a new policy that promoted class warfare and made the creation of proletarian solidarity the supreme goal. This policy reached its zenith during the Cultural Revolution (1966–76), when Tibetan customs were attacked and, in many cases, banned. Chinese policy in Tibet now denigrated Tibetan culture and civilization, characterizing them as feudal and backward. The 1950s policy of trying to persuade Tibetans to modernize and adopt socialist political and economic institutions while permitting them to retain all of their language, religion, and culture was over. Tibetans were encouraged to internalize the universalistic values of socialism and discard the particularistic values of Tibetan ethnicity. The primary identity for the overwhelming majority of Tibetans who were members of the proletariat, therefore, was socialist, not Tibetan; their core loyalty was to be with proletarian Han and other proletarian *minzu* (peoples) rather than with other Tibetans who were not members of the proletariat. Cultural identity was now marginalized and trivialized.

The eight-year transition period from 1951 to 1959, therefore, ended poorly for both Tibet and China. On the Tibetan side, the Dalai Lama and his government were unable to develop and implement a realistic compromise strategy that could persuade the Chinese to allow them a niche within China in which they could maximize Tibetan long-term autonomy and institutions. Different elements in the Tibetan elite pursued contradictory policies, the result of which was a premature and ineffective military confrontation that resulted in the destruction of the old society, including Buddhism and all that they were seeking to preserve. On the Chinese side, ideological zeal in prematurely implementing socialist changes in Tibetan areas in Sichuan thwarted the goal of gradually winning over Tibetans to accept being part of socialist China. Tibet and the Dalai Lama were now under the wing of the United States, and the Tibet question was again visible on the international stage.

The events of the 1950s also gave credence to the views of those in the CCP who had advocated a more hard-line approach to dealing with the question of how best to integrate Tibet into China. The hard-liners had argued that the best way to integrate Tibet into China and win over the people was rapidly to eliminate the system of serfdom (together with the elites who ruled the system, since they would never accept socialist reforms on their own). Consequently, another, less explicit consequence of the failure of Sino-Tibetan relations in the 1950s was that within the CCP, many now came to accept that it had been a mistake for the Party to coddle Tibet's religious elites and institutions. They discretely mentioned that the Party had been misguided in its views about the progressive attitudes of the Dalai Lama. The Dalai Lama, they asserted, had been duplicitous when he met Mao and Zhou Enlai in Beijing and gave them the impression he was a progressive in favor of reforming Tibet when in reality he was pursuing "splittist" policies. Although this view was not accurate with regard to the Dalai Lama, these cadres blamed the Party's gradualist strategy for the 1959 rebellion and the reinternationalization of the Tibet question; today, some in China consider this "moderation" policy to be one of the Party's (Mao's) greatest failures. If China had eliminated the old system quickly, they say, there would have been no revolt and no Dalai Lama in exile.

The hard-line, anti-Tibetan cultural policy of the post-1959 era appeared on the surface to achieve China's basic strategic goals in Tibet. The Chinese leadership in Tibet believed that the Tibetan masses, the previously exploited classes, were grateful and happy to have the old system ended. The view projected to Beijing from Lhasa was that the Tibetan proletarian masses had been won over to being loyal citizens of China and to socialist values and institutions. Hatred of the old society and hatred of class exploitation had supplanted ethnic and religious solidarity.

POST-MAO TIBET, 1978–

The rise to power of Deng Xiaoping produced major changes in China. Communes were disbanded and land was returned to the peasants under a long-term lease arrangement called the "household-responsibility" system, wherein the household again became the basic unit of production. Major changes also occurred in the cultural arena, as prohibitory rules about dress, customs, and religion were gradually ended. Similarly, normalization of relations with the United States and new initiatives to reconcile two outstanding conflicts that concerned the unity of the PRC— Taiwan and the Tibet question—were launched.

With regard to Tibet, China made a number of unilateral gestures in 1978, including releasing a group of prisoners and announcing that Tibetans would be able to visit relatives abroad. This developed quickly into a move to try to resolve the Tibet question by persuading the Dalai Lama and his followers to return to China. In 1979, Deng Xiaoping invited Gyalo Thondup to Beijing. Deng told the Dalai Lama's Chinese-speaking elder brother that apart from the question of total independence, all other issues could be discussed and all problems could be resolved. He also invited the Dalai Lama to send fact-finding delegations to Tibet. Beijing obviously believed that the delegations would be impressed by the progress that had been made in Tibet since 1959 and by the solidarity of the Tibetan people with the nation. It also believed that after twenty years in exile, the Dalai Lama would be eager to reach an agreement that would permit his return to Tibet. They were wrong.

Contrary to what the Chinese expected, the fact-finding delegations revealed to the exiles that Chinese proclamations of socialist progress in Tibet had little substance. The living standard of the Tibetan people was poor, economic development was minimal, and the Tibetan masses, despite twenty years of communist propaganda, still believed strongly in the Dalai Lama and had strong feelings for Tibetan religion and nationalism. Proletarian solidarity, in fact, had not replaced ethnic loyalties. Thus, the overall impact of the delegations' visits was precisely the opposite of what Beijing had hoped for, in that it bolstered the confidence of the exiles.

Beijing's external Dalai Lama strategy was paralleled by the development of a new internal strategy. Pushed by Party secretary Hu Yaobang, who admitted that the CCP had made serious mistakes in Tibet, the strategy had two main components: (1) an economic component—rapidly to improve the standard of living of individual Tibetans, and (2) a cultural or ethnic component—to make the Tibet Autonomous Region (TAR) more Tibetan in overall character by fostering a revitalization of Tibetan culture and religion (including more extensive use of the Tibetan language) and the withdrawal of large numbers of Chinese cadres, who would be replaced with Tibetans. In a speech in Lhasa, Hu announced a 180-degree shift from the antiethnic, antiminority cultural ideology of the Cultural Revolution, saying,

> So long as the socialist orientation is upheld, vigorous efforts must be made to revive and develop Tibetan culture, education, and science. The Tibetan people have a long history and a rich culture. The world-renowned ancient Tibetan culture included fine Buddhism, graceful music and dance, as well as medicine and opera, all of which are worthy of serious study and development. All ideas that ignore and weaken Tibetan culture are wrong. It is necessary to do a good job in inheriting and developing Tibetan culture.[11]

After the hard-line policies of the post-1959 era, this was a partial return to Mao's policy of moderation in the 1950s. Being "Tibetan" was again publicly valued by the state as an end in itself.

Not surprisingly, this ethnically conciliatory strategy evinced strong objections from a faction of hard-line Chinese and Tibetan civil and military leaders, who insisted that allowing religion and monasteries to flourish again in Tibet would inevitably fan the flames of nationalism and "split-tism." Nevertheless, Beijing started to liberalize within Tibet. It also invited the Dalai Lama to send a negotiating delegation to Beijing. The Dalai Lama accepted, and in October 1982, three exile representatives arrived in Beijing. This was their first official contact since 1959. An end to the Tibet question seemed at hand.

The problem facing the Dalai Lama and his leaders was what kind of a compromise to seek. They genuinely felt that they deserved self-determination and independence. However, they also understood that China was a powerful nation and they had few bargaining chips. The focal decision, therefore, was whether they should take a tough approach, demanding semi-independence (i.e., total internal political control and a reunification of all Tibetans in China under one government as part of a "Greater Tibet"), or whether they should adopt a more conciliatory and realistic posture wherein they would accept far less (in the belief that this was a unique moment for them to secure a deal that would allow the Dalai Lama and the exiles to return to Tibet). These very difficult choices prompted months of in-depth discussions in Dharamsala, but in the end, there was no consensus as to how low the Dalai Lama's "bottom line" should be drawn regarding political concessions. The Dalai Lama, consequently, sent high-level representatives to Beijing with a brief to talk only in general terms—for example, to present historical arguments about Tibet and Sino-Tibetan relations and issues such as the "priest-patron" relationship. The discussions, therefore, did not get down to substantive issues about terms for the Dalai Lama's return, and from the beginning, there were tensions that revealed the enormous gap that existed in thinking (e.g., the Chinese insisted that the Tibetans refer to Tibet as "the local area of Tibet," while the exiles used the term meaning "Tibet as a separate country"). In the end, the Tibetans made only a single comment about their political position, stating in passing that if China was willing to offer Taiwan the "one country–two systems" option, then Tibet should receive far more, since Tibetans are different culturally, linguistically, and racially.[12] The Chinese response to this is revealing of Beijing's thinking—Tibet is already liberated and Taiwan is not.[13]

Thus, though Deng Xiaoping had announced that anything other than independence could be discussed, Beijing had no intention of allowing real political autonomy in Tibet. The extent to which Tibetan language, culture, and religion could be practiced was negotiable, but a different political system was not. Beijing was thinking about the Dalai Lama and the exiles returning to China and being integrated into the existing institutions of the TAR as loyal citizens of a multiethnic nation, whereas the Dalai Lama's representatives appeared intent on returning to Tibet as rulers of an autonomous region. The Chinese, therefore, were disappointed by the Tibetans' attitude and by the exile's unwillingness to accept their fundamental given—that Tibet would remain ruled by the CCP. Beijing, which had power and international acceptance on its side, wanted rapprochement, but only on its terms. It did not want to enter into a genuine give-and-take with the exiles over the issue of making changes in the political control of the TAR, let alone about the possibility of reuniting all ethnic Tibetans in China, as the exiles wanted.

In the end, therefore, this historic meeting not only produced no new movement toward resolving the Tibet question, but it began to raise serious questions in Beijing about the feasibility of rapprochement with the Dalai Lama. And when the exiled leadership continued to attack Chinese policies and human-rights violations in Tibet (e.g., with charges of Chinese genocide),[14] opponents of the new "moderation" policy in China interpreted the Dalai Lama's response as a sign of his insincerity. In fact, those who believed that China should settle the Tibet problem without the Dalai Lama explicitly saw this as déjà vu—as a replay of what they considered the duplicitous behavior of the Dalai Lama and his government in the 1950s. This may not be fair, but given the history of the two poles of Chinese strategic thinking about how to end the Tibet problem, it is not surprising.

Nevertheless, a second face-to-face meeting between Tibetan representatives and China was held in Beijing in 1984. At this meeting, the Tibetans came with a developed negotiating position that included the creation of a Greater Tibet, comprising all ethnic Tibetans in China (i.e., the 1.8 million in Tibet proper and the 2.1 million in the neighboring Chinese provinces).[15] This Greater Tibet would be demilitarized and would have a different political system than the rest of China. This strategy turned out to be unsuccessful. Beijing was seeking to enhance its stability and security in Tibet, not lessen it by turning over political control of Tibet to its adversaries in Dharamsala, let alone give up control over a Greater Tibet. If China let Tibet have a different political system, how could it refuse requests from Xinjiang or Shanghai? Dharamsala's leaders, in one sense, had misjudged both their own leverage and Beijing's desire for an agreement, but in another sense, the exile leaders *simply could not bring themselves to contemplate accepting anything less.* They were not sure they wanted to make any agreement that would entail their renouncing independence, much less, one where they would simply return as citizens of

China. Both, therefore, became angry and frustrated by the other's intransigence. In this strained atmosphere, a proposed visit of the Dalai Lama to China (Tibet) fell by the wayside.

Beijing, in the meantime, continued its "internal" reform strategy by allocating increased funds for economic development and allowing greater expression of minority culture (e.g., allowing monasteries to reopen as religious centers). Dharamsala, therefore, found itself in an awkward situation. It was clear that Beijing had no intention of allowing them to rule Tibet with a different political system, and it was also clear that Beijing was pursuing, with at least some success, their worst-case scenario, in that its new reforms and valorization of "being Tibetan" might gradually win the support of Tibetans. At the same time, China's economic power and international prestige and stature were increasing. Thus, there was a danger that the exile's role in the Tibet question would be marginalized.

Dharamsala and the Dalai Lama responded in 1986–87 by launching a new political offensive. In what we might think of as their "international campaign,"[16] they sought to secure new Western political and economic leverage that would force Beijing to offer concessions. In essence, they were trying to move the Tibet question from the cloistered realm of the U.S. State Department to the front stage of American domestic politics. At the same time, they thought that the campaign would give Tibetans in Tibet new hope that the Dalai Lama was on the verge of securing U.S. and Western assistance to settle the Tibet question (i.e., that it would shift Tibetans' attention from Beijing to the Dalai Lama). It was a dangerous undertaking, since having the Dalai Lama make an international appeal was certain to infuriate Beijing and further inflame the distrust that many in Beijing and Lhasa had about his and the exiles' motives.

DHARAMSALA'S INTERNATIONAL CAMPAIGN

The key innovation in the campaign was having the Dalai Lama for the first time carry the exiles' political message to the United States and Europe. Prior to this, he had traveled and spoken only as a religious leader and in fact, first visited the United States only in 1979, having previously been denied a visa for ten years. Now, with the help of Western supporters and sympathetic U.S. congressmen and congressional aides, a campaign was launched in the United States (and Europe) to gain support for the exiles' cause and enhance the stature of the Dalai Lama.

The Dalai Lama made his first political speech in America before the U.S. Congressional Human Rights Caucus in September 1987. It laid out the argument that Tibet had been independent when China invaded and began what the Dalai Lama called China's "illegal occupation" of the country. Specifically, he said, "Though Tibetans lost their freedom, under international law, Tibet today is still an independent state under illegal occupation."[17] The speech also raised serious human-rights charges, referring twice to a Chinese-inflicted "holocaust" on the Tibetan people. The Dalai Lama's speech and visit stunned the leaders in Beijing and had an almost immediate impact in Tibet, where less than a week afterward, nationalistic monks from Drepung Monastery in Lhasa staged a political demonstration in support of Tibetan independence and the Dalai Lama's initiative. They were arrested, but four days later, on the morning of 1 October, another group of twenty to thirty monks demonstrated in Lhasa to show their support for the Dalai Lama and the first group of demonstrators. When they demanded the latter's release from jail, police quickly took them into custody and started beating them. A crowd of Tibetans who had gathered outside the police headquarters demanded these monks be released, and before long, this escalated into a full-scale riot. In the end, the police station and a number of vehicles and shops were burnt down, and anywhere from six to twenty Tibetans were killed when police (including ethnic Tibetans) fired at the crowds.

Beijing was taken aback by the riot and the anti-Chinese anger it expressed. There had been clandestine nationalistic incidents for years in Lhasa, but now Beijing had to face the reality that thousands upon thousands of average Tibetans were angry enough to defy death and prison by participating in a massive riot against the government and Chinese rule in Tibet. Although there was no specific issue Tibetans wanted resolved, anger with the past twenty-five years of harsh Chinese rule and with the privations suffered under the Cultural Revolution and the communes was coupled with resentment over the increasing numbers of Han and Hui (Chinese Muslims) coming to Lhasa to work. These feelings coalesced when the Dalai Lama's successful visit to the United States offered Tibetans what seemed like a realistic alternative to China to achieve their aspirations—it gave them new hope that with the work of the Dalai Lama and the power of the United States, some form of independence or total autonomy was just around the corner. While this might seem naive, it was what the monks and common Tibetans believed. In addition, Lhasa Tibetans generally felt that this was the time that they should show Beijing and the world the extent of their support for the Dalai Lama.

In the months after the riot, Lhasa saw more demonstrations by monks and nuns, and another major riot occurred in February 1988. The situation in Tibet had become an international embarrassment to China. A few months later, in June 1988, the Dalai Lama made the first *public* announcement of his conditions for returning to Tibet in a speech in Strasbourg. Its main points were that a Greater Tibet should become a self-governing political entity founded on a constitution that granted Western-style democratic rights. This enlarged political Tibet would operate under a different system of government than the rest of China and would have the right to decide on all affairs relating to Tibet and Tibetans. China would remain responsible for Tibet's foreign policy, although Tibet would maintain and develop relations through its own Foreign Affairs Bureau in nonpolitical fields such as commerce, sports, education, and so forth. China could maintain a limited number of troops in Tibet until a regional peace conference was convened and Tibet was converted into a demilitarized zone. This came to be called the Dalai Lama's "middle way," that is, his compromise between the current Chinese system and independence. The Dalai Lama indicated he was ready to talk with the Chinese about this.

Although this proposal was simply a restatement of Dharamsala's position in the 1984 Beijing talks, that position had never been publicly discussed, and it created a stir in exile politics, where it was criticized by some as a sell-out.[18] This public offer for new talks evinced some initial interest in Beijing, but the more hard-line view predominated, and Strasbourg was rejected as an indirect form of independence. The Dalai Lama's inclusion of a Dutch national as the negotiating team's legal advisor clearly did not help convince Beijing of his sincerity.

Meanwhile, in Tibet, the situation deteriorated further when a third bloody riot in Lhasa was precipitated by monks demonstrating in commemoration of International Human Rights Day in December 1988. Soon after this, the sudden death of Tibet's second highest incarnate lama, the Panchen Lama, produced an unexpected new initiative from Beijing. In early 1989, China secretly invited the Dalai Lama to visit Beijing to participate in the memorial ceremony for the Panchen Lama. This initiative was meant to give the Dalai Lama an opportunity to return for a visit to China without any overt political connotations or preconditions. He would go ostensibly as a religious figure but would informally hold discussions with top Chinese officials. The rationale behind this approach was the belief by some in China that the negotiations had failed because Beijing had been unable to talk directly with the Dalai Lama, who they felt was more moderate than his officials and was being held back by them. Beijing was interested primarily in the Dalai Lama, not the exile community, so coming to an agreement with him to return to China would have met their strategic needs. Consequently, it was thought that given the poor situation in Tibet, allowing the Dalai Lama to visit China informally was worth the risks, since it might provide an opportunity to break the deadlock.

Dharamsala, however, was reluctant simply to accept the invitation. The Chinese had indicated the Dalai Lama would not be allowed to visit Tibet, so there was some concern that Tibetans in Lhasa would feel abandoned if he went to China but not to Tibet. Some exile-government officials also worried that China might treat the Dalai Lama in a humiliating way, ignoring him or treating him as a minor figure. And there was suspicion that it would yield nothing of value in terms of settling the Tibet question but would provide the Chinese with a propaganda victory. With events going well in their view, the Dalai Lama, in essence, declined. An extraordinary opportunity to meet face-to-face with no preconditions had been lost.

Meanwhile, Beijing's situation in Tibet deteriorated still further in 1989. Tibetans in Lhasa continued to mount repeated small nationalistic demonstrations, one of which, on 5 March, turned into a fourth Lhasa riot. At this juncture, Beijing accepted the fact that the situation in Tibet was out of control and initiated strong measures to quell the unrest—it took the drastic step of declaring martial law.

Nineteen eighty-nine brought another dramatic setback for Beijing when the Dalai Lama was awarded the Nobel Peace Prize. Tibetans everywhere considered this a major victory—an indirect but powerful statement that their cause was just and valid and a sign that the world was lining up behind the Dalai Lama in his fight with China. On top of all this, 1989 also brought the Tiananmen debacle. Although this had no direct impact on the situation in Tibet because Tibetans had little interest or sympathy in what they considered a "Han" affair, it fostered a more hard-line political policy in China and made it easier to use such a policy in Tibet.

By 1989, therefore, Beijing's internal and external strategies for Tibet were in disarray. Unless China was willing to agree to relinquish direct political control in Tibet and accept a Strasbourg-like dominion status there, the exiles appeared bent on continuing their international campaign. This would certainly encourage more demonstrations internally and new accusations internationally. The momentum appeared to have shifted to the Dalai Lama. The Dalai Lama's international initiative had successfully turned the tables on China, placing Beijing on the defensive both internationally and within Tibet. Forty years after the Seventeen-Point Agreement had brought Tibet within the PRC's fold, Beijing had not attained the popular acceptance and legitimacy that were the goal of Mao's gradualist policy.

BEIJING'S SHIFT BACK TO A HARD-LINE STRATEGY IN TIBET

The separatist threats in Tibet directly affected China's national identity and strategic interests and were not taken lightly in Beijing. Just as it had after the 1903–04 invasion and the 1959 revolt, China now moved to a more hard-line policy that emphasized national integration and downplayed ethnic differences. The historical parallelism of Mao's policy to support the Dalai Lama precipitating the 1959 rebellion and Hu Yaobang's cultural and religious liberalization precipitating the 1987–89 riots was not lost in Beijing. The consensus was that it had to stop coddling the "reactionary" and "superstitious" Tibetans before matters got completely out of hand. Operationally, this had come to mean that allowing too much minority culture was creating an unwanted divide between Tibetans and Han, so Tibetan culture and religion should be carefully regulated and constrained. Once again, political reality determined how Beijing would implement its ideology regarding *minzu* autonomy.

The new strategy had a number of dimensions, the most obvious of which was the enhancement of the security apparatus in Tibet. These measures have been extremely effective: during the twelve years since martial law was lifted in 1990, there have been no new riots. This success has created confidence in Beijing that it can handle whatever tactics Tibetan dissidents (or exiles) try. A second aspect of the new strategy involved strengthening the leadership of the party in Tibet by appointing better-educated and more highly skilled personnel (non-Tibetans) who could help to modernize the area and its people. As a result of this approach, Han officials have come to play an even more dominant role in Tibet than they had in the 1980s.

A cornerstone of the Chinese government's new policy was (and is) economic growth and modernization—that is, accelerating economic development in Tibet by providing large subsidies for development projects aimed at building infrastructure and productive capacity. The new strategy is premised on the view that the key to winning the loyalty of Tibetans is to improve their standard of living and modernize their society and that to do this effectively, Tibet has to be rapidly developed. Over the past decade, Beijing has expended billions of yuan for new infrastructure and development projects and has just begun building a multibillion yuan railway to Lhasa. Thus, Beijing seeks to solidify its position in Tibet by investing substantial funds for development rather than by making more concessions to ethnic sensibilities.

Many Tibetans have benefited economically from this program, but the policy has also created resentment, as it has greatly increased the influx of non-Tibetan laborers and businessmen into Tibet. There are no accurate data on the numbers of such people in Tibet, but they have dramatically changed the demographic composition and atmosphere of cities like Lhasa, and the process is beginning to expand to smaller "urban" towns and even county seats. The number of these non-Tibetans is unprecedented in Tibetan history and has turned Lhasa, the heart of Tibet, into a city where non-Tibetan residents appear to equal or exceed the number of Tibetans.

This influx has also resulted in non-Tibetans controlling a large segment of the local economy at all levels, from street-corner bicycle repairmen to firms doing major construction projects. There have been many complaints about this from Tibetans who argue that this influx should be stopped or severely curtailed because Tibet is a special minority "autonomous region" where Tibetans, not outsiders, should be the primary beneficiaries of the new-market economic growth. There is also a strong feeling among Tibetans that they cannot compete economically with the more industrious and skilled Han and Hui, so without government intervention to ensure the welfare of the citizens of the autonomous region, they will become increasingly marginalized, economically as well as demographically. It has also been argued that allowing this process to continue is counterproductive, as it will fuel anti-Chinese hatred in Tibetans and make Tibet less secure in the long run. Notwithstanding these criticisms, Beijing has not agreed to stop or impede the flow of non-Tibetan workers coming to Tibet. Instead, it has responded to critics by saying that Tibet is poor and that these people have more skills and business know-how than Tibetans and thus are necessary to develop Tibet quickly.

To some extent, Beijing's refusal is, of course, political. The large numbers of non-Tibetans living and working in Tibet inextricably link Tibet closely to the rest of China and provide Beijing with a new and significant pro-China "constituency" that increases its security there. Although these Chinese do not see themselves as permanent colonists, the reality is that at any given time, there are a large number of ethnic Chinese residents in key urban areas in Tibet. This has created a kind of "facts on the ground" for Beijing. One can easily imagine China promulgating new laws to make the large Han presence permanent if its control over Tibet was seriously threatened.

Equally important to the hard-line strategy is the expectation that these Chinese will provide a powerful model of modern thinking and behavior that Tibetans will see and gradually emulate. Based on the history of other minority areas, this strategy is banking on a process of acculturation, in which the more "advanced" Han will open Tibet to new ideas and attitudes and create a new, "modern" Tibetan in the process, one who will not be so influenced by religion and lamas. It valorizes a national identity as a citizen of China over a specific identity as a Tibetan living in a Tibetan Autonomous Region. Thus, although Beijing realizes that its open-door policy will likely create hostility among many Tibetans in the short run, proponents of the view feel that this is the price they must pay for modernizing Tibetan society so as to succeed in the long run. To this end, Beijing has also tried to use the education system to create a "modern" Tibetan elite who are comfortable being a part of China. For example, besides operating the standard school system in Tibet, Beijing initiated a program to create special Tibetan lower-middle schools in other parts of China in 1985, and the program was expanded substantially after 1987. Today, there are roughly ten thousand Tibetan youths attending such schools throughout the rest of China, and more attend special Tibetan upper-middle and vocational schools.

Finally, as mentioned above, Beijing's current policy also seeks to curtail the extent to which Tibet is dominated by Tibetan language and culture. Tibetans are still free to speak Tibetan and adhere to Tibetan customs, but Beijing has not permitted additional changes that were under consideration in 1987–88 that would have enhanced the cultural distinctness of Tibet. For example, reforms that would have made Tibetan an official language, along with Chinese, in government offices have not been pursued, and a plan to use written Tibetan in the secondary-school science curriculum has been set aside in favor of continuing the dominance of Chinese. Similarly, the commitment of CCP first secretary Hu Yaobang in the early 1980s to require Han officials in Tibet to learn Tibetan has been ignored. The government has also become far more intrusive in the organization and operation of monasteries. It has been unwilling to eliminate or substantially increase its limits on the number of monks and nuns and has also carried out divisive political-education campaigns in the monasteries. The operating notion is that Beijing should not allow changes that make Tibet more isolated in language, culture, and values from the rest of China because they will impede the diffusion of a national identity wherein Tibetans see themselves primarily as loyal citizens of a multiethnic state. Elevating and inculcating national culture while constraining and de-emphasizing *minzu* culture is the essence of the approach.

Nor is Beijing willing to consider the argument that relative demographic homogeneity is needed for Tibetan culture to flourish. In essence, Beijing's post-1989 hard-line policy has implicitly redefined and diminished what is meant by ethnic or cultural autonomy in Tibet. There are still some subsidies and preferential treatment for Tibetans, but the basic policy has moved from the view that Tibet and Tibetan culture has a special status in China because of Tibet's past history and the Seventeen-Point Agreement to the view that Tibetans are just another ethnic group in a multiethnic state. Tibet is now seen as a region in which Tibetans can practice their culture if they wish, but there are no special commitments on the part of the government to limit the number of non-Tibetans living and working there, to make Tibetan the language of higher government offices and secondary schools, or to allow monasteries and religion to flourish freely. Recently, for example, a new campaign in Tibet prohibited all Tibetans earning government salaries from keeping religious chapels in their homes or participating in other religious activities. Such campaigns reinforce the hard-line message that Beijing will determine what aspects of Tibetan culture will be permitted, and if some Tibetans do not like it, too bad. If this is autonomy, it's autonomy with a small *a*.

For Tibetans, one of the most disturbing aspects of the intensification of the hard-line policy in the 1990s was the vocal and vitriolic campaign to attack and demean the Dalai Lama. In addition to banning the popular annual celebration of the Dalai Lama's birthday (held in a park in Lhasa) and the sale of his photograph, top officials in Tibet repeatedly attacked his integrity and honesty in the media. Insulting Tibetan religion, the Dalai Lama, and Tibetans as an ethnic group was no longer taboo for Beijing's top leaders in Tibet. This was a new, "in-your-face" Tibet policy that sent the clear message to Tibetans that *you* have to adapt to *our* sensibilities, not vice versa. It was a far cry from the sympathetic rhetoric of Hu Yaobang.

Thus, although the cultural freedoms given to individual Tibetans were not rescinded in the 1990s and rural Tibet is still Tibetan in language, custom, religion, and demographic composition, the overall thrust of the Hu Yaobang approach of the early 1980s was rejected by Beijing as counterproductive, since it appeared to enhance rather than reduce separatist sentiments. In its place, a more hard-line policy was implemented in which crushing dissidence, modernizing Tibet, and creating a new breed of "modern," less ethnic Tibetans took precedence over catering to ethnic sensibilities and interests.

The international campaign of the Dalai Lama, therefore, had failed. It sought to compel Beijing to resolve the conflict by giving Tibet more political and ethnic autonomy, but it achieved the opposite. Now, Tibetans in Tibet and in exile see their demographic and cultural homogeneity being lost right before their eyes. The Dalai Lama continues to experience great international sympathy and has tremendous influence over the attitudes and emotions of the local Tibetans in Tibet, but his strategy did not compel China to yield to his demands. Beijing, therefore, has turned the tables on Dharamsala, and the triumphs won by the Dalai Lama's international campaign look more and more like pyrrhic victories.

However, in another sense, China's hard-line policy itself can be said to have failed. It appears to have alienated many Tibetans, in all walks of life, including educated Tibetan cadres who once supported modernization and Tibet as a part of China. Tibetans are incensed by Han cadres' lack of respect for their culture and by the Han chauvinism evinced by some over the past decade. The tacit categorization of Tibetans who advocate a more Tibetan TAR as enemies who are putting the interests of their own nationality above those of the nation has embittered Tibetan cadres, since it means that to succeed in Tibet, they have to minimize their ethnicity. The hard-line policy of the last decade, therefore, has illuminated for many Tibetans the reality that twenty years after the fall of Maoist leftism in China, they are still not equal partners and cannot control the ethnic character of their own autonomous region. It has heightened their feeling of powerlessness and has evinced troubling memories of the anti-ethnicity policies of the Cultural Revolution, when Han leaders looked down on and deprecated the worth of Tibetan culture. As such, some say it has stimulated more Tibetan nationalism among educated younger Tibetans than existed a decade earlier.

FUTURE PROSPECTS

At one level, both Beijing and the Dalai Lama would like to settle the Tibet question. The Dalai Lama finds himself standing on the sidelines, unable to impede or reverse changes in Tibet that he deplores and feels threaten the future of his homeland and culture. Time seems to be running out. A settlement could reverse this trend and preserve the kind of culturally and demographically intact Tibet he desires.

The Chinese government also has good reasons for wanting the conflict settled. Beijing finds itself continuously embarrassed and under attack internationally because of its policies in Tibet, and, as mentioned above, animosity in Tibet has probably been increased as a result of its hard-line policies. The recent flight of two high-profile lamas (Arjia Lobsang Thubten from Kumbum [Taer] Monastery, in Qinghai, in 1998 and the Karmapa Lama from Tshurpu Monastery, near Lhasa, in 2000) reflected this discontent with Chinese hard-line policies. These defections shocked Beijing, since this could not be passed off facilely as exile lies or Western misunderstandings of events in China. These were favored lamas who were considered loyal to China, yet they secretly fled to exile because of their anger with Chinese nationality and religious policies for Tibetans. Thus, despite its hard-line approach to the Tibetan issue, Beijing continues to actively scrutinize conditions to see if the settlement it wants can be made, and on a number of occasions, such as in 1993, 1997–1998, and again in 2000 and 2001, it flirted with restarting talks with the Dalai Lama. However, in the end, Beijing and the exiles were unable to go forward. Though this is not the appropriate place to examine in depth each of these failed "flirtations," there are several general issues that warrant mentioning.

Despite rhetoric in the West asserting that if China would only agree to sit down with the Dalai Lama, both sides could solve the conflict to their mutual satisfaction, as this chapter has shown, there are actually enormous hurdles that will have to be overcome before a settlement of this conflict can occur, or even before meaningful talks can be held.

One enormous hurdle, of course, is the issue that undermined the 1982 and 1984 talks, namely, the kind of autonomy a TAR in China should exercise. This issue includes the amount of internal autonomy Tibet should have, the role of the exile Tibetans in a TAR government, and whether the agreement should reunite all ethnic Tibetans in China into a new Greater Tibet autonomous region.

The Dalai Lama has publicly stated and restated that a settlement should allow Tibet real political autonomy, but this, as was discussed earlier, is far more than China is willing to give (and has been since 1979, when attempts at rapprochement began). Consequently, if the Dalai Lama is firmly wedded to this view, given the current balance of power, he will not get a settlement. He can continue to inflict public embarrassment on China in the international arena, but there is no compelling reason to believe that one more award, one more high-profile glitterati benefit, or one more protest demonstration when China's top leaders travel abroad will change Beijing's policies any more than they have in the past. Despite his outward public stance that "sooner or later, China will have to understand the global sentiments on the Tibetan issue,"[19] depending on global opinion seems unrealistic. To force major concessions from China, the Dalai Lama will have to escalate his campaign and inflict far greater pain on Beijing than he has been able to do to date. Thus, if real political autonomy is the least the Dalai Lama will agree to, there is little point to a new round of discussions at this time. They would simply be a replay of the 1982 and 1984 negotiations.

However, informed sources suggest that the Dalai Lama's public demand for political autonomy is merely a negotiating ploy and that in reality he is ready to accept substantially less than that. Thus, the idea of face-to-face talks and an eventual compromise settlement is not completely unrealistic.

What such a compromise settlement would look like is difficult to specify, as there are many conceivable permutations, but there are a number of basic issues that would likely have to be addressed. For many Tibetans, the key to an acceptable compromise is to ensure the preservation of a Tibetan homeland, where ethnic Tibetans predominate demographically and Tibet language, culture, and religion flourish. This is what Tibet has always been, regardless of whether it was subordinate to Mongols or Manchus or was de facto independent. Such a compromise, moreover, is possible within the current political and legal structure of China. For example, Beijing could move in stages to appoint reform-minded, ethnically sensitive Tibetan cadres to head major party and government offices, including the first party secretary position, and it could gradually increase the overall percent of Tibetans in the government. In the cultural sphere, a variety of measures could be implemented to enhance substantially the degree to which Tibetan culture predominates (e.g., eliminating or reducing restrictions on the number of monks in monasteries and mandating far greater use of written Tibetan language in government, high school, and college). And in the critical demographic and economic spheres, Beijing could take measures that would decrease substantially the number of non-Tibetans living in Tibet and reduce outside economic competition so that Tibetans become the main beneficiaries of economic development in the TAR. The end result of such a process would be a Tibet that was predominantly Tibetan in culture, language, and demographic composition. It would continue to modernize and would also continue to be run by the CCP, albeit a CCP headed by a new, reform type of Tibetan cadre. This kind of Tibet would likely meet with the approval of the overwhelming majority of Tibetans in Tibet. But is this enough for the Dalai Lama?

The Dalai Lama's overt abandonment of the quest for independence at Strasbourg in 1988 produced strong criticism in the exile community. Tibetan independence "hard-liners" objected, contending, among other things, that if the Dalai Lama accepted Chinese sovereignty and returned to China he would be throwing away the last hope of Tibetans to ultimately attain an independent Tibet. Influential Tibetan-exile groups, such as the Tibetan Youth Congress, today continue to advocate independence rather than a compromise that would leave the CCP in control in Tibet. While such views seem naive and unrealistic, given the power of the PRC, the history of the collapse of the U.S.S.R. is a powerful legitimizing precedent for these Tibetans and their projected scenario. Consequently, if the Dalai Lama were to accept a cultural-autonomy compromise, such as the one outlined above, he could well undermine the already fragile unity of the exile community. This would be the case especially if such a compromise did not unite all Tibetans into a new Greater Tibet autonomous region, something that is unlikely to occur because Beijing fears that uniting all Tibetans in China under one government would create a greater danger of separatism. Because of these real issues, the Dalai Lama would have to be convinced that the payoff for making painful concessions would be worth the risks, and he would have to be ready to move forward without the support of important segments of the exile community.

But even if we assume the Dalai Lama would be willing to make such concessions to reverse the hard-line policy that he deplores, an enormously difficult hurdle remains—trust. If the Dalai Lama worked out terms for his return to China, could he trust the Chinese to implement the agreement honestly, given all the enmity the conflict has engendered over the past century and the history of major shifts in Chinese politics? This is an issue that looms large for the Dalai Lama and his supporters, who fear that China's leaders will change their minds after he returns and renege on key terms of the agreement or that new leaders will come to power with different views on Tibet. This is the nightmare "lose-lose" scenario: the Dalai Lama definitively accepts Chinese sovereignty over Tibet, ends the international campaign, returns to China, and a few years later, finds that policies change and that he (and the Tibetans) end up with something far less than they agreed to. Consequently, it is difficult to see how he could return to China without some guarantees (for example, involvement by the U.N.). China, however, has defined the Tibet question as an internal matter and has been adamantly opposed to mediation or interference from outside countries or organizations. Nothing is insurmountable if both sides genuinely desire a solution, but this is a major issue that will not be easy to finesse.

There are also many problems that make China dubious about entering into new talks, let alone making major concessions to bring about a resolution to the Tibet question. It is essential to understand that for the past decade, one of the aims of the hard-line policy has been to convince Tibetans in Tibet that the Dalai Lama is unable to help them and that Beijing is in total control of their future—that they must look to Beijing, not India or the United States. Consequently, they will not readily enhance the Dalai Lama's stature in Tibetans' eyes by agreeing to hold talks with him unless they are convinced he is sincere about returning to China on their terms. This means the Dalai Lama must not only publicly accept a major compromise but also demonstrate that his acceptance is genuine.

If he returned, the Dalai Lama would be an even more towering figure in the eyes of Tibetans and would have enormous influence with them. He would also likely become a major religious figure for Chinese spiritual seekers. The crux of the matter for Beijing, therefore, is how he would use this power. Would he genuinely use his stature to heal the enmity of Tibetans and induce them to accept being loyal and patriotic citizens of China? Or would he use the agreement and his return as a stepping stone, that is, as a time for coalescing, unifying, and positioning Tibet and Tibetans to separate from China when the first opportunity arose? When the Dalai Lama speaks in the West of peace and reconciliation, leaders in China wonder: Is this the Dalai Lama who told Mao in 1955 that he wanted reforms and a modern Tibet but then did not deliver and allowed the 1958–59 revolt to occur? Or is this a new Dalai Lama, one who genuinely wants to return to China and heal old wounds? One of the unpublicized reasons for the breakdown in communications in 1998 is said to have been China's discovery of a Dharamsala document that discussed compromise with China as merely a preliminary step in a long-term strategy to attain independence. It is hard for Beijing to know what the Dalai Lama will do, so consequently, it scrutinizes not only everything the Dalai Lama says, publicly and privately, but also everything he does and *does not do* that is relevant to China. They are forever looking for a major sign that he is genuinely committed to a new course, such as stopping all or a major part of the international campaign or agreeing to various preconditions.

The Dalai Lama has been reluctant to do this publicly without guarantees from Beijing that they will reciprocate, and as of now, Beijing has declined. It has not been persuaded by the Dalai Lama's words and actions that the potential benefits of reopening talks outweigh the potential risks. In large part, this is because many in China distrust the Dalai Lama's motives and argue that it is not in China's best interests to permit him to return. The hard-liners believe that China will be better able to settle the Tibet question to its advantage after the Dalai Lama dies and Tibetans have no unifying leader. Since he is now 67 years of age, they argue it is well worth the wait, given that the current policy is, in their eyes, working. Time, they feel, is on their side.

This strategy is attractive to Beijing because it engenders few risks, at least in the short term, and it can solidify China's position in Tibet regardless of what the Dalai Lama or Tibetans think or do. Hard-liners in Beijing and Lhasa argue that this strategy will ultimately create a new generation of Tibetans who will consider themselves loyal citizens of China. Moreover, even if it does not, it will so radically change the demographic composition of Tibet and the nature of its economy that this failure will not weaken Beijing's control over Tibet. Beijing's security measures are functioning effectively, and in the absence of a credible U.S. or Western threat of sanctions, they are free to pursue the hard-line policy with impunity. Consequently, the dominant opinion on the Chinese side holds that conditions now are not conducive to making a serious compromise to meet the needs of the Dalai Lama.

Thus, though there are good reasons for each side to desire a settlement, the prospects are not good for one, notwithstanding the repeated calls of the Dalai Lama and other world leaders for new talks, as well as the backdoor signals from the Chinese side that they are still interested in a settlement. The Tibet question, therefore, appears to have reached a stalemate. Both sides seem incapable of taking the risks necessary to work out a compromise solution, preferring instead to continue adversarial strategies and tactics designed to thwart their opponent and register gains for their own side. However, while Dharamsala and Beijing's efforts to achieve rapprochement are stalemated, the hard-line policy in Tibet is moving forward inexorably.

Where does that leave Tibet and the Tibetans living there? Although the dominant view in Beijing is that the hard-line policy serves the long-term interests of the PRC, other elements in China believe this policy is creating ethnic anger and enmity among both the Tibetan masses and cadres and is not creating the long-term security and goodwill China wants. For example, a group of retired former military officials who served in Tibet in the 1950 and 1960s (in the Sichuan-based Eighteenth Army) submitted a ten-thousand-character critique of current policy in Tibet that, among other things, tried to refute the contention that the Dalai Lama had been duplicitous in the 1955–59 period and argue that he is someone China can negotiate with today.

If Tibetans and Chinese are to ever reach a secure and meaningful rapprochement, at the very least, the Tibetans' deep-seated ethnic sensitivities must be addressed. Since a settlement with the Dalai Lama is remote, the most likely avenue to accomplish this would be the revival in China of an ethnically conciliatory "internal" strategy that would answer most of the issues that currently concern and anger Tibetans. Such an internal policy would reverse the hard-line policies of the 1990s with regard to cultural, linguistic, and religious issues and make a major shift in economic policy by creating a new set of ground rules that restrict Han and other non-Tibetan workers and businesses in Tibet, or at least begin a process of doing that. For Tibetans to feel they are equal partners in a multiethnic state, they need to believe that the state views them with respect and dignity and that they are in control over policies in the TAR to a greater extent than exists today. To accomplish that, Beijing needs to empower a new breed of ethnically sensitive Tibetan leaders who have pride in their culture and civilization and who can give voice to the feelings and aspirations of Tibetans residing there. This would, of course, entail risks, but it holds out the possibility of enormous gains, as it could provide the very security and loyalty Beijing has sought, without great success, since it incorporated Tibet in 1951. It would also silence Western criticism of China's treatment of Tibetan religion and culture and greatly enhance China's moral stature on the international stage. Tibetans in Tibet have reached a point in their thinking where such a unilateral "internal" policy would likely be genuinely welcomed.

THE UNITED STATES AND THE TIBET QUESTION

The United States has had a long, and at times, intimate, involvement with Tibet, and the Tibet question in part is the result of its policies regarding China and Asia.

U.S. interest in Tibet began during World War II, when the United States conveyed its position on Tibet's political status in a 1942 response to Britain:

> For its part, the Government of the United States has borne in mind the fact that the Chinese Government has long claimed suzerainty over Tibet and that the Chinese constitution lists Tibet among areas constituting the territory of the Republic of China. This Government has at no time raised a question regarding either of these claims.[20]

The following year, the United States, as part of the war effort, decided to send two officers from the Office of Strategic Services (OSS) through Tibet to China. Washington quickly found that notwithstanding Chinese claims that Tibet was a part of China, Chiang Kai-shek exercised no authority there and could not secure Tibetan permission to admit such a U.S. mission. The United States turned to the British to recommend them to Lhasa and then, for the first time, dealt directly with the Tibetan government. Lhasa agreed to the U.S. request and the two officers visited Lhasa in 1943, carrying a letter from President Roosevelt to the Dalai Lama. The OSS officers were sympathetic to Tibet's needs, but the United States remained unwilling to recognize and support Tibet as an independent country after the visit, despite the fact that Washington now had first-hand evidence of Tibet's de facto independence.

In 1948, the Tibetan government wanted to send an official trade mission to the United States, using its own passports. When they approached the U.S. Embassy in New Delhi, the State Department instructed its ambassador that the Tibetan trade mission could be received in the United States only on an informal basis and that the United States would not recognize the Tibetan passports, since it did not recognize Tibet as a country:

> It should be recalled that China claims sovereignty over Tibet and that this Government has never questioned that claim; accordingly it would not be possible for this government to accord members of the projected mission other than an informal reception unless the mission enjoyed the official sanction of the Chinese Government.[21]

Consequently, during the period of Nationalist Party (Guomindang) rule in China, the United States supported the position of its ally Chiang Kai-shek. Knowing that China did not exercise authority over Tibet, and had not since the fall of the Qing dynasty, the United States dealt directly with the Tibetan government (without reference to China) when it had to. But it refused to recognize Tibet's de facto status as de jure because it felt that its larger national interests lay with China.

In 1949, as the Guomindang government was collapsing and about to flee to Taiwan, the United States reexamined its Tibet policy. The State Department now showed some new flexibility regarding Tibet's status vis-à-vis China, although it still considered the "sensibilities" of Chiang Kai-shek to be paramount:

1. It is believed to be clearly to our advantage under any circumstances to have Tibet as a friend if possible. We should accordingly maintain a friendly attitude toward Tibet in ways short of giving China [the Guomindang] cause for offense. We should encourage so far as feasible Tibet's orientation toward the West rather than toward the East.

2. For the present we should avoid giving the impression of any alteration in our position toward Chinese authority over Tibet such as for example steps which would clearly indicate that we regard Tibet as independent, etc. We should however keep our policy as flexible as possible by avoiding references to Chinese sovereignty or suzerainty unless references are clearly called for and by informing China of our proposed moves in connection with Tibet, rather than asking China's consent for them.[22]

The inauguration of the PRC on 1 October 1949 quickly changed the situation. Tibet was now facing a communist regime to which the United States was hostile, and it was about to become embroiled in the Cold War. The PRC set the "liberation" of Tibet as an immediate goal. From the Chinese perspective, Tibet had been, and should again be, an integral part of China, so this was really the reunification of a wayward part of greater China. The Dalai Lama's government disagreed and desperately sought diplomatic and military aid from India and the West, especially the United States. It received none.

In the meantime, the Tibetan government stalled sending a delegation to negotiate its "liberation" with China, so Beijing sent in troops to invade Tibet's eastern province. There, they defeated the Tibet army in a two-week campaign, forcing the Dalai Lama to send a negotiating team to Beijing, where in May 1951, its members signed the Seventeen-Point Agreement. At this time, the Dalai Lama was living in a Tibetan town on the Indian border waiting to decide if it was best for him to flee into exile or return to Lhasa.

In Washington, Tibet was now a victim of communist aggression, and the United States was eager to enlist the Dalai Lama in its Asian anti-communist crusade. It actively sought to persuade him to renounce the Seventeen-Point Agreement, the terms of which he had not approved before finalization, and flee into exile. Washington conveyed to the Dalai Lama that the

US Govmt believes Tibet shld not be compelled by duress accept violation its autonomy and that Tib people should enjoy rights of self determination commensurate with autonomy Tibet has had many years. US therefore will indicate publicly its understanding of the position of DL as head of an autonomous Tibet.[23]

This was more than the United States had indicated previously but fell short of what Tibet wanted. Tibet insisted it was independent, not autonomous, and did not want to be a part of China. Although the United States wanted to use the Dalai Lama against the PRC, at the same time, it did not want to undercut the position of Chiang Kai-shek's Republic of China on Taiwan, which continued to claim Tibet as part of China, nor did it want a dispute with Indian prime minister Jawaharlal Nehru, who strongly opposed U.S. intervention in Tibet. The United States, therefore, would not commit itself to support more than autonomy for Tibet under China, and it would not agree to recognize the Dalai Lama as the head of a government-in-exile if he left Tibet.

The Dalai Lama and the Tibetan government considered this offer inadequate and returned to Lhasa in August 1951 to live under the terms of the Seventeen-Point Agreement.[24] Despite this disappointment, the United States made another effort to persuade the Dalai Lama to flee from Lhasa, sweetening the offer by agreeing, for the first time, to allow him to live in exile in the United States. But it was not enough. U.S. claims of friendship and support rang hollow to the Tibetan government, inexperienced as it was in international diplomacy. The Tibetans felt that Washington wanted to use the Dalai Lama in the Cold War, not wield its tremendous power and international influence to support Tibet's aspiration to continue living freely. Consequently, the Dalai Lama decided that the interests of Tibetans were better served by trying to work with Beijing than by depending on Washington.

The refusal of the Dalai Lama to leave Lhasa was a setback that temporarily dampened the enthusiasm of the United States. However, an outbreak of rebellion in the ethnic-Tibetan areas of Sichuan Province in 1956 brought the United States back actively. The CIA quickly became involved in a covert initiative, and by 1957, it was providing training and support for Tibetan guerrilla forces (without the permission of the Dalai Lama). Nevertheless, the situation in Tibet deteriorated and led the Dalai Lama to flee to India in 1959.

With the Dalai Lama in exile, the United States now had to decide how to deal with him. This led to a new discussion in Washington about whether its Tibetan policy should change and if so, how much.

The United States covertly helped the Dalai Lama bring his case to the U.N., helped set up Tibetan guerrillas on the Nepal-Tibet border, and helped finance the guerrillas and the Dalai Lama,[25] but it continued to accept that Tibet was jurally part of China. Moreover, it insisted that the Tibetans focus their publicity on the communists' violations of human rights rather than on the core political issues the Tibetans wanted to raise, that is, Beijing's invasion and occupation of their country. The U.S. ambassador in New Delhi, Winthrop Brown, for example, told the Dalai Lama that the United States felt that the Tibetan case at the U.N. would command the greatest support if it was presented primarily in terms of human rights.[26]

Thus, even at this juncture, the United States still would not recognize the Dalai Lama as the head of a Tibetan government-in-exile or support his political goal of getting the international community to recognize Tibet as an independent country that had been illegally invaded and conquered. The U.S. strategic goal for Tibet was to generate "sympathy for the Tibetan people on human rights grounds"[27] around the world. This was just the kind of limited response the Tibetan government had feared would happen when it was considering the U.S. plea to leave Tibet in 1951.

However, within these limits, the United States now began to call Tibet "an autonomous country under Chinese suzerainty," although it did not spell out what "autonomous country" meant:

> As to the position which the U.S. government takes with regard to the status of Tibet, the historical position of the United States has been that Tibet is an autonomous country under Chinese suzerainty. However, the U.S. government has consistently held that the autonomy of Tibet should not be impaired by force.[28]

The United States has never recognized the pretension to sovereignty over Tibet put forward by the Chinese Communist regime.

And for a brief period, there were indications that Washington was willing to go even further by saying it would support the Tibetans' right to self-determination. On 20 February 1960, Secretary of State Christian Herter, in a letter to the Dalai Lama, wrote:

> As you know, while it has been the historical position of the U.S. to consider Tibet as an autonomous country under the suzerainty of China, the American people have also traditionally stood for the principle of self-determination. It is the belief of the U.S. government that this principle should apply to the people of Tibet

and that they should have the determining voice in their own political destiny.[29]

This letter, however, turned out to be an aberration and was not the start of a new, proactive U.S. policy for Tibet. So the Dalai Lama found himself in exile in India, with strong U.S. support for a campaign to castigate the PRC for genocide and the like, but no support for Tibet's claim that Tibet was now a captive nation. The reasons for this reluctance to launch a new policy appear to have been laid out in a State Department internal memo written the previous year:

> FE [Far Eastern Affairs] has completed a study . . . of the question of the United States' recognition of the independence of Tibet in which the considerations both for and against such action are examined in detail. Taking these factors into account, we have concluded that on balance the arguments against recognition of Tibetan independence under present conditions are stronger than those in favor. I consider this conclusion valid from the standpoint of both United States national interest and from that of the Tibetans. We share with the Tibetans the objective of keeping the Tibetans' cause alive in the consciousness of the world and maintaining the Dalai Lama as an effective spokesman of the Tibetan people. I believe that United States recognition of the Dalai Lama's government as that of an independent country would serve neither purpose well. Since very few countries could be expected to follow our lead, our recognition now would make the Dalai Lama the leader of a government-in-exile obviously dependent on the United States for political support. This would almost certainly damage the prestige and influence he now enjoys as one of Asia's revered leaders and would hamper his activities on behalf of the Tibetan people.[30]

In the late 1960s, the shift in China policy initiated by President Richard Nixon and Secretary of State Henry Kissinger led to the United States stopping all funding for the Tibetan guerrillas in Nepal,[31] as well as to diminished American interest in and involvement with the Tibet question in general. For the decade of the 1970s, Tibet remained an obscure issue in U.S. foreign policy. The Dalai Lama was not even granted a visa to visit the United States until 1979, and then only as a religious leader.

The early record of U.S. involvement with Tibet is, therefore, mixed. At the same time that the United States was arming and training Tibetan insurgents to fight the PRC, it was also spurning the Dalai Lama's request for U.S. political recognition of Tibetan independence or a Tibetan government-in-exile. With the isolated exception of Herter's 1960 letter to the Dalai Lama, U.S. policy toward the Tibet question supported the position that Tibet was rightly a part of China, albeit an autonomous part. This lack of support was frustrating for Tibetans, who saw and read of America's international crusade for democracy and self-determination yet found in their case that the United States was unwilling to support it politically or militarily. Thus, although the United States was in one sense clearly a friend and supporter of Tibet, it is hard not to conclude that in a more basic sense, it was a "bad" friend or at least not a "good" friend. This is particularly clear when we compare the United States' support for Tibet with the U.S.S.R.'s support for Mongolia. Stalin, at Yalta, persuaded Roosevelt and Churchill to support a plebiscite for Mongolia and then compelled Chiang Kai-shek to accept it. That is why, although Tibet and Mongolia were politically similar at the end of the Qing dynasty, in 1911–12, Mongolia is today independent and a member of the United Nations and Tibet is not.

Events in the 1980s brought the Tibet question to the forefront again. The riots in Lhasa and the Dalai Lama's international initiative garnered strong sympathy and support for Tibet in Congress, in the human-rights community, and among citizens' lobbying groups. U.S. policy toward Tibet now acquired a new dimension, with Congress expressing strong pro-Tibetan political views independent of administration or State Department foreign policy.

The following quotes illustrate these two "policies." The first is from a 1991 Congressional (nonbinding) resolution on Tibet that was attached to a State Department authorization act (and signed into law by the first President Bush at the end of that year):

> It is the sense of the Congress that . . . Tibet, including those areas incorporated into the Chinese provinces of Sichuan, Yunnan, Gansu and Qinghai, is an occupied country under established principles of international law.
>
> Tibet's true representatives are the Dalai Lama and the Tibetan Government in Exile as recognized by the Tibetan people.[32]

By contrast, a State Department report on Tibet prepared for Congress (in 1994) included a tough statement on Tibet with the United States categorically accepting Chinese sovereignty:

Historically, the United States has acknowledged Chinese sovereignty over Tibet. Since at least 1966, U.S. policy has explicitly
recognized the Tibetan Autonomous Region . . . as part of the
People's Republic of China. This long-standing policy is consistent with the view of the entire international community, including all China's neighbors: no country recognizes Tibet as a
sovereign state. Because we do not recognize Tibet as an independent state, the United States does not conduct diplomatic relations with the self-styled "Tibetan government-in-exile."[33]

The start of the Clinton administration appeared to usher in major
changes in U.S. foreign policy on Tibet. As part of President Clinton's
new policy of giving high priority to human-rights issues in foreign affairs,
he took a tough stance with China, announcing on 28 May 1993, for example, that the secretary of state would not recommend Most Favored Nation
(MFN) status for China in 1994 unless China made significant progress
with respect to a series of human-rights problems. What was striking was
that he included among these "protecting Tibet's distinctive religious and
cultural heritage." Six months later, when President Clinton met CCP
general secretary Jiang Zemin face-to-face in Seattle, he urged Jiang to
improve cultural and religious freedom in Tibet and to open talks with
the Dalai Lama.[34] The United States, for the first time since rapprochement with the People's Republic of China in 1971, appeared willing to try
to force changes in Chinese policy toward Tibetans in China, although
the United States was careful to focus on cultural and religious survival
rather than political status. Nevertheless, 1993 seemed a turning point in
U.S.-Tibetan relations—if MFN status was denied to China in part
because of its policies in Tibet, the Tibetan exiles would have attained the
kind of new leverage they had been seeking through their international
campaign. However, as we know, Clinton was forced to back down and
in 1994 announced he would not use economic sanctions to try to induce
political changes in China, let alone Tibet.

After that, the Clinton administration's China policy reverted to previous policy, placing geopolitical and economic interests ahead of human
rights–democracy issues and steering away from a public, confrontational
style that could harm Sino-American relations. Consequently, although
some involved with U.S. foreign policy still contended that assisting Tibet
was a matter of principle and conscience—that Tibet was an important
test of the United States' will to take the lead in forging a new, more
democratic and morally just post–Cold War world—the dominant view

was that the United States had no intrinsic strategic interest in Tibet so should avoid worsening relations with China by supporting Tibet or the Dalai Lama.

However, the new domestic realities (especially the strong interest of Congress in this issue) meant that Tibet could no longer be ignored, as it had been in the 1970s. So while the Clinton administration refused to support the Dalai Lama's political goals vis-à-vis China, it supported the Dalai Lama by criticizing Chinese human-rights violations in Tibet, calling for Beijing to take steps to ensure the preservation of Tibetan religion and culture, urging Beijing to reopen talks with the Dalai Lama, and quietly working behind the scenes to try to bring this about. For example, the State Department's report cited above also stated:

> The United States continues, however, to urge Beijing and the Dalai Lama to hold serious discussions at an early date, without preconditions, and on a fixed agenda. The United States also urges China to respect Tibet's unique religious, linguistic and cultural traditions as it formulated policies for Tibet.[35]

Ideologically, the Clinton administration rationalized its approach by arguing that the best way to influence China regarding Tibet was by developing good relations with China. Confrontation would not work:

> The ability of the United States to promote respect for human rights by the Chinese authorities is closely related to the strength of our bilateral relations with China. A serious disruption of U.S.-China relations would gravely undermine any hope for the United States to foster greater respect for the human rights of ethnic Tibetans in China.[36]

Nevertheless, the Clinton administration also took a number of steps in response to pressure from Congress and the Tibet lobby. For example, it authorized a separate section on Tibet in the annual State Department world human-rights assessment and appointed a special coordinator for Tibetan affairs in the State Department (to promote Sino-Tibetan dialogue and facilitate the preservation of Tibetan religion and culture). Although these moves irritated China, which denounced them as interference in its domestic affairs, they were crafted in a way that did not contest China's sovereignty over Tibet.

Consequently, after the 1987–89 riots and martial law, questions about how China was treating and should treat its Tibetan minority became part of the United States' China policy, first in Congress and then in the Clinton administration. It became a visible part of Sino-American relations.

The Clinton administration, therefore, forged a new, more nuanced, dual-level Tibet policy. Tibet was no longer ignored but was supported only in a relatively "safe" way. The United States would not use its power to try to force China to change its policies in Tibet, nor would it deviate from the United States' absolute recognition of Chinese sovereignty over Tibet. And the administration worked hard to prevent the Tibet question from disturbing the more important economic and security dimensions of Sino-American relations. But at the same time, the benign neglect of the 1970s and the first Bush administration ended. The Clinton administration supported the Dalai Lama by publicly committing the United States to the goal of preserving Tibet's unique religion and culture while it sought behind the scenes to foster a resolution to the conflict.

In the end, however, the Clinton administration's China-Tibet policy failed. It failed to produce a new set of direct talks between the Dalai Lama and China, and according to most assessments, it was unable to protect Tibet's cultural and religious heritage by impeding or restraining China's hard-line policy in Tibet. If the Dalai Lama is correct, the future of Tibetan society and culture was at far greater risk at the end of the Clinton administration than when President Clinton took office in 1992.

The second Bush administration, therefore, inherited a difficult situation. The Dalai Lama and the pro-Tibet lobby were charging that the conditions in Tibet were deteriorating and the future of Tibetan religion and culture was in doubt. In the face of this, the new administration had to decide whether to continue the nonconfrontational policies of the previous administration or to play a more proactive, confrontational role to reverse the hard-line policies employed in Tibet.

Initially, the new administration set out to take a much tougher line with China and, apparently, the Tibet question. Bush referred to China no longer as a partner but rather as a "strategic competitor," and although Bush himself did not publicly comment on Tibet, Secretary of State Colin Powell gave some inkling of the early thinking of the administration at his confirmation hearing on 17 January 2001, when he made a very strong statement in support of Tibetans in Tibet and of the Dalai Lama:

> It's a very difficult situation right now with the Chinese sending more and more Han Chinese in to settle Tibet. What seems to be a policy that might well destroy that society. I think we have to

> reenergize our discussions with the Chinese to let them know that
> this is another example of the kind of behavior that will effect [*sic*]
> our entire relationship. And show our interest in solidarity with
> the Dalai Lama and the people of Tibet.[37]

These tough comments are eerily reminiscent of the early days of the Clinton administration. As with the Clinton administration, however, over the past year, the tough Bush rhetoric on China has vanished in the face of real issues affecting U.S. national interests. Even before the 11 September 2001 terrorist attack, the Bush administration was back-pedaling, and after the warming of Sino-American relations following 11 September, it is not likely that the administration will risk a worsening of Sino-American relations by taking major steps in support of Tibet (such as by threatening to change its position on Chinese sovereignty over Tibet or by recognizing Dharamsala as a government-in-exile if China does not improve its policies in Tibet). So although President Bush, like Clinton, is quietly trying to persuade both sides to open new talks, as of now, he has been unsuccessful. The dual policy honed by the Clinton administration appears to have been appropriated by the Bush administration, but with no greater success.

In conclusion, there are no simple solutions to the Tibet question in either its internal or international dimensions, and the future of Tibetans in Tibet and China is uncertain. Tibetan villages (in which 85 percent of the population live) are entirely Tibetan in ethnicity, language, and culture and will certainly remain so in the near future. Life is changing, as the amount of land per capita decreases and villagers are pushed to supplement farm income by seeking jobs as migrant laborers, but the essential character of village life is still completely Tibetan.[38] The urban areas, however, are very different. The growing sinicization of Tibet's cities and towns (and probably, in the next decade, its county seats as well) may create a situation that is somewhat analogous to the situation in Inner Mongolia, where the cities are demographically and culturally dominated by Han, and Mongolians predominate only in the more distant rural-grass-land herding areas.[39] Thus, unless a resolution with the Dalai Lama is reached or Beijing unilaterally returns to an ethnically conciliatory internal approach, the future for a predominantly Tibetan Tibet is not good.

NOTES

Parts of this chapter are adapted from Melvyn C. Goldstein, *A History of Modern Tibet, 1913–1951* (Berkeley and Los Angeles: University of California Press, 1989);

idem, *The Snow Lion and the Dragon* (Berkeley and Los Angeles: University of California Press, 1997); and idem, *The History of Modern Tibet, 1951–1955* (forthcoming).

1. Tibet here refers to political Tibet, the polity ruled by the Dalai Lama. It does not include the various ethnic Tibetan areas in Kham and Amdo.

2. It is interesting to note that in January 2002, China announced it was starting the population transfers using its own funds (Agence France-Presse, "China Revives").

3. Lamb, *Britain and Chinese Central Asia.*

4. See Goldstein, *History of Modern Tibet: 1913–51,* and Lamb, *Britain and Chinese Central Asia.*

5. See Goldstein, *Snow Lion.*

6. Goldstein, *History of Modern Tibet, 1913–1951,* 767–768.

7. Ibid., 703ff.

8. Gyalo Thondup, author interview, May 1987.

9. Department of Information and International Relations, "Dalai Lama."

10. See Knaus, *Orphans of the Cold War.*

11. New China News Agency, *Summary of World Broadcasts.*

12. Anonymous Tibetan exile-government official, author interview. See also the comment of delegation member Jurchen Thupten Namgyal cited in "News Report," 5.

13. Department of Information and International Relations, "Dalai Lama."

14. In October 1982, the Office of Tibet in New York City submitted a fourteen-page document titled "Chinese Human Rights Abuses in Tibet: 1959–1982."

15. These population figures come from Zhang and Zhang, "Present Population," 48.

16. The new strategy was finalized, it appears, after a series of high-level meetings between key Tibetan and Western supporters in New York, Washington, and London. The history of these developments has not yet been well documented.

17. Cited in Goldstein, *Snow Lion,* 77.

18. It was strongly criticized by, for example, the Tibetan Youth Congress, the European Tibetan Youth Association, and another of the Dalai Lama's elder brothers, Thupten Norbu. The latter sent a letter to Tibetans throughout the world attacking his brother's decision to relinquish the goal of independence.

19. McElroy, "No Response."

20. "Aide-Memoire Sent by State Department."

21. U.S. National Archives: USFR, 693.0031 Tibet/8–2147, dispatch no. 46, 28 October 1947.

22. U.S. National Archives: USFR, 693.0031 Tibet/1–849, 12 April 1949.

23. U.S. National Archives: USFR, 793B.00/7–1251 telegram no. 107, 12 July 1951.

24. U.S. offers of military aid also were perceived as inadequate because they were contingent on agreement by the Government of India, which was on record as being against this.

25. In 1964, for example, the CIA provided a total of $1,735,000 in support, including $500,000 for the support of twenty-one hundred Tibetan guerrillas in Nepal, $180,000 as a subsidy for the Dalai Lama, $225,000 for equipment, trans-

portation, and training, and $400,000 for covert training in Colorado ("Memorandum for the Special Group, 9 January 1964," in U.S. Department of State, *Foreign Relations of the United States, 1964–68, 731*).

26. "Telegram from Ambassador Brown to the State Department, 4 September 1959," in U.S. Department of State, *Foreign Relations of the United States, 1958–60, 778.*

27. Ibid.

28. On 3 November 1959, the Republic of China's ambassador to the United States, Dr. George Yeh, was informed by the director of the Office of Chinese Affairs and the assistant secretary for Far Eastern Affairs that "the United States had made a decision to go somewhat beyond its previous position with regard to Tibet, namely that it is an autonomous country under the suzerainty of China" ("Memorandum of Conversation," in U.S. Department of State, *Foreign Relations of the United States, 1958–60,* 801).

29. U.S. Department of State, *Foreign Relations of the United States, 1958–60, 809.*

30. "Memorandum from Assistant Secretary of State for Far Eastern Affairs (Parsons) to Secretary of State (Herter), 14 October 1959," in U.S. Department of State, *Foreign Relations of the United States, 1958–60,* 798.

31. Gyalo Thondup, the Dalai Lama's brother and his liaison with the CIA, said that the United States came to tell him in 1969 that they had to discontinue Tibet's assistance. He said that Kissinger made a promise to the Chinese to cut off diplomatic ties with Taiwan and cease support for the Dalai Lama and the Tibetan resistance (Author interview, Hong Kong, 11 April 1994).

32. *Tibet Press Watch.*

33. U.S. Department of State, *Relations of the United States with Tibet,* Washington, D.C.: 1995, 4.

34. *International Herald Tribune,* 22 November 1993, 1.

35. U.S. Department of State, *Relations of the United States with Tibet,* Washington, D.C.: 1995, 4.

36. *International Herald Tribune,* 22 November 1993, 1.

37. Phillips and Meserve, "Senate Foreign Relations Committee."

38. Goldstein, Jiao, Beall, and Tsering, "Fertility and Family Planning."

39. The percentage of Han in Tibet, however, will not soon approach the levels found in Inner Mongolia, where 81 percent of the total population is Han.

7 / A Thorn in the Dragon's Side

Tibetan Buddhist Culture in China

MATTHEW T. KAPSTEIN

We have by now grown accustomed to an ongoing war of representations concerning contemporary Tibetan religion in China. According to what is no doubt the most prominent perspective in the United States and Western Europe, the brutal machinery of Chinese communism is determined to eradicate any trace of the Buddhist tradition among Tibetans in China, while some one hundred thousand exiles led by the Dalai Lama, together with their foreign supporters, struggle to preserve an enlightened religion against all odds.[1] The Chinese government, of course, sees things quite differently. In its view, Tibetans in China now enjoy unprecedented religious liberty. This is compromised, according to the official viewpoint, only in the case of Chinese Communist Party (CCP) members (who are required by virtue of their avowal of Marxist-Leninism to be atheists) and the small minority of Tibetans who the authorities believe to be using religion merely to cloak illicit political activity, above all by remaining expressly loyal to (and not just religiously respectful of) the exiled Dalai Lama. The latter's real aims, according to the CCP, have little in fact to do with religion but are seditiously motivated: he intends to split China apart.[2]

One of the unremarked ironies in the background of this opposition is that there are now in fact more Tibetan Buddhist monks in China than there are Tibetan exiles, including both monks and laypersons, in all the rest of the world. Let me restate this unambiguously: in China today there are more than one hundred thousand Tibetan Buddhist monks.[3] This, of course, is not to say that official Chinese representations of the situation are unobjectionable; many religious Tibetans in China maintain that they continue to experience significant constraints and sometimes harsh oppression, despite whatever freedoms they now enjoy. In some instances, alleged abuses have been sufficiently credible and sufficiently egregious to attract the sustained attention of international organizations dedicated to issues of human rights.[4] This chapter attempts to describe the present conflicted situation and its origins and discover what it has to tell us of the uneasy balance between religious freedom and religious restriction in contemporary China.

POLITICAL AND CULTURAL TIBET

"Tibet," as we use the term in English, is an ambiguous designation. It refers both to a political entity and to the entire territory inhabited by ethnic Tibetans and bound together not by political union but by commonalities of language, history, and cultural tradition. These two Tibets are not now, and indeed seldom have been, geographically congruent. The ambiguity of Tibet may be explained in part historically: During some periods in Tibet's earlier history and under the regime of the fifth Dalai Lama, founded in 1642, political Tibet did correspond closely with the Tibetan cultural area, the vast region known in Tibetan as "the three provinces" *(chölka sum)*.[5] Since then, the fifth Dalai Lama's successors and their regents have insisted in principle upon the legitimacy of their authority throughout this whole area. But less than a half century after the "Great Fifth's" death, in 1682, large parts of the eastern Tibetan provinces of Amdo and Kham were incorporated by the growing Manchu empire into administrative units apart from Tibet, and they thus came under the jurisdiction of local provincial officials appointed in Beijing and not by the Lhasa government.[6] When the thirteenth Dalai Lama declared his independence, following the fall of the Manchus in 1911, he therefore effectively held sway in central and western Tibet but not throughout the eastern regions of the Tibetan cultural sphere. Despite efforts by his government to consolidate its authority in these areas, which resulted in some fluctuation of the borders, the Chinese Republicans, who came to power in 1912, never entirely relinquished their hold over them (nor, indeed, their claim to Tibet as a whole). When the People's Republic of China (PRC) was founded in October 1949, the realm constituting the independent Tibetan polity governed from Lhasa corresponded territorially to what is today the Tibet Autonomous Region (TAR). The eastern Tibetan populations of Amdo and Kham for the most part inhabited not Tibet but prefectures belonging to the Chinese provinces of Qinghai, Gansu, Sichuan, and Yunnan.[7]

The people of these eastern Tibetan regions traditionally related to the central Tibetan regime in a number of ways.[8] For the most part, they revered the Dalai Lama and regarded Lhasa and its shrines as the center of their spiritual and cultural world. Pilgrimage to Lhasa was an important practice for them, and virtually all Tibetans desired to visit the sacred city at some point in their lives. Certainly there were numerous easterners—particularly among the adherents of the Gelukpa sect, with which the Dalai Lamas were affiliated and which therefore dominated the political life of central Tibet—who believed the Dalai Lama to be their rightful political leader and who favored some form of political union with central Tibet. Nevertheless, the immediate political allegiance of most was to local Tibetan princes and chieftains, who enjoyed a high degree of autonomy under both the Manchus and the Republicans. The people of Amdo and Kham were proud of their own independent traditions, and sometimes also of their alliances with Chinese governmental authorities, who were often thought to buttress their local autonomy: the ruler of the principality of Nangchen, for instance, styled himself Nangchen Chinghu Gyelpo, the "king of Nangchen in Qinghai."

There is reason to believe that eastern Tibetan populations, in accord with their traditions of local rule, sometimes also enjoyed less rigidly hierarchical social relations than did the populations of political Tibet.[9] One ramification may have been somewhat greater scope for economic enterprise among eastern Tibetan entrepreneurs. (It seems true, at the very least, that traditional Tibet's greatest mercantile fortunes were won by eastern Tibetan trading families. Some eastern Tibetans have been able to draw on this commercial history to achieve a relatively high degree of success in Tibetan exile communities.) Tribal and clan affiliations formed the fundamental organizational structures in the east, whereas the division of land and people into aristocratic and monastic estates was more characteristic of the central Tibetan polity. In their expressions of self-identity, eastern Tibetans tended to portray themselves as belonging to strong and free confederations of warriors, in contrast with central Tibetans, whom they saw as weak and subject to the whims of their lords.

The political and economic variation of the Tibetan world was complemented by a measure of religious diversity as well. Though the 17th century consolidation of Tibetan rule by the fifth Dalai Lama was accompanied by some effort to mandate adherence to the Gelukpa sect, to whose hierarchy the Dalai Lamas belonged, this effort was generally less thoroughgoing in the eastern Tibetan regions than in central Tibet, and the older Tibetan religious orders accordingly were more prominent here than they were in the center.[10] The Karmapa, for example, a line of very important hierarchs of the Kagyüpa order, had been prominent in central Tibetan affairs from the thirteenth century onward. Though their authority was much diminished in the central regions following the rise of the Dalai

Lamas, they continued to enjoy extensive, and even growing, prestige—down to our time—among Tibetans throughout the districts of Kham that now belong to Sichuan and Yunnan. This has had significant ramifications in recent years; with the decimation of the central Tibetan religious leadership during the 1960s and 1970s, it was the young seventeenth Karmapa—who hailed from far-eastern Tibet (specifically, western Sichuan) and whose investiture was widely supported by religious Tibetans in the east—who emerged as the most revered figure in central Tibetan religious life following the death of the Panchen Lama in 1989. (The implications of the Karmapa's flight to India in 1999 will be considered in brief below.)

During the eighteenth and nineteenth centuries, new centers of religious learning and art developed in some parts of eastern Tibet, with patronage from local rulers, traders, and chiefs. Examples included the huge Gelukpa monastery of Labrang (Ch. Labulangsi), in Gansu Province, and the monasteries and printery of the formerly independent principality of Derge, in Sichuan. For the non-Gelukpa orders especially, the newly founded monastic colleges in the east came to function as the primary centers of religious education and scholarship, though the great Gelukpa institutions of the Lhasa region continued to attract large numbers of eastern Tibetan monks as well. In some parts of eastern Tibet, the extent of monasticism was truly staggering: in present-day Aba County (Tib. Rnga-ba-rdzong), for example, in 1951 at least 25 percent of the entire population (or roughly half of the males) were monks living in monasteries.[11] This number was no doubt somewhat inflated, owing to the presence of large numbers of monks from neighboring districts who had joined one or another of Aba's famous monastic communities. Nevertheless, it does reflect the great importance that monastic Buddhism had assumed in the culture and economy of eastern Tibet, as it had throughout the Tibetan world and Mongolia more generally.[12]

RELIGION IN TIBETAN LIFE

The institutional heart of Tibetan Buddhism is the monastery. Mass monasticism was encouraged in traditional Tibetan society, particularly after the consolidation of political power by the fifth Dalai Lama.[13] This was justified ideologically by the notion that the monk was in an especially privileged position to avoid evil and to achieve merit, so that by maximizing monasticism the maximum merit accrued to Tibetan society as a whole and especially to those individuals and families who most contributed to the monastic system by dedicating sons to the religious life and wealth to support religious activities. Nomadic groups in the east often felt this to be a particularly urgent matter, for the merit earned by supporting good monks and their monasteries was believed to counterbalance to some extent the burden of sin that one acquired through actions prohibited by the system of religious ethics, especially the slaughter of animals, which were nevertheless unavoidable in a nomadic livelihood.[14] Though worldly life was thought to be inevitably ensnared in various evils, a family could still better itself spiritually by committing some sons to the clergy. And if those sons achieved religious distinction, this could sometimes also impact favorably upon the status of the family concerned. This outlook helped to sustain the large or small monasteries and shrines of various kinds that were to be found in nearly every locale.

In practical terms, the monastery fostered a concentration of cultural resources, serving as a center for education and the cultivation of the arts (though in most cases only a minority of the monks participated in these pursuits). Significantly, too, the monastery absorbed surplus labor. Whenever the rate of fertility outpaced the expansion of economic activity—and there is reason to believe that this was a regular tendency throughout much of the Tibetan world—monasticism provided a socially valued alternative to production.[15] For religious girls and women, nunneries also existed, though nuns appear to have been less numerous than monks and seldom had access to resources for more than a rudimentary education.[16] However, it is also true that nuns more often than monks continued to live with their families, contributing to household work while also pursuing their devotions. The apparent numerical discrepancy between the male and female religious, therefore, may be due in part to the fact that relatively fewer religious women lived in specifically religious institutions.

The religious life of Tibet embraced a wide range of ritual practices whose origins and purposes were diverse. Among them were the important rituals of the central Tibetan state and of the local Tibetan polities, such as those concerned with the state oracles and protective deities, which had developed over the course of centuries as solemn rites of national or regional significance. On the other end of the scale, daily observances, such as the offering of the fragrant smoke of burnt juniper to the gods and spirits of the local environment, were and continue to be performed in virtually every Tibetan household. Rituals of these and other types have long been incorporated within the Buddhist religion in Tibet and have been formulated over the centuries to accord, more or less, with Buddhist doctrinal norms. The importance of religious ritual for the maintenance of health, prosperity, and peace in this life, and for securing a positive course of rebirth in the next, ensured that many types of religious specialists enjoyed an essential and honored place in traditional Tibetan society.

Most monks entered the monastery as children and did so at the wish of their parents. Such children were granted the essential vows of the Buddhist novitiate and became eligible to receive full ordination only in later adolescence. Rudimentary knowledge of the alphabet seems to have been relatively widespread among monks and nuns, though the numbers able or inclined to pursue a higher education in Buddhist philosophy, or in such disciplines as medicine, art, or astrology, were few. The majority of the monks participated, when possible, in prayer services sponsored by lay patrons, who offered tea, butter, grain, and cash to the assembled congregation. Monks also pursued economic or administrative activities required for their own support or for that of the monastic community. They therefore were regularly involved in commerce and in various trades. Larger monasteries had their own complex bureaucracies, in which some offices were filled according to merit and ability, and others were occupied by *tülku*s (incarnates), groomed for the task since childhood.[17]

Some monasteries housed colleges where advanced studies could be pursued by those motivated to do so. Aspirant monk-scholars sometimes traveled for months across the whole of the Tibetan world to enter an especially famous college, such as the Gelukpa Gomang College of Drepung Monastery, near Lhasa, or the Nyingmapa Shrisimha College of Dzokchen Monastery, near Derge, in modern Sichuan. Besides the economic and ritual functions of the monastery, therefore, almost the entire apparatus of Tibetan formal education was concentrated within the monasteries as well. Literacy in traditional Tibet was a preeminently religious affair, and so, not surprisingly, the clerical services of trained monks were required by the old Lhasa government and by the administrations of the eastern Tibetan principalities as well.[18]

TIBETAN BUDDHISM UNDER THE EARLY PEOPLE'S REPUBLIC

As seen above, the monastic institution was central to the formation of Tibetan culture, and the monastic hierarchy, culminating in the Dalai Lama, was the focal point of cultural authority, both within and outside the territory ruled from Lhasa. Despite the very broad Tibetan consensus along these lines, there were nevertheless many variations in the ways in which particular individuals and communities positioned themselves in relation to it. Not all Tibetans lived within the central Tibetan religio-political system, and what's more, by the 1930s in various parts of the Tibetan world there were proponents of modernization, as well as some political dissidents, who were looking to China or to the West for inspiration.[19] When the course of events in China turned decisively in favor of the Communists after World War II, there were those among the Tibetan modernists who felt that the revolutionary programs of the CCP offered the Tibetans the best opportunity for modernization and reform. An example was the celebrated monk-scholar Dobi Sherab Gyatso (1884–1968), who after allying himself with the Nationalists during the 1930s, later turned to the Communists.[20] In 1952 he would become the first chairman of the Chinese Buddhist Association.[21]

Throughout the 1950s, Sherab sought to encourage the Tibetan clergy to see that the best hope for the future of their religion lay with Mao Zedong and the CCP. His motivations may well have been in part opportunistic, but they were also pragmatic and protective of the Buddhist religious tradition in which he had been educated and which he always saw as his first loyalty. In a letter addressed to the administration of Serko Monastery in Qinghai, for instance, responding to reports that some of the monks were misappropriating the monastery's wealth for private gain, he wrote:

> Now, at this time when throughout the world there shines the sunlight of Chairman Mao's good system, in which there is freedom of religious faith and protection for the teaching [of Buddhism], there have been some bad monks who—taking account of neither the Triple Gem, nor karma and its results, nor the laws of the state—have disloyally looted the monastery and have in other ways opened the door to evil rebirth. On hearing such things, [I must respond that] from this very day forward this cannot be allowed, and what was done already must be brought to a stop. You must beware, for this [behavior] is evidently reactionary [*hphan tos*] rebellion against both the ways of the Communist Party's United Front and the great policy [*krin tshe*] of protection for the teaching. You should each think about both your present and future lives! One may well be a monk, but it is not permitted for you to engage in trade or destruction [of property], regardless of the size of the monastic residence unit [to which you belong], nor are others allowed to sell or to destroy [on your behalf]. Bear all this in mind! It is not good if you deliberately neglect either the Buddha's teaching or the customs of the Communist Party.[22]

Sherab's attempt to find a common ground between the policies of the CCP and the interests of Tibetan Buddhism came to represent in some measure the norm among educated Tibetan clergy during the 1950s. Both the Dalai Lama and the Panchen Lama embraced the hopeful idea that Mao Zedong's revolution had room for their religion and indeed, that the ethical concern of Mahayana Buddhism for universal well-being—which, though widely preached in theory, was imperfectly actualized in traditional society—would be realized by the dawning socialist order.[23] Such hopes, of course, were naive, and it seems likely that Sherab recognized this early on; besides his praise for Mao in the letter quoted above, one detects a distinct element of fear for what will befall the religious establishment should they fail to toe the line.

During the late 1950s, the promise of a harmonious relationship between Chinese Communism and Tibetan Buddhism progressively came undone. The difference of circumstances prevailing between political Tibet and the eastern Tibetan districts incorporated into Chinese provincial units was of crucial importance here. In political Tibet, Mao had insisted on a policy of gradualism, convincing many Tibetans that China would desist from forcibly overturning Tibet's traditional ways. In the east, on the other hand, provincial authorities were already aggressively pursuing policies of communalization, which provoked a chain of violent reactions, culminating in the formation of the "Four Rivers, Six Ranges" (Chu Bzhi, Gangs Drug) guerrilla movement. As the monasteries were considered to be among the centers of resistance to the implementation of Communist programs and also to be giving shelter to the rebels, they became increasingly prone to direct attack, and in 1956, a number of eastern Tibetan monasteries were actually subjected to aerial bombardment. These circumstances were deeply shocking to Tibetan sensibilities and led to the flight of large numbers of easterners, both monks and laypersons, to central Tibet.[24]

It has been estimated that by the start of the Tibetan New Year in early 1959, some fifty thousand refugees from Kham and Amdo were camping in and around the capital. For many of these people, the gradualist policy pursued by the CCP in central Tibet was seen as a mere sham; their harsh experiences in the east had demonstrated the true nature of Chinese Communism in its policies toward Tibetan society and toward religion in particular. Their reports of the fighting in the east contributed directly to the volatility that was then building in Lhasa. With the events surrounding the so-called Lhasa Uprising of 1959 and the subsequent flight of the Dalai Lama to India, the steadily worsening relations between the

Fig. 7.1. Following the Cultural Revolution: a temple mural effaced by Maoist slogans (Photo by Matthew T. Kapstein)

Tibetan Buddhist establishment and the Chinese Communists spun altogether out of control. Ordinary monks and religious hierarchs formed a prominent constituency among the Tibetan exiles who followed the Dalai Lama, and these included many of the eastern Tibetans who had moved into central Tibet during the late 1950s. Religious persons who remained behind in Tibet were mostly forced to leave their monasteries, some only to return to their homes, but many others were classed as rebels and reactionaries and imprisoned as a result. By 1962, both the Panchen Lama and Sherab, certainly the two most renowned Tibetan clerics remaining in China, were openly expressing their disillusionment, and both would be shortly dismissed from their posts.[25] The efforts of the CCP to find an accommodation with Tibetan Buddhists and the efforts of some Tibetan Buddhist leaders to find a patron in the CCP were now decisively finished. It remained only for the Cultural Revolution to undertake the wholesale destruction of whatever remained of Tibetan religious culture.[26]

Having dominated Tibetan politics, economic life, and society for centuries, the monasteries now had to cede the last vestiges of their power and privilege to the secular force of the CCP. The assault on religion intensified throughout the 1960s, and all but a few of the thousands of Tibetan temples and monasteries were razed, their artistic treasures and libraries destroyed or plundered. Tens of thousands of monks and nuns were forced to undergo "reeducation," and many perished under extraordinarily harsh conditions or suffered prolonged maltreatment in prison. The religious institutions of Tibet's old society were annihilated, and few could have imagined that they would ever return. Tibet had been dragged, kicking and screaming, into one version of modernity.

A REVIVAL AND ITS VICISSITUDES

The conclusion of the Cultural Revolution in 1976 and the subsequent consolidation of power within the CCP by Deng Xiaoping two years later brought great changes to cultural and religious affairs throughout China. It was now generally recognized that the unrestrained assault on traditional cultural values and institutions had done more harm than good—it represented what the official jargon characterized as a "leftist deviation"—and that some measure of restoration in these spheres was warranted. However, it was not the case that any and all such activity was to be immediately sanctioned anew. In some cultural fields—for instance, in the study of local history—it was clear to all that renewal was essential for the contemporary social sciences, as well as for reasons of cultural preservation, and this was accordingly given sufficiently broad encouragement to usher in a veritable "local history movement."[27] In other pursuits, especially in the religious sphere, where ideological differences between the traditional religions and the CCP could not be readily ignored, liberalization of cultural policy proceeded with greater caution. Though there were many regional differences in the manner in which new policy directives were carried out, cultural revival in Tibet unfolded within the same general parameters as it did in the rest of China. During the late 1970s and early 1980s, Tibetans—who had witnessed the destruction of their monasteries, religious artworks, and libraries, the exile of many leading authorities in areas of both religious and secular culture, and the persecution of most such persons who had remained behind—found themselves pondering both the wreckage of their civilization and the prospects for renewal that Dengist reform seemed to promise.

It was the visit to Tibet in 1980 by Party Secretary Hu Yaobang that clearly signaled that a cultural revival was now possible.[28] Hu was reported to have been genuinely appalled by conditions in the TAR in all spheres and urged that sweeping reforms be enacted. At the same time, a cautious series of contacts between Beijing and the representatives of the Dalai Lama raised hopes that the Chinese leadership was eager to find a basis for reconciliation with the exiled Tibetan leader. In tandem with this opening, China also began to permit some Tibetans to visit relatives and places of Buddhist pilgrimage in Nepal and India, and Tibetans living abroad, including some religious leaders, were allowed to visit their original homes for the first time in over two decades. Renewed contacts between Tibetans in China and the exile community directly encouraged the restoration of aspects of traditional religious culture, and exiles who had the means to do so contributed financial as well as moral incentives. Once more, this was particularly true in eastern Tibet, where beginning in the early 1980s, important religious leaders living abroad were sometimes able to become directly involved in the restoration of their communities. (The central Tibetan religious leadership in exile, by contrast, was severely constrained in this regard.) In addition, older Tibetan religious leaders who had remained in China and had survived the Cultural Revolution were now being rehabilitated and in some cases permitted to resume their religious activities. Foremost among them was the Panchen Lama, who used his regained prestige and influence to support the religious revival to the extent possible.[29]

Besides these developments, the post–Cultural Revolution evolution of Chinese law offered further grounds for hope. The Chinese constitution promulgated in 1982 discussed freedom of faith in its thirty-sixth article. I cite the text here according to the official Tibetan-language version:

> Citizens of the People's Republic of China have freedom of religious faith.
>
> It is not permitted for any state office, social organization, or private individual whatsoever to coerce a citizen by force to have religious faith or not to have religious faith. It is not permitted to discriminate against a citizen who has religious faith or a citizen who does not have religious faith.
>
> The basis for state protection of regular religious activity [is this]: it is forbidden for anyone, on the basis of a religion, to destroy social regulations or to harm the physical health of a citizen or to obstruct the educational programs of the state.
>
> Religious associations and religious work must not be subject to foreign influence.[30]

Of course, the mere fact that the constitution offered a qualified legal protection for religious *faith* was no guarantee that freedom of religious *practice* would be respected. Earlier Chinese constitutions had done the

Fig. 7.2. A revival begins: pilgrims picnicking at Ganden Monastery in 1985 (Photo by Matthew T. Kapstein)

same, and as we have seen above, Tibetan religious leaders during the 1950s believed that they enjoyed similar protections. Nevertheless, in this case, additional reinforcement was offered by the CCP's promulgation, also in 1982, of Document 19, said to have been drafted by Hu Yaobang.[31] Though religion is of course incompatible with the Communist ideology of atheism, Document 19 made it clear that this warranted a prohibition on the practice of religion by Party members, but that otherwise, freedom of belief was genuinely to be protected. In view of such policy directives and of the many remarkable and rapid changes taking place under Deng's leadership, a dramatic revival of Tibetan Buddhism now ensued.

This revival in fact took many different forms. At its most basic level, it meant that ordinary believers could now engage publicly once more in a variety of devotional and ritual activities: performing prostrations and circumambulations, making offerings, and saying prayers at temples and other sacred sites; erecting prayer flags and stone walls with prayers carved upon them; copying and distributing prayer books and religious icons. The small number of temples and monasteries that had survived the Cultural Revolution in more or less usable condition began to be refurbished and reopened, and efforts were made to rebuild some that had been destroyed. In some cases, it was even possible to secure aid from the government or some payment in compensation for the damage that had earlier been done. As the monasteries reopened, the small numbers of aged monks who remained were joined by numerous young new recruits, some entering the order in a wave of religious enthusiasm and others, following tradition, sent by their families. The restoration of religious festivals and pilgrimages was also a development welcomed by both monks and laypersons.[32]

Religious revival unfolded in tandem with, and in relation to, a number of other developments in the increasingly open cultural scene. Of particular importance in this regard were Tibetan-language publications, education, and cultural-relics preservation. The provincial governments that controlled eastern Tibet for the most part also began to accept a more liberal view of traditional Tibetan culture, and in these regions, in particular, religious-revival activities proceeded rapidly and on an astonishingly large scale. Later, we shall turn to examine aspects of the revival in the east in greater detail.

The revival of Buddhism among Tibetans, as with religious revival in other parts of China, was an unwelcome surprise within some quarters in the CCP. Though the policy of liberalization was encouraged by Hu Yaobang and those most closely associated with him, many believed that after decades of communism, few would be interested in religion any longer. The liberalization was intended to provide an opportunity for the last vestiges of superstitious belief to quietly wither away. It came as a shock, therefore, to discover that religion could still appeal to large numbers of people and, above all, to large numbers of the young. When I first began to visit Tibet, in 1984, Chinese cadres posted in Lhasa often commented to me that they had to conclude that there was something genetically defective about the Tibetans that caused them to embrace the irrational beliefs that supposedly had long since ceased to dominate their society! (Being stationed in Tibet, of course, they were perhaps unaware that analogous "mutations" were expressing themselves among Muslims, Christians, Buddhists, and Daoists throughout China.)

The revival of Tibetan Buddhism that began over two decades ago has continued to the present, but it has nevertheless been marked by repeated tensions with the Chinese political leadership, especially in the TAR. Most dramatically, a series of demonstrations in support of the exiled Dalai Lama, staged by monks in Lhasa beginning in 1987, led to rioting culminating in the declaration of a state of emergency in 1989.[33] Since that time, the government's view of the Dalai Lama has steadily hardened, and after a period in which the expression of purely religious devotion to him was tolerated, any explicit manifestation of loyalty to him is now treated as fundamentally political in nature.

In 1989, the highest-ranking Buddhist hierarch who had remained in Tibet after 1959, the Panchen Lama, died suddenly, and his passing led to new disputes between Chinese authorities and the partisans of the Dalai Lama. This received worldwide attention when, on 14 May 1995, the Dalai Lama and the Tibetan government-in-exile announced the discovery of the young incarnate Panchen in Tibet. The Chinese responded harshly: the acting abbot of Tashi Lhünpo Monastery, Chadrel Rinpoche, was placed under house arrest in Chengdu, Sichuan, and Gendun Choekyi Nyima, the young boy who had been recognized as the Panchen Lama by the Dalai Lama, was detained with his family. Shortly thereafter, his recognition was rejected by the Chinese government, and a lottery was held on 29 November 1995 to choose a new Panchen Lama from among several officially approved candidates. For his role in the affair, Chadrel Rinpoche was imprisoned without recognizable due process; meanwhile, the precise circumstances of the boy he had championed as the Dalai Lama's candidate remain uncertain and have become a topic of much rumor. Both the case of Chadrel Rinpoche and that of Gendun Choekyi Nyima are among those that are of particular concern to the human-rights community.[34]

The Dalai Lama remains of course the best-known symbol of Tibetan aspirations in the world at large and also for Tibetans themselves. One result of religious revival in post–Cultural Revolution Tibet was an outpouring of new-felt devotion to him, manifest frequently in the distribution and display of his image. During the late 1980s and early 1990s, photographs of the Dalai Lama were ubiquitous and could be seen in temples, homes, shops and markets. In reaction to the Panchen Lama affair, the Party launched a campaign in April 1996 to remove such images from view, particularly from public and otherwise high-prestige venues such as schools and the homes and offices of Tibetan officials. A protest riot was reported to have broken out at Ganden Monastery, which resulted in some deaths, many arrests, and new restrictions placed upon the monastery. Nevertheless, the campaign directed against the Dalai Lama has continued unabated, and by the summer of 2000, it was reported that even the homes of ordinary villagers in some districts had been searched for offending images and publications. Outside of the TAR, too, the Dalai Lama's likeness is now rarely displayed. Devotion to him continues to be evident primarily in such unostentatious practices as the recitation of prayers on behalf of his health and longevity.[35]

There has been other fallout from the Panchen Lama affair as well. Because the Dalai Lama's recognition is believed to be crucial for the legitimation of a new Panchen, few of the Tibetan Buddhist clergy in China have wished to affirm the legitimacy of the child enthroned with government approval. But at the same time, the government has sought to secure its position among Tibetan Buddhist believers by insisting that leading monks do make their acquiescence in this matter public and clear. The ensuing conflict is widely thought to have contributed to the decision of two of the leading hierarchs remaining in China to leave the country: the Agya Rinpoche, abbot of Kumbum Monastery in Qinghai, in 1998, and the seventeenth Karmapa, at the end of 1999. In response, the CCP has moved to limit contact between Tibetan Buddhists in China and lamas living abroad, so that even some who have regularly visited their home monasteries throughout the past two decades now find themselves subject to increased restrictions.[36]

The government has also sought to promote a following for their Panchen among ordinary monks and believers, widely distributing his photograph and glowing reports of his good character and educational progress. Nevertheless, popular opinion is universally cynical. As a monk in Ganze (Sichuan) told me, "For all we care, they can dress up a monkey in lama's robes and enthrone him. But they can't make us feel faith." In fact, throughout my travels in Sichuan in the summer of 2000, I was told of the mass distribution to the monks of Tibetan New Year's cards bearing the likeness of the government's Panchen. "On New Year's we were given these cards, and by the very next day, they were all in the trash," one of the recipients told me.

Given all this, I was astonished to discover that in some of the Gelukpa monasteries in Sichuan that I visited, the monks were proudly sporting pins with photos of the state-recognized Panchen. Closer inspection, however, revealed that some clever individual had manufactured them using the face of Gendun Choekyi Nyima, the Dalai Lama's candidate, superimposed upon one of the government Panchen's ubiquitous official photographs. From a few yards' distance, one therefore had the impression that the monks were expressing their support of the government's position in this affair, whereas the opposite was in fact true. There now appears to be a certain agreement that public protests of the type we saw during the late 1980s are pointless and invite only repression; religious dissent now takes subtler forms. The deceptive Panchen Lama pin serves as an excellent metaphor for the general condition of Tibetan Buddhism in China at present—depending upon one's perspective, a single set of facts can often be read in opposite ways.

RELIGION AND CONTEMPORARY EDUCATION

I wish to turn now to survey a number of topics that have grown out of my observations during research visits in 1998 and 2000. These include Tibetan religion in its relation to contemporary education, apparent discrepancies between religious affairs in the TAR and in the eastern Tibetan districts, and aspects of the representation of Tibetan religion in contemporary Chinese culture.

Policies and programs bearing upon Tibetan affairs during the post–Cultural Revolution era have been set by a series of "work forums."[37] One of the projects undertaken under directives from the first, and especially the second, forum was a thoroughgoing overhaul of Tibetan-language texts for instruction at the primary and middle-school levels. Though it is not true, as has sometimes been reported, that Tibetan-language instruction had been entirely prohibited during the Cultural Revolution, it was clear enough by the early 1980s that educational development in Tibet as a whole had been neglected and that available instructional materials were inadequate and out of date. In response, a new educational consortium among the "five autonomous regions and provinces" (Tib. *ljongs dang zhing chen lnga*) with Tibetan populations— the TAR, Qinghai, Gansu, Sichuan, and Yunnan—embarked upon an ambitious effort to create suitable textbooks not only for learning written Tibetan but for the whole range of required classes, including science, math, civics, geography, history, and art. For the middle-school textbooks, in particular, this demanded a remarkable effort to standardize a largely new vocabulary for subjects such as algebra, trigonometry, calculus, chemistry, biology, and physics. The publication of the resulting second-forum textbooks during the 1990s marks a signal achievement in the renewal of Tibetan as vehicle for culture and learning in contemporary China.[38]

As might be expected, traditional Tibetan religion and subjects closely associated with religion are not among the topics prominently discussed in the new texts.[39] Nevertheless, neither are they avoided altogether. In the elective senior-middle language and literature texts, topics relating to Tibetan religious traditions are indeed represented. In one of these we find, for instance, a survey of key points in the system of logic that forms the basis for the practice of Buddhist monastic philosophical debate. Consider the manner in which this branch of Buddhist learning is introduced here to Tibetan high schoolers:

> Concerning the science of logic: there are many texts on the science of logic written by non-Buddhists of the noble land [Aryadesha, a traditional Sanskrit designation for India as the Buddhist holy land]. Moreover, the great Buddhist scholar Dignaga composed the *Compendium of Logic,* and Master Dharmakirti the *Seven Logical Treatises.* There are many commentaries upon them, which the gracious translators and scholars have rendered into Tibetan and which now form about twenty volumes in the Tanjur [the canon of Indian Buddhist commentaries translated into Tibetan]. As for the commentaries on their meaning by Tibetan authors, there are many texts authored by scholars of all the sectarian traditions, such as the *Treasury of Reason,* by Sakya Pandita. . . .
>
> The reason for studying the science of logic, that is, the science of inference, is this: provisionally, it contributes to the agility of intelligence, so that the intellect enters [new subjects] clearly and quickly, making it easy to understand the textbooks studied. Ultimately, when you investigate the underlying nature of outer objects and of the mind within, you are not like those who accept foolishness, but on the basis of your intelligence, you come to understand the real nature of outer and inner matters.[40]

Even more striking is an account of the hardships endured by the eleventh-century poet-saint Milarepa during his apprenticeship to his guru, Marpa. This might have seemed a fine opportunity to depict traditional religious discipleship as exemplifying the injustices of the old Tibetan society. However, the text's authors adhere closely to the traditional story line, which accentuates the values of the disciple's faith and determination and the tantric master Marpa's compassion and skill in using harsh discipline to bring about Milarepa's spiritual rebirth.[41] (The fact that tantrism is even mentioned, let alone positively valued, in a high-school text is in itself quite remarkable.)

Taken by themselves, the second-forum textbooks may therefore be seen as a hopeful sign that Tibetan-language education in China is being developed along lines that will ensure that Tibetan high-school graduates, at least, will be able both to use their native language for modern pursuits and at the same time to enjoy a wide range of traditional cultural resources, including, to some extent, the rich textual traditions of Tibetan Buddhism. Clearly, the educators involved in carrying out the second-forum program

Fig. 7.3. Monks browsing at a Ganze bookshop under the Party's vigilant eyes (Photo by Matthew T. Kapstein)

were aiming to achieve this encompassing end. However, the implementation of the second-forum educational program has not lived up to the potential represented by the texts, and there are many signs that the program as a whole is giving way to an increasing emphasis on Chinese-language education and a return to the promotion of ideological indoctrination, whether in Tibetan or Chinese.

The only Tibetan-language texts produced under the second forum that have come into relatively wide circulation appear to be those in the primary-school (K-6) language and literature series and in some places, the elementary arithmetic texts as well. These continue to be widely used, especially in rural Tibetan grade schools. The middle-school language and literature texts have had some currency in Tibetan high-school programs, but the tendency in education has been overwhelmingly to favor Chinese-language texts at this level. Tibetan middle school–level texts on special subjects, such as math and sciences, have only infrequently been adopted for classroom use. Educators and officials with whom I have discussed this issue generally maintain that a shortage of teachers trained to offer Tibetan-language instruction in these subjects is the primary reason for the neglect of Tibetan in such contexts. The lack of qualified teachers is no doubt a big problem here, but Tibetan-language education in China faces other obstacles as well.

To begin with, there are some very strong prejudices, articulated by both Chinese and Tibetans, regarding the value of Tibetan at the present time. The Chinese headmistress of a Lhasa grade school whom I interviewed in 1998, for instance, categorically affirmed what officials in Beijing have often stated to me, namely, that the Tibetan language is, by its very nature, unsuited to be a language of modern science, technology, and commerce. (Of course, there was a time not long ago when many people would have said the same thing of Chinese!) This is not an exclusively Chinese prejudice, however, and one meets many Tibetans in China who affirm it as well.[42] The conviction leads many, regardless of their ethnic background, to believe that the education of Tibetan children should now be conducted in Chinese to the fullest extent possible. For contemporary Tibetan parents and students, this is generally reinforced by the feeling that, regardless of linguistic considerations, it is an undeniable matter of fact that Chinese is the language needed to succeed in China today. The questions raised in this context in some respects resemble those raised wherever bilingualism has become a contested issue in education. Whatever the pedagogical arguments in this case, however, it is clear that in Lhasa, as in larger towns throughout the eastern Tibetan districts outside the TAR, many and perhaps most Tibetan students are being educated primarily or exclusively in Chinese. In some cases, one notes a reticence (or perhaps an inability) among younger Tibetans to use their native language at all.

Thus, despite the best efforts of the second-forum educators to effect some measure of accord between traditional educational values and modern educational needs, in actual practice, their program has enjoyed only restricted success. In some families, the new Tibetan textbooks have been privately purchased and are being used for supplemental lessons at home. Some Tibetans I have interviewed expressly favor this approach because it provides a means for their children to maintain something of their Tibetan identity, even while growing up in a rapidly sinicizing public culture, as exemplified at school. Not all families, however, have the means or the determination to do this, and many of the second-forum texts have in any case fallen out of print or are unavailable in local bookshops. All in all, maintaining and improving Tibetan-language education has proven to be a difficult uphill struggle.

At the same time, religion has become involved in education in other ways. Because the monastery was traditionally the educational center of the Tibetan world, and because in many regions public education is still only poorly developed, if at all, the monasteries in some cases have begun to take up the slack. This is particularly evident, once more, outside of the TAR. Indeed, throughout eastern Tibet it is possible to speak of a "*she-dra* (monastic college) movement."

THE BUDDHIST REVIVAL IN EASTERN TIBET

Earlier, we noted some of the historical discrepancies between central and eastern Tibet. The division of the Tibetan world into five distinct provincial units has resulted, in the sphere of religion at least, in a broad distinction between the TAR and the eastern Tibetan regions that are contained within the four Chinese provinces of Qinghai, Gansu, Sichuan, and Yunnan. Agitation in favor of the Dalai Lama has been most persistent in the TAR,[43] and accordingly, it is the TAR that has been subject to the greatest degree of scrutiny and control.

But there are other pertinent differences as well: whereas Tibet is effectively ruled from Beijing, by an administration that has included many figures who are not from the TAR and often not Tibetans, the Tibetan administration in the other provinces, being conducted largely at lower levels of government (chiefly at county and prefectural levels), often appears to have a more genuinely local character.[44] Hence, although general principles of policy are of course common to the TAR and other Tibetan regions, their interpretation and application tend nevertheless to vary regionally. One result has been that religious and cultural matters reflect a greater degree of local discretion in the east, and officials in these parts have sometimes been content to pursue a far more moderate path than in the TAR.[45] In the early 1980s, the discrepancy between the TAR and the eastern Tibetan regions was already evident in Tibetan publishing: whereas the official publishing houses (chiefly the various *minzu chubanshe*, or "ethnic publishing houses") in the TAR shied away from purely religious matters at that time, as well as from modern literature that might be considered too daring, editors in Qinghai, Gansu, and Sichuan permitted far greater leeway in both genre and content. This difference in the application of recently liberalized publishing policy— marked conservatism in the TAR versus a relatively liberal approach in the east—has continued to characterize cultural and religious affairs overall.[46] In the field of monastic education, the most remarkable developments in eastern Tibet during the 1980s and 1990s were no doubt the reestablishment of the monastic colleges of Labrang in Gansu and the foundation of the Higher Buddhist Studies Institute by Khenpo Jikphün in Serta County, Sichuan. These centers have been studied elsewhere, so I will offer only a few remarks about them here.[47]

Labrang, founded early in the eighteenth century, was long renowned as the greatest center of Gelukpa learning and hierarchical authority in far northeastern Tibet and, given its strategic location, played an important role in relations among Tibetans, Mongols, and Chinese governments from the Qing dynasty onwards (and among the often-warring Buddhist and Muslim tribal groups of Qinghai and Gansu, such as the Mongour (Tuzu and Salar). Its elaborate college system included six specialized faculties, teaching not only the standard Buddhist doctrinal topics (chiefly logic, metaphysics, and the monastic code) but medicine and astrology as well. During the 1980s, the monastery was permitted to revive these programs, and by 1990, when I first visited it, the provincial government had accepted Labrang's *geshe*—its highest academic degree—as equivalent to a doctorate (Ch. *boshi*). Indeed, when I visited the Muslim Madrassah in Lanzhou that same year, one of the complaints I heard was that whereas the Buddhists were permitted to grant doctoral degrees, the highest recognized Muslim degree was considered equivalent only to a master's (Ch. *shuoshi*). Labrang continues to attract large numbers of aspirants today and is no doubt the finest Gelukpa educational institution in China.

This has become a problem of sorts, however, for traditionally, only those whose monasteries were directly affiliated with Labrang pursued their higher studies there. For scholars at many of the other Gelukpa centers in eastern Tibet, it would have been inappropriate to enroll at Labrang; instead, enrollment at one or another of the major monasteries in central Tibet would have been the proper path to follow.[48] However, the political situation in the TAR and the related failure of the Lhasa monasteries to establish viable educational programs on a significant scale have meant that for many of the brightest young Gelukpa monks in Kham and Amdo, the only alternative is to find some means to travel to India to continue their studies. The hierarchy of Labrang, which wishes neither to be seen as usurping the traditional role of the central Tibetan colleges, its historical superiors in the order, nor to become involved in current Tibetan political contests, has therefore sought to distance itself from Gelukpa affairs elsewhere.[49]

The Buddhist Studies Institute in Serta, a remote Tibetan county in Sichuan, bordering on Qinghai, emerged in the 1990s as one of the most dynamic centers for the study of Buddhist philosophy and meditation, not just in Tibetan regions but in China overall. During the summer of

Fig. 7.4. Debate practice at Labrang Monastery, Gansu (Photo by Matthew T. Kapstein)

2000, when I passed nearby, there were 9,300 residents, including several hundred Han Buddhists from China's eastern provinces.[50] Khenpo Jikphün's reputation as a charismatic, visionary teacher, one who has reached out to embrace all of China's Buddhist communities, has, together with knowledge of his efforts to establish Buddhist education at a high level, spread throughout China, and his followers now constitute a virtually identifiable movement. In accordance with the traditions of the Nyingmapa order, with which Khenpo Jikphün is affiliated, those who complete the institute's curriculum receive the degree of *khenpo* (literally, preceptor).

The restoration of Buddhist teaching activities on a significant scale, as represented both by Labrang and by the institute at Serta, has done much to inspire a widespread Buddhist educational movement in eastern Tibet. Most important, however, is that these and other major centers have produced a new generation of educated Buddhist clergy—*geshe*s and *khenpo*s— who have begun to teach in their own right throughout the eastern districts. At the same time, too, other, smaller religious establishments have also begun to produce new teachers.[51] In the course of my travels in July 2000 and October 2001, I was able to visit more than a dozen such establishments, as well as two secular schools established by religious leaders on behalf of the lay community, located in the Aba and Ganze Autonomous Prefectures (AAP and GAP) of Sichuan Province.[52] A few examples will illustrate some of the diversity among current religiously motivated educational projects.

Soon after I arrived at the county seat of Barkham in July 2000, Tibetan acquaintances told me enthusiastically of the development of a monastic school at the meditation cave of Vairocana,[53] a famous pilgrimage place located about fifteen kilometers from the town. Established by Akhu Dorlo, a lama originally from Mewa (modern Hongyuan County), who is widely respected for his learning and strict adherence to the code of monastic discipline, the small school and retreat center hosts a community of some thirty dedicated disciples who have come for training in Buddhist philosophy and contemplative practice.

After hiking up the wooded trail to the cave, I found that it was sufficiently expansive for a small temple and the lama's personal residence to have been built within its mouth. Its walls were decorated with colorfully painted reliefs depicting the renowned saints of Indian and Tibetan Buddhism, and prominently posted at the entrance was a list of the texts students are expected to master as part of the curriculum, including the classics of the Indian Mahayana and the works of famed Tibetan teachers. A num-

Fig. 7.5. Class photo at a *shedra* in western Sichuan (Photo by Matthew T. Kapstein)

ber of small cottages were constructed nearby to house the resident monks, as well as an open pavilion where Akhu Dorlo received guests. The lama himself struck me as an extremely reserved and humble man, who evidently runs a tight ship. He has no aspiration to attract large numbers of disciples and would prefer to devote himself to the instruction of just those who are dedicated to mastering thoroughly the instruction in Buddhist philosophy that he is prepared to offer. During my visit with him, I was repeatedly reminded of the accounts of older refugee lamas from Kham and of their own studies under celebrated masters in eastern Tibet before 1959. Akhu Dorlo, it seems, has succeeded remarkably well in reconstituting a traditional *shedra,* whose purpose is to guide the studies and spiritual development of a self-selecting monastic elite.

A contrast to this small and unassuming *shedra* at the Vairocana Cave near Barkham is offered by the revived Shrisimha College at Dzokchen Monastery, in Ganze Prefecture in the far west of Sichuan Province. The Shrisimha College must address itself not only to the education of advanced students of Buddhism but also to primary education in a largely nomadic region. The leadership of Dzokchen wished at first to restore it to the prestige it enjoyed through the 1950s, when it was one of the preeminent centers of learning for the Nyingmapa order. In those days, the Shrisimha College was virtually a postgraduate institution, a place where the best Nyingmapa scholars would enroll to complete their studies of advanced subjects in Buddhist doctrine and philosophy. In the course of its revival, however, it soon emerged that while there was indeed a constituency among Nyingmapa adherents who wished to enter Shrisimha with such higher studies in mind, there were also large numbers of families in the surrounding area who wanted to send their young children to Dzokchen to be cared for and educated. At present, Shrisimha has roughly four hundred students, more than half of whom are such children, in need of primary schooling. Necessarily, its *shedra* has assumed a rather different character from Akhu Dorlo's much smaller establishment.

Dzokchen Monastery has become involved in primary education in large part because the mostly nomadic families who send their children there do not have ready access to other schools. Indeed, this is the case throughout much of eastern Tibet and helps to account for an important dimension of the *shedra* movement. At monasteries like Dzokchen, where religious leaders have recognized that primary education is now an essential task for their communities overall, the monastic schools have slowly attempted to adapt to these circumstances. At Dzokchen, for instance, it is acknowledged that many of the children now in the monastery will not continue a religious vocation throughout their lives. The monastery's leaders believe that these children should receive an education that will serve them well if and when they leave monastic life and indeed, that those who remain monks will benefit as well by studying some of the subjects that are part of the compulsory curriculum for Chinese schools. Hence, in addition to their prayers, Tibetan grammar, and Mahayana Buddhist ethics and metaphysics, the novices at Dzokchen now also have lessons in math and Chinese.

The *shedra*s near Barkham and at Dzokchen represent the primary poles around which religious education in eastern Tibet now revolves, on the one hand focusing strictly upon the needs and interests of advanced Buddhist scholars, and on the other, becoming more actively engaged in general education. Indeed, in some cases, eastern Tibetan religious leaders have fully embraced the latter course and have founded schools whose pupils are ordinary children, not even novice monks. At Lhagang, for example, a young and progressive Nyingmapa *tülku* has established a boarding school for orphaned nomad children. And at Dhargyay Monastery, near Ganze, the head lama, drawing on Ganze's famous tradition as a center of painting and sculpture, founded an art school for local youth that in recent years has begun to offer general vocational training. Given the evident commitment of many eastern Tibetan clergymen to Tibetan education overall, it is not unimaginable that should sufficiently liberal conditions be allowed to develop and to prevail, a loosely organized Buddhist parochial-school system might flourish in eastern Tibet. It remains questionable, however, whether or not the local and provincial governments would permit such developments to proceed unabated.

Whatever the future holds in store, some patterns may be observed that help us to understand why currently there are some eastern Tibetan religious communities that seem to enjoy relatively liberal conditions while others are far more restricted. I shall attempt to characterize these here in terms of a small number of fundamental oppositions, but the reader must bear in mind that the real-world conditions prevailing in any given community cannot be predicted directly from any one of these oppositions alone. Indeed, there may be some cases that prove to be entirely exceptional, and which reflect solely the vagaries of local circumstance.

The conditions prevailing in "Tibet outside the TAR" suggest that when it comes to Tibetan religious and cultural revival, distance from Lhasa is a valuable asset. Lhasa, as the traditional center for Tibetan religion and politics, remains an important focus of pilgrimage but also an important focus of national sentiment; hence, conditions there can be especially volatile. Demonstrations for Tibetan freedom occurred in many parts of the Tibetan world during the 1980s and 1990s, and they were harshly suppressed, but the ones in Lhasa were particularly heated and became internationally known. For this reason, Lhasa's place in contemporary China is that of a city subject to especially close scrutiny. Religious activity, owing to the manner in which it has been tied to political activity in and around Lhasa, is a matter of special sensitivity there. One factor that has assisted the religious in eastern Tibet, therefore, is the simple fact that their activities are greatly removed from Lhasa.

The tensions that inform the scene in Lhasa, however, are recapitulated to one degree or another in the larger towns throughout the Tibetan world. Shigatse (TAR), Derge (Sichuan), Ganze (Sichuan), Xiahe (the location of Labrang Monastery, in Gansu), and Aba County (Sichuan), among many others, all have had—and Shigatse, by virtue of its special ties to the Panchen Lama, certainly continues to have—the potential for religion and politics to blend together in an explosive brew. As a result, even in the eastern Tibetan districts, religious centers in close proximity to the towns are frequently more constrained than are their rural counterparts.

A second point of relevance is highlighted by the saying "Small is beautiful." Though there are a number of large monastic communities that have succeeded in achieving remarkable success in recent years, small- and middle-sized institutions seem often to enjoy greater freedom from close supervision. Despite this, given the traditional ethos of mass monasticism, many larger monasteries have wished to return to their former size, even while recognizing that this might create new difficulties for them. The Ganze Monastery, for instance, is now allowed by the government to have 600 resident monks but in fact had only 400 when I visited in 2000. It may appear that this is a relatively positive situation, for the local government has clearly left some scope for growth, and this contrasts favorably with the circumstances one regularly encounters in the TAR, where the numbers permitted are often far lower than the numbers actually in residence.[54] Still, some monks at Ganze complained to me about the numerical restriction, saying that before 1959, there were 2,000 monks in their community, and so 2,000 it should still be.

Moreover, absolute numbers are not by themselves the crucial matter. In some cases involving religious communities in remote districts, removed from important towns, the numbers of residents are astonishingly large. The institute at Serta, as we have seen, was until very recently a case in point. What does seem to be crucial in such instances, however, is that a low profile is maintained and that political activism is scrupulously avoided. A small number of dissident monks surely do more to arouse official interest (and wrath) than does a large cohort of unobtrusive students and meditators.

A further opposition of importance here is that between the Gelukpa and non-Gelukpa orders of Tibetan Buddhism. Though the Dalai Lama is revered by virtually all religious Tibetans, he belongs to a preeminent incarnation line of the Gelukpa order and thus enjoys a special position within the Gelukpa hierarchy.[55] Owing to this, it is virtually impossible for Gelukpa monks to minimize or to disguise their allegiance and devotion to the Dalai Lama, though monks of the other orders can often remain diffident on this score. For similar reasons, Gelukpa monks tend to be more demonstrative of their support for Dharamsala's position in the Panchen Lama affair—this was illustrated above with reference to the intentionally deceptive buttons sported by some of the monks I met. It comes as no surprise, therefore, to learn that political-education campaigns have been especially intensive in the larger Gelukpa monasteries and that accordingly, the discontent of the Gelukpa clergy is most overt. Once more, however, it must be emphasized that this is not an absolute point of division: Gelukpa monks and monasteries have sometimes found viable accommodations with the state—Labrang is perhaps the best example—and members of the other orders have at times come into conflict with political authority as well.[56]

The last variable I wish to mention turns on relations with the Tibetan community in exile. Since the early 1980s, when contacts were renewed between exiles and their native homes, the revival of some monasteries has depended to a very great degree on such connections. Direct financial aid from the outside is not all that is at stake here; the return visit of a renowned lama now living abroad will often galvanize local devotion and donations to the monastery with which he is affiliated. The knowledge, on the part of both monks and lay believers, that they are connected to an institution that derives its spiritual prestige from a known living master, whether at home or abroad, can do much to reinforce their motivation and sense of purpose. In general, once more, the discrepancy between the TAR and the other Tibetan districts is apparent; monasteries that have been able to sustain strong connections with their leadership in exile seem to be far more numerous outside of the TAR.[57]

The manner in which the oppositions noted here influence the freedoms or restrictions felt in particular communities varies considerably. Local conditions in general play some role in this regard, as do the ad hoc decisions of local officials and the savvy of the local religious leadership. Though provincial and prefectural governments exercise a large measure of authority in this regard, the determination of the number of residents permitted at a given monastery, permission for or refusal of an exiled lama's visit, the duration of such a visit if it is permitted, restrictions placed on the visiting teacher's activities—these and more are frequently within the purview of prefectural or county officials, and inconsistencies from one district to the next are therefore by no means unknown.

TIBETAN BUDDHISM ENTERS THE CHINESE MAINSTREAM

The day before I left Beijing, at the end of July 2000, I strolled through the bustling newly renovated commercial district of Wangfujing. It was a Sunday, and there was a beer fest in progress. Chinese brands, such as Tsingtao, and foreign labels, including Asahi and Heineken, had set up stands serving snacks and beer on tap. Thousands of people stopped at the nearby parasol-shaded tables to rest and beat the July heat with a cold brew. Most were young, and many appeared to be educated and relatively prosperous (an impression reinforced in the course of my making small talk with some in the crowd). Virtually no one seemed consciously to notice that the music blaring from loudspeakers in the background was sung by the Tibetan pop star Jamyang Drölma and that drifting through the laughter and foam in China's capital and following each verse sung in Chinese, her refrain was the Tibetan Buddhist mantra of compassion: "Om mani-padme hum." On calling the attention of one of my companions at a beer stall to the music, he immediately signaled his recognition: "It's that Tibetan singer, isn't it? She's really good!"

Besides Jamyang Drölma, there are other Tibetan artists who have succeeded in breaking into mainstream Chinese media in recent years. Dechen Wangmo can often be seen in her popular music-video performance "Wo shi Xizangde haize" (I am a child of Tibet). The travel-brochure imagery of the video suggests a nostalgic and idealized Tibet, a Tibet now also frequently depicted in beer and beverage ads, where images of glacial purity suggest, perhaps, both a paradise and a frontier to east-coast Chinese viewers, for whom both snow and vast, open spaces often belong only in dreams. If the "shangrilaification" of Tibet is a cultural phenomenon that is sufficiently advanced in the West as to have drawn deconstructive criticism,[58] it is a phenomenon just now beginning in China.

Besides purity, the Tibet of the contemporary Chinese imagination— like other places of the imagination that are at once both dangerous and alluring—conveys also associations of uncanny powers, whether erotic, thaumaturgic, or spiritual. Sex shops in China's cities and towns prominently display a male potency–enhancing product called Vajra Divinity Oil (Jingang Shen You), sold in colorful packages adorned with a photograph of the Potala Palace in Lhasa, above which is superimposed, incongruously, a blond couple in steamy embrace. Current fascination with Tibetan Buddhism and especially tantrism is in evidence in the bookshops as well: popular introductions to Tibetan religion, colorful picture books filled with images of Tibetan *thangka* paintings, and some serious scholarship, including Chinese translations of Tibetan Buddhist texts, have all become notably plentiful. Recent televised documentaries, such as one about the Chamdo region of the TAR, seen on a Chengdu station, now tend to depict not only Tibetan scenery and folklore but also Tibetan Buddhist devotional practice, in an idealized manner that would have been unimaginable just a decade ago.

Corresponding with all of this is a remarkable upsurge of involvement in Tibetan spirituality on the part of Chinese seekers, who in many respects resemble their counterparts among the Westerners who flock to attend the teachings of lamas in Europe and the Americas. To some degree, they represent a general interest in Tibetan Buddhism that one now finds expressed

Fig. 7.6. Buddhism sells: a billboard advertisement for China Telecom featuring three young monks showing off their cell phones (Photo by Matthew T. Kapstein)

in Chinese communities throughout the world, but most especially in Southeast Asia, Hong Kong, and Taiwan,[59] that is to say, in precisely those communities that interact most intensively with the Chinese mainland over-all. Chinese Buddhist pilgrims from these places are now counted among the most frequent visitors to the TAR (of course, together with large num-bers of nonreligious Chinese tourists of various stripes). And during my journeys in eastern Tibet, I met Chinese students of Buddhism at many of the monasteries I visited. Though the majority were of college age, not all were young by any means. At one Nyingmapa center, for instance, I enjoyed a teatime conversation with the chairman of a major academic department at one of China's most prestigious east-coast universities, who had come to seek the resident lama's guidance in meditation.

Whatever official representations of Tibet and Tibetan culture may be, some Chinese are now encountering Tibet in other terms—whether through advertising and media or owing to their own interest and incli-nation. Ironically, therefore—despite all the trials Tibetans have faced and continue to face in attempting to secure the survival of their culture in China—Tibetan culture has begun to emerge in some respects as part of Chinese culture overall. This may yet prove to be an ephemeral and rela-tively unimportant development, but it is a trend that has the potential to affect (for better or for worse) China's policies toward Tibetan religion and culture in the future.

CONCLUSION

What general lessons can we draw from the foregoing observations? Given the extraordinary dynamism of contemporary China, which is subject to an unprecedented torrent of economic and cultural forces, one hesitates to draw any firm conclusions at all. Nevertheless, I think that a few points clearly warrant my touching on them.

Despite the view of some in the CCP that religion was effectively sup-planted by socialism and persisted only among the most backward, the cultural role of religion has continued or even expanded in many com-munities in China. That Tibetan nomads and yuppies from the eastern cities may be found assembling together to receive lamas' blessings speaks miles for the broad sweep of new-found religiosity in China. This is not to say, of course, that all are similarly motivated. Whereas the recent upsurge of consumerism has many young Tibetans, like their Chinese coun-terparts, more interested in the latest model DVD players than in their reli-gion, the reverse may also be true—more than once did I find modern gadgetry used to play prayer services, not rock. And the east-coast Chinese professionals who now, on pilgrimage, sometimes rub shoulders with people from the eastern province of Khampa are not, after all, traditional believers; rather, they are the first beneficiaries of the prosperity ushered in by Dengist reform.

In part, one is impressed that there has been a genuine, though halting, progress of religious freedom in China (particularly if one's time frame extends back to the period of the Cultural Revolution and just after). Tibetan monks, traditional lay devotees, and young Chinese enthusiasts are all enjoying a degree of liberty and openness in their spiritual lives that would have been unimaginable just two decades ago. This is not to say, however, that China is, by any measure, a place of religious freedom as we conceive of it. Nor is it to deny the plentiful evidence of tightening control of Tibetan Buddhism throughout the 1990s, particularly following the contested recognition of the Panchen Lama. The twin phenomena of increasing freedom and continuing repression in China's religious life may appear paradoxical, but in some respects, this only mirrors deeper paradoxes at the heart of China's ongoing experiment with economic opening and reform under a Communist regime.

It is clear that the relationship of the CCP to the developments within Tibetan Buddhism that I have described here remains an uneasy one. If some within the Party have been at times prepared to adopt a liberal standpoint, holding in effect that it serves no purpose to make trouble with believers unless believers make trouble first, there are also those who regard the new rise of religion to be inherently problematic. Thus, over and against the relatively liberal environment for Tibetan religion in Sichuan, one also hears the Party leadership in that province declaring that Tibetans have been devoting too much of their energy and resources to their religion and that this is felt to be wasteful. On occasion, too, there are official interventions that appear to compromise religious liberties that elsewhere would be considered unobjectionable. In the often conflicting reports regarding attempts by the government to limit the size of Khenpo Jikphün's institute in Serta, for instance, one of the constant themes heard is that the presence there of large numbers of east-coast Chinese disciples is regarded as a matter of special concern.

Besides the questions pertaining to religious freedom per se, the reassertion of religion in Tibetan communities raises other pertinent issues. One of these is a question central to sociologist Richard Madsen's recent work on China's Catholic communities:[60] how, he asks, might contemporary Chinese religious communities contribute to the formation of civil society in China? Reflected here is a preoccupation on the part of many who study the liberalization of authoritarian regimes with the emergence of new forms of association thought to be consistent with and supportive of further liberalization and eventual democratization. Civil society, manifest particularly in the growth of local, nongovernmental aid organizations, is the paradigmatic exemplification of these new forms of association.[61] Of course, it remains questionable whether any phenomena that we would wish unreservedly to characterize as belonging to civil society have so far emerged in China. And in the Tibetan regions, which are among China's most politically and economically backward, the prospects for civil society are particularly poor. Nevertheless, the question helps us to discern an additional point of interest in some of the developments we have surveyed above.

In the TAR, where religious affairs seem largely bifurcated between institutions that are thoroughly controlled or monitored by the government and individual agents (or ephemeral collectivities of such agents) that function either in explicit or tacit opposition to political authority, it appears that the Buddhist revival contributes little to the formation of civil society and has only a meager potential to do so. There has been virtually no scope in the TAR for more or less independent religious institution building of a type that would contribute to progressive developments within contemporary Tibetan society. Moreover, given the traditional Tibetan Buddhist insistence upon the unalterably benighted condition of most worldly life and monasticism as an almost exclusive remedy for that condition, purely traditional ways of thought provide few resources for tackling the problems that aid organizations in contemporary society must address.

In the east, however, religious revival has so far advanced under sufficiently liberal conditions (at least, when compared to the TAR) that a new generation of enterprising and forward-looking clergymen have been able to begin to address communal needs for welfare and education. Where this has occurred, as it has at the vocational school in Dhargyay, the orphanage at Lhagang, or the primary-school facilities of the Dzokchen *shedra*, there is the emerging promise of a form of institution building that is reasonably independent from, though at the same time constructively related to, the official administration. Under such circumstances, the advancement of Buddhist religious institutions does appear potentially to support the formation of civil associations. Whether the potential we note here will be realized in the coming years, however, cannot as yet be determined. Indications that some within the present CCP leadership in

Sichuan wish to promote a harder line with respect to Tibetan Buddhism suggest that promising developments may yet be stillborn.

NOTES

I am grateful to the Committee for Scholarly Communication with China and to the Smith Richardson Foundation for summer research support in 1998 and 2000, respectively. This chapter is largely based on work completed under these awards.

1. For an example of this perspective, see Powers, *Introduction to Tibetan Buddhism,* 18: "Due to the diaspora of the Tibetan people brought about by the invasion and occupation of Tibet by China, today Tibetan religion and culture are being spread all over the world, and increasing numbers of people in the West consider themselves to be adherents of Tibetan Buddhism. Millions more have heard teachings or read books and articles by Tibetan teachers, with the result that Tibetan culture is attracting unprecedented attention outside its homeland at the same time that it is being systematically eradicated in the land of its origin."

2. See, for instance, "Comrade Li Ruihuan's Speech": "As a ruler, the Dalai Lama was the upholder. [In] 1959, he betrayed the motherland and fled abroad. Since then he has been engaged in activities aimed at splitting the motherland and has served as a . . . tool of the international anti China forces. What the Dalai Lama has done in this Tenth Panchen Lama incident has proved once again that he has neither given up his old dream of becoming the 'king of Tibet', nor changed his ethnic separatist stance in defiance of the central government. Hence the . . . [1.2] billion Chinese people including the masses of Tibetan compatriots will by no means let the Dalai Lama get away with his scheme."

3. The most recent published official figures I have at my disposal are those given in *Les religions,* 3–5. Here, it states that for all forms of Buddhism in China, there are at present 13,000 monasteries and 200,000 monks. The breakdown that follows, however, supports somewhat lower figures: Chinese Buddhism is said to account for over 5,000 temples and 40,000 monks and nuns. "Lamaism," used here to designate the Buddhism practiced by Tibetans, Mongols, Tu, Yugu, Naxi, Pumi, and Menba, accounts for 120,000 monks and nuns, more than 1,700 "living Buddhas" (Tib. *tülku,* Ch. *huofo*), and 3,000 lamaseries. In addition, there are about 9,000 Theravada monks and nuns and 1,400 temples among the Dai and other ethnic groups in southern China. In other words, this yields a total of approximately 170,000 monks and nuns and at least 9,400 temples and monasteries.

Whatever the basis for these published figures, my own observations suggest that there are now likely to be over 100,000 monks and nuns in eastern Tibet, omitting the TAR. The basis for my assessment is as follows: Labrang Monastery in Gannan Prefecture (Gansu) and its branch monasteries in Gansu, Aba (Sichuan), and the adjacent counties of southeastern Qinghai have 20,000 monks. The Jonangpa monasteries of Aba Prefecture (Sichuan) and Darlag and Gabde Counties (Qinghai) have 15,000 monks. Khenpo Jikphün's Higher Buddhist Studies Institute in Serta County (Sichuan) had 9,300 monks and nuns in residence in

July 2000. At the same time, Lhartse Monastery and its branches in Serta had 3,000 monks, of whom as many as half were then studying at Khenpo Jikphün's Institute. These figures, all of which came from sources I regard as highly reliable, yield a total of 45,800 monks and nuns. But this represents only a minority of the eastern Tibetan prefectures and monastic systems. Other than Labrang and its affiliates, it includes none of the eastern Tibetan Gelukpa monasteries, even such major centers as Kumbum (Qinghai), Kirti (Aba), Lithang, Bathang, Ganze, Dargyay, and Drango. Nor does it include any of the monasteries of the Sakyapa or Kagyüpa orders, or of the Bön religion. Among the Nyingmapa, it omits Katok, Dzokchen, Zhechen, and Dodrup Monasteries and their numerous affiliates; and it omits the entire widespread Peyül monastic system with the exception of Lhartse, which is affiliated with Peyül. Approximations supplied by local officials and monastic leaders suggest that the monasteries and monastic systems just mentioned would add 40,000 to 60,000 to the total number of monks and nuns, and there are many monasteries that still are not included in these groupings.

In sum, I am inclined to hold that the official figure of 120,000 Tibetan Buddhist monks and nuns given in *Les religions* in 1997 may well be reasonably correct and is not the product of a deliberate attempt to fluff up the numbers for propaganda purposes. It is notable, moreover, that the official figures firmly support the general impression that monastic revival has proceeded much further among Tibetans and other adherents of Tibetan Buddhism in China than among other Buddhist groups.

4. Relevant reports include Asia Watch Committee, *Human Rights Tibet;* Tibet Information Network and Human Rights Watch/Asia, *Cutting off the Serpent's Head;* Human Rights Watch/Asia, *China: State Control*, chap. 6; Spiegel, *Tibet since 1950;* and Marshall, *Rukhag 3.*

5. The three provinces are Ütsang (central Tibet), corresponding to the present TAR, excepting its easternmost counties; Amdo, embracing Qinghai, Gannan, and Tianzhu Prefectures in Gansu and Aba Prefecture in Sichuan; and Kham, including the remaining Tibetan districts of Sichuan, Yunnan, and the eastern parts of the TAR. (Note that in this grouping, the western Tibetan districts of Ngari and adjacent regions are tacitly included in Ütsang, though they are not, properly speaking, parts of central Tibet.)

6. The finest study of this period in Sino-Tibetan relations remains Petech, *China and Tibet.*

7. For the perspective of an official of the old Tibetan government on the shifting political status of the eastern Tibetan regions, see Shakabpa, *Tibet,* chaps. 9 and 16. Goldstein, *History of Modern Tibet: 1913–51,* map 6, illustrates the de facto border fluctuations in Kham. See also the remarks of Shakya, *Dragon in the Land of Snows,* 136.

8. Ethnographic data on Kham and Amdo are surveyed in Samuel, *Civilized Shamans,* chaps. 4 and 5. Note that there are substantial populations in these regions who were adherents of Tibetan Buddhism but were not ethnically Tibetan. Examples include the Mongol and Mongour (Tuzu) peoples of Qinghai and at least some among the Yi of Sichuan. To speak only of Tibetans in the present context, as I do here, is therefore to some degree a simplification.

9. This is not to say, of course, that eastern Tibetan society was indeed egali-

tarian. Local hierarchies, both political and religious, played important roles here as well. The impression remains, however, that stratification was far less rigid than it was within the central Tibetan estate system.

10. The religious changes mandated by the fifth Dalai Lama's regime have yet to be studied in depth. A point of departure may be found in Dung-dkar Blo-bzang-'phrin-las, *Bod-kyi chos-srid zung-'brel skor bshad-pa*, 97–117.

11. According to information supplied to me by the Aba County Religious Affairs Bureau in August 1990, there were 7,000 monks in the total 1951 population of 25,000. At the time of my visit, there were estimated to be 5,000 monks in a total of 37,000, or approximately 25 percent of the males.

12. Samuel, *Civilized Shamans*, app. 1, summarizes the current rather tenuous state of knowledge of pre-1959 levels of monasticism in the various Tibetan regions. For Tibet proper (the region now comprising the TAR), see also Goldstein, *History of Modern Tibet: 1913–51*, 5, n. 13.

13. See n. 10, above, and Goldstein and Kapstein, *Buddhism in Contemporary Tibet*, chap. 2.

14. Animal slaughter is often the subject of sermonizing in eastern Tibetan religious literature and was clearly felt to pose a moral dilemma. See my remarks on this in Huber, *Proceedings of the Ninth Seminar*. During my travels in October 2001, I noticed that a recent sermon by Khenpo Jikphün that condemned the development of slaughterhouses in eastern Tibetan nomadic districts was prominently posted at many monasteries.

15. The development of monasticism among the Sherpa people of Nepal is a well-documented case in point. See especially Ortner, *High Religion*.

16. Havnevik, *Tibetan Buddhist Nuns*.

17. For an ethnography of a large traditional Tibetan monastery, see Li, *Labrang*. Li's fieldwork was carried out in 1938–1941.

18. On monk officials in general, refer to Goldstein, *History of Modern Tibet: 1913–51*, 8–10.

19. See, especially, Goldstein, *History of Modern Tibet: 1913–51*, 449–63, on the Tibet Improvement Party. For a detailed study of the celebrated progressive artist and intellectual Gendün Chömpel (1905–1951), refer to Stoddard, *Le Mendiant*.

20. Welch, *Buddhist Revival*, 177, describes his early career in brief: "Early in 1937 the Nationalists invited Shirob Jaltso [Sherab Gyatso], an eminent scholar, to lecture at five Chinese universities. 'This was the first time a Tibetan instructor had been provided for Chinese university students.' Shirob, like the Panchen and No-na, was at odds with Lhasa. Soon he too received a series of official posts." Sherab's troubles with Lhasa had been due to an editorial disagreement with the thirteenth Dalai Lama, who had appointed him editor-in-chief for a new Lhasa edition of the Tibetan Buddhist canon. Welch went on to observe: "I was also told that Shirob Jaltso . . . was never listed as *persona non grata* [i.e., by the Lhasa government]. I myself have heard the Dalai Lama express deep respect for Shirob as an eminent scholar whose only fault was the pride that had led him to make rash emendations in the Tripitaka, thus incurring the censure of the previous Dalai Lama. Despite Shirob's collaboration with the Nationalists and later with the Communists, 'one had no right to say he was pro-Chinese.'" Tibetans do not like to air their dirty linen in public, and Tibetan lamas in particular observe the rule that

no monk should speak ill of another. Therefore, even more than in the case of Chinese Buddhism, it is difficult for the outsider to get an accurate picture of factional struggles" (336–37, n. 42).

21. For remarks on his activities during this period, see Welch, *Buddhism under Mao,* 10, 19, 54, 65–66, 111, 114, 174–76, 211, 286–87, 325–28, 355.

22. Shes-rab-rgya-mtsho, *Rje btsun Shes-rab-rgya-mtsho,* 470–71. Note that some of the political terms used in this passage are directly transcribed from Chinese, for example, *hphan tos* (reactionary) (Ch. *fandong*) and *krin tshe* (policy) (Ch. *zhengce*).

23. The Dalai Lama has continued to espouse a markedly generous view of Marxist theory, as is reflected in a characteristic statement cited in Avedon, *In Exile,* 106: "Now, theoretically, Marxism also stands for the majority—the working class. This touches me, yet there is something wrong with its implementation in the present Communist states."

24. Shakya, *Dragon in the Land of Snows,* chaps. 4–6, surveys the transformations of Tibetan relations with China during this period.

25. Ibid., 270–71 and 290–301; and Hilton, *Search,* 154–55. (Hilton's eminently readable account of the life of the tenth Panchen Lama and his conflicted succession offers the fullest discussion of these matters to date, though it is occasionally marred by a penchant for journalistic hyperbole.)

26. Shakya, *Dragon in the Land of Snows,* chap. 12, surveys the Cultural Revolution in Tibet. For personal testimonies, see Kunsang, *Tibet;* and Goldstein, Siebenschuh, and Tsering, *Struggle for Modern Tibet.*

27. Aspects of recent Chinese historiography are studied in Unger, *Using the Past.*

28. Wang Yao, "Hu Yaobang's Visit."

29. Goldstein and Kapstein, *Buddhism in Contemporary Tibet,* 147; Shakya, *Dragon in the Land of Snows,* 372, 392; Hilton, *Search,* 173–86.

30. *Krung hwa mi dmangs spyi mthun rgyal khab kyi khrims yig phyogs bsgrigs,* 498.

31. The translated text of Document 19 is given in McInnis, *Religion in China,* 8–26.

32. Four case studies documenting particular aspects of the religious revival in the TAR, Sichuan, and Qinghai may be found in Goldstein and Kapstein, *Buddhism in Contemporary Tibet.*

33. For an analysis of these events, see Schwartz, *Circle of Protest.*

34. On Chadrel Rinpoche's denunciation, see Hilton, *Search,* 299–301. At present, he is reported to be imprisoned in Sichuan Province near Dazu (now part of Chongqing City). The fate of Gendun Choekyi Nyima is unknown.

35. Nevertheless, in some parts of Sichuan, images of the Dalai Lama were returning to public view during the summer and autumn of 2001.

36. It appears that this new, restrictive policy vis-à-vis visits of lamas living abroad was decided upon by a Party meeting in May 2000.

37. The first and second Tibetan work forums are surveyed in Shakya, *Dragon in the Land of Snows,* 380–398. Their implications for education policy, in particular, are discussed in Bass, *Education in Tibet,* 51–54.

38. On the development of Tibetan education in the TAR, see Bass, *Education in Tibet.* Upton, "Schooling Shar-khog," explores the use of modern literature in

Tibetan education in parts of Sichuan. My knowledge of the textbooks developed under the directives of the second work forum is due to research in Lhasa during the summer of 1998, which allowed me to survey and collect these texts and to interview educators and families about them.

39. Bass, *Education in Tibet,* 95–106, tells how religion has been a problematic issue in primary-school curriculum development.

40. Skad-yig, *Mtho rim slob 'bring slob deb dang po tshod ltar spyod rgyu,* 21–23.

41. Skad-yig, *Mtho rim slob 'bring slob deb gsum pa tshod ltar spyod rgyu,* 71–102.

42. I should note, too, that I have encountered Chinese educators in Tibet who are quite insistent that instruction in the Tibetan language yields better results in Tibetan schools, even where one of the main concerns is learning Chinese as a second language. A Lhasa high-school principal, originally from Jiangsu, expressed considerable frustration that both the educational bureaucracy and popular opinion were now effectively conspiring to undermine the development of Tibetan-language education in Lhasa. On the question of Tibetan-language education, see Bass, *Education in Tibet,* chap. 12, esp. 235–237, on the Tibetan secondary-school pilot project.

43. There has been also some agitation in the eastern Tibetan regions, for instance, at Ganze Monastery, and at Kirti Monastery in Aba County. On the tensions between the state and Tibetan Buddhist communities in Qinghai and Sichuan, see Tibet Information Network, *Sea of Bitterness* and *Relative Freedom?* As these reports indicate, there has actually been a retrenchment of liberalizing tendencies in these regions over the past decade. Nevertheless, I believe that the conclusion that the "prospects for the survival of Tibetan Buddhism within the PRC seem bleak" (*Relative Freedom?* 99) is premature.

44. Note, too, that although all Tibetan regions in China have been subject to some degree of immigration from other parts of China and to development favoring such immigration, Chinese immigrants in the eastern Tibetan districts are often likely to be persons from places close by (in contrast with the TAR, where new immigrants generally have no connections at all in Tibet). This is particularly so in places like Barkham, where Tibetans have always lived in close proximity to Han and Hui populations. The immigrants one meets here are often from towns just a few hours away and have long had sustained connections in the region. As one travels westward, however, the intrusive nature of recent immigration seems increasingly glaring.

45. We should note, however, that there have been regular efforts to promote political education within the monasteries and that this always emphasizes the denunciation of the Dalai Lama and the "splittism" he is accused of espousing. This and other governmental intrusions in monastic life are profoundly resented throughout the religious community.

46. The general trend in Tibetan publication in the TAR, however, has gradually liberalized over the years. See Stoddard, "Tibetan Publications," and Kapstein, "Indian Literary."

47. For an attractive, general introduction to Labrang Monastery, making extensive use of pre-1949 photographic documentation, see Nietupski, *Labrang.* On Khenpo Jikphün and the development of his institute in Serta County, see Goldstein and Kapstein, *Buddhism in Contemporary Tibet,* chap. 3.

48. Eastern Tibetan Gelukpa monasteries generally were affiliated with specific colleges in the three great central Tibetan monasteries or, in some cases, with Tashi Lhünpo, the Panchen Lama's monastery in Shigatse. Labrang and its branches, for instance, were themselves affiliated with the Gomang College of Drepung Monastery, so that even though Labrang was itself a distinguished center of learning, many Labrang monks would traditionally travel to Lhasa to finish their studies at Gomang.

49. The late Gungtang Rinpoche (d. 1999) compensated to some extent for Labrang's aloofness by traveling widely throughout China, including Hong Kong, where he had a very wide network of disciples and patrons. He was one of the most beloved of Tibetan religious leaders remaining in China after 1959, and he survived to resume his activities after the Maoist era.

50. The figure of 9,300 came from monks working for the administration of the institute whom I interviewed in Barkham. I was unable to visit the institute itself, as the Serta road was washed out shortly before I arrived in the region in July 2000. During the autumn of 2000, rumors were circulated that the institute was being closed down by the authorities because it had grown unacceptably large. Inquiries directed to the Bureau of Religious Affairs in Beijing brought the response that these rumors were false and that there was no plan to shut the institute. However, my informant continued, the large size of the institute had aroused public-health concerns—the water supply was considered inadequate, and there were no sewage facilities—so that some of the residents were encouraged to return to their homes for the winter. In 2001, it was widely reported that the authorities had in fact moved to limit the size of the institute to 1,500 residents and had burned the houses of those it had expelled. In particular, large numbers of nuns, as well as monks whose residence permits were from outside of Sichuan, were instructed to leave. Khenpo Jikphün's health was reported to have been adversely affected by this turn of events, and during the summer of 2001, he was said to be convalescing in Barkham.

51. An example of a successful, smaller Buddhist college is the *shedra* in Lhagang, founded by Khenpo Chödrak. There are now important *shedra,* as well, at Kathok and Peyül, in Sichuan, and at Darthang, in Qinghai, among others.

52. The AAP and GAP together include most of Sichuan's ethnic-Tibetan population. The counties of which the AAP is comprised embrace, according to traditional Tibetan geography, some of the southern parts of Amdo, the northeastern region of geographical and cultural Tibet that is now divided among Qinghai, Gansu, and Sichuan. The AAP also includes the region known in Tibetan as Gyelmorong, an ethnic patchwork in which, until the Chinese revolution at least, Tibetan religion was the predominant cultural system. The GAP corresponds in large measure to the eastern reaches of the old Tibetan province of Kham and is home to many of the most famous centers of eastern Tibetan religion and culture, including Derge, with its renowned printing establishment and the great Sakyapa monastery of Gönchen; Palpung, the eastern seat of the Karmapa order; and four of the six major seats of the Nyingmapa order.

53. Pa-gor Vairocana, an eighth-century Tibetan translator, is one of the cultural heroes in the region: during a period of exile from central Tibet, the result of an altercation with one of the queens, Vairocana is said to have traveled to Gyel-

morong, where he transmitted his unique system of meditation to local Buddhist disciples. His sojourn in the area is considered to be one of the important founding moments in Gyelmorong religious history.

54. For instance, in one case familiar to me, in Nyingchi County in the TAR, there were in 1998 200 monks and nuns in residence when the local government set a limit of just 8!

55. Contrary to popular belief, the Dalai Lama is not in fact the head of the Gelukpa order. The Gelukpa are led by neither a particular line of incarnations (as is the Karma Kagyüpa order), nor by the scion of an aristocratic religious family (as is the Sakyapa). Instead, they are headed by the chief abbot of Ganden Monastery, the Ganden Tripa, who is elected to hold that office for a term of five years. The office is in large measure a ceremonial and symbolic one, representing the direct succession of Tsongkhapa (1357–1419), the founder of Ganden Monastery and of the Gelukpa order. At present, there are two Ganden Tripa, one recognized within the Tibetan exile community in India, and the second by the Bureau of Religious Affairs in the TAR.

56. In the region of Lhasa, for instance, many of the nuns who have been engaged in political activism (and on occasion, have been imprisoned and tortured for this) have belonged to the non-Gelukpa orders.

57. One of the monasteries in the TAR that was allowed to cultivate cautious relations with its counterparts in exile was Tsurpu, the seat of the Karmapa. Not surprisingly, it was the Karmapa's flight in late 1999 that is said to have provided the catalyst for the Party's reassessment of such connections and the new restrictions placed on them in the months that followed.

58. See, especially, Lopez, *Prisoners.*

59. The intensive involvement of ethnic Chinese in Tibetan Buddhism, and their importance for the patronage of Tibetan monasteries and masters in China, South Asia, and the West, has been little remarked to date. It is a topic that deserves detailed consideration from students of both contemporary Chinese religion and Tibetan affairs. According to one estimate I have been given, in Taipei, there are now as many as 500 Tibetan monks (including those from both China and South Asia) teaching or performing ritual functions at any one time.

60. Madsen, *China's Catholics.*

61. Ruffin and Waugh, *Civil Society.*

Bibliography

Abdiiaev, Iskandar. *"Disaster Zone."* Resource 7, no. 11 (2000): 13.

Agence France-Presse. "Chinese Muslims Bury Five Shot in Clash with Police." 15 December 2000. Uyghur-1. http://www/uyghurinfo.com (10 December 2000).

Agence France-Presse. "China Revives Controversial Tibetan Migration Project." World Tibet Network News, 23 January 2002. http://www.tibet.ca/wtnarchive/2002/1/23_1.html (4 February 2002).

Agence France-Presse. "China to Deploy Demobilized Officers in Xinjiang Region." 31 March 2000. http://ww1.cnd.org/CND-Global00.2nd/CND-Global.00 –04–02.html (4 April 2000).

Agence France-Presse. "Karzai Agrees to Repatriate Any Chinese Separatists in Afghanistan." 24 January 2002.

Agence France-Presse. "Muslims Placed under Tight Control in Xinjiang." 24 January 2002.

"Aide Memoire Sent by State Department to the British Embassy, 13 July 1942." British Foreign Office Records. FO371/35756.

Allés, Elizabeth. *Musulmans de Chine: Une anthropologie des Hui du Henan.* Paris: Editions de l'École des Hautes Études en Sciences Sociales, 2000.

Amnesty International. "People's Republic of China: Gross Violations of Human Rights in Xinjiang Uyghur Autonomous Region." Report ASA 17/18/99. http://www.web.amnesty.org/ai.nsf/index/ASA170181999 (21 March 2003).

Anon. "Guanyu minzu lilun wenti de zhengming: Shoujie Quanguo Minzu Lilun Kexue Taolunhui jianjie" (A debate concerning problems of *minzu* theory: A brief account of the First Annual National Scientific Symposium on *Minzu* Theory). *Minzu yanjiu* 1 (1981): 74–79.

Asia Watch. *Crackdown in Inner Mongolia.* New York: Human Rights Watch, 1991.

Asia Watch Committee, *Human Rights Tibet.* Washington, D.C.: Asia Watch, 1988.

Associated Press. "Chinese Police Fire on Muslim Demonstrators, Killing Five." Eurasianet, 14 December 2000. http://www.eurasianet.org/resource/cenasia/hypermail/200012/0061.html (18 December 2000).

Atwood, Christopher P. "Revolutionary Nationalist Mobilization in Inner Mongolia, 1925–1929." Ph.D. diss., Indiana University, 1994.

———. "'Worshiping Grace': The Language of Loyalty in Qing Mongolia." *Late Imperial China* 21, no. 2 (2001).

Avedon, John. *In Exile from the Land of Snows*. New York: Alfred Knopf, 1984.

Bao [Borchigud], Wurlig. "When Is a Mongol? The Process of Learning in Inner Mongolia." Ph.D. diss., University of Washington, 1994.

Bass, Catriona. *Education in Tibet: Policy and Practice since 1950*. London: Zed Books, 1998.

Bawden, Charles. *The Modern History of Mongolia*. New York: Frederick Praeger, 1968.

Becquelin, Nicolas. "Xinjiang in the Nineties." *China Journal* 44 (2000): 65–90.

Bell, Charles. *Tibet Past and Present*. 1924. Reprint, Oxford: Oxford University Press, 1966.

Ben-Dor, Zvi. "The 'Dao of Muhammad': Education, Scholarship, and Chinese Muslim Literati Identity in Late Imperial China." Ph.D. diss., University of California, Los Angeles, 2000.

Benson, Linda. *The Ili Rebellion: The Moslem Challenge to Chinese Authority in Xinjiang, 1944–1949*. Armonk, N.Y.: M. E. Sharpe, 1990.

Borchigud [Bao], Wurlig. "The Impact of Urban Ethnic Education on Modern Mongolian Ethnicity, 1949–1966." In *Cultural Encounters on China's Ethnic Frontiers*, pp. 278–300. Ed. Stevan Harrell. Seattle: University of Washington Press, 1995.

Bovingdon, Gardner. "Strangers in Their Own Land: The Politics of Uyghur Identity in Chinese Central Asia." Ph.D. diss., Cornell University, 2002.

———. "The Not-so-silent Majority: Everyday Resistance to Han Rule in Xinjiang." *Modern China* 28, no. 1 (2002): 39–78.

Brown, Lester R. "Dust Bowl Threatening China's Future." Earth Policy Institute, 23 May 2001. http://www.earth-policy.org/Alerts/Alert13.htm (3 July 2001).

Brown, Melissa J., ed. *Negotiating Ethnicities in China and Taiwan*. Berkeley: Institute of East Asian Studies, University of California, Berkeley, 1996.

Bulag, Uradyn E. *Nationalism and Hybridity in Mongolia*. Oxford: Clarendon Press, 1998.

———. *The Mongols at China's Edge: History and the Politics of National Unity*. Lanham: Rowman and Littlefield, 2002.

———. "Municipalization and Ethnopolitics in Inner Mongolia." In *Mongolia from Countryside to City*. Ed. Li Narangoa and Ole Bruun. London: Curzon Press, in press.

Cai Hua. *Une société sans père ni mari: Les Na de Chine* (A society without fathers or husbands: The Na of China). Paris: Presses Universitaires de France, 1997.

Chen Hongmou. "Huahui Huihui tiaoyue" (A covenant to instruct and admonish the Muslims). In *Peiyuan tang oucun gao* (Randomly preserved manuscripts from the Peiyuan Hall), pp. 30:13a–22a. N.p., n.d.

Chen Li and Wang Xun. *Zhongxibu de shuguang: E'erduosi xianxiang touxi* (The dawn of central and western China: A thorough analysis of the Ordos phenomenon). Huhehaote: Nei Menggu Jiaoyu Chubanshe, 1998.

Cheung Po-ling. "'More Autonomy' for Xinjiang to Resist Separatism." *The Standard* (Hong Kong), 1 April 1992, A5.

Chia Ning. "The Li-fan Yuan in the Early Ch'ing Dynasty." Ph.D. diss., Johns Hopkins University, 1991.

China News Agency. "Xinjiang Mobilizes the Whole People to Launch Antiseparatism Struggle in the Ideological Field." 1 February 2002.

"China Reports Popular Support for Propaganda Work in Xinjiang's Ili Region." *BBC Monitoring Asia Pacific-Political,* 17 February 2000. Xinjua News Agency Domestic Service, Beijing (in Chinese). 0813. 1 February 2000.

"China: Xinjiang Receives Rising Numbers of Migrant Farmers." *World News Connection,* FBIS-CHI-93-139.

Chindamani. "Shi lun Menggu minzu tedian yu xiandaihua wenti" (A preliminary discussion of the modernization of the Mongol nationality). In *Nei Menggu Zizhiqu Minzu Yanjiu Xuehui Shoujie Nianhui lunwen xuanji* (The proceedings of the First Annual Conference of the Association for Nationality Studies of the Inner Mongolian Autonomous Region), 28–43. Comp. Nei Menggu Zizhiqu Minzu Yanjiu Xuehui. Huhehaote: Nei Menggu Zizhiqu Minzu Yanjiu Xuehui, 1981.

"Chinese Tomb May Have Belonged to Genghis Khan." National Geographic, 15 September 2000. http://www.ngnews.com/news/2000/09/09152000/ghengis_3035.asp (23 September 2000).

Christoffersen, Gaye. "China's Intentions for Russia and Central Asian Oil and Gas." *NBR Analysis* 9, no. 2 (1998): 130–51.

Clark, William C. "Ibrahim's Story." Unpublished manuscript.

"Comrade Li Ruihuan's Speech at the Third Meeting of the Leading Group for Locating the Reincarnated Soul Boy of the Panchen Lama." 10 November 1995. http://china-window.com/Area/Xizang/part2/title2 (6 January 1996).

Constable, Nicole, ed. *Guest People: Hakka Identity in China and Abroad.* Seattle: University of Washington Press, 1996.

Crossley, Pamela. *A Translucent Mirror: History and Identity in Qing Imperial Ideology.* Berkeley: University of California Press, 1999.

Davin, Delia. *Internal Migration in Contemporary China.* New York: Macmillan Press, 1999.

Davis, Sara. "Never Say 'Dai': Listening to Minority Oral Literature in Yunnan, China." Paper presented at the annual meeting of the Association of Asian Studies, San Diego, Calif., March 2000.

Department of Information and International Relations, Central Tibetan Administration, Dharamsala. "Dalai Lama on Contacts with China." World Tibet Network News, 26 December 2000. http://www.tibet.ca/wtnarchive/2000/12/26_1.html (28 December 2000).

Dikotter, Frank. *The Discourse of Race in Modern China.* Stanford: Stanford University Press, 1992.

Dillon, Michael. "Xinjiang: Ethnicity, Separatism, and Control in Chinese Central Asia." Durham, England: Department of East Asian Studies, University of Durham, 1995. Photocopy.

Dreyer, June. "Traditional Minority Elites and the CPR Elite Engaged in Minority Nationalities Work." In *Elites in the People's Republic of China,* pp. 416–50. Ed. Robert Scalapino. Seattle: University of Washington Press, 1972.

———. *China's Forty Millions: Minority Nationalities and National Integration in the People's Republic of China.* Cambridge: Harvard University Press, 1976.

———. "The PLA and Regionalism in Xinjiang." *Pacific Review* 7, no. 1 (1994): 41–56.

Dung-dkar Blo-bzang-'phrin-las, *Bod-kyi chos-srid zung-'brel skor bshad-pa.* Beijing: Minzu Chubanshe, 1981.

Economy Department of National Minzu Commission et al., ed. *Zhongguo minzu tongji* (Statistics on China's *minzu*). Beijing: Zhongguo Tongji Chubanshe, 1992.

Esposito, Bruce J. "China's West in the Twentieth Century." *Military Review* 54, no. 1 (1974): 64–75.

Ewing, Thomas. *Between the Hammer and the Anvil? Chinese and Russian Policies in Outer Mongolia, 1911–1921.* Indiana University Uralic and Altaic Series, no. 138. Bloomington: Indiana University Research Institute for Inner Asian Studies, 1980.

Farquhar, David. "Emperor as Bodhisattva in the Governance of the Qing Empire." *Harvard Journal of Asiatic Studies* 38 (1978): 5–34.

Fei Xiaotong. *Fei Xiaotong xuanji* (Selected works of Fei Xiaotong). Fuzhou: Haixian Wenyi Chubanshe, 1996.

Fletcher, Joseph. "Ch'ing Inner Asia, c. 1800." In *The Cambridge History of China.* Vol. 10, part 1, pp. 35–106. Ed. John K. Fairbank. Cambridge: Cambridge University Press, 1978.

Forbes, Andrew. *Warlords and Muslims in Chinese Central Asia: A Political History of Republican Sinkiang, 1911–1949.* Cambridge: Cambridge University Press, 1986.

Frolic, B. Michael. *Mao's People: Sixteen Portraits of Life in Revolutionary China.* Cambridge: Harvard University Press, 1980.

Fu Wen, ed. *Dangdai Zhongguo de Xinjiang* (Contemporary China's Xinjiang). Beijing: Dangdai Zhongguo Chubanshe, 1991.

Gillette, Maris Boyd. *Between Mecca and Beijing: Modernization and Consumption among Urban Chinese Muslims.* Stanford: Stanford University Press, 2000.

Gladney, Dru. "The Ethnogenesis of the Uighur." *Central Asian Survey* 9, no. 1 (1990): 1–28.

———. *Muslim Chinese: Ethnic Nationalism in the People's Republic.* Cambridge: Harvard University Press, 1991.

———. "Representing the Nationality in China." *Journal of Asian Studies* 53, no. 1 (1994): 92–123.

———. "The Salafiyya Movement in Northwest China: Islamic Fundamentalism among the Muslim Chinese?" In *Muslim Diversity: Local Islam in Global Contexts,* pp. 102–49. Ed. Leif Manger. London: Curzon, 1999.

Goldstein, Melvyn C. *A History of Modern Tibet: 1913–1951.* Berkeley: University of California Press, 1989.

——. *The History of Modern Tibet, 1951–1955.* Forthcoming.

——. *The Snow Lion and the Dragon: China, Tibet, and the Dalai Lama.* Berkeley: University of California Press, 1997.

Goldstein, Melvyn C., and Matthew T. Kapstein, eds. *Buddhism in Contemporary Tibet.* Berkeley: University of California Press, 1998.

Goldstein, Melvyn C., William Siebenschuh, and P. Tsering, *The Struggle for Modern Tibet.* Armonk, N.Y.: M. E. Sharpe, 1997.

Goldstein, Melvyn C., Ben Jiao, C. M. Beall, and P. Tsering. "Fertility and Family Planning in Rural Tibet." *China Journal* 47 (January 2002): 19–39.

Goncharov, Sergei, John Wilson Lewis, and Xue Litai. *Uncertain Partners.* Stanford: Stanford University Press, 1993.

Goodrich, L. C., and C. Y. Fang, eds. *A Dictionary of Ming Biography.* New York: Columbia University Press, 1976.

Guangxi guofang gongye. (The National Defense Industry in Guangxi.) Nanning(?): N.p., 1996.

Guanyu minzu lilun wenti de zhengming: Shoujie Quanguo Minzu Lilun Kexue Taolunhui jianjie (A debate concerning problems of *minzu* theory: A brief account of the First Annual Scientific Symposium on *Minzu* Theory). Beijing: N.p., 1981.

Guo Qingsheng. *Zhongguo shuangyu renkou goucheng* (The structure of China's bilingual population). N.p., n.d.

Guo Zhengli. *Zhongguo tese de minzu quyu zizhi lilun yu shijian* (The theory and practice of *minzu* regional autonomy [with] Chinese characteristics). Urumqi: Xinjiang Daxue Chubanshe, 1992.

Hannum, Emily, and Yu Xie. "Ethnic Stratification in Northwest China: Occupational Differences between Han Chinese and National Minorities in Xinjiang, 1982–1990." *Demography* 35, no. 3 (1998): 323–34.

Hansen, Mette Halskov. *Lessons in Being Chinese: State Education and Ethnic Identity in Southwest China.* Seattle: University of Washington Press, 1999.

——. "The Call of Mao or Money?: Han Chinese Settlers on China's Southwestern Borders." *China Quarterly* 158 (1999): 394–413.

——. "Ethnic Minority Girls on Chinese School Benches: Gender Perspectives on Minority Education." In *Education, Culture, and Identity in Twentieth-Century China,* pp. 403–30. Ed. Lu Yongling, R. Hayhoe, and G. Petersen. Ann Arbor: University of Michigan Press, 2001.

——. *Majorities as Minorities: Han Chinese in Ethnic Minority Areas of China.* Forthcoming.

Hao Fan. *Nei Menggu Menggu minzu de shehuizhuyi guodu* (The socialist transformation of the Mongolian nationality in Inner Mongolia). Huhehaote: Nei Menggu Renmin Chubanshe, 1987.

Harrell, Stevan. "Introduction: Civilizing Projects and the Reaction to Them."

In *Cultural Encounters on China's Ethnic Frontiers,* pp. 3–36. Ed. Stevan Harrell. Seattle: University of Washington Press, 1995.

——. "The Nationalities Question and the Prmi Problem." In *Negotiating Ethnicities in China and Taiwan,* pp. 274–96. Ed. Melissa Brown. Berkeley: Institute for East Asian Studies, University of California, Berkeley, 1996.

Harrell, Stevan, ed. *Cultural Encounters on China's Ethnic Frontiers.* Seattle: University of Washington Press, 1995.

Harrell, Stevan, and Ma Erzi. "Folk Theories of Success: Where Han Aren't Always the Best." In *China's National Minority Education: Culture, Schooling, and Development,* pp. 213–43. Ed. G. A. Postiglione. New York and London: Falmer Press, 1999.

Harris, Lillian Craig. "Xinjiang, Central Asia, and the Implications for China's Policy in the Islamic World." *China Quarterly* 133 (1993): 111–29.

Havnevik, Hanna. *Tibetan Buddhist Nuns.* Oslo: Norwegian University Press, 1989.

He, Qinglian. "China's Listing Social Structure." *New Left Review* 5 (2000): 201–26.

Hewitt, Duncan. "China Clampdown on Muslim Region." BBC News Online, 29 May 2000. http://news.bbc.co.uk/hi/english/world/asia-pacific/newsid _768000/768815.stm (22 April 2001).

Hilton, Isabel. *The Search for the Panchen Lama.* New York: W. W. Norton, 1999.

Hirsch, Francine. "Toward an Empire of Nations: Border-Making and the Formation of Soviet National Identities." *Russian Review* 59, no. 2 (April 2000): 201–26.

Holloway, David. *Stalin and the Bomb.* New Haven: Yale University Press, 1994.

Hsu, Immanuel C. K. *The Ili Crisis.* Oxford: Oxford University Press, 1965.

Huang Tianming. *Bianjiang xiao ge* (Song of dawn at the borders). Beijing: Zuojia Chubanshe, 1965.

Huber, Toni, ed. *Proceedings of the Ninth Seminar of the International Association for Tibetan Studies.* Leiden: E. J. Brill, in press.

Human Rights Watch/Asia. "China: Human Rights Concerns in Xinjiang." New York: Human Rights Watch, October 2001.

——. *China: State Control of Religion.* New York: Human Rights Watch, 1997.

Humphrey, Caroline, and David Sneath. *The End of Nomadism? Society, State, and the Environment in Inner Asia.* Durham, N.C.: Duke University Press, 1999.

Hyde, Sandra Teresa. "Sex Tourism Practices on the Periphery: Eroticizing Ethnicity and Pathologizing Sex on the Lancang." In *China Urban: Ethnographies of Contemporary Culture,* pp. 143–65. Ed. Nancy N. Chen, Constance D. Clark, Suzanne Z. Gottschang, and L. Jeffrey. Durham, N.C.: Duke University Press, 2001.

Information Office of the State Council. *White Paper: Tibet—Its Ownership and Human Rights Situation.* State Council, 1992 (as cited in FBIS, Daily Report, FBIS-CHI-92, 197S).

Information Office of the State Council, People's Republic of China. "'East Turkistan' Terrorist Forces Cannot Get Away with Impunity." People's Daily, 21

January 2002. http://www.peopledaily.com.cn/200201/21/print200020121_89078 .htm (22 January 2002).

"Intelligence: China Urged to Spurn Taliban." *Far Eastern Economic Review*, 30 November 2000, 8.

Jagchid, Sechin. *The Last Mongol Prince: The Life and Times of Demchugdongrob, 1902–1966*. Bellingham: Center for East Asian Studies, 1999.

Jaschok, Maria, and Shui Jingjun. *The History of Women's Mosques in Chinese Islam: A Mosque of Their Own*. London: Curzon, 2001.

Jin Yijiu. *Zhongguo Yisilan tanmi* (Exploring the mystery of Islam in China). Beijing: Dongfang, 1999.

Kapstein, Matthew T. "The Indian Literary Identity in Tibet." In *Literary Cultures in History*. Ed. S. Pollock. Berkeley: University of California Press, 2002.

Kashi Diwei Xuanchuan Bu, ed. *Fandui minzu fenlie, weihu zuguo tongyi, weihu minzu tuanjie, weihu shehui wending xuanchuan jiaoyu cailiao* (Propaganda education materials on opposing *minzu* separatism, protecting the unification of the motherland, protecting *minzu* unity, and protecting social stability). Kashi: N.p., 1995.

Kaup, Katherine Palmer. *Creating the Zhuang: Ethnic Politics in China*. Boulder: Lynne Rienner, 2000.

Khan, Almaz. "Who Are the Mongols? State, Ethnicity, and the Politics of Representation in the PRC." In *Negotiating Ethnicities in China and Taiwan*, pp. 125–59. Ed. Melissa Brown. Berkeley: Institute of East Asian Studies, University of California, Berkeley, 1996.

Knaus, Kenneth. J. *Orphans of the Cold War: America and the Tibetan Struggle for Survival*. New York: Public Affairs, 1999.

Krekel, Bryan A. "Cross Border Trade and Ethnic Unrest in Xinjiang: Conflict and Cooperation in the Origins of Chinese-Kazakh Energy Relations." Master's thesis, University of Washington, 1998.

Krung hwa mi dmangs spyi mthun rgyal khab kyi khrims yig phyogs bsgrigs, 1991 lo nas 1993 lo'i bar (Collected legislation of the People's Republic of China, 1991 through 1993). Beijing: Mi rigs dpe skrun khang, 1996.

Kunsang Paljor. *Tibet: The Undying Flame*. Dharamsala: Information Office of H. H. the Dalai Lama, 1977.

Kwang, Mary. "Outpost Set to Rise." *Straits Times*. 3 September 2000.

Lamb, Alistair. *Britain and Chinese Central Asia: The Road to Lhasa, 1767 to 1905*. London: Routledge and Kegan Paul, 1960.

Lateline News (Beijing). http://latelinenews.com/ps/english (15 and 18 December 2000).

Lawrence, Susan V. "Where Beijing Fears Kosovo." *Far Eastern Economic Review*, 7 September 2000. http://www.feer.com/articles/2000/0907/p22region.html. (21 March 2003).

Lee, James. "Migration and Expansion in Chinese History." In *Human Migration:*

Patterns and Policies, pp. 20–47. Ed. W. H. McNeill and R. S. Adams. Bloomington: Indiana University Press, 1978.

Li An-che. *Labrang: A Study in the Field.* Ed. Chie Nakane. Tokyo: University of Tokyo Institute of Oriental Culture, 1982.

Li Debin, Shi Fang, and Gao Lin. *Jindai Zhongguo yimin shiyao* (Essentials in the history of migration in modern China). Harbin: Harbin Chubanshe, 1994.

Li Jue et al., eds. *Dangdai Zhongguo de he gongye* (The nuclear industry of contemporary China). Beijing: Zhongguo Shehui Kexue Chubanshe, 1987.

Li Weihan. *Huihui minzu wenti* (The problem of the Huihui *minzu*). N.p., 1940.

Li Xiaofang. *Neidi ren zai Xizang* (People from the interior of China living in Tibet). Lhasa: Xizang Renmin Chubanshe, 1996.

Liao Zeyu. "Dui Xinjiang Weiwu'er Zizhiqu shuangyu zhi de taidu diaocha" (An investigation of attitudes toward the bilingual system in the XUAR). In *Yuyan de jiechu yu yingxiang* (Language contact and influence), pp. 407–18. Ed. Xu Siyi. Urumqi: Xinjiang Renmin Chubanshe, 1997.

Lipman, Jonathan N. "Ethnicity and Politics in Republican China: The Ma Family Warlords of Gansu." *Modern China* 10, no. 3 (1984): 285–316.

——. "Ethnic Conflict in Modern China: Hans and Huis in Gansu, 1781–1929." In *Violence in China,* pp. 65–86. Ed. Jonathan N. Lipman and Stevan Harrell. Albany: State University of New York Press, 1990.

——. *Familiar Strangers: A History of the Muslims of Northwest China.* Seattle: University of Washington Press, 1997.

——. "Sufism in the Chinese Courts: Islam and Qing Law in the Eighteenth and Nineteenth Centuries." In *Islamic Mysticism Contested: Thirteen Centuries of Controversies and Polemics,* pp. 553–75. Ed. F. de Jong and B. Radtke. Leiden: Brill, 1999.

Litzinger, Ralph A. *Other Chinas: The Yao and the Politics of National Belonging.* Durham, N.C.: Duke University Press, 2000.

Liu Zhongkang. "Feifa zongjiao huodong ji qi weihai" (Illegal religious activities and what they threaten). *Xinjiang shehui jingji* 5 (1996): 66–69.

Lo Jung-pang. "Policy Formulation and Decision-Making on Issues Respecting Peace and War." In *Chinese Government in Ming Times,* pp. 41–72. Ed. Charles O. Hucker. New York: Columbia University Press, 1969.

Long Fei. "Cong Yining shijian kan Zhong Gong 'minzu zizhi' wenti" (Looking at the CCP's *"minzu* self-rule" question from the perspective of the Yining incident). *Zhong Gong yanjiu* 31, no. 5 (1997): 13–25.

Lopez, Donald. *Prisoners of Shangri-la: Tibetan Buddhism and the West.* Chicago: University of Chicago Press, 1998.

Luo Yingfu. *Zongjiao wenti jianlun* (A brief discussion of the religious question). Urumqi: Xinjiang Renmin Chubanshe, 1992.

Ma Rong and Zhou Xin. *Zhonghua minzu ningjuli xingcheng yu fazhan* (The formation and development of the cohesion of the Chinese nation). Beijing: Beijing Daxue Chubanshe, 1999.

Ma Xueliang. "The Relationship between the Plan for Phonetic Spelling of Chinese and National Minority Written Languages." In *Language Reform in China: Documents and Commentary*, pp. 221–27. Ed. Peter J. Seybolt and Gregory Kueike Chiang. White Plains, N.Y.: M. E. Sharpe, 1979.

Ma Yan, Li Ailing, Li Hongxun, and Zhang Guolin. *Ate'izm tarbiyisi toghrisida qisqichä oqushluq* (A concise text concerning education in atheism). Trans. Tursun Sadiq. Urumqi: Shinjang Yashlar Ösmürir Näshriyati, 1992.

Madsen, Richard. *China's Catholics.* Berkeley: University of California Press, 1998.

Mao Yongfu and Li Ling. "Nanjiang san dizhou shehui jingji fazhan de shehuixue sikao" (Sociological reflections on socioeconomic development in three regions of southern Xinjiang). In *Xinjiang minzu guanxi yanjiu* (Research on *minzu* relations in Xinjiang), pp. 169–82. Ed. Yin Zhuguang and Mao Yongfu. Urumqi: Xinjiang Renmin Chubanshe, 1996.

Marshall, Steven. *Rukhag 3: The News of Dragchi Prison.* London: Tibet Information Network, 2000.

Matsumoto, Masumi. *Chūgoku minzoku seisaku no kenkyū: Shinmatsu kara 1945 made no "minzokuron" o chūshin ni* (China's nationality policies: Discussions of nationality from the late Qing to 1945). Tokyo: Taga, 1999.

McElroy, Damien. "No Response from China to Dalai Lama Talks Offer." World Tibet Network News, 29 January 2001. *http://www.tibet.ca/wtnarchive/2001/1/29_3 .html* (30 January 2001).

McInnis, Donald. *Religion in China Today: Policy and Practice.* Maryknoll, N.Y.: Orbis Books, 1989.

McMillen, Donald. *Communist Power and Policy in Xinjiang, 1949–1977.* Boulder: Westview Press, 1979.

——. "Xinjiang and the Production and Construction Corps: A Han Organization in a Non-Han Region." *Australian Journal of Chinese Affairs* 6 (1981): 65–96.

——. "Xinjiang and Wang Enmao: New Directions in Power, Policy, and Integration?" *China Quarterly* 99 (1984): 569–93.

Micklin, Philip P. "Desiccation of the Aral Sea." *Science* 281, no. 4870 (1988): 1170–77.

Nasr, S. V. "The Rise of Sunni Militancy in Pakistan." *Modern Asian Studies* 34, no. 1 (2000): 139–80.

National People's Congress. *Law of the People's Republic of China on Regional National Autonomy.* Beijing: Chinalaw Computer-Assisted Legal Research Center, Beijing University, 1984. Photocopy.

Naughton, Barry. "The Third Front: Defense Industrialization in the Chinese Interior." *China Quarterly* 115 (1988): 351–86.

Nietupski, Paul. *Labrang: A Tibetan Buddhist Monastery at the Crossroads of Four Civilizations.* Ithaca, N.Y.: Snow Lion Publications, 1999.

New China News Agency. *Summary of World Broadcasts.* 30 May 1980.

"News Report." *Tibetan Review* 18, no. 5 (May 1983): 3–5.

Oakes, Tim. *Tourism and Modernity in China*. London and New York: Routledge, 1998.

Onon, Urgunge, and Derrick Pritchatt. *Asia's First Modern Revolution: Mongolia Proclaims Its Independence in 1911*. Leiden: E. J. Brill, 1989.

Ortner, Sherry. *High Religion: A Cultural and Political History of Sherpa Buddhism*. Princeton, N.J.: Princeton University Press, 1999.

Petech, Luciano. *China and Tibet in the Early Eighteenth Century: A History of the Establishment of the Chinese Protectorate in Tibet*. Leiden: E. J. Brill, 1950.

Phillips, Kyra, and Jeanne Meserve. "Senate Foreign Relations Committee Questions Secretary of State Designee Colin Powell." World Tibet Network News, 18 January 2001. http://www.tibet.ca/wtnarchive/2001/1/18_3.html (20 January 2001).

Pomfret, John. "In China's Wild West, a Face-off between Development and Unrest." *International Herald Tribune,* 18 September 2000, p. 5.

Postiglione, Gerard A., ed. *China's National Minority Education: Culture, Schooling and Development*. New York and London: Falmer Press, 1999.

Powers, John. *Introduction to Tibetan Buddhism*. Ithaca, N.Y.: Snow Lion Publications, 1995.

Quanguo ge sheng, zizhiqu, zhixiashi lishi tongji ziliao (Historical statistics for all provinces, autonomous regions, and centrally administered cities). Beijing: Zhongguo Tongji Chubanshe, 1990.

Rawski, Evelyn Sakakida. *The Last Emperors: A Social History of Qing Imperial Institutions*. Berkeley: University of California Press, 1999.

Les religions et la liberté de croyance en Chine. Beijing: Nouvelles Etoiles, 1997.

Reuters, "Hijack Foiled, Lone Suspect Killed," 27 September 2000.

Rossabi, Morris. *China and Inner Asia from 1368 to the Present Day*. London: Thames and Hudson, 1975.

Rudelson, Justin Jon. *Oasis Identities: Uyghur Nationalism along China's Silk Road*. New York: Columbia University Press, 1997.

Ruffin, M. Holt, and Daniel Waugh, eds. *Civil Society in Central Asia*. Seattle: University of Washington Press, 1995.

Samuel, Geoffrey. *Civilized Shamans: Buddhism in Tibetan Societies*. Washington, D.C.: Smithsonian Institution Press, 1993.

Sanjdorj, M. *Manchu Chinese Colonial Rule in Northern Mongolia*. Translated by Urgunge Onon. New York: St. Martin's Press, 1980.

Sautman, Barry. "Preferential Policies for Ethnic Minorities in China: The Case of Xinjiang." *Nationalism and Ethnic Politics* 4, nos. 1–2 (1998): 86–118.

———. "Is Xinjiang an Internal Colony?" *Inner Asia* 2, no. 2 (2000): 239–71.

Schein, Louisa. *Minority Rules: The Miao and the Feminine in China's Cultural Politics*. Durham, N.C.: Duke University Press, 2000.

Schram, Stuart, trans. *Mao's Road to Power: Revolutionary Writings, 1912–1949: Toward the Second United Front, January 1935–July 1937*. Armonk, N.Y.: M. E. Sharpe, 1999.

Schwartz, Ronald. *Circle of Protest: Political Ritual in the Tibetan Uprising.* New York: Columbia University Press, 1994.

Selden, Mark. *The Yenan Way in Revolutionary China.* Cambridge: Harvard University Press, 1971.

Seybolt, Peter J., and Gregory Kuei-ke Chiang, eds. *Language Reform in China: Documents and Commentary.* White Plains, N.Y.: M. E. Sharpe, 1979.

Seymour, James D. "Xinjiang's Production and Construction Corps and the Sinification of Eastern Turkestan." *Inner Asia* 2, no. 2 (2000): 171–93.

Seymour, James, and Richard Anderson. *New Ghosts, Old Ghosts.* Armonk, N.Y.: M. E. Sharpe, 1998.

Shakabpa, Tsebon. *Tibet: A Political History.* New Haven, Conn.: Yale University Press, 1967.

Shakya, Tsering. *The Dragon in the Land of Snows: A History of Modern Tibet since 1947.* New York: Columbia University Press, 1999.

Shes-rab-rgya-mtsho. *Rje btsun Shes-rab-rgya-mtsho-'jam-dpal-dgyes-pa'i-blo-gros kyi gsung rtsom pod gsum pa* (Volume three of the works of the venerable Shes-rab-rgya-mtsho-'jam-dpal-dgyes-pa'i-blo-gros). Xining: Mtsho-sngon-mi-rigs-dpe-skrun-khang, 1984.

Skad-yig. *Mtho rim slob 'bring slob deb dang po tshod ltar spyod rgyu* (Language and literature: Elective senior-middle textbook no. 1). Lhasa: Bod ljongs mi dmangs dpe skrun khang, 1998.

Skad-yig. *Mtho rim slob 'bring slob deb gsum pa tshod ltar spyod rgyu* (Language and literature: Elective senior-middle textbook no. 3). Lhasa: Bod ljongs mi dmangs dpe skrun khang, 1998.

Slezkine, Yuri. "The USSR as a Communal Apartment, or How a Socialist State Promoted Ethnic Particularism." In *Becoming National: A Reader,* pp. 203–28. Ed. Geoff Eley and Ronald Suny. Oxford: Oxford University Press, 1996.

Snow, Edgar. *Red Star over China.* New York: Random House, 1938.

Solinger, Dorothy J. *Contesting Citizenship in Urban China: Peasant Migrants, the State, and the Logic of the Market.* Berkeley: University of California Press, 1999.

Song Naigong, ed. *Zhongguo renkou: Nei Menggu fence* (China's Population: Inner Mongolia). Beijing: Zhongguo Caizheng Jingji Chubanshe, 1987.

Spiegel, Mickey. *Tibet since 1950: Silence, Prison, or Exile.* New York: Human Rights Watch, 2000.

Stoddard, Heather. *Le Mendiant de l'Amdo.* Paris: Société d' Ethnographique, 1985.

———. "Tibetan Publications." In *Resistance and Reform,* pp. 121–56. Ed. Robert Barnett and Shirin Akiner. London: Hurst and Co., 1994.

Stone, Richard. "Coming to Grips with the Aral Sea's Grim Legacy." *Science* 284, no. 5411 (1999): 30–33.

Sun, Tao. "Qinghai Huizu yuanliu kao" (On the origins of the Hui of Qinghai Province). *Huizu yanjiu* 36, no. 4 (1999): 12–21.

Taylor, Jeffrey. "Foreign Affairs: China's Wild West." *Atlantic,* September 1999, 22–29.

Tibet Information Network. *A Sea of Bitterness: Patriotic Education in Qinghai Monasteries*. London: Tibet Information Network, 1999.

Tibet Information Network. *Relative Freedom? Tibetan Buddhism and Religious Policy in Kardze, Sichuan, 1987–1999*. London: Tibet Information Network, 1999.

Tibet Information Network and Human Rights Watch/Asia, *Cutting off the Serpent's Head: Tightening Control in Tibet, 1994–1995*. New York: Human Rights Watch, 1996.

Tibet Press Watch 3, no. 17 (1991).

Toops, Stanley. "Recent Uygur Leaders in Xinjiang." *Central Asian Survey* 11, no. 2 (1992): 77–99.

Tumen and Zhu Dongli. *Kang Sheng yu Neirendang yuanan* (Kang Sheng and the Unjust Case of the Inner Mongolian People's Revolution). Beijing: Zhonggong Zhongyang Dangxiao Chubanshe, 1995.

Unger, Jonathan, ed. *Using the Past to Serve the Present: Historiography and Politics in Contemporary China*. Armonk, N.Y.: M. E. Sharpe, 1993.

Upton, Janet. "Schooling Shar-khog: Time, Space, and the Place of Pedagogy in the Making of the Tibetan Modern." Ph.D. diss., University of Washington, 1999.

U.S. Department of State. *Foreign Relations of the United States, 1958–1960*. Vol. 19. Washington, D.C.: GPO, 1996.

U.S. Department of State. *Foreign Relations of the United States, 1964–1968*. Vol. 30. Washington, D.C.: GPO, 1998.

U.S. Department of State. *Relations of the United States with Tibet*. Washington, D.C.: GPO, 1995.

U.S. Embassy, Beijing. "PRC Desertification: Inner Mongolian Range Wars and the Ningxia Population Boom." American Embassy in China, April 1998. http://www.usembassychina.org.cn/english/sandt/desmngca.htm (6 May 1998).

Verrengia, Joseph B. "No Real Public Health Threat—Yet Pollution, Dust Cross Pacific," ABC News, 7 December 1998. http://abcnews.go.com/sections/science/DailyNews/longdistancedust981206.html (9 December 1998).

Walder, Andrew. *Communist Neo-Traditionalism: Work and Authority in Chinese Industry*. Berkeley: University of California Press, 1986.

"Wang Enmao, Song Hanliang, deng kanwang Zepu *minzu* tuanjie mofan danwei qunzhong shi zhichu ge *minzu* huxue yuyan wenzi shi jian hao shi" (While visiting the masses at Zepu [County] *minzu*-unity model work units, Wang Enmao, Song Hanliang, and others point out that mutual language study by the various *minzu* is a good thing). *Xinjiang ribao*, 6 May 1986, 1.

Wang Gungwu. "The Rhetoric of a Lesser Empire: Early Sung Relations with Its Neighbors." In *China among Equals*, pp. 47–65. Ed. Morris Rossabi. Berkeley: University of California Press, 1983.

Wang Lixiong. *Tianzang: Xizang de mingyun* (Sky burial: The fate of Tibet). Brampton, Ont.: Mingjing Chubanshe, 1998.

Wang Xien. "Globalization and China's Regional Autonomy." In *International Workshop on Regional Autonomy of Ethnic Minorities, Dissertation Collection,* pp. 331–52. Beijing: State Nationalities Affairs Commission, 2001.

Wang Yao. "Hu Yaobang's Visit to Tibet, May 22–31, 1980." In *Resistance and Reform,* pp. 285–89. Ed. Robert Barnett and Shirin Akiner. London: Hurst and Co., 1994.

Watson, James. "Rites or Beliefs? The Construction of a Unified Culture in Late Imperial China." In *China's Quest for National Identity,* pp. 80–103. Ed. Lowell Dittmer and Samuel S. Kim. Ithaca, N.Y.: Cornell University Press, 1993.

Wei Cuiyi. "A Historical Survey of Modern Uighur Writing since the 1950s in Xinjiang, China." *Central Asiatic Journal* 37, nos. 3–4 (1993): 249–322.

Welch, Holmes. *The Buddhist Revival in China.* Cambridge, Mass.: Harvard University Press, 1968.

Welch, Holmes. *Buddhism under Mao.* Cambridge, Mass.: Harvard University Press, 1972.

Wellens, Koen. "What's in a Name? The Premi in Southwest China and the Consequences of Defining Ethnic Identity." *Nations and Nationalism* 4, no. 1 (1998): 17–34.

Wen Hui, Wang Peng, and Li Bengang, eds. *Dangdai xin ciyu da cidian* (The big dictionary of contemporary neologisms). Dalian: Dalian Chubanshe, 1992.

Williams, Dee Mack. "The Barbed Walls of China: A Contemporary Grassland Drama." *Journal of Asian Studies* 55, no. 6 (1996): 665–91.

Woodside, Alexander. "Early Ming Expansionism (1406–1427): China's Abortive Conquest of Vietnam." *Harvard University Papers on China* 17 (1963): 1–37.

Woody, W. [pseud.]. *The Cultural Revolution in Inner Mongolia.* Occasional Paper 20. Stockholm: Center for Pacific Asian Studies, Stockholm University, 1993.

Wu Jianwei, ed. *Zhongguo qingzhensi conglan xubian* (Supplementary catalogue of China's mosques). Yinchuan: Ningxia Renmin Chubanshe, 1998.

Xinhua News Agency. "Chinese News Agency Says Islamic Community Condemns 'East Turkistan' Terrorist Force." 25 January 2002.

Xinhua News Agency. "Genghis Khan's Tomb Tourism Zone to Be Upgraded." Hohhot, 10 December 2001.

Xinjiang nianjian (Xinjiang yearbook). Urumqi: Xinjiang Renmin Chubanshe, 1988–2000.

Xinjiang Shengchan Jianshe Bingtuan 1997 nianjian (1997 yearbook of the Xinjiang Production and Construction Corps). Urumqi: Xinjiang Renmin Chubanshe, 1997.

Xinjiang Shengchan Jianshe Bingtuan 1998 tongji nianjian (1998 statistical yearbook of the Xinjiang Production and Construction Corps). Beijing: Zhongguo Tongji Chubanshe, 1997, 1998.

Xinjiang tongji nianjian (Xinjiang statistical yearbook). Beijing: Zhongguo Tongji Chubanshe, 1989–1999.

XUAR Dangwei Xuanchuanbu, ed. *Minzu tuanjie jiaoyu duben* (A reader on education in *minzu* unity). Urumqi: Xinjiang Qingshaonian Chubanshe, 1997.

XUAR Difangzhi Bianzuan Weiyuanhui, ed. *Xinjiang nianjian, 1988* (1988 Xinjiang yearbook). Urumqi: Xinjiang Renmin Chubanshe, 1988.

XUAR Difangzhi Bianzuan Weiyuanhui, ed. *Xinjiang nianjian, 1995* (1995 Xinjiang yearbook). Urumqi: Xinjiang Renmin Chubanshe, 1995.

XUAR Gaikuang Bianxiezu, ed. *Xinjiang Weiwuer Zizhiqu gaikuang* (An overview of conditions in the XUAR). Urumqi: Xinjiang Renmin Chubanshe, 1985.

XUAR Minzu Shiwu Weiyuanhui and XUAR Laodong Ting, eds. *Minzu lilun he minzu zhengce duben* (A reader on *minzu* theory and policy). Urumqi: Minzu Shiwu Weiyuanhui, 1992 (internal circulation).

XUAR Party Committee Propaganda Bureau Report (in Chinese). Beijing: N.p., 1997.

XUAR Renmin Zhengfu Bangong Ting and XUAR Tongjiju, eds. *Xinjiang xian shi zhuyao shehui jingji zhibiao paixu* (Rank orderings of key socioeconomic indicators in counties and cities of Xinjiang). Urumqi: N.p., 1994.

XUAR Statistical Bureau and CCP XUAR Party Committee Propaganda Bureau, eds. *Doujin de sishi nian: Xinjiang fence* (Forty years' struggle for progress: Xinjiang volume). Beijing: Zhongguo Tongji Chubanshe, 1989.

Xu Ke and Zainu'er (Zaynur). "Pingxi '5–19' dazaqiang saoluan shijian" (Putting down the 'May 19' beating, smashing, and looting riot). In *Xinjiang nianjian* (Xinjiang yearbook). Urumqi: Xinjiang Renmin Chubanshe, 1990.

Xu Siyi, ed. *Yuyan de jiechu yu yingxiang* (Language contact and influence). Urumqi: Xinjiang Renmin Chubanshe, 1997.

Yang Shengming. "'Ru shi' hou, wo guo ying caiqu de duice jianyi" (Suggestions for counterpolicies our country should adopt after entering the WTO). Guangming ribao, 9 May 2000. http://www.gmw.com.cn. (14 May 2000).

Yang, Zhanwu. *Huizu yuyan wenhua* (The language culture of the Hui). Yinchuan: Ningxia Renmin Chubanshe, 1996.

Yuan Qing-li. "Population Changes in the Xinjiang Uyghur Autonomous Region (1949–1984)." *Central Asian Survey* 9, no. 1 (1990): 49–73.

Zhang, Tianlu, and Mei Zhang. "The Present Population of the Tibetan Nationality in China." *Social Sciences in China* 15 (1994): 46–65.

Zhang Yuxi. "Xinjiang jiefang yilai fandui minzu fenliezhuyi de douzheng ji qi lishi jingyan" (The struggle and historical experience of opposition to *minzu* separatism in Xinjiang since liberation). In *Fan Yisilanzhuyi, fan Tujuezhuyi yanjiu* (Research on Pan-Islamism and Pan-Turkism), pp. 331–63. Ed. Yang Fajen. Urumqi: N.p., 1993.

Zhongguo binggong nianjian, 1986–1990 (China ordinance industry yearbook, 1986–1990). Beijing: Bingqi Gongye Chubanshe, 1991.

Zhongguo diminglu. (Record of Chinese place names). Beijing: Ditu Chubanshe, 1994.

Zhongguo Disanci Gongye Pucha ziliao guangpan. (CD-ROM of material on China's Third Industrial Census). Beijing: China Statistics Consultants (BJ) Limited, 1997. CD-ROM.

Zhongguo Gongchangdang Nei Menggu Zizhiqu zuzhishi ziliao (1925.3–1987.12) (Materials on the organizational development of the Chinese Communist Party in Inner Mongolia from March 1925 to December 1987). Huhehaote: Nei Menggu Renmin Chubanshe, 1995.

Zhongguo Gongchandang Xinjiang Weiwuer Zizhiqu zuzhi fazhan jianshi (A simplified history of the organizational development of the Chinese Communist Party in the Xinjiang Uygur Autonomous Region). Urumqi: Xinjiang Renmin Chubanshe, 1993.

Zhongguo guding zichan touzi tongji nianjian, 1995 (1995 statistical yearbook on fixed asset investment in China). Beijing: Zhongguo Tongji Chubanshe, 1996.

Zhongguo guding zichan touzi tongji ziliao, 1950–1985 (Statistical materials on Chinese fixed assets investment, 1950–1985). Beijing: Zhongguo Tongji Chubanshe, 1987.

Zhongguo guonei shengchan zongzhi hesuan lishi ziliao (Historical materials on gross domestic product accounting in China). Dalian: Dongbei Caijing Daxue Chubanshe, 1997.

Zhongguo tongji nianjian (China statistical yearbook). Beijing: Zhongguo Tongji Chubanshe, 1997, 1998, 1999, 2000.

Zhonghua Renmin Gongheguo 1985 nian Quanguo Gongye Pucha ziliao, Di yi ce (Materials on the 1985 National Industrial Census of the People's Republic of China, Vol. 1). Beijing: Zhongguo Tongji Chubanshe, 1987.

Zhonghua Renmin Gongheguo 1995 nian Disanci Quanguo Gongye Pucha ziliao huibian, Diqu juan (A compendium of materials on the Third National Industrial Census of the People's Republic of China in 1995, Regional volume). Beijingguo Tongji Chubanshe, 1997.

Zhonghua Renmin Gongheguo Minzu Quyu Zizhifa (Law of the People's Republic of China on Regional Ethnic Autonomy). Beijing: Zhongguo Fazhi Chubanshe, 1998.

Zhu Songli. "Guanyu Xi'an Huifang gaijian de shexiang" (On the tentative plan for the rebuilding of Xian's Hui quarter). In *Yisilan wenhua yanjiu* (Studies on Muslim culture). Ed. Zhu Songli et al. Yinchuan: Ningxia Renmin Chubanshe, 1998.

Contributors

DAVID BACHMAN is professor of political science at the University of Washington. He has written *Bureaucracy, Economy, and Leadership in China: The Institutional Origins of the Great Leap Forward* (1991) and numerous articles on contemporary China.

GARDNER BOVINGDON is assistant professor of political science at Indiana University and is preparing a book on Chinese policy in Xinjiang.

URADYN E. BULAG is associate professor of anthropology at Hunter College of the City University of New York. He is the author of *Nationalism and Hybridity in Mongolia* (1998) and *The Mongols at China's Edge* (2002).

MELVYN C. GOLDSTEIN is professor of anthropology at Case Western Reserve University. He is the author of numerous books on modern Tibet, including *A History of Modern Tibet, 1913–1951* (1989) and *The Snow Lion and the Dragon* (1997).

METTE HALSKOV HANSEN is associate professor in the department of East European and Oriental studies at Oslo University and has written *Lessons in Being Chinese: State Education and Ethnic Identity in Southwest China* (1999).

MATTHEW T. KAPSTEIN is professor of religion at the University of Chicago and is the author of *The Tibetan Assimilation of Buddhism: Conversion, Contestation, and Memory* (2000), as well as other works on Tibetan religion and society.

JONATHAN N. LIPMAN is professor of history at Mount Holyoke College and has written *Familiar Strangers: A History of Muslims in Northwest China* (1997), among other works.

MORRIS ROSSABI is professor of history at the City University of New York and visiting professor of Chinese and Inner Asian history at Columbia University. He is the author of *Khubilai Khan: His Life and Times* (1988) and *Voyager from Xanadu* (1992), as well as chapters for exhibition catalogs of Mongol and Yuan art at the Metropolitan Museum of Art and the Asian Art Museum in San Francisco.

Index

Aba Autonomous Prefecture, 252
Aba County (Rnga-ba-rdzong), and
    monasticism, 233, 255
Afghanistan, 42, 159, 183–84; U.S. pres-
    ence in, 10
African Americans, 49
Agya Rinpoche, 244
Akha (Hani), 56–57, 73, 75; and lack of
    written script, 67
Akhu Dorlo, 252–54
Akto County, 138
Amban (Imperial Commissioner), 189
Amdo, 196, 231–32, 237, 250
American Indians, 109
Amnesty International, 140, 187
Anglo-Russian Agreement, 190
Anglo-Tibetan Convention, 189
Anhui Province, 94
Aqsu, 127–28, 158, 165, 168, 172–73
Arabic script, 133–35
Arabs and Arabic, 25, 29, 32, 42, 47
Aral Sea, 170, 172
Arjia Lobsang Thubten, 212
Aryadesha, 246
Asia Watch, 187
Atlas Mountains, 29
Azeri-Armenian wars, 11

Baatar, 96
Bachman, David, 9, 15–16
Bangladesh, 48
Banqiao Sufis, 39
Baoliudi ("reservation"), 109
Baotou, 104
Baren incident, 132, 138, 144
Barkham, 252–54
Batubagan, 95, 111
Bayanbuur, 107
Bayanchuluu, 96
Bayin, 96
Bayinguoleng, 118
Beijing, 5, 6, 22–24, 30, 38, 41, 48, 59, 73,
    86, 99, 104, 107–8, 128, 142, 149, 160,
    172, 189–90, 193–94, 196, 212, 219;

policy of in Tibet, 198–206, 207–10,
    215–16, 221, 225, 227, 248, 249
Beimen, 144
Bhutan, 189
Biligbaatar, 97
Bilingual education, 69
Biyao, 75
Blang, 56–57
Boroldui, 101
Boshi (doctorate), 250
Bovingdon, Gardner, 14–16
Boxer Indemnity, 86
Brown, Winthrop, U.S. Ambassador
    to India, 221
Buddhism, 13, 14, 86, 110; revival of in
    Sipsong Panna, 77–79; Tibetan, 16
Buhe (Ulanhu's son), 99
Bulag, Uradyn, 13–14
Bulang, 54
Burhan Shāhidi, 122
Burma, 55, 76; Chinese migration into,
    61; relations of with Tai, 66
Bush, George H. W., administration
    of, 226–27
Bush, George W., administration of, 187,
    226–27

Cashmere trade, 106–7
Catholics in China, 261
Caucasus, 29
Central Asia, 15, 31–32, 42, 133–34, 138, 155,
    174, 183; Chinese investment in, 10;
    and independence from U.S.S.R., 9
Central Ethnic Affairs Commission
    (Minwei), 30–31, 47
Central Intelligence Agency (CIA), in
    Tibet, 16, 197, 220
Chadrel Rinpoche, detention of, 243
Chahar Province, 86, 91
Chengbao ("privately owned shops"), 75
Chengdu, 243, 258
Chiang Kai-shek, 87, 218, 220
Chibuliao zhei yang de ku ("eat bitter-
    ness"), 62

Chifeng Municipality, 105
Chinese Buddhist Association, 236
Chinese Communist Party (CCP): and
    Chinese Communists, 21, 25–27, 33,
    54, 56, 58, 102, 113, 132, 147, 174, 191–
    92, 198, 202, 213; early policy of
    toward Inner Mongolia, 89; hard
    line policy of in Tibet, 207–10, 215–
    16; *minzu* policy of, 47–48, 62; policy
    of in Xinjiang, 117, 118–20, 123–24;
    and Tibetan Buddhism, 230, 236–37,
    238–39, 244, 260
Chinese Islamic Association (Yixie), 30–
    31, 34, 40, 47, 122
Chinggis Khan, 14, 110; mausoleum,
    104
Chölka sum ("three provinces"), 231
Chongqing, 59
Christianity, 242
Chu Bo, 94
Churchill, Winston, 223
Clinton, William Jefferson, administra-
    tion of, and Tibet, 224–27
Cold War, 193, 197, 219–20, 224
Comintern (Communist International),
    88; and minorities, 27
Communist minorities policy, 7–8, 9;
    in Southwest, 79–81; in Tibet, 161;
    in Xinjiang, 122
Cotton cultivation (Xinjiang), 170
Cultural Revolution, 9, 14, 42, 44, 56–
    67, 59, 77, 85, 107; and destruction
    of monasteries, 238–39; in Sipsong
    Panna, 64; in Tibet, 16–17, 198, 200,
    204, 211, 240–41, 243–45, 261; in Xin-
    jiang, 127, 130, 134–35, 143; in Yin-
    chuan, 37
Cyrillic script, 134

Daghuor, 118
Da hanzuzhuyi ("Han chauvinism"), 63
Dai *minzu* (Daizu), 55, 137
Dalad banner, 105
Dalai Lama, 10, 17, 47, 89, 99, 125, 182,
    186–87, 189–90, 193–94, 195–200,
    207, 230–36, 238–43, 249, 256; award-
    ing of Nobel Peace Price to, 206;
    Chinese attacks on, 210–11; and com-
    promise settlement, 213–15; desire of
    for autonomy, 212; flight of to India,
    16; negotiating position of, 201,
    221–27; visit of to U.S., 204

Dali, 5, 43
Da Muminggan banner, 87
Dang jia zuo zhu ("masters of their own
    house"), 119
Daoists, 23, 242
Daqing, 107
Darjeeling, 189
Dazhai, 101
Dechen Wangmo, 258
Dehong, 55
Dehqan bolmaq tas ("It's hard to be a
    peasant"), 133
Demchugdongroba (Prince), and Japa-
    nese, 88
Deng Nan (daughter of Deng Xiaoping),
    95
Deng Xiaoping, 95, 125, 127, 143; and
    Tibet, 199, 201, 239
Derge, 233, 235, 255
Dharamsala, 201–3, 205–6, 211, 215–16,
    227, 256
Dhargyay, 262
Dhargyay Monastery, 254
Di er dai ("second generation"), 60
Dignaga, 246
Dobi Sherab Gyatso, and support of
    Chinese Communists, 236
Drepung Monastery, 204, 233
Drug trade, 41–42, 58
Duguilong movement, 102, 105
Dulong, 54
Durben Huhed banner, 87
Du Wenxiu, 6, 43
Dzokchen Monastery, 235, 262; educa-
    tion in, 253–54
Dzungaria, 174

Eastern Mongolian Autonomous
    Government, founding of, 89–90
Eastern Tibet, 249
Eastern Turkistan Republic and move-
    ment, 7, 47, 121, 160
Education (Sipsong Panna), 64–70
Egypt, 23
Eighth Route Army (Chinese Commu-
    nists), 26
Ejen Horoo banner, 104
Eleventh Party Congress, 140
Emin County Autonomous District, 118
Environmental problems (Southwest
    China), 70–72, 80–81
Europe, 146, 159, 203, 258

Facai, 106
Fan Changjiang, definition of Hui, 24
Fan Han pai wai ("oppose the Chinese
    and reject outsiders"), 102–3
Fan Ming, 195
Fatwa ("religious opinion"), 29
Fei Xiaotong, 58
Feifa zuzhi ("illegal organization"), 34
Fengtian, 87
Foreign relations, traditional, 3–4
Forests and logging, 70–71
Four Rivers, Six Ranges (Chu Bzhi
    Gangs Drug) guerrillas, 237
Fox, Richard, 132
Fujian Province, 76

Gada Meijen, 102, 105
Ganden Monastery, riot at, 243
Gang of Four, 45, 124, 130, 144
Gansu Province, 26, 32, 34, 39, 48, 91, 93,
    159; Tibetans in, 231, 233, 245, 249–
    50, 255; violence in, 41, 43, 162–63
Ganze, 244, 249, 254, 255; Autonomous
    Prefecture, 252–53
Ganze Monastery, 256
Gelukpa Gomang College, 235
Gelukpa sect, 232–33, 244, 250, 256
Gendun Choekyi Nyima, detention of,
    243–44
Geshe (academic degree), 250, 252
Gillette, Maris Boyd, 37
Gladney, Dru, 41, 45
Golden Triangle, 42, 58
Goldstein, Melvyn, 16
Great Britain, and Tibet, 189, 191, 217–18
Great Leap Forward, 9, 56, 70, 123, 134–35
Great Mosque: Xi'an, 33, 36; Zhengzhou
    21
Guangdong Province, 76, 106
Guangxi Province, 5, 7, 54, 158, 162–64
Guisui. *See* Hohhot
Guizhou Province, 5, 7, 27, 54, 58, 76
Gu Jiegang, definition of Hui, 24
Gulja, 121, 144
Guomingdang (Nationalist Party, KMT),
    6, 24, 26, 89–91, 122, 128, 144, 146,
    157, 175, 218
Gyalo Thondup (brother of Dalai Lama),
    196, 199

Hafenga, 97
Hajj ("religious pilgrimage"), 30

Hamid Karzai, 183
Han dynasty (206 B.C.E.–C.E. 220), 3
Hangzhou, 32, 73
Han Hui, 22
Hani, 76
Han migrants, 17
Hansen, Mette, 11, 13
Hebei Province, 46
Hebrew, 112
Heilongjiang Province, 87, 93
Helan Mountains, 39
Helms, Jesse, 186
Henan Province, 24, 34, 39, 48, 164
Herter, Christian (U.S. Secretary of
    State), 221, 223
Higher Buddhist Studies Institute, 249–50
Himalayas, 189
Hingan Army, 89, 97
Hirsch, Francine, on Soviet nationality
    policy, 90
Hohhot, 91, 110; early history of, 92
Hong Kong, 106, 126, 260
Hotan, 140, 144, 165–66, 168, 173
Houtao, 87
Hui, 7, 13, 23–25, 33–34, 39, 42, 46, 84,
    137, 144, 168, 204, 208; attitude of
    toward exhibits, 28–29; as brokers,
    31–32; *Chantou*, 22; and conflict with
    Mongols, 106; and confrontations
    with Han, 19–21, 38–46, 118; food
    and restaurants, 32; Huibu, 22; iden-
    tity, 22, 24–28; localization (*diquhua*),
    46–47; in Ningxia, 39–40; occupa-
    tions of, 32; in Sanpo, 34; and simi-
    larities to Han, 11–12; in Xi'an, 35–37;
    in Yinchuan, 37
Huihui *minzu*, 24
Huijiao, 24
hukou ("household registration"), 127,
    166, 176
Hulunbuir, 100, 109
Hunan Province, 60, 72, 76
Hundred Flowers campaign, 92, 123
Hu Yaobang: purge of, 125; trip of to
    Tibet, 125, 158, 200, 207, 209–10, 239,
    241–42

Ibrahim Mutte'i, 124
Ili district, 165; and splittist activities, 173,
    175
India, 16, 189–91, 215, 219, 233, 240, 246;
    Muslims in, 48

Inner Asia, 175

Inner Mongolia, 4, 6, 8, 10, 11, 13, 89, 158, 162–63, 227; and Chinese Communist Party Working Committee, 97; and Chinese crackdown, 107–8; and Chinese migration, 86, 92, 100–107; Chinese population of, 87; decline of pastoralism in, 103–5, 107; economic development in, 104; ethnic and tribal splits in, 96–99; land reform and collectives in, 100–107; and loss of autonomy, 92; nationalism in, 111–12; Organization Department (*Zuzhibu*) of, 98; qualities of leadership in, 99; and reduction of territory, 93, 95–96

Inner Mongolian Autonomous Government, 100–101; early structure of, 90–91

Inner Mongolian Autonomous Region, founding of, 7, 9, 13, 85, 92

Inner Mongolian People's Congress, 111

Inner Mongolian People's Revolutionary Party, founding of, 88

Inner Mongolian Youth League, 96

International Campaign for Tibet, 186, 203–7, 211

International Committee of Lawyers for Tibet, 187

International Human Rights Day, 205

Islam, 15, 23–26, 28–30, 33–34, 40–41, 43, 47–48, 134, 139–40, 156, 159; organization of, 28–30

Islam magazine, 24

Isma'il Āhmād, 125, 131, 141–42

Israel, 112

Jahriya Sufis, 39

Jāmia ("mosque"), 29

Jamyang Drolma, 258

Janabil, 135

Jangiya Hutagt, 86

Japan, 23, 27, 96, 107, 114; in Manchuria, 88–89

Jargal, 96

Jebtsundamba Hutagt, 86

Jews: compared with Mongols, 112–13; French, 49

Jiang Zemin, 224

Jilin Province, 87, 93

Jinan, 35

Jingdong, 62

Jinghong, 60; private businesses in, 74–76; prostitution in, 74; street survey in, 75–76; tourism in, 73–74

jinghua ("elite"), 110

Jingpeng, 87

Jinuo, 54, 56–57; and lack of written script, 67

Jirim League, 87, 91, 105

Jo'uda League, 87, 91, 105

Kagyüpa, 232

Kailu, 87

Kapstein, Matthew, 17

Karamay, 173

Karmapa Lama and sect, 212, 232–33

Kashgar, 121, 128, 138, 140, 165–66, 168, 172–73

Kashgar Literature, 132

Kashgar Youth Press, 132

Kazakhs and Kazakhstan, 118, 121, 124, 126, 129, 134–36, 144, 160; oil in, 15, 161

Khalkha (Halh) Mongols, 5, 86

Kham, 196, 231–33, 237, 252, 253

Khampa, 260

Khenpo ("preceptor"), 252

Khenpo Jikphun, 249, 252, 261

Khitans, 3

Khrushchev, Nikita, and virgin lands, 170

Khubilai Khan, 5, 43

Kirghiz and Kirghizstan, 118, 121, 126, 160

Kissinger, Henry (U.S. Secretary of State), 222

Kitab, 42

Kizilsu (Kezilesu), 166, 173

Koran, 133

Korean War, 91

Korla, 158, 168

Kuibi, 97

Kumbun (Taer) monastery, 104, 212, 244

Kumul, 128

Kunming, 19, 30, 44–45, 59

Kuytun, 173

Labrang (Labulangsi), 233, 251–52, 256; organization and studies, 251

Lahu, 56–57

Lancang, 62

Lantos, Tom, 186

Lanzhou, 34, 41

Laos, 55; relations with Tai, 66
Law on Regional National Autonomy, 64, 68, 77–78, 94, 96, 98–99, 108, 113
Lhagang Monastery, 254, 262
Lhasa, 190, 193, 195, 197, 199, 200, 203–6, 208, 210, 212, 216, 218, 220, 223, 231, 233, 235, 242, 248, 250, 255, 258; and Chinese immigration, 208–9; uprising in, 237
Liang ge libukai ("the two inseparables"), 146
Liangshan Prefecture, 67, 71
Liaobei Province, 91
Liao dynasty (907–1115), 3
Liaoning Province, 93
Lifanyuan, 5
Li Ling, 118
Liling, 60
Lindong, 87
Lintan Jiucheng, 32; and lack of violence, 42–43
Linxi, 87
Linxia, trade and drug addiction in, 41–42
Li Peng, 105
Lipman, Jonathan, 11–12
Liu Chun, 97
Liu Mingzu, 94
Liupan Mountains, 39
Ljongs dang zhing chen lnga ("five autonomous regions and provinces"), 245
London, 189
Long March, 26–27
Lop Nor, 146
Los Angeles, 48
Lupei, 87

Mädräsa ("theological school"), 138
Madsen, Richard, 261
Mahayana Buddhism, 236, 254
Ma Jong, 95
Malaysia, 106
Ma Liangji, 36
Ma Liangxun, 35
Manchukuo, 96
Manchus and Manchuria, 4–5, 22, 24, 110, 155, 188–90, 195, 213, 231–32
Mao Yongfu, 118
Mao Zedong, 89, 123, 155, 175; and Tibet, 193–94, 195–200, 207, 215, 236
Ma Qixi, 42
Marxist-Leninists, 230

Matsumoto Matsui, and views on *minzu*, 21
McMillen, Donald, description of Communist policy in Xinjiang, 122, 130
Mecca, 30
Meigu county, 71
Mekong River, 77
Mengcun, 46
Menghai, 76
Mengla, 76
Mewa (Hongyuan County), 252
Miao, 5, 7, 54
Middle East, 23–24, 28, 47–48
Milarepa, 246
Ming dynasty (1368–1644), 4, 22, 47, 188
Min Han jiantong ("equal competence in Han and minority languages"), 136
Ministry of Coal, 104
Ministry of Land Reclamation, 100
Ministry of Petroleum (China National Oil Corporation), 159, 169
Minjian ("popular organizations"), 36
Minzu Affairs Commission, 142
Minzu chuban she ("ethnic publishing houses"), 249
Minzu fenliehzhu fenzi ("ethnic splittists"), 111
Minzu ganbu ("ethnic functionaries"), 25, 30, 39, 46; ineffectiveness of, 30–31
Minzu hua ("ethnicization"), 46
Minzu jinghua ("ethnic elites"), 111
Minzu shibie ("ethnic identification") 25
Minzu xuexiao ("ethnic schools") 68
Minzu youpai ("ethnic rightists"), 92
Minzu zhengce ("ethnic policy"), 121
Mojiang, 62
Mongolian People's Republic (MPR), 89, 92–93, 98–100; founding, 6
Mongolian-Tibetan Affairs Commission, 85
Mongols, in Manchuria, 88–89
Mongols and Mongolia, 21–22, 24, 27–28, 31, 40, 43, 47, 53, 118, 129, 157, 188, 213, 223, 227, 233, 250; and Mongour (Tuzu), 250; and nationalism, 88
Most Favored Nation (MFN), 224
Muli County, 71
Muslims, 12, 19, 21–24, 27–28, 30–31, 33–34, 36–38, 41–45, 124, 140, 144, 183, 242; and Chinese Communists, 26; divisions among, 23

Najiaying, 45, 48
Namaz ("prayers"), 140
Nangchen Chinghu Gyelpo ("king of Nangchen in Qinghai"), 232
Nanjiang, 181
Nanjing, 23
Nanniwan, 175
National People's Congress (NPC), 98
Native language instruction, in Sipsong Panna, 66–70
Nehru, Jawaharlal, 220
Neidi ("the interior"), 42
Nepal, 189, 197, 240
New Delhi, 221
New York City, 110
Ningxia, 26, 30–31, 43, 48, 162–64; violence in, 39–40
Ningxia Hui Autonomous Region, 11, 37, 39, 93, 106
Nixon, Richard, 222
Nongjiang ("state farms"), 59
Nyingmapa order, 253–54, 260
Nyingmapa Shrisimha College, 235

Oakes, Tim, and tourism in Guizhou, 74
Office of Strategic Services (OSS), 218
Ordos Desert, 39, 89, 106–8
Ordos Mongols, 94, 96–97, 101, 104–5
Ordos Municipality, 105
Osama bin Laden, 183
Otog Front banner, 104–5
Ötkür, Abdurehim, 132–33
Ottoman Empire, 23
Outer Mongolia, 85, 88, 189
Oyunchimeg, 96, 100

Pakistan, 48
Panchen Lama, 195, 205, 233, 238, 240, 255–56, 261; conflict over, 243–44; death of, 243
Panthay rebellion, 6
Pastoralism, and Mongol heritage, 101–2
People's Armed Police, 175
People's Liberation Army (PLA), 7, 129, 144, 146, 155, 157, 161, 175–76, 180; and invasion of Tibet, 193; and suppression of Shadian, 44–45; in Xinjiang, 122
People's Republic of China (PRC), 28–31, 38, 59, 70, 91, 110, 113, 117, 155–58,

160–62, 164, 167, 174, 181–82, 187–88; early policy of toward Hui, 25; founding of, 231; policy of toward Tibet, 186–88, 192–93, 214, 216, 219–20, 222–24
Persian and Persians, 25, 29, 47
Pighan, 144
Pingnan Guo ("the State that pacifies the South"), 43
Political Consultative Congress, ineffectiveness of, 93–95
Potala Palace, 258
Powell, Colin (U.S. Secretary of State), 226
Premi, 54
Production and Construction Corps (PCC), 16, 122–23, 146–47, 158, 164, 168, 170, 172–73, 175; composition of, 128–29; and economic power, 180; objectives of, 156–57

Qian Fengyun, 93
Qidong, 60
Qing dynasty (1644–1911), 8, 13, 22–24, 27, 32, 38, 42–43, 46, 155, 175; collapse of, 6; expansionist policy of, 4–5; and Muslim and Panthay rebellions, 6; policy of in Mongolia, 85–86; policy of in Tibet, 188–89, 218, 223, 250
Qinghai Province, 26, 39, 43, 162–64, 187, 197, 212, 244; Tibetans in, 231, 236, 245, 249–50; violence in, 40–41
Qingzhen (*halāl*), 22, 29, 32, 49

Radio Free Asia, 186
Red Guards, 124
Rehe Province 86, 91
Religious Affairs Office (Zongjiao Shiwu Ju), 30
Rencai ("talented individuals"), 111
Republican China, 23, 46, 117, 121, 155, 191, 231–32; policy of in Inner Mongolia, 86–88
Republic of Mongolia, 107–8, 110; and splits with Inner Mongolia, 109
Roosevelt, Franklin, 218, 223
Rubber plantations, 72
Rudelson, Justin, 132
Ruohua minzu yishi ("reduce ethnic consciousness"), 113
Ruoqiang, 168

Russia, 126, 160, 191
Russian language and script, 134–35

Sakya Pandita, 246
Sala Hui (Salars), 22, 250
Sanpo, 34; and tanning and fur industries, 34; and women's mosques (*nusi*), 34
Saudi Arabia, 23
Sautman, Barry, 141, 174
Sāypidin (Saifudin) Āzizi, 122, 131
Sayyid Ajall Shams ad-Din (Sai Dianchi), 43
Serko Monastery, 236
Serta County, 250, 252, 256, 261
Seventeen-Point Agreement for the Peaceful Liberation of Tibet, 193–94, 195–97, 206, 210, 219, 220
Shaanxi Province, 36, 39, 89, 162–63
Shadian, 46, 48; Communist suppression of, 44–45
Shandong Province, violence in, 45–46
Shanghai, 59, 76, 104, 127, 202
Shanghai Five, 126
Shanghen wenxue ("scar literature"), 132
Shanshan County, 167
Shantou Hanzu ("mountain Han"), 59
Shari'a (religious law), 29
Shedra (religious school), 253–54
Sheikh (*shaykh, she-hai, laorenjia*), 23
Shenyang, 35
Shenzhen, 104–5
Sherab, 238
Shigatse, 255
Shihezi, 173
Shirisimha College, 253–54
Shuoshi (master's degree), 250
Siberia, 27
Sichuan Province, 27, 33, 40, 54, 67, 71, 76, 190, 197–98, 216, 220, 243, 244–45; and migrants to Panna, 60; Tibetans in, 231, 233, 235, 249, 250, 252–53, 255, 261, 263; women sex workers in, 74
Sikkim, 189
Silingol, 88, 95, 106, 109
Simla Convention, 191
Sine Lama, 102, 105
Singapore, 106
Sino-American relations, 186–88, 223–27
Sino-Arabian calligraphy, 28

Sino-Arabic schools, 24
Sino-Soviet split: influence of in Inner Mongolia, 92–93, 98, 100; impact of in Xinjiang, 124, 156–57
Sino-Tibetan relations: early history of, 188; independent status of, 190–92; in Qing era, 188–90; and rebellion, 198
Sipsong Panna (Panna): and attitudes toward independence, 81; Buddhist education in, 65; and Chinese "civilizing mission," 63; Chinese migration into, 57–64; drug trade in, 58; education in, 64–70; and natural resource management, 70–72; in pre-Communist era, 55–56; prostitution in, 58; and religion, 77–79; tourism in, 72–79
Sishi (personal matter), 138
Slezkine, Yuri, on Soviet nationality policy, 90
Snow, Edgar, 26
Social Darwinism, definition of Hui, 24
Socialist Education campaign, 124
Song dynasty (960–1279), 4
Song Hanliang, 135
Southeast Asia, 11, 31, 43, 73, 260
South Korea, 195
Soviet Central Asia, 169, 172
Soviet Far East, 155
Soviet Union, 27, 42, 84, 90, 92, 98–99, 113, 123–24, 126, 134, 138, 160, 156–59, 191–92, 214, 223; and aid to Inner Mongolia, 93; and privileges in Xinjiang, 155
Splittism, 17, 181–82
Stalin, Josef, 21, 24–25, 27, 155, 223
State Council Information Office, 183
State Department (U.S.). *See* United States
State Nationalities Affairs Commission, 8
Strasbourg, 205–6, 214
Students for a Free Tibet, 187
Sufi orders (*tariqa*) 25, 29, 31, 38, 40; spread and influence of, 23
Suiyuan Province, 86, 91, 97
Sunni Islam, 29
Sun Yat-sen, 27
Su Qianyi, 97–98
Suzhou, 23, 73

Tacheng County Autonomous District, 118, 158

Ta Chung Kuo (Da Zhongguo), 27

Tai, 13, 54–56, 63, 72–73, 75; Buddhism in, 57; Chinese images of, 62; Communist policy toward, 56–57, 59; language and script of, 65–70; shop owners in, 76

Tai Autonomous Prefecture, 55; founding of, 56

Tai Lüe, 55

Tai Na, 55

Taiwan, 85, 199, 218, 220, 260

Tajiks and Tajikistan, 118, 121, 126, 160

Taliban, 183

Talip (religious pupils), 138

Tang dynasty (618–907), 3, 28, 175

Tanjur, 246

Tao River, 41

Tarim basin, 22

Tashi Lhunpo Monastery, 243

Tatars, 122

Thailand, 13, 60; and contact with Tai Buddhists, 78–79; relations of with Tai, 57, 65–66; and *thangka* painting, 258

Theravada Buddhism, 57, 65

Tiananmen Square, 159, 206

Tianshan Mountains, 158, 165, 168

Tianxinglong, 42

Tibet and Tibetans 11, 16–17, 24, 27, 31–32, 40, 41–43, 47, 53–54, 68, 84–85, 89, 99, 110, 113, 124–25, 137, 156, 158–59, 162–63, 174, 182, 250, 258; and advocates of hardline policy toward, 195, 197–98; and Buddhism, 198, 230; and contact with Tibetan exiles, 240; and economic growth, 207; and insults to Chinese, 199; and and language and education, 209; and Manchu invasion, 5; and Military Administration Bureau, 193; and Military Area Headquarters, 193; and monasteries, 234–35; and preservation of Tibetan language, 246–48; and rebellion, 197; and religion, 233–35; and religious revival, 240–42; and riots, 204–6, 223, 237, 242; sinicization of, 227; Sino-Tibetan negotiations with, 201–2; and tighter security, 207; and writing of textbooks, 245–47

Tibet Information Network, 187

Tibetan Autonomous Region (TAR), 10, 18, 200, 202, 209, 213, 217, 231, 239, 243, 248–49, 255–57, 258, 261; and plans for autonomy, 212

Tibetan Buddhism, 17–18, 238, 241–42; revival, 244, 249–57, 258–62

Tibetan monasteries, Chinese in, 252–53

Tibetan People's Party, 196

Tibetan Youth League, 214

Ting Mao, 9

Tokyo, 24

Tomorbagan, 97

Tömür Dawamät, 131, 141

Tongliao municipality, 105

Toops, Stanley, 131

Tourism, problems with in Sipsong Panna, 73–79

Treaty of Friendship, Alliance, and Mutual Understanding (1950), 155

Tshurpu Monastery, 212

Tuanjie ("unity"), 40

Tulkus ("incarnation"), 235, 254

Tumed Mongols, 89, 91, 96

Turghun Almas, 132

Turkic languages, 133–34

Turkish Islamic Republic of Eastern Turkistan, 121

Turkistan, 182

Turks and Turkic peoples, 12, 14–16, 22, 29, 32, 40, 47, 48, 126, 129, 160

Ulaanchab League, 87, 91, 106

Ulaanhot (Wangiin Sume), 89, 91, 110

'Ulamā (ahong, akhund) (Muslim leader), 29, 33, 42, 44–45, 47, 49; role of, 31, 40

Ulanhu, 87, 93, 106, 108, 110; as chair of Inner Mongolian government, 97–98; removal of, 98–99

Ulji, 99

Umma, 26, 49

United Front Department, 140

United Front policy, 27, 122

United Nations, 214, 221, 223

United States, 107, 146, 183, 203–4; Congress of, 187, 223, 225–26; Congressional Human Rights Caucus of, 203; embassy of in New Delhi, 218; relations of with Tibet, 186–88, 191, 192–94, 196–97, 215, 217–27, 230; and sovereignty for Tibet, 223–24; State Department of, 186, 203, 218, 225; strategy of in Tibet, 221

Ürümchi kechlik gäziti (Urumqi Evening News), 145
Urumqi, 126–27, 130, 132, 144–45, 158, 168–70, 173, 181
Urumqi County, 167
Ushenju, 101
Uygurs, 14, 22, 47, 53, 84, 117, 119–23, 125–29, 131–33, 136, 139–40, 141–48, 166, 181–83; discrimination against, 129–30; flight of to Soviet Union, 123; separatists among, 126

Vairochana cave, 252–53
Vajra Divinity Oil (Jingang Shen You), 258
Vietnam, 4
Voice of America (VOA), 186

Wahhabism, 140
Wang Enmao, 122, 131, 135, 157
Wang Fengqi, 96
Wangfujing, 257
Wang Qun, 94
Wang Zhen, 125, 127, 175
Waqf ("endowment"), 37
War on Terrorism, and China, 183
Washington, D.C., 187, 194, 218–20
Water Splashing Festival, 73
Wei River Valley, 39
Western Europe, 109
White Russians, 6
World Bank, 187
World War II, 114, 191, 236
Wuchuan County, 87
Wuhai, 94, 104–5

Xiafang ("sent down"), 127
Xiahe, 255
Xi'an, 30, 39, 46, 73; Muslim quarter of, 33–34; urban renewal in, 35–37
Xi'an Islamic Cultural Study Society (Xi'an Shi Yisilan Wenhua Yanjiuhui), 36–37
Xibo, 129
Xibu da kifa ("develop the western regions"), 61, 80, 104, 128
Xidaotang, role of in mediation and trade, 42
Ximeng, 62
Xincun ("public housing"), 21
Xing Fengsu (Sexual Customs), 144
Xinghuibian magazine, 24
Xining, 31, 40–41

Xinjiang, 10, 11, 12, 14–17, 32, 42, 47, 85, 113, 125–35, 137, 140, 145–48, 155–56, 158–59, 202; and Arabic script, 134; censorship in, 132–33; and Chinese immigration, 124, 126–27, 143, 175–80; and Chinese industrial managers, 168; Chinese majority in, 165; and collectivization, 123; as a colony, 174–75, 176, 180–84; cotton cultivation in, 170–72; economic and educational disparities in, 173; environmental problems in, 156, 170, 172; and growth in foreign trade, 169–71; integration of into China, 160; investment in, 182; investment of in Kazakhstan, 162–65; language policy of, 134–37; and Manchu annexation, 5; oil exploration in, 159; People's Congress of, 130; per capita income in, 166–67; reform efforts in, 158; relations of with Central Asia, 160; and relations of Uygurs and Chinese, 143–46; religious policy of, 137–41; and resource development and conflicts, 161, 169; scarcity of minority leaders in, 131; and state domination of economy, 168–69; and "tomb" of Chinggis Khan, 110
Xinjiang Academy of Social Sciences, 137
Xinjiang Statistical Yearbook, 166
Xinjiang University, 140, 142
Xinjiang Uygur Autonomous Region, 7, 15, 125, 137, 141, 156, 161, 172–73; founding of, 7, 118, 120
Xuanyuan Guoxin, 168

Yakub Beg, 155
Yalta, 223
Yan'an (northern Shaanxi), 21, 96, 175
Yan da ("strike hard"), 126
Yangjin County, 45–46
Yang Zhilin, 97–98
Yangzi River, 190
Yanyuan County, 67
Yao, 7
Yekeju League, 87, 91; and economic development, 104
Yellow River, 38, 87
Yi, 7, 54, 75
Yinchuan, 40, 48; Hui in, 37; Religious Affairs Office of, 38; urban renewal in, 37–38

Yining, 166, 168, 181
Youhui zhengce ("preferential policies"), 141–42
Younong ("nomadic agriculture"), 101
Youxiang ("deep-fried dough"), 26
Yuan dynasty (1271–1368), 3, 188
Yuehua magazine, 24
Yugoslavia, 11, 84
Yun Bulong, 99; death of, 96–96
Yunnan and Yunnanese, 5, 6, 7, 19–20, 26–27, 33, 36, 38–39, 46, 54–55; 57–59, 76, 79, 137, 158, 245, 249; and ban on logging, 71; and Chinese migrants, 54, 60–64; in Cultural Revolution, 44–45; and drug trade, 41, 43; and Tibetans, 231, 237
Yuxi, 19–20, 44, 46, 48

Zepu County, 135
Zhang Xianliang, 132
Zhangjiakou, 91

Zhao Erfeng, 190
Zhaotong, 43
Zhejiang, 76
Zhengzhou, 20, 34–35, 46, 48
Zhishi qingnian ("young intellectuals"), 59
Zhongdian xuexiao ("key schools"), 68
Zhonghua minzu ("Chinese ethnicity"), 24, 27
Zhou Enlai, 198
Zhou Hui, 93
Zhou Xin, 95
Zhuang, 7, 54, 84
Zhu Rongyi, 95
Zhushi ("grain foods"), 33
Zhu Songli, 36
Zizhi ("self-government"), 120
Zonghe zhili ("comprehensive management"), 126
Zunghar Mongols, 5
Zuo Zongtang, 155